GERARD MANLEY HOPKINS

A COMPREHENSIVE BIBLIOGRAPHY

GERARD MANLEY HOPKINS

A COMPREHENSIVE BIBLIOGRAPHY

TOM DUNNE

CLARENDON PRESS · OXFORD
1976

Oxford University Press, Ely House, London W.1

GLASGOW   NEW YORK   TORONTO   MELBOURNE   WELLINGTON
CAPE TOWN   IBADAN   NAIROBI   DAR ES SALAAM   LUSAKA   ADDIS ABABA
DELHI   BOMBAY   CALCUTTA   MADRAS   KARACHI   LAHORE   DACCA
KUALA LUMPUR   SINGAPORE   HONG KONG   TOKYO

ISBN 0 19 818158 2

Printed in Great Britain by
Richard Clay (The Chaucer Press), Ltd.
Bungay, Suffolk

278/134

*This book is gratefully
dedicated to
my wife, Gillian,
for all her patience
and help.*

PREFACE

This bibliography of Gerard Manley Hopkins is comprehensive but not complete. To compile a complete bibliography of Hopkins is probably impossible. I have excluded all but a very few 'association items'—material which does not mention Hopkins but relates to persons or places with which he was associated—because in spite of its undoubted value to researchers, inclusion of this type of material expands the scope of a bibliography indefinitely. It would have been possible to produce a substantial bibliography limited to books and articles in which Hopkins was the sole or main subject, but the results would have been emasculated: some of the most penetrating observations on Hopkins have been made *passim*, in books and articles in which he takes a secondary place. I have therefore not hesitated to include brief references, even two-line comments; if in my judgement they showed enough insight to make them worth including, or if they seemed to be of historical importance. My listing of writings about Hopkins in English is as comprehensive as I could make it within this framework, and my listing of writings about him in other languages is selective. The terminal date for the bibliography is 1969–70.

A comprehensive bibliography must be used with discrimination if it is to be used with profit, and the entries in this bibliography are annotated to make discrimination easier. The annotations are usually descriptive, and often consist of quotations from the item concerned. I have used quotations, not because I always agree with what I quote, but as the easiest way of passing on the *flavour* of the original. Occasionally I have attempted to criticize or evaluate: since this practice will undoubtedly irritate those users of the bibliography who do not agree with my opinions, I have resorted to it only when it seemed most justified. Any student of Hopkins has plenty to read: some indication of quality may at least help him to arrange his priorities.

The arrangement of the entries groups similar materials together, and places them chronologically in each group. The logical progression of strict chronological arrangement is lost, but the benefits of having (for example) all the criticism of individual poems together as a group seems in practice to outweigh this disadvantage. Cross-references have been provided between sections where they seemed likely to be useful.

The full descriptions of primary works are largely conventional, but several points should be noted. The transcriptions of title-pages are as exact as they could be made in typescript, but do not show different sizes of type. The spacing of words in these transcriptions does not attempt to reproduce the originals: any irregularities are due to the printer's justification of the type for this book, and should be ignored. The size of the book is given in centimetres, and is the measurement of the title-page or of a typical leaf. The bulk is the thickness of the book, measured first without including the binding and secondly with the binding included. The shorter forms of entry for secondary works are entirely conventional, and do not call for special comment.

In order to simplify this Preface, any points of scope or arrangement peculiar to individual sections of the bibliography have been dealt with at the beginning of each separate section. One other general point can be made here: I have tried to examine as many items as possible before including them in the bibliography, and where I have failed to do so the sign * is placed at the beginning of the entry. When it has proved impossible for me to examine an item myself, I have tried to ensure accuracy by asking someone else to examine it for me, and confirm the various details. In my Acknowledgements I have paid tribute to the many librarians and correspondents who have helped me in this way and in others. For any errors which remain, I am alone responsible.

ACKNOWLEDGEMENTS

My debts are so various and so heavy that to enumerate them individually is hardly possible. No bibliographer could have wished for more good will or co-operation.

Firstly I must thank my predecessors in the field, the other bibliographers of Hopkins; for their labours have done much to lighten mine. I am particularly grateful to Professor Edward H. Cohen, who has been most generous in sharing information and has provided photostats of some very rare items, to Mrs. Ruth Seelhammer, and to Professor Elgin W. Mellown, whose M.A. thesis (J173) helped me, *inter alia*, to plan my Introduction.

I owe special thanks, also, to the many scholars and academics who have freely offered help and advice; in particular to Father Anthony Bischoff, Mr. Kazuyoshi Enozawa, the late Professor W. H. Gardner, Mr. F. N. Lees, Professor N. H. MacKenzie, Professor J. G. Ritz, Father Alfred Thomas, and Dr. Norman White.

The staffs of the numerous libraries I have used have proved unfailingly courteous and efficient despite the large amount of work I have caused them, and I have received prompt and careful replies to almost every letter of inquiry I have sent out, which places me under obligation to over two hundred correspondents.

This book is a revised form of a Fellowship Thesis written for the Library Association. For the thesis, Dr. W. R. Aitken was my supervisor, and my work could not have been completed without the support of his expert knowledge and warm encouragement. In preparing the book for the press I have continued to benefit from his kindness, generosity, and unstinted help.

CONTENTS

CONTENTS

PART FOUR: NOTES ON LOCATIONS OF
SOURCE MATERIALS

ABBREVIATIONS

P1   *Poems of Gerard Manley Hopkins,* 1st edition, 1918.

P2   *Poems of Gerard Manley Hopkins,* 2nd edition, 1930.

P3   *Poems of Gerard Manley Hopkins,* 3rd edition, 1948.

P4   *Poems of Gerard Manley Hopkins,* 4th edition, 1967.

LL1   *The letters of Gerard Manley Hopkins to Robert Bridges,* 1935.

LL2   *The correspondence of Gerard Manley Hopkins and Richard Watson Dixon,* 1935.

FL   *Further letters of Gerard Manley Hopkins,* 1938.

FL2   *Further letters of Gerard Manley Hopkins,* 2nd edition, 1956.

NP   *The note-books and papers of Gerard Manley Hopkins,* 1937.

JP   *The journals and papers of Gerard Manley Hopkins,* 1959.

SD   *The sermons and devotional writings of Gerard Manley Hopkins,* 1959.

Hopkins himself is referred to throughout as GMH.

The sign * at the beginning of an entry indicates that the material referred to has not been seen by the compiler.

Where 'p.' without a number occurs in an entry, the compiler has been unable to trace the page-reference.

INTRODUCTION

In setting out to write this Introduction I had to make some difficult decisions about its form and content. The purpose of an introduction is to introduce what it precedes: having surveyed the whole field of Hopkins studies in compiling this bibliography (however deficient my coverage may have been), I thought it desirable to record my impressions of the growth and development of Hopkins's reputation, because Hopkins's reputation is largely what the bibliography is about. But it was evident that a connected account and analysis of such a complex subject would require many thousands of words. If it could not be done in detail, was it worth doing at all? And if it was, how could it best be done? My answers to these questions were arrived at after some reflection about the effect of certain special factors and events on the critical acceptance of Hopkins's work. I think that I can best introduce this bibliography to its users by drawing attention to these factors and events, by explaining their significance, and by trying to relate them to the main trends of Hopkins criticism. This method will be discursive, and perhaps superficial, because there will not always be room for adequate qualification and amplification where both are needed, but it still seems the most useful approach.

I begin with Hopkins's religion. This seems inevitable, because it was the centripetal force in his life and the fulcrum of his poetry. Hopkins, in F. R. Leavis's phrase, was 'the devotional poet of a dogmatic Christianity'.[1] This does not mean that interest in his poetry has been predominantly religious—far from it—but it does mean that much Hopkins criticism has been written within a religious framework. Now some of the material entered in this bibliography demonstrates (if demonstration is required) that it is possible to write literary criticism of very high standards within such a framework, but the method inevitably imposes its own restrictions. In particular, it sometimes leads to special pleading; and in criticism any special pleading, whether religious, agnostic, political, or esoteric, weakens the general validity of all conclusions reached. The whole question is very much one of degree. Some critics of Hopkins have been too concerned with

[1] F. R. Leavis, *The Common Pursuit* (London, 1952), p. 48.

defending his religious position to pay much attention to his poetry (there were some Dunciad-like exchanges over Bridges's 'Preface to Notes' for the first edition); some have vitiated otherwise excellent criticism by super-fluous anti-Jesuit or anti-Catholic sniping; others have wasted their time in meaningless speculations about the kind of poetry Hopkins might have written if he had not become a Jesuit and a religious poet. (He *did* become a Jesuit and he *was* a religious poet. Who can possibly say what else he might have done, or what he might have written? Who cares?) Some Catholic readers, moreover, will always turn to Hopkins as much for his religious message as for his poetry; and thus he is often written about by Catholics, for Catholics, in purely Catholic terms. This kind of criticism has an obvious place in a comprehensive bibliography, but it has contri-buted nothing to Hopkins's literary status. The relevance of Hopkins's religion to his reputation as a whole is therefore mainly this: some Hopkins criticism has had only limited influence because of religious bias, or has not been literary criticism at all. Literary criticism is one thing. Religious controversy is another. I have tried to distinguish between them in annotat-ing my entries.

The next point requiring emphasis is one which nobody writing about Hopkins can avoid for long. Hopkins died in 1889, but his poems were not published until 1918, just after the First World War. In literature, as in life, the effect of what a man does sometimes depends on when he does it. Without belittling Hopkins's splendid talent, this can to some extent fairly be said of him. The First World War was for the whole of Europe a turning-point in social and intellectual attitudes. In England, after the war, most Victorian and Edwardian achievements seemed to have been built on sand; their foundations were everywhere crumbling. The general mood was a cynical one, and literature (both in England and America) reflected it, as literature anywhere always does. In poetry, the result was an in-creasing contempt for traditional standards. Since one of the most durable myths about Hopkins suggests that his immediate impact on English poetry resembled an exploding bomb, I may perhaps point out that this rejection of tradition was not as cathartic as is sometimes suggested. On the one hand, deliberate efforts to combat the Romantic and Victorian tra-ditions had occasionally been made before the war began; and on the other hand, the popularity of the Georgian poets (those staunch upholders of the established order) continued unabated for almost a decade after it ended: the term 'Georgian' only became a critical insult from around 1930. (It is worth noting that the original volumes of *Georgian Poetry* sold in large numbers—enormous ones, by present-day standards. This means that between 1912 and 1922 there was a known, substantial poetry-reading public in England. Hopkins sold slowly at first, admittedly; but without this public he might never have been published at all.)

'Modernist' poetry, then, which prepared the way for Hopkins, took hold gradually. It did not shatter traditional ideas about acceptable standards and practice, it eroded them. It owed much to the Symbolists and Imagists, and more to Eliot and Pound; but the war, and what the war did to the English and American ethos, really gave it impetus. The war produced a change in sensibility. And in this new critical climate Hopkins appeared so much at odds with the Victorian tradition that he seemed to belong more to the age in which he was published than to his own. The most far-reaching effect of Hopkins's posthumous publication is therefore the dual role in which he now appears: by 1930 (when he finally achieved full recognition) Hopkins the Victorian had become Hopkins the modern. Since then he has attracted a wider *range* of criticism than most poets, because he appeals to students of both periods.

If it is impossible to write about Hopkins without eventual reference to his posthumous publication, it is equally impossible to write without reference to Robert Bridges. Bridges was both shrewd and perceptive in waiting until 1918 before publishing Hopkins's collected poems. He could easily have published them earlier, and certainly thought of doing so.[2] But my research on this bibliography has convinced me that if he had, the growth of Hopkins's reputation would have been retarded. The cautious and gradual manner in which Bridges chose to make the poems public—by recommending them to his literary friends, and securing publication of selected poems in anthologies at intervals over thirty years—has laid him open to some very astringent criticism. The main charge, usually, is that he was perversely blind to the greatness of Hopkins's poetry, and ought to have known better. Well, perhaps he was; and I dare say he ought. But those critics who go on to berate him for not publishing the poems earlier in a collected edition have surely never examined the reviews of the books in which he published selected ones. Those included in this bibliography have to the best of my knowledge not previously been located, and their importance seems to me considerable.[3]

Bridges withheld the poems until 1918 because he wanted to be sure that the poetry-reading public, and the critics, were ready for Hopkins; and would not be antagonized by the poems' innovations and idiosyn-

---

[2] He discussed the idea with the printer C. H. O. Daniel: see S. Nowell-Smith, 'Bridges, Hopkins, and Dr. Daniel', *Times Literary Supplement*, 13 Dec. 1957, p. 764.

[3] These reviews will be found with the entries for the books, in Section A.

crasies. This motive emerges clearly from his letters (now in the Bodleian Library) to Hopkins's mother, Mrs. Kate Hopkins.[4] Anything the reviewers had to say about Hopkins before 1918 must therefore throw light in one way or another on the quality of Bridges's judgement. And the reviewers had quite a lot to say: if this bibliography achieves nothing else, it should help to explode another myth about Hopkins; one insisting that he was quite unknown in the literary world before 1918. Some of the reviewers' comments were very brief (but can be significant, in context, for what they do *not* say); some were religiously motivated, and some merely biographical anecdotes; but together they help to show how, during Bridges's watchful custody, a steady mellowing of critical attitudes to the poems took place; from early hostility (or, worse, indifference) to pleased, if sometimes puzzled, admiration. Even allowing for the fact that the poems which Bridges published in anthologies were all simpler ones, free from Hopkins's more ebullient innovations, their reception still vindicates Bridges's caution. Reviewers in the 1890s (I am speaking of the reviews which I have seen, knowing only too well that there may be others I have missed) mostly tended to ignore Hopkins's inclusion in the book under review. Only three of them mentioned his presence, and the *Manchester Guardian* reviewer dismissed him as a 'curiosity', who should have been excluded. By 1916, when Hopkins appeared in Bridges's own anthology, *The Spirit of Man*, the change in critical attitudes was startling; though admittedly Bridges's elevation to Poet Laureate probably influenced the reviewers of that particular book. It is time that Bridges receives more credit for his part in all this: if he had published the poems thirty, twenty, or even ten years earlier, their reception would almost certainly have been impeded by ridicule and censure from the reviewers. Bridges may never have realized the true worth and potential of Hopkins's poetry, but he unquestionably valued it highly; and if he was motivated more by the memory of a friendship than by real confidence in the poems, that surely is in itself a tribute to the qualities which distinguished him both as a friend and as a man.

If Bridges was partly responsible for making a 'modern' poet of Hopkins, he was entirely responsible for the famous 'Preface to Notes' with which the poems were launched: another extremely influential factor in the growth of Hopkins's reputation. This Preface, over the years, has generated a great deal of heat. It is certainly difficult to understand why, after preserving his friend's poems for so long, and editing them with such skill,

---

[4] An extract from one of these letters is published in N. White *and* T. Dunne, 'A Hopkins discovery', *Library*, vol. 24, no. 1, Mar. 1969, pp. 56–8.

Bridges should then have so efficiently damned them with faint praise: my own impression is that he hoped to disarm criticism in advance. Bridges's critical acumen was lively, and his erudition considerable, but he had a tendency to pedantry which sometimes got the better of him when he was faced with the unconventional. (I once heard a memorable suggestion made about the criticism of Matthew Arnold: that Arnold was a little inclined to inspect poets as he inspected schools—for their educational value. It now occurs to me that in this matter Bridges reveals a rather similar attitude of mind.) The question, besides, centres not only on Bridges's critical sense but on his taste, and taste is a very personal thing. Bridges found some of the religious attitudes in Hopkins's poetry distasteful, and also some features of Hopkins's style. Being a plain-spoken man, he said so. His religious aversions no longer matter; their relevance ended with the offence that they at first caused. And he had a perfect right to apply his own standards of taste to Hopkins's poems, though he should not have made those standards sound like moral imperatives. What is important is the effect of his criticism.

Bridges's strictures on Hopkins's style have been so influential that Maurice Charney, in his survey of Hopkins criticism, began with the 'Preface to Notes' in the belief that 'much of the later work developed, in a schematic sense, as a defense of Hopkins against Bridges'.[5] Certainly anyone who studies the Hopkins criticism written between 1919 and the 1940s will find it echoing Bridges everywhere. His influence on the reviewers of Hopkins's poems in 1919 was particularly strong: time and again they took their stand with him in censuring Hopkins's 'oddity' and 'obscurity'. But time and again, too, they acknowledged warmly Hopkins's 'rare masterly beauties'; and this was all that Bridges wanted. Since the 1940s his influence on Hopkins criticism has declined, probably because the new critical methods have made him seem old-fashioned. But the fourth edition of Hopkins's poems in 1967 was the first not to include his 'Preface to Notes' in full—and even there the most controversial passages were still retained. The following comment on them by the late W. H. Gardner seems well fitted to be the last word on the subject here:

. . . the last four pages of R.B.'s original *Preface* still retain their historical and critical interest: in their combination of qualified praise and modified censure they indicate the kind of critical reservation or opposition which Hopkins's poetry has succeeded, largely, in overcoming or circumventing.[6]

[5] M. Charney, 'A bibliographical study of Hopkins criticism, 1918–1949', *Thought*, vol. 25, no. 97, June 1950, p. 298.
[6] *Poems of Gerard Manley Hopkins*, 4th edition (London, 1967), p. 240.

After the reviews of the first edition, not much was heard of Hopkins for a few years. But just before and just after the publication of the second edition, he was discovered by the 'Cambridge Critics'; in particular, by Richards and Leavis, who laid the foundations of academic acceptance for him. From about 1930 onwards he began to be discussed in scholarly and university-based periodicals, both in England and America, and the first of the full-length books about him began to appear. The second edition of the poems was reviewed very enthusiastically indeed. These things helped to make Hopkins into an example of a phenomenon common to all the contemporary arts: in the 1930s, he became a cult.

The cult of Hopkins, like all cults, has had mixed results. The first was that the trickle of Hopkins criticism became a deluge. Some very enduring work was written, but many critics tended to be over-preoccupied with Hopkins's innovations in technique, and a few others tended to be generally over-enthusiastic. Excessive praise of Hopkins is a product of the Hopkins cult, and has done his reputation little good. Certain over-effusive tributes which have appeared, despite the obvious intelligence and sincerity of their writers, can to my mind be brought within no definition of criticism known or discoverable: they are completely *un*critical in their extremes of enthusiasm. Hopkins has had to pay for these, like any other poet (Burns and Shelley are examples) whose admirers have been unduly ardent. And though his acceptance since the 1930s as a major poet has been on the whole surprisingly rapid, some of the dissent has probably been provoked by irritation at the more extravagant claims which have been made for him.

Another outcome of the Hopkins cult was a spate of imitation by poets and poetasters. Writing in 1935, Professor C. C. Abbott commented crisply on this:

He is accepted by the young as one of their contemporaries, and—a more doubtful privilege—he has even been affiliated to the Martin Tuppers of our day, whose scrannel pipes have infected the field of poetry with mildew and blight.[7]

Hopkins's appeal to the young remains; a fact which is unlikely to surprise anybody. And his appeal to the young poets of the 1930s was intense. He gave them ideas, and they tried them out gleefully, but it is essential here to distinguish between influence and imitation. The first is always the harder to recognize, usually because imitation cannot escape a suggestion of parody if its model is worth imitating in the first place. Hopkins's influence

---

[7] *The Letters of Gerard Manley Hopkins to Robert Bridges* (London, 1935), p. xx.

has been a liberating force in English literature: it can be seen in poets as diverse as Dylan Thomas and Robert Lowell. This influence has strengthened as imitations have waned, and the imitations began to wane as the novelty of what Hopkins had done to English poetry began to wear off. Familiarity with his style bred, not contempt, but a thoughtful rather than an excited response. (I do not mean to imply that Hopkins has lost his power to excite, or that he has in any way become dull—even though he is now a G.C.E. 'A' Level set book, which might be considered the hallmark of conventional respectability.)

Imitations of Hopkins were not confined to the 1930s (one which would have undoubtedly both amused and horrified him, had he been able to see it, was published as early as 1927;[8] and examples still occasionally appear), but there was a concentration of them then. And this led some critics to accuse Hopkins of being a pernicious influence, thus setting up another milestone in his reputation's progress. In retrospect, it seems to me that these critics were wrong. The good poets who were drawn into imitation of Hopkins soon grew out of the phase, but carried over his influence into their mature work; where it emerges, time and again, in supple rhythm and concrete language. His other imitators can simply be forgotten, since they have had no more effect on the course of English literature than Nahum Tate's bland provision of a happy ending for *King Lear*. However, the critics who did take this view were only concerned about the health of English poetry. We should not blame them—and certainly nobody should blame Hopkins's imitators for trying. Hopkins was an innovator, and he seemed much more so then than he does now. Imitation follows innovation, not only in poetry but in all the other arts. This is simply a fact of life. Not one of the imitations was very successful, not even the efforts of good poets, because Hopkins's style is so extremely personal. Hopkins thought and felt so intensely about so many things—about God, about man, about nature, about life and death—and had such wide and curious, if sometimes faulty, knowledge of poetic technique, that to write like him successfully would require not only his technical equipment, but his temperament and outlook too. Nobody has ever managed to think and feel quite in the way Hopkins did. Nobody ever will. And without this, all imitations seem overdressed; as though they are tricked out for show in Hopkins's style. For Hopkins, that style was everyday wear, and not merely the trappings of a gilded hour.

---

[8] In *Cambridge Review*, vol. 49, no. 1198, 4 Nov. 1927, p. 75. A correspondent, sheltering behind the singularly inapt pen-name 'Pro Bono Publico', attempted to pass the poem off as GMH's own.

Hopkins's poetry therefore provided a source of technical ideas for the younger poets of the 1930s; and throughout the decade, despite some dissident voices, his reputation continued to rise. The next important event in its development was the publication (between 1935 and 1938) of his letters, journals, and papers. These books altered the basic attitudes of much Hopkins criticism as soon as they appeared. Critics began to pay less attention to the poems and more to the man behind them, and for Hopkins studies at that time, this shift in emphasis was beneficial. Until Hopkins's prose was published, very little was known about him: there was Lahey's biography, which is superficial and not very reliable, and a number of biographical articles of varying quality; but practically nothing was available that revealed much of Hopkins's personality. Once having read his letters and journals, some critics returned to the poems with newly opened eyes. This brought Hopkins criticism away from an excessive preoccupation with technique. The poems began to be examined not only as poems, but in relation to their spiritual, aesthetic, and biographical background. Special aspects of Hopkins's thought, such as his theory of inscape and its relation to Scotist philosophy, began to be examined in depth. The 1940s, therefore, were a most fruitful period for Hopkins's reputation, and the best of the criticism written then is likely to be of permanent value. By no means all of it, however, was written on traditional lines, or from a biographical standpoint. In the 1940s established critical methods were fighting a rearguard action (lately they have begun to recover lost ground) against the advance of the 'New Criticism'. Since the 'New Critics' have contributed a great deal to Hopkins's present status, some discussion of them is necessary, but so much has already been written about this subject in general that a few words here will be enough.

The 'New Criticism' had been accelerating since the turn of the century: in England and America, it really began with Eliot, though Eliot in turn owed much to the anti-Romanticism of T. E. Hulme. In 1919, Eliot had declared in a famous lecture that 'honest criticism and sensitive appreciation is directed not upon the poet but upon the poetry'.[9] Basically, it seems to me, the whole system rests on that concept: only form, style, and meaning (taking all three in their broadest sense) are relevant in critical processes; nothing else matters. The 'New Criticism' has grown up from there, sometimes in directions which Eliot himself would not have sanctioned, but never departing from that first principle. It has been developed by the 'Cambridge Critics', by the 'Kenyon Critics', and by the 'Chicago

[9] T. S. Eliot, *Tradition and the Individual Talent*, in his *The Sacred Wood* (London, 1920), p. 47.

Critics'; and by others to whom no collective label has yet been affixed. In poetry, it involves close, and often exceedingly subtle, attention to the structure, meaning, and aesthetics of a poet's work. It is now mainly an academic activity, though it has also permeated into journalism. And its influence in Hopkins studies from about 1950 onwards has been altogether dominant.

I have no wish to take sides here in any quarrel between advocates of different critical methods. A critic of poetry, be his object a two-volume study or a two-column review, can reasonably and profitably approach his subject in a variety of ways, depending only on what he is trying to do, and why. Therefore it has always seemed to me absurd to assert the superiority of any approach *a priori*: far too many issues are involved. The 'New Critics' have done a great amount of good by stiffening and reinforcing the fibre of English criticism through their insistence on clarity, precision, and an unemotional, objective attitude to literature. But one of the results of their work, and one acutely obvious in Hopkins criticism throughout the last twenty years, has been a steadily increasing emphasis on interpretation; or, to use the movement's own idiom, explication. The results of this have been noted perceptively by Allen Tate:

Our critics, since Mr. Richards started them off with 'The Principles of Literary Criticism' in 1924, have been perfecting an apparatus for 'explicating' poems (not a bad thing to do) in a kind of prelapsarian innocence of the permanently larger ends of criticism.[10]

That remark concisely expresses my feelings about the effect of this trend in Hopkins studies. Explication of Hopkins's poems is certainly not a bad thing to do, and Hopkins's style is made to measure for it. But unless the process of explication includes some attempt to evaluate, I think it can contribute very little, in the long term, to the development of Hopkins's reputation. Its short-term effect can be considerable, because as long as explication remains fashionable it helps to keep Hopkins fashionable; at least in university English departments, where (since the tradition of academic criticism is now so firmly established) current literary reputations are made and lost. But the kind of criticism that has done most to secure acceptance for Hopkins as a major poet is evaluative criticism; the kind which says, fundamentally, 'Hopkins is a major poet, and I will tell you why.' This is extremely difficult to do well, but when it is done well it is likely to be remembered long after all the explication is forgotten.

[10] A. Tate, 'Reflections on American Poetry, 1900–1950', *Sewanee Review*, vol. 64, 1956, p. 61.

Those are perhaps rather strong words, so I must point out that I am
not attempting to minimize the intrinsic value of explication. At its best, it
is thoroughly worthwhile because it increases understanding of Hopkins's
poems. But at its worst it is too often merely irritating: some practitioners
appear bent on obfuscation rather than explication, and where no difficulties exist they find it necessary to invent them. Altogether too much has
been made of Hopkins's obscurity. He is not allusive like Yeats; he does
not embellish his poetry with Chinese ideographs like Pound; he was
never drunk with the sound of words like Dylan Thomas. And he was
quite definitely never intentionally obscure: his letters show that when he
recognized his obscurity, he regretted it. If he were still able to give his
opinion, he would probably no more relish having his poems explicated
than William McGonagall would relish being treasured by connoisseurs
of incomparable bathos. Each would feel that he was being read for the
wrong reasons. The present close focus of attention on meaning and interpretation in Hopkins criticism seems to me to have gone far enough. But
anyone can define 'the permanently larger ends of criticism' according to
his own schemes of valuation. I merely underline the difference between
analysis and judgement.

Throughout the 1950s and 1960s, then, Hopkins has been holding an
established position as a major poet, and the criticism of his work has been
comparable both in scope and in depth to that accorded to other major
poets. Apart from the frequent studies of individual poems just mentioned,
his critics have been mainly interested in the various aspects of his style,
with special attention to rhythm; in his imagery, with special attention to
metaphor; in his thought and spirituality, in relation to his poems; and in
his life, though there is still no complete biography. Books and book-
length studies of varied scope and quality have been appearing steadily, and
during the last few years the first scholarly tools of the kind provided
sooner or later for every major poet have been published: bibliographies
and concordances are now available, and a definitive edition of the poems
is in preparation. Because Hopkins criticism is so varied and extensive, a
survey of current critical attitudes can be nothing more than an outline
sketch. What follows is offered with that provision.

A glance at Hopkins's entry in the *New Cambridge Bibliography of
English Literature* (1969) is probably as good a way as any of placing his
present relative importance in perspective. The sheer size of the entry
speaks for itself. Hopkins, moreover, is now virtually always given major
status in poetry textbooks and literary histories. Articles and studies usually
take this major status as a *fait accompli*, and get on with the job in hand

without attempting to explain or justify it in detail. But critical approval of Hopkins is neither unanimous nor unqualified; a few critics still regard him as essentially a minor poet, and it is common for even very admiring ones to stress the limitations of his achievement; usually by demonstrating (in one way or another) that his poetic range was narrow, and that his style was often strained and overloaded. There has been a tendency lately to suggest that his most successful work was written in his last years, and that his earlier work has been overrated. It seems possible, in fact, that the next decade may see a downward trend in his reputation: at the moment the signs of this are nothing more than straws in the wind, but it seems to me that they show which way the wind is blowing. If a slump occurs, however, I am convinced that it will mainly be a reaction against Hopkins's comparatively rapid rise in critical favour. I doubt if any serious or lasting rejection of him is now possible.

It may reasonably be argued that one who attempts to write on Hopkins's reputation should be capable of saying exactly what his present reputation is. I realize that there is a lack of precision in my use of the term 'major poet', but I find it very difficult to say just where Hopkins now stands in relation to other poets, because the point is one upon which most critics are wary of committing themselves. Perhaps the most representative recent opinion I have seen is George MacBeth's. In his introduction to the Hopkins section in a recent anthology, Mr. MacBeth draws attention to the 'grotesque over-carved effect' of some of Hopkins's poetry and continues:

Despite these qualifications, Hopkins remains a major Victorian poet, though more important for his form than his content. What finally places him a little lower than Tennyson or Arnold is his lack of any coherent original set of things to say . . . with the passage of time he may begin to seem less like the Donne of the nineteenth century than its Crashaw.[11]

I must take issue here with Mr. MacBeth over one important point. Hopkins probably is, at the moment, placed a little lower than Tennyson or Arnold, and this may (though I doubt it) be because of his lack of 'any coherent original set of things to say'. But he is not *finally* placed anywhere. Hopkins studies are still in their young days by historical standards, and I cannot see that anything like a final judgement on him will be possible for many years yet; if indeed one is ever possible on any poet when relationships between poet and critic are so easily conditioned by ever-changing social and intellectual environment.

[11] G. MacBeth (editor). *The Penguin Book of Victorian Verse* (Harmondsworth, Middlesex, 1969), p. 306.

In writing this introduction I have been uneasily aware that I have had one foot in my own province as a bibliographer and one in the province of the literary historian. It would be nothing but presumption for me to invade the province of the critic, because I have no business there. But after spending so much time in Hopkins's company during the compilation of this bibliography, I have formed strong personal opinions about him, and I would like to end now with a simple statement of my strongest opinion: I believe that Hopkins was not only a major poet, but a great poet. Having said this, I must attempt to justify it, but explicit justification is certainly impossible for me, and probably for anyone else; because nobody, so far as I know, has ever yet managed to explain precisely what great poetry is, or how poets write it, or why individual reaction to it varies so much. This is hardly surprising: we know little enough, really, about the processes of thought and reason, let alone about the creative impulse and emotional response. And however informed the judgement, however scientific its criteria, in the end it is emotional response that matters. Poetry is an emotional form of expression. Hopkins, to me, is a great poet because the emotional response he activates in those who are attuned to his poetry is so intense and lasting. And this, I think, is because his poetry expresses so magnificently his unwavering awareness of the human condition and the human predicament, and of his own involvement in both. Hopkins cared passionately about people, and he knew what people were: the patina of Victorian convention over his attitudes towards them only proves, with its patches of condescension and spots of sentimentality, that he was a man of his time; just as his Christian-moralist ethics prove that he was a conscientious priest. Human nature occasionally disgusted him; human beings, never. Hopkins simply loved his fellow men, and this was not merely something his religion taught him. Nothing and nobody can teach a man to love. Many poets have had a wider experience of life than Hopkins, and a better knowledge of the world. Some have written better poetry. But no poet has ever shown a deeper concern for 'dear and dogged man':

> And what is Earth's eye, tongue, or heart else, where
> Else, but in dear and dogged man?—Ah, the heir
> To his own selfbent so bound, so tied to his turn,
>
> To thriftless reave both our rich round world bare
> And none reck of world after, this bids wear
> Earth brows of such care, care and dear concern.

PART ONE

PUBLISHED WRITINGS BY HOPKINS

SECTION A
POETRY

THIS section is a chronological list of published poetry by GMH. It includes every poem known to the compiler to have been published before 1918, but from 1918 onwards only poems not previously published are recorded. Books containing the first published version of any poem, and all primary editions and selected editions, are described in full. Later impressions are not described unless they differ significantly in form or content. Reviews in English of these books are listed following the entries for the books; reviews in foreign languages are in Section M, and cross-references to them have been provided.

The numbers in parentheses following the titles of poems are the identification-numbers allocated to the poems in P4.

WINTER WITH THE GULF STREAM (3)

A1 Winter with the Gulf Stream. *Once a Week*, vol. 8, 14 Feb. 1863, p. 210.

Signed 'G.M.H.', this version is quoted in FL2, Note B, pp. 437–8. For GMH's comments on its publication, see FL2, p. 16. Full textual notes in P4, p. 247.

BARNFLOOR AND WINEPRESS (6)

A2 Barnfloor and Winepress. *Union Review*, vol. 3, 1865, pp. 579–80. Signed 'G.M.H.' See comments by GMH in FL2, pp. 35–6, 41–2, 213 note 6. Full textual notes in P4, pp. 247–8.

THE SILVER JUBILEE (29)

A3 A SERMON/*Preached at St. Beuno's College, July 30, 1876*, ON THE OCCASION OF/The Silver Jubilee/OF THE/LORD

BISHOP OF SHREWSBURY./BY/JOHN MORRIS,/*Priest of the Society of Jesus.*/[rule]/PUBLISHED AT HIS LORDSHIP'S REQUEST, WITH THE/ADDRESS THEN PRESENTED./[rule]/ LONDON:/BURNS AND OATES, PORTMAN STREET/AND PATERNOSTER ROW./[rule]/1876.

10 unsigned leaves, comprising p. [1] title; p. [2] printer's notice; pp. [3]–4 introductory letter; pp. [5]–14 text; pp. 15–18 text of Address; p. 19 text of THE SILVER JUBILEE, signed 'G.M.H.'; p. [20] blank.

20·5 × 13 cm. Unbound pamphlet printed on white laid paper. The copy described here (the only one located by the compiler) has no covers, but the compiler's attempts to establish whether or not the sermon was originally issued in covers have been inconclusive.

Notes. The text of the poem as published here is identical with P4, apart from details of punctuation. For GMH's own comments see LL1, pp. 65, 77–8; FL2, pp. 139–41. Brief textual notes in P4, p. 263. The poem was originally written for inclusion in an album presented to the Bishop by the Jesuits of St. Beuno's: for a detailed description of this album, with commentary, see 1648.

MILTON (Translated from Dryden) (181)

A4   Milton (translated from Dryden). *Stonyhurst Magazine*, vol. 1, no. 2, July 1881, p. 34.

Signed 'G.H.' Five Latin versions of Dryden's epigram on Milton are printed, GMH's being the fifth. A note with these poems explains: 'The following versions were made by boys on occasion of an examination. That which comes last is from an older pen.' Brief textual note in P4, p. 339.

ANGELUS AD VIRGINEM (Appendix D)

A5   The Song of Chaucer's Clerk of Oxenford, '*Angelus ad Virginem*'. *Month*, vol. 44, no. 211, Jan. 1882, pp. 100–11.

Published anonymously: GMH's contribution was limited to a modernization of the English text and some footnotes. See his comments in FL2, pp. 161, 162; and Professor Abbott's comments on these letters, p. 444 note H. Full textual notes in P4, pp. 237–8, 341–3.

THE CHILD IS FATHER TO THE MAN (147); COCKLE'S ANTIBILIOUS PILLS; NO NEWS IN THE *TIMES* TO-DAY.

A6   A trio of triolets. *Stonyhurst Magazine*, vol. 1, no. 9, Mar. 1883, p. 162.

> Signed 'Bran'. For G M H's own comments, see LL1, p. 178, 190–1. Textual notes in P4, pp. 312–13. See also K14, K15.

SONGS FROM SHAKESPEARE, IN LATIN (182)

A7   Songs from Shakspeare [*sic*] in Latin. No. I. 'Full fathom five thy father lies'. *Irish Monthly*, vol. 14, no. 161, Nov. 1886, p. 628.
> Published anonymously. English text, and G M H's Latin translation. For G M H's own comments, see LL1, p. 230. Full textual notes in P4, pp. 339–40.

A8   Songs from Shakspere [*sic*] in Latin. No. II. 'Come unto these yellow sands'. *Irish Monthly*, vol. 15, no. 164, Feb. 1887, p. 92.
> Signed 'G.H.' English text, and G M H's Latin translation. For G M H's own comments, see LL1, p. 230. Full textual notes in P4, pp. 339–40.

MORNING MIDDAY AND EVENING SACRIFICE (49)

A9   *Dixon, Richard Watson, *compiler*. The Bible birthday book; arranged by . . . Canon Dixon. London, G. Routledge & Sons, 1887. 252 pp. 16°.
> *See* entry for 25 May. The first stanza only is given, printed over 'Hopkins'. For G M H's own comments see LL1, pp. 87, 92, 97–8, and LL2, pp. 130, 132, 138. Textual notes in P4, pp. 276–7. The compiler has been unable to trace a copy of this book for examination. The British Museum copy (shelf-mark 3128. aa. 3) is missing, and after repeated inquiries the compiler was informed in January 1971 that it had been destroyed by bombing in the last war.

AD MARIAM (26)

A10 *Ad Mariam. *Blandyke Papers*, vol. 26, May 1890, p. 130. Textual notes in P4, p. 253. The *Blandyke Papers* is a private Jesuit publication of very limited circulation: see also A14.

THOU ART INDEED JUST, LORD . . . (74); THEE, GOD, I COME FROM . . . (155); TO SEEM THE STRANGER . . . (66); A VISION OF THE MERMAIDS (2); THE HABIT OF PERFEC-TION (22); THE STARLIGHT NIGHT (32); SPRING (33); THE CANDLE INDOORS (46); SPRING AND FALL (55); INVERS-NAID (56); TO R.B. (76).

A11 The/[in red]POETS/and the/[in red]POETRY/of the/[in red] CENTURY/[rule]/Robert Bridges/and/Contemporary Poets/[two rules]/ [in red] Edited by/[in red]ALFRED H. MILES/[rule]/HUTCHIN-SON & CO./34, PATERNOSTER ROW, LONDON

[a]^8, b^4, 1–45^8, 46^1. 373 leaves, comprising p. [i] half-title: The/ POETS/and the/POETRY/of the/CENTURY; p. [ii] blank; p. [iii] title; p. [iv] blank; pp. v–viii PREFATORY.; pp. ix–xxii INDEX.; p. [xxiii] fly-title: [in red] Robert Bridges/and/Contemporary Poets; p. [xxiv] blank; pp. 1–714 text, with printer's notice at foot of p. 714; pp. [715]–[722] publisher's descriptive note on the plan of the ten-volume set, with contents of each volume and details of different editions.

16·8 × 10·8 cm. Bulk 4 × 4·5 cm. White laid paper, top edge gilt, other edges untrimmed. In some copies paper of two different weights has been used: some leaves are thicker than others. White laid end-papers. Bound in olive-green cloth, lettered in gold on front: The Poets/and the Poetry/of the Century/Alfred H. Miles; and in gold on spine: The/POETS/and the/POETRY/of the/CENTURY/[rule]/ Miles/Robert/Bridges/and/Contemporary/Poets/HUTCHINSON & Co.

Notes. The eleven poems by G M H are printed with a short introduction by Bridges on pp. 161–70. Poems 74 (partial text), 155, and 66 (partial text) are quoted in Bridges's introduction, pp. 162–3. The main selection of poems is on pp. 165–70: all except the first (2) are given in full. This book is volume 8 in the ten-volume set. It was published in August 1893, price 4*s*. (£2 the set) and belongs to the 'Popular' edition. There was also an edition on special paper, bound in vellum, gilt top, limited to 100 copies, each book numbered, sold in sets only at £3. 15*s*. 0*d*. the set; and an edition limited to 300 copies, on fine paper, bound in buckram gilt, gilt top, sold at £3. 0*s*. 0*d*. the set, separate volumes 10*s*. each. No further information has been available owing to the destruction of the publisher's records by bombing in the last war. The book was reprinted in 1898, on coated paper with a different title-page and binding.

Reviews:

A12   Anon. in *Manchester Guardian*, 29 Aug. 1893, p. 9.
The reviewer challenged G M H's claim to a place in this type of anthology: 'Curiosities like the verses of the late Gerard Hopkins should be excluded, while introductions like those contributed to his work by Mr. Bridges should, if possible, be multiplied, but employed on worthier objects.'

A13   Anon. in *Athenaeum*, no. 3439, 23 Sept. 1893, pp. 411–13.
This review simply mentions G M H's inclusion in the anthology, but without censure.

AD MARIAM (26)

A14   Ad Mariam. *Stonyhurst Magazine*, vol. 5, no. 72, Feb. 1894, p. 233.
The poem is printed with a covering letter from a correspondent who signed himself 'O.S.J.' Full textual note in P4, p. 253.

BARNFLOOR AND WINEPRESS (6); GOD'S GRANDEUR (31); HEAVEN-HAVEN (9); MORNING, MIDDAY AND EVENING SACRIFICE (49); THEE, GOD, I COME FROM (155)

A15   [first line in red] LYRA SACRA/A BOOK OF RELIGIOUS VERSE/SELECTED AND ARRANGED BY/H. C. BEECHING, M.A./METHUEN & CO./36 ESSEX STREET, W.C./LONDON/ 1895

[*a*]², *b*⁸, 1–22⁸, 23⁶. 192 leaves, comprising p. [i] half-title: LYRA SACRA; p. [ii] printer's notice; p. [iii] title; p. [iv] blank; pp. v–x

PREFACE; pp. xi–xx CONTENTS; pp. [1]–336 text; pp. [337]–356 NOTES; pp. 357–64 INDEX, with printer's notice at foot of p. 364.

19 × 12·5 cm. Bulk 2·8 × 3·3 cm. White laid paper, top edge gilt, other edges untrimmed. White laid endpapers. Bound in dark blue cloth, lettered in gold on spine: LYRA/SACRA/SELECTED &/ ARRANGED BY/H. C. BEECHING/METHUEN/LONDON

Notes. The first four of the five poems by G M H (6, 31, 9, 49) are given in full, printed over 'Gerard Hopkins' on pp. 313–16. See also Beeching's notes, p. 354: 'A selection of poems by the late Father Hopkins, S.J. appeared, with a critical notice by Mr. Robert Bridges, in Miles's *Poets of the Century*, vol. viii. Those in this anthology, which are all now printed for the first time, [*sic*] are given by kind leave of the poet's father, Mr. Manley Hopkins . . .' The final poem (155) is printed with this note. The book was published in March 1895.

In the second edition, published in 1903 in Methuen's 'Library of Devotion' series, 'Spring and Fall' (55) was added to the five poems mentioned above—see p. 346. The text is identical with the one printed in A11, the eighth line reading 'Though world of wanhood leafmeal lie;' but Beeching added a note: 'An earlier and plainer reading is, "Though forests low and leafmeal lie." ' This reading was rejected by G M H in drafting the poem: see P4, p. 280.

Reviews:

A16   Anon. Some recent books of verse. *Speaker*, vol. 11, 20 Apr. 1895, pp. 443–4.

'One omission is Mr. Aubrey de Vere . . . Also, in a selection which included the late Father Hopkins and Mr. Digby Mackworth Dolben, room might well have been made for Mr. Lionel Johnson, Miss Probyn, and Mrs. Meynell.'

THE BLESSED VIRGIN COMPARED TO THE AIR WE BREATHE (60)

A17   A BOOK OF/[in red]CHRISTMAS VERSE/SELECTED BY H. C. BEECHING: WITH/TEN DESIGNS BY WALTER CRANE/ [design]/LONDON: METHUEN AND COMPANY/36 ESSEX ST. STRAND: MDCCCXCV

[a]–b⁴, A–Y⁴. 96 leaves, comprising pp. [i]–[ii] blank; p. [iii] half-title: CHRISTMAS VERSE; p. [iv] blank; p. [v] title; p. [vi] blank; pp. vii–ix PREFACE; p. [x] blank; pp. xi–xvi CONTENTS: p. [1] fly-title: LATIN HYMNS; p. [2] blank; pp. 3–10 text; p. [11] fly-title: EARLY CAROLS; p. [12] blank; pp. 13–22 text; p. [23] fly-title: LATER POEMS AND CAROLS; p. [24] blank; pp. 25–136 text; p. [137] fly-title: POEMS ON CHRISTMAS MERRY-/MAKING; p. [138] blank; pp. 139–65 text; p. [166] blank; p. [167] fly-title: NOTES; p. [168] blank; pp. 169–[174] text of Notes; with printer's notice at foot of p. [174]; one blank leaf.

18·6 × 12·5 cm. Bulk 2·2 × 2·7 cm. White wove paper, top edge gilt, other edges untrimmed. White laid endpapers. Bound in green cloth, blocked with red on spine. Embossed designs on front and spine. Lettered on front: [in relief on a red panel] A BOOK OF/CHRIST-MAS/VERSE; and on spine: [in gold] A BOOK/OF/XMAS/VERSE/ [in black] SELECTED/BY/H. C./BEECHING/10 DESIGNS/BY/ WALTER/CRANE/1895/LONDON/METHUEN/& CO

The designs by Walter Crane are printed on pp. [20], 27, [38], 41, [50], 118, [126], 139, [144], 154. The design on p. 27 is also printed on the title-page.

Notes. The poem is published here under its original title, 'Mary Mother of Divine Grace Compared to the Air we Breathe'; see P4, p. 283. It is printed over 'Gerard Hopkins', and Beeching's brief note on the poem is on p. 173. In some copies a publisher's catalogue of 32 pages is bound in at the back of the book between the last leaf and the endpaper. This catalogue is dated September 1895.

THE ELOPEMENT (135)

A18   Anon. Early Magazines. *Oratory School Magazine*, no. 13, Nov. 1895, pp. 5–8.

The poem first appeared in a handwritten school magazine produced at the Oratory School, Birmingham. This essay quotes the poem together with a parody of it. Textual notes in P4, p. 309.

ROSA MYSTICA (27)

A19 Rosa Mystica. *Irish Monthly*, vol. 26, no. 299, May 1898, pp. 234–5.

  Textual notes in P4, p. 253.

A20 *Rosa Mystica. *Weekly Register* (Diocese of Westminster, London), 7 May 1898.

THEE, GOD, I COME FROM ... (155)

A21 Magnus, Laurie, *and* Headlam, Cecil, *compilers.*
  Prayers from the poets: a calendar of devotion.
  Edinburgh and London, William Blackwood and Sons, 1899. ix, 369 pp.
  The poem is printed on pp. 234–5. For a detailed discussion of the text and comparison with other printed versions, see I 706.

ROSA MYSTICA (27); MARY MOTHER OF DIVINE GRACE COMPARED TO THE AIR WE BREATHE (60)

A22 Shipley, Orby, *editor.* Carmina Mariana ... *2nd edition, 2nd series.*
  London, Burns and Oates, 1902. liv, 528 pp.
  See pp. 183–9.

HEAVEN-HAVEN (9)

A23 Waterhouse, Elizabeth. A little book of life and death. London, Methuen & Co., 1902. xi, 287 pp.
  See p. 70. The poem is printed over 'Gerard Hopkins, S.J.'

Review:

A24 Thompson, Francis. The preferential anthology. *Academy and Literature*, vol. 63, no. 1576, 19 July 1902, pp. 88–9.
  'Lastly, perhaps, we may end these citations on solitude with a very quiet and restrained little poem which is unknown to us, from the pen of Father Gerard Hopkins, called "Heaven-Haven"—' Full quotation of the poem follows. This is the only reference to GMH

by Thompson discovered by the compiler. Thompson's authorship of this review has been established by Terence L. Connolly in *Literary Criticisms by Francis Thompson* (New York, E. P. Dutton & Co., 1948).

A25   *Heaven-Haven. *Living Age*, vol. 18 (7th series), 10 Jan. 1903, p. 128.

THE BLESSED VIRGIN COMPARED TO THE AIR WE BREATHE (60)

A26   Bartle, Anita, *compiler*. The Madonna of the poets. London, Burns and Oates, 1906. 126, xix pp.
   See pp. 88–9. Partial text only.

HEAVEN-HAVEN (9)

A27   Tynan, Katharine, *compiler*. A book of memory: the birthday book of the blessed dead. London, Hodder & Stoughton, 1906. xi, 216 pp.
   See p. 210.

THE STARLIGHT NIGHT (32)

A28   Quiller-Couch, Arthur, *editor*. The Oxford book of Victorian verse. Oxford, Clarendon Press, 1912. xv, 1023 pp.
   See p. 691.

NONDUM (23)

A29   Nondum. *Month*, vol. 126, no. 615, Sept. 1915, pp. 246–7.
   'The above verses, dated 1866, were found in a second-hand classical book, lately purchased in Dublin. They are in the handwriting of the late Father Gerard Hopkins S.J., and on the inner evidence of style may perhaps be attributed to his composition.' Brief textual notes in P4, p. 252.

SPRING AND FALL (55); THE WRECK OF THE DEUTSCH-
LAND, STANZA 1 (28); THE CANDLE INDOORS (46); IN THE
VALLEY OF THE ELWY (34); THE HANDSOME HEART (47);
THE HABIT OF PERFECTION (22)

A 30   The/Spirit of Man/An Anthology in English & French/from the
Philosophers & Poets/made by the Poet Laureate in/1915/& dedicated by
gracious permission/to His Majesty/The King/[ornament]/Longmans
Green & Co London/New York, Bombay, Calcutta & Madras/1916
[title-page printed in fancy italics]

[A]⁶, B–X⁸, Y⁴. 170 leaves, comprising an unpaginated text consisting
of 449 numbered items, preceded by PREFACE; CONTENTS
[on recto of one leaf, with brief introductory poem on verso]; and
followed by PREFACE TO THE INDEX; INDEX; LIST OF
AUTHORS; and printer's notice on verso of penultimate leaf.

17 × 11·5 cm. Bulk 2·5 × 2·9 cm. White wove paper, all edges
trimmed. White wove endpapers. Bound in fawn paper boards, with
parchment spine. White paper label on spine, lettered in black: The/
Spirit/of/Man/Robert Bridges [this lettering in fancy italics]

Notes. The six poems by GMH are items 9, 53, 269, 358, 369, 385.
Of these; 'The Candle Indoors', 'In the Valley of the Elwy', and 'The
Handsome Heart' are given in full. 'Spring and Fall' and 'The Habit of
Perfection' are partial texts, and Stanza 1 of 'The Wreck of the
Deutschland' can only be described as mutilated, presumably by
Bridges. The book was published on 20 Jan. 1916, price 5*s.*, in an
edition of 3,000 copies. A further 1,000 copies were printed on India
paper, and bound in cloth, price 6*s.* 6*d.*, and leather, price 9*s.*

Reviews:
A 31   [De la Mare, Walter.] The spirit of man. *Times Literary Supplement*,
    3 Feb. 1916, pp. 49–50.
       'As regards more modern writers, the book is singularly rich in the
    work of Dolben, R.W. Dixon, and Gerard Hopkins—and friendship
    needs no better tribute and loyalty—and these . . . are among (in its
    exact sense) the most egregious craftsmen of Dr. Bridges' flock.'
    This review was reprinted in *Littell's Living Age*, vol. 289, 29 Apr.

1916, p. 298. De la Mare's authorship is confirmed by his book
Private view (London, Faber, 1953), pp. 185–93.

A 32   Anon. The spirit of man. *New Statesman*, vol. 6, no. 148, 5 Feb.
1916, pp. 427–8.

'There are several poems by Gerard Hopkins which are not to be
found elsewhere. In these there is a curious sincerity and elaborate-
ness of diction which, if it delights at all, delights the reader deeply.
He is little known; but he was one of the most original of modern
poets.'

A 33   Anon. The growth of man's soul through the ages. *New York Times
Review of Books*, 26 Mar. 1916, p. 105.

'And then there is Gerard Hopkins who was Walter Pater's pupil, a
poet whose craftsmanship was as elaborate as his inspiration was
genuine . . .

"The Habit of Perfection" in its entirety is Gerard Hopkins's
best claim to literary immortality, and the best poetry ever written
about the religious life.'

A 34   Martindale, C. C. Anthologia Laureata. *Dublin Review*, vol. 158,
no. 317, Apr. 1916, pp. 259–65.

'. . . the Jesuit poet Gerard Hopkins . . . is, astonishingly, more
pessimistic over "the blight man was born for" even than Rimbaud
. . .'

A 35   Anon. in *Catholic World*, vol. 103, June 1916, pp. 394–5.

'. . . the great men are always accessible, and the gain is ours when a
man of true taste and discernment brings forth . . . the best things from
second or third rate poets . . . and so we are thankful that Mr.
Bridges has a fondness for Darley and Dixon and Dolben and Hopkins and Yeats . . .'

THE HABIT OF PERFECTION (22); GOD'S GRANDEUR (31);
MARY MOTHER OF DIVINE GRACE COMPARED TO THE
AIR WE BREATHE (60)

A 36   Nicholson, D. H. S., *and* Lee, A. H. E., *editors*. The Oxford
book of English mystical verse. Oxford, Clarendon Press, 1917. xv,
644 pp.

See pp. 353–9.

THE STARLIGHT NIGHT (32); THE HABIT OF PERFECTION
(22); SPRING (33)

A 37 *Kilmer, Joyce, *editor*. Dreams and images: an anthology of
Catholic poets. New York, Boni and Liveright, 1917. xvii, 286 pp.
> See pp. 99–101.

POEMS OF GMH (FIRST EDITION, 1918)

A 38 [within an ornamental border] Poems/of/Gerard Manley Hopkins/
now first published/Edited with notes/by/ROBERT BRIDGES/Poet
Laureate/[ornament]/LONDON/HUMPHREY MILFORD [title-page
printed in italics]

[A]⁴, B–H⁸, I⁶. 66 leaves, comprising p. [i] half-title: *Poems/of/Gerard
Manley Hopkins/*1918; p. [ii] printer's notice; p. [iii] title; p. [iv]
blank; p. [v] dedication; p. [vi] blank; p. [vii] CONTENTS; p. [viii]
Robert Bridges's sonnet 'Our generation already is overpast . . .'; pp.
[1]–6 AUTHOR'S PREFACE; pp. [7]–9 EARLY POEMS; p. [10]
blank; pp. [11]–70 POEMS 1876–1889; pp. [71]–92 UNFINISHED
POEMS & FRAGMENTS; p. [93] fly-title: EDITOR'S NOTES;
pp. [94]–124 text of Editor's Notes.

19·2 × 12·5 cm. Bulk 1 × 1·4 cm. White wove paper, edges of some
leaves trimmed, edges of others untrimmed. White wove endpapers.
Bound in light-blue paper boards, with cream cloth spine. Cream
paper label on spine, lettered in black: *Poems/of/Gerard/Manley/
Hopkins/*[ornament]/*Bridges*
Illustrations are inserted facing pp. 7, 41, 71, 92.

Notes. This book was published in an edition of 750 copies. Of these,
50 were given away; 180 were sold in the first year; 240 in the second
year; then an average of 30 a year for six years, rising to 90 in 1927.
The last four copies were sold in 1928. The price was 12s. 6d. (See
LL1, p. xx.) It is now scarce, and the few copies which appear for sale
or auction command very high prices.

Reviews :
A 39 [Bain, Robert.] in *Glasgow Herald*, 2 Jan. 1919, p. 3.
> 'The book is a hard nut to crack, and a lecturer on English literature

might make a week's work out of it . . . The crudities obscure the intellectual swiftness and the imaginative boldness which are the note of the book . . .' The *probable* authorship of this review has been established by E. W. Mellown (see F 9).

A40 [Clutton-Brock, Arthur.] Gerard Hopkins. *Times Literary Supplement*, 9 Jan. 1919, p. 19.

A generally favourable review. 'It is as if he heard everywhere a music too difficult, because too beautiful, for our ears and noted down what he could catch of it . . .' Some stress is laid on G M H's defects (Bridges's influence is clear) but the over-all tone is one of pleased acceptance. The authorship of this review has again been established by E. W. Mellown (F 9).

A41 Maynard, Theodore. The artist as hero. *New Witness*, vol. 13, no. 325, 24 Jan. 1919, pp. 259–60.

'A shy mid-Victorian priest, writing while Tennyson, Swinburne and Patmore led their various schools, was more modern than the most freakish modern would dare to be . . . He is the last word in technical development.' This review was strongly influenced by Bridges: thus we are told that G M H's style '. . . has its own original beauty, but it is a style no-one should use again . . . the oddities of rhyme and rhythm are sometimes repellently ugly.' None the less, the over-all tone is one of admiration, perhaps slightly prompted by religious sympathy.

A42 Anon. in *Book Monthly*, vol. 14, no. 3, Feb. 1919, p. 214.

A brief comment, here given in full: 'Hopkins, a Jesuit, was only forty-four at his death thirty years ago. These distinguished poems (with notes by the Poet Laureate) are now first published.'

A43 Henry, Michael. Sweet discord. *Everyman*, vol. 13, no. 330, 8 Feb. 1919, pp. 416–17.

Another review clearly influenced by Bridges, but again stressing the beauties to be found in the poems.

A44 Guiney, Louise Imogen. Gerard Hopkins: a rediscovered poet. *Month*, vol. 133, no. 657, Mar. 1919, pp. 205–14.

This review pays handsome tribute to Bridges's skill and care in editing the poems, though Miss Guiney was distressed by his lack of tolerance towards G M H's religion. The poems are evaluated very favourably.

A45 Maynard, Theodore. Solitary of song. *America*, vol. 20, no. 21, 1 Mar. 1919, pp. 533–4.

'Hopkins is, upon the whole, the most densely obscure poet who ever wrote in English. Where Blake and Browning leave off, there Hopkins begins.' See also A67.

A46   Anon. Gerard Hopkins. *Saturday Westminster Gazette*, vol. 53, no. 8022, 8 Mar. 1919, pp. 13–14.

This review is very critical of Bridges for omitting some of G M H's poems on grounds of immaturity or inferiority. 'There may, of course, be good reason why it was held necessary to reserve for this long period the most important work of a distinguished writer; but there can surely be none for its publication in an incomplete form . . .' See also A47, A49, A50, A52, A53.

A47   Anon. Improper editing. *Universe*, 14 Mar. 1919, p. 2.

Another attack on Bridges as editor, which quotes with approval the views of the *Saturday Westminster Gazette*'s reviewer (A46) as a prelude to an onslaught on Bridges for excluding some purely religious poems. A correspondence followed in which literary criticism and religious controversy became decidedly entangled: see A49, A50, A52, A53.

A48   [Shanks, Edward.] The prophet unveiled. *New Statesman*, vol. 12, no. 310, 15 Mar. 1919, p. 530.

This is probably the least favourable of all the reviews.

A49   Guiney, Louise Imogen. 'Improper editing'—a counter-thrust. *Universe*, 21 Mar. 1919, p. 10.

A long and reasoned defence of Bridges as editor of G M H's poems, in reply to A47. See also A50, A52, A53.

A50   Anon. Improper editing. *Universe*, 28 Mar. 1919, p. 4.

Two letters refuting Guiney's defence of Bridges (A49), the first from 'The Writer of the Note' (i.e. the author of A47) and the second from 'A Member of the University of Oxford'. See also A52, A53.

A51   *Anon. in *Catholic Book Club Notes*, vol. 23, no. 246, Apr. 1919, pp. 52–3.

A52   Holden, Edward. Improper editing. *Universe*, 4 Apr. 1919, p. 4. A letter in support of Guiney (A49).

A53   Robinson, Gertrude. Improper editing. *Universe*, 4 Apr. 1919, p. 4.

Another letter in support of Guiney (A49).

A54   [Bliss, Geoffrey] Gerard Hopkins' poems. *Tablet*, vol. 133, no. 4117, 5 Apr. 1919, pp. 420, 422.

A favourable review which includes some detailed and perceptive criticism of G M H's style and technique. Written for a Catholic audience but by no means partisan. The authorship of this review

has been confirmed by Father David Hoy, in a letter to the compiler.

A55 *Guiney, Louise Imogen. A lost and recovered poet. *Ave Maria*,
vol. 9 (n.s.), no. 14, 5 Apr. 1919, pp. 433–5.

A56 [Moore, F. C.] A medley of verse. *Spectator*, vol. 122, no. 4741,
10 May 1919, pp. 598–9.

Bridges's influence is again clearly evident. 'The poems . . . are too
often needlessly obscure, harsh and perverse . . .' The authorship of
this review has been established by E. W. Mellown (see F9).

A57 Anon. in *Oxford Magazine*, vol. 37, no. 20, 23 May 1919, pp.
310–11.

An unenthusiastic review, strongly influenced by Bridges. The
reviewer's standards and general attitude are perhaps summed up in
his comment on 'Harry Ploughman': 'There are many who will turn
with relief to, say, Masefield's sketch of the ploughman at the end of
The Everlasting Mercy; all those at any rate who believe in the
inevitable quality of real poetry.'

A58 Anon. in *Methodist Recorder*, 29 May 1919, p. 9.
'It is scarcely likely the book will have a very wide circulation. It is quite
certain to find its place on the shelf of the discerning . . .'

A59 Anon. in *Dial* (New York), vol. 66, no. 791, 31 May 1919,
p. 572.
'These poems . . . show a kinship with the roughness and obscurity,
as well as with the force, of Browning and Meredith. They express a
strange talent, but will claim few readers.'

A60 *McBrien, Peter. in *Irish Rosary* (Literary Supplement), vol. 23,
June 1919, pp. 473–8.

A61 O'Neill, George. in *Studies* (Dublin), vol. 8, no. 30, June 1919,
pp. 331–3.
G M H had '. . . an exquisitely refined literary sense, but it permitted
him to lapse into nearly every literary fault . . .'

A62 M[urry], J[ohn] M[iddleton]. Gerard Manley Hopkins. *Athenaeum*, no. 4649, 6 June 1919, pp. 425–6.
Thoughtful and subtle criticism, showing enthusiasm tempered by
misgivings about the more unusual features in the poems. Reprinted
in H16.

A63 *Lappin, Henry A. Gerard Hopkins and his poetry. *Catholic
World*, vol. 109, no. 652, July 1919, pp. 501–12.

A64 *Russell, Matthew. in *Irish Monthly*, vol. 47, no. 554, Aug. 1919,
pp. 441–8.

A65   Page, Frederick. Father Gerard Hopkins: I—his poetry. *Dublin Review*, vol. 167, no. 334, July–Sept. 1920, pp. 40–5.

This review is almost entirely preoccupied with G M H's religion, and with defending it against Bridges's comments and attitudes. As literary criticism it is negligible.

A66   Sapir, Edward. Gerard Hopkins. *Poetry*, vol. 18, no. 6, Sept. 1921, pp. 330–6.

Influential and important review, which contains some of the earliest *balanced* criticism of G M H. Sapir admits that 'To a certain extent Hopkins undoubtedly loved difficulty, even obscurity, for its own sake . . .', but asserts that 'Hopkins's poetry is of the most precious. His voice is easily one of the half-dozen most individual voices in the whole course of English nineteenth-century poetry'.

A67   *Maynard, Theodore. The poetry of Father Hopkins. *Freeman*, vol. 8, no. 189, 24 Oct. 1923, pp. 156–7.

Condensed reprint of A45.

A68   *Putnam, Sam. Gerard Manley Hopkins. *Chicago Post*, 30 May 1924, p. 7.

ROSA MYSTICA (27)

A69   Rosa Mystica. *Month*, vol. 133, no. 659, May 1919, pp. 339–40.

DOROTHEA AND THEOPHILUS (25)

A70   Dorothea and Theophilus. *Dublin Review*, vol. 167, no. 334, July–Sept. 1920, pp. 45–6.

There is no annotation and the source is not given, but this version corresponds very closely to that published in P3 and P4. The small variations are probably mistranscriptions—e.g. 'shy' for 'sky' in stanza 4. Textual notes in P4, p. 252.

A VISION OF THE MERMAIDS (2)

A71   Gerard Manley Hopkins/A Vision of the Mermaids/A prize poem dated Christmas, 1862, partially/printed in A. H. Miles' 'Poets and Poetry of/the Nineteenth Century' (Robert Bridges and/Contemporary Poets), and in the Notes to the/'Poems of Gerard Manley Hopkins' edited/by Robert Bridges (1918) and now for the/first time printed in full. *The poem is here/published in a complete facsimile, by Humphrey/Milford at the Oxford University Press/London. The edition is limited/to 250 copies, of which/this is No. /*MCMXXIX

6 unsigned and unpaginated leaves, comprising one blank leaf; p. [1] title; p. [2] blank; pp. [3]–6 text; p. [7] blank; p. [8] printer's notice; one blank leaf.

32·5 × 21 cm. Text paper 30·7 × 19·3 cm. Prelims and end-pages printed on white wove paper; text printed on smoother and heavier paper. All edges of text paper trimmed, all other edges untrimmed. White wove endpapers. Bound in paper boards, patterned in black and white, black cloth spine. White paper label on front, lettered in black: [within a border of black rules] A VISION/OF/THE/MERMAIDS/ *by/G. M. Hopkins*

The text is headed by a circular pen-and-ink drawing, 6 in. in diameter.

Notes. Despite the title-page, this was probably *not* a prize poem: see P4, p. 246. The drawing by G M H which heads the text is reproduced in P4 on the plate facing p. 8. This book received little attention from reviewers, but is included in some reviews of A72—see A77, A84, A89, B24.

POEMS OF G M H (SECOND EDITION, 1930)

A72   *Poems of/*GERARD MANLEY/HOPKINS/*Edited with notes/ by/*ROBERT *BRIDGES/*[ornament]/SECOND EDITION/*With an Appendix of Additional/Poems, and a Critical/Introduction by/CHARLES WILLIAMS/*OXFORD   UNIVERSITY   PRESS/*LONDON: HUMPHREY MILFORD/*1930

[a]⁴, b⁶, B–X⁴. 90 leaves, comprising p. [i] half-title: *Poems of/* GERARD MANLEY/HOPKINS; p. [ii] blank; p. [iii] title; p. [iv] printer's notice; pp. [v]–viii CONTENTS; pp. [ix]–xvi INTRODUC-TION TO THE/SECOND EDITION; p. [xvii] fly-title: Poems of/ *GERARD MANLEY/HOPKINS*; p. [xviii] blank; p. [xix] dedi-cation; p. [xx] Robert Bridges's sonnet 'Our generation already is over-

past . . .'; pp. [1]–6 AUTHOR'S PREFACE; pp. [7]–9 EARLY
POEMS; p. [10] blank; pp. [11]–69 POEMS 1876–1889; pp. [70]–
92 UNFINISHED POEMS/& FRAGMENTS; p. [93] fly-title:
EDITOR'S NOTES; pp. [94]–122 text of Editor's Notes; p. [123]
fly-title: APPENDIX; p. [124] blank; pp. 125–53 text of Appendix;
pp. [154]–6 NOTES TO THE ADDITIONAL/POEMS; pp. [157]
–9 INDEX OF FIRST LINES; p. [160] printer's notice.

19·2 × 12·6 cm. Bulk 1·1 × 1·4 cm. White wove paper, edges untrimmed, white wove endpapers. Bound in dark-blue cloth, lettered in
gold on front: POEMS OF/GERARD MANLEY/HOPKINS/
ROBERT BRIDGES; and in gold on spine: POEMS/OF/GERARD/
MANLEY/HOPKINS/BRIDGES/OXFORD

Notes. This book is essentially an expanded reprint of the first edition
(A38). The arrangement and numbering of the poems in the first
edition are retained, and the 16 additional poems in the Appendix
continue the numbering consecutively, as follows: 75 Spring and
Death; 76 The Escorial; 77 A Vision of the Mermaids; 78 Barnfloor
and Winepress; 79 The Nightingale; 80 Nondum; 81 Easter; 82 Lines
for a Picture of St. Dorothea; 83 Winter with the Gulf Stream; 84 Ad
Mariam; 85 Rosa Mystica; 86 Margaret Cliteroe; 87 On St. Winefred;
88 O Deus, ego amo te; 89 S. Thomae Aquinatis; 90 Oratio Patris
Condren. Published in November 1930; reprinted in March 1931,
January 1933, March 1935; reissued in the 'Oxford Bookshelf' series
May 1937, reprinted in 1938, 1940, 1941, 1943 (smaller format), and
1944. The 1944 impression was taken out of the 'Oxford Bookshelf'
series, but was in the same format and from the same plates as the 1943
impression.

POEMS OF GMH (SECOND EDITION, LIMITED, 1930)

A73   *Poems of*/GERARD MANLEY/HOPKINS/*Edited with notes*/
by/*ROBERT BRIDGES*/[ornament]/SECOND EDITION/*With an*
Appendix of Additional/*Poems, and a Critical Introduction by*/*CHARLES*
WILLIAMS/OXFORD UNIVERSITY PRESS/ *LONDON: HUM-*
PHREY MILFORD/1930

[a]⁴, b⁶, B–X⁴. 90 leaves, comprising p. [i] half-title: *Poems of*/
GERARD MANLEY/HOPKINS; p. [ii] blank; p. [iii] title; p. [iv]

certificate: THIS EDITION, PRINTED ON HAND-/MADE PAPER, IS LIMITED TO 250 COPIES, OF WHICH THIS IS/ NO. , [and] printer's notice; pp. [v]–viii CONTENTS [and] ILLUSTRATIONS; pp. [ix]–xvi INTRODUCTION TO THE/ SECOND EDITION; p. [xvii] fly-title: Poems of/*GERARD MANLEY/HOPKINS*; p. [xviii] blank; p. [xix] dedication; p. [xx] Robert Bridges's sonnet 'Our generation already is overpast . . .'; pp. [1]–6 AUTHOR'S PREFACE; pp. [7]–9 EARLY POEMS; p. [10] blank; pp. [11]–69 POEMS 1876–1889; pp. [70]–92 UN-FINISHED POEMS/& FRAGMENTS; p. [93] fly-title: EDITOR'S NOTES; pp. [94]–122 text of Editor's Notes; p. [123] fly-title: APPENDIX; p. [124] blank; pp. 125–53 text of Appendix; pp. [154]–6 NOTES TO THE ADDITIONAL/POEMS; pp. [157]–9 INDEX OF FIRST LINES; p. [160] printer's notice.

20·7 × 13·4 cm. Bulk 1·8 × 2·2 cm. White wove paper, watermarked MILLBOURN/BRITISH HAND MADE PURE RAG with de-vice, grey laid endpapers patterned in black to match binding. Top edge trimmed, others untrimmed. Bound in paper boards, patterned in grey and black, parchment spine. Lettered in gold on spine: POEMS/ OF / GERARD / MANLEY / HOPKINS / [ornament] / BRIDGES / OXFORD

Illustrations are inserted facing pp. 7, 40, and 130, and between pp. 70–1 and 92–3. The leaves bearing these are sewn in, not gummed, but the illustrations facing p. 7 and 40 are portraits lightly gummed to the leaf. For contents and arrangement, see the notes to A72. This book is now rare.

Reviews of A72:

A74 *Pickman, Hester. in *Hound and Horn*, vol. 4, no. 1, Oct.–Dec. 1930, pp. 118–27.

A75 *Anon. in *Commonweal*, vol. 13, no. 2, 12 Nov. 1930, pp. 32–3.

A76 [Kunitz, Stanley J.] Dilly Tante observes. *Wilson Bulletin*, vol. 5, no. 4, Dec. 1930, pp. 256–8.
   Review of A72 and B23.

A77 O., E. The poet Hopkins. *Tablet*, vol. 124 (n.s.), no. 4125, 6 Dec. 1930, pp. 767–8.
   Review of A72, B23, and A71. '. . . the works and theories of Hop-kins have been keenly discussed by indisputable poets for nearly fifty

years, and have been well known in literary circles since the Poet
Laureate . . . brought out an annotated selection from the poems
twelve years ago.'

A78   Anon. Gerard Manley Hopkins. *Times Literary Supplement*, 25
Dec. 1930, p. 1099.

Review of A72 and B23. 'Not until . . . 1918 did the world know
that the second half of the nineteenth century had possessed another
major poet whose achievement in bulk and quality can perhaps best
be compared with Matthew Arnold's.'

A79   Anon. [Review of A72] *Month*, vol. 157, no. 799, Jan. 1931,
pp. 93–4.

'A contemporary poet, Alice Meynell, excelled in the point in which
Hopkins was most deficient, limpidity of expression.'

A80   Schappes, Morris U. in *Symposium*, vol. 2, no. 1, Jan. 1931, pp.
129–36.

Some unfavourable comments on B23, and a detailed critical assessment of A72. 'Hopkins was a genius of repelling originality. But the
weighty adjective "great" cannot, I feel, be any longer denied him . . .
the bulk of his achievements forms a glorious pinnacle of poetry.'

A81   W., K. R. Not to be forgotten. *Liverpool Post*, 7 Jan. 1931, p. 4.
'There is a revival of interest in Hopkins at present, and he seems
assured eventually of a high place in the hierarchy of English poets.'

A82   Anon. in *Nation* (New York), vol. 132, no. 3421, 28 Jan. 1931,
p. 105.

'No other poet in the entire range of English literature has brought
sense and sound into so perfect or beautiful a unity.'

A83   Turner, W. J. Some modern poetry. *Nineteenth Century*, vol. 109,
no. 648, Feb. 1931, pp. 243–52.

'Whatever defects Hopkins had (and he is certainly deficient in some
of the elements of poetry) his mature work . . . had the perfect integrity of a poet of genius.'

A84   Flanner, Hildegarde. Gerard Manley Hopkins. *New Republic*,
vol. 65, no. 844, 4 Feb. 1931, pp. 331–2.

Review of A72, B23, and A71. 'His poetry was essentially en-
lightened, honest, and rebellious, and made to last.'

A85   Grigson, Geoffrey. A poet of surprise. *Saturday Review*, vol. 151,
no. 3929, 14 Feb. 1931, pp. 237–8.

G M H's verbal obscurities '. . . are often the boldest compressions of
fine thought that, once explained . . . provoke, most of them, respect
rather than impatience.'

A86   *Anon. in *Booklist*, vol. 27, no. 7, Mar. 1931, p. 322.

A87   L[ittle], A[rthur]. in *Studies* (Dublin), vol. 20, no. 77, Mar. 1931, and pp. 165–7.

> 'Since . . . the first edition in 1918 his admirers, though ardent and discriminating, have been all too few. Now he bids fair to win wide and permanent devotion.'

A88   *Meagher, Margaret C. in *Catholic World*, vol. 132, no. 792, Mar. 1931, pp. 754–6.

> Review of A72 and B23.

A89   Cowley, Malcolm. Resurrection of a poet. *New York Herald Tribune Books*, 8 Mar. 1931, pp. 1, 6.

> Review of A72, B23, and A71, with much original critical comment.

A90   *Deutsch, Babette. Poems of Gerard Manley Hopkins. *New York Evening Post*, 14 Mar. 1931, p. 7.

A91   Read, Herbert. in *Criterion*, vol. 10, no. 40, Apr. 1931, pp. 552–9.

> 'When the history of the last decade of English poetry comes to be written by a dispassionate critic, no influence will rank in importance with that of Gerard Manley Hopkins.' Also reviews B23.

A92   O'Brien, Justin. in *Bookman* (New York), vol. 73, no. 2, Apr. 1931, pp. 206–8.

> 'Like many another great writer he merely had to wait for the world to catch up with him.'

A93   Pritchard, Guy. in *Venerabile* (Venerable English College, Rome), vol. 5, no. 2, Apr. 1931, pp. 219–25.

> 'True, the little book of Gerard Hopkins' poetry, sonnets nearly all, is slender enough. But never since the exciting days that followed the publishing of Swinburne's *Poems and Ballads* . . . has so small a book contained so brave a challenge.' Also reviews B23.

A94   Pryce-Jones, Alan. Gerard Manley Hopkins. *London Mercury*, vol. 24, no. 139, May 1931, pp. 45–52.

> 'It must be easy to swallow every fault in this small book . . . when so much intact beauty remains.' This appreciative reviewer also makes a point which still needs making: 'When solemnity makes a fool of him it is never because he has nothing to say. It is easy to laugh often at a line, impossible . . . ever to laugh at a poem.'

A95   Grisewood, Harman. Gerard Manley Hopkins S.J. *Dublin Review*, vol. 189, no. 379, Oct. 1931, pp. 213–26.

> General critical essay, including review of A72 and B23.

A96   Stonier, G. W. Gerard Manley Hopkins. *New Statesman and Nation*, vol. 3 (n.s.), no. 70, 25 June 1932, pp. 836–8.

'He was a great poet; how great, I shall not venture to guess until I have read him a dozen times more, and a lonely one . . . alone in his art . . . and yet characteristic of his time.' Reprinted with revisions in H31.

For other reviews, see M16, M114.

A SOLILOQUY OF ONE OF THE SPIES LEFT IN THE WILDERNESS (5); NEW READINGS (7); Opening of A VOICE FROM THE WORLD (81); WHERE ART THOU FRIEND . . . (13); THE BEGINNING OF THE END (14); SEE HOW SPRING OPENS WITH DISABLING COLD . . . (17); I AM LIKE A SLIP OF COMET . . . (103); THE COLD WHIP-ADDER UNESPIED . . . (106); SOME MEN MAY HATE THEIR RIVALS AND DESIRE . . .

A97   H[ouse], H[umphry], *editor*. Early poems and extracts from the notebooks and papers of Gerard Manley Hopkins. *Criterion*, vol. 15, no. 58, Oct. 1935, pp. 1–17.

A critical introduction, and first publication of these poems from GMH's early diaries. Textual notes are in P4, as follows: (5)—p. 247, (7)—p. 248, (81)—pp. 298–9, (13)—pp. 249–50, (14)—p. 250, (17)—p. 251, (103)—p. 304, (106)—p. 304, 'Some men may hate . . .' —p. 250. For details of the prose extracts here published with the poems, see B78.

AD MATREM VIRGINEM (178)

A98   Nativity Hymn . . . *Tablet*, vol. 168, no. 5042, 26 Dec. 1936, pp. 897–8.

First publication of the Latin text, with a fine English verse translation by Father Ronald Knox. Textual notes in P4, pp. 337–8.

POEMS OF GMH (OXFORD BOOKSHELF, 1938)

Note. The second edition of 1930 (A72) was re-issued in the 'Oxford Bookshelf' series in 1937. The compiler has been unable to locate a copy of that first printing for examination, and the description which follows is taken from a copy belonging to the first reprint, 1938.

A99   *Poems of*/GERARD MANLEY/HOPKINS/*Edited with notes*/
by/*ROBERT BRIDGES*/[ornament]/SECOND EDITION/*With an*
Appendix of Additional/*Poems, and a Critical*/*Introduction by*/CHARLES
WILLIAMS/OXFORD UNIVERSITY PRESS/LONDON NEW
YORK TORONTO

[a]⁴, b⁶, B–X⁴. 90 leaves, comprising p. [i] half-title: *Poems of*/
GERARD MANLEY/HOPKINS; p. [ii] blank; p. [iii] title; p. [iv]
bibliographical and printer's notices; pp. [v]–viii CONTENTS;
pp. [ix]–xvi INTRODUCTION TO THE/SECOND EDITION;
p. [xvii] fly-title: Poems of/*GERARD MANLEY*/*HOPKINS*;
p. [xviii] blank; p. [xix] dedication; p. [xx] Robert Bridges's sonnet
'Our generation already is overpast . . .'; pp. [1]–6 AUTHOR'S
PREFACE; pp. [7]–9 EARLY POEMS; p. [10] blank; pp. [11]–69
POEMS 1876–1889; pp. [70]–92 UNFINISHED POEMS/&
FRAGMENTS; p. [93] fly-title: EDITOR'S NOTES; pp. [94]–122
text of Editor's Notes; p. [123] fly-title: APPENDIX; p. [124]
blank; pp. 125–53 text of Appendix; pp. [154]–6 NOTES TO THE
ADDITIONAL/POEMS; pp. [157]–9 INDEX OF FIRST LINES;
p. [160] printer's notice.

19 × 12·5 cm. Bulk 1·7 × 2·1 cm. White wove paper, top edge
trimmed and stained red, other edges irregularly trimmed. White wove
endpapers. Bound in light-brown cloth, lettered in red on front:
The Oxford/[ornament]/*Bookshelf*; and in red on spine: [treble rule]/
THE/POEMS/OF/GERARD/MANLEY/HOPKINS/[treble rule]/
[double rule]/*The Oxford*/[ornament]/*Bookshelf*/[double rule]

Notes. The 'Oxford Bookshelf' edition is essentially a reprint of the second
edition of 1930 (A72) in a different binding. First published in May
1937, it was reprinted in 1938, 1940, 1941, 1943 (small format, see
A102), 1944. The 1944 reprint was taken out of the 'Oxford Bookshelf' series, but was in the same format and from the same plates as the
1943 reprint (see A103).

LINES FOR A PICTURE OF ST. DOROTHEA (25); THE HABIT
OF PERFECTION (22)

A100   Abbott, Claude Colleer. Gerard Manley Hopkins: a letter and
drafts of early poems. *Durham University Journal*, vol. 1 (n.s.), no. 1,
Jan. 1940, pp. 65–73.

Carefully annotated transcripts, with commentary, of (*a*) A letter from G M H to A. W. Garrett, dated 22 March, 1872, reprinted in FL2, pp. 55–7; (*b*) 'St. Dorothea: Lines for a Picture', from MS. book A—see P4, p. 249; (*c*) An early version of 'The Habit of Perfection', from MS. book A—see P4, p. 251–2; (*d*) The Stony-hurst MS. of 'The Kind Betrothal', i.e. 'The Habit of Perfection'—see N4. Comparisons are made with other known versions.

CYWYDD (172)

A101   Gardner, W. H. G. Manley Hopkins as a Cywyddwr. *Transactions of the Honourable Society of Cymmrodorion.* Session 1940, 1941, pp. 184–8.

An emended and skilfully edited text of G M H's Welsh poem in honour of the Silver Jubilee of the Bishop of Shrewsbury; with an English translation. For very detailed textual notes, see P4, pp. 325–8.

POEMS OF G M H (OXFORD BOOKSHELF, SMALL FORMAT, 1943)

A102   *Poems of*/GERARD MANLEY/HOPKINS/*Edited with notes*/*by*/*ROBERT BRIDGES*/[ornament]/SECOND EDITION/*With an Appendix of Additional*/*Poems, and a Critical*/*Introduction by*/*CHARLES WILLIAMS*/OXFORD UNIVERSITY PRESS/LONDON NEW YORK TORONTO

[a]⁴, b⁶, B–E⁴, F⁸, H–X⁴. 90 leaves, comprising p. [i] half-title: *Poems of*/GERARD MANLEY/HOPKINS; p. [ii] blank; p. [iii] title; p. [iv] bibliographical and printer's notices; pp. [v]–viii CONTENTS; pp. [ix]–xvi INTRODUCTION TO THE/SECOND EDITION; p. [xvii] fly-title: Poems of/*GERARD MANLEY*/*HOPKINS*; p. [xviii] blank; p. [xix] dedication; p. [xx] Robert Bridges's sonnet 'Our generation already is overpast . . .'; pp. [1]–6 AUTHOR'S PREFACE; pp. [7]–9 EARLY POEMS; p. [10] blank; pp. [11]–69 POEMS 1876–1889; pp. [70]–92 UNFINISHED POEMS/& FRAGMENTS; p. [93] fly-title: EDITOR'S NOTES; pp. [94]–122 text of Editor's Notes; p. [123] fly-title: APPENDIX; p. [124] blank; pp. 125–53 text of Appendix; pp. [154]–6 NOTES TO THE

ADDITIONAL/POEMS; pp. [157]–9 INDEX OF FIRST LINES; p. [160] printer's notice.

16·5 × 10·4 cm. Bulk 1·1 × 1·3 cm. Text printed on three different grades of paper, all white wove, but of varying weight and bulk. White wove endpapers. All edges trimmed. Bound in light-brown cloth, lettered in red on front: *The Oxford*/[ornament]/*Bookshelf*; and in red on spine, vertically: [within double rules at head and foot] THE POEMS OF GERARD MANLEY HOPKINS

Issued in cream dust-jacket printed in red. Price 6*s*.

POEMS OF GMH (SMALL FORMAT, 1944)

A103   *Poems of*/GERARD MANLEY/HOPKINS/*Edited with notes*/*by*/*ROBERT BRIDGES*/[ornament]/SECOND EDITION/*With an Appendix of Additional*/*Poems, and a Critical*/*Introduction by*/*CHARLES WILLIAMS*/OXFORD UNIVERSITY PRESS/LONDON NEW YORK TORONTO

[a]⁴, b⁶, B–X⁴. 90 leaves, comprising p. [i] half-title: *Poems of*/ GERARD MANLEY/HOPKINS; p. [ii] blank; p. [iii] title; p. [iv] bibliographical and printer's notices; pp. [v]–viii CONTENTS; pp. [ix]–xvi INTRODUCTION TO THE/SECOND EDITION; p. [xvii] fly-title: Poems of/*GERARD MANLEY*/*HOPKINS*; p. [xviii] blank; p. [xix] dedication; p. [xx] Robert Bridges's sonnet 'Our generation already is overpast...'; pp. [1]–6 AUTHOR'S PREFACE; pp. [7]–9 EARLY POEMS; p. [10] blank; pp. [11]–69 POEMS 1876–1889; pp. [70]–92 UNFINISHED POEMS/& FRAGMENTS; p. [93] fly-title: EDITOR'S NOTES; pp. [94]–122 text of Editor's Notes; p. [123] fly-title: APPENDIX; p. [124] blank; pp. 125–53 text of Appendix; pp. [154]–6 NOTES TO THE ADDITIONAL/POEMS; pp. [157]–9 INDEX OF FIRST LINES; p. [160] printer's notice.

16·5 × 10·4 cm. Bulk 0·9 × 1·2 cm. White wove paper, all edges trimmed. White wove endpapers. Bound in dark-blue cloth, lettered in gold on spine: [horizontally at foot] OXFORD [vertically] THE POEMS OF GERARD MANLEY HOPKINS

Notes. Issued in light-blue dust-jacket printed in blue. Price 6*s*.

SELECTED POEMS OF GMH (WHITE, 1945)

A104   Some Poems of /Gerard Manley /Hopkins /Michael White/ London/1945

16 unsigned leaves, comprising p. [1] title; p. [2] blank; p. 3 CONTENTS; p. [4] blank; pp. 5–32 text.

18·4 × 12·2 cm. Bulk 0·2 cm. White wove paper, all edges trimmed. Bound in emerald-green paper covers, lettered in black on front: Some/ Poems of/Gerard/Manley/Hopkins; printer's notice at foot of back cover.

Notes. This selection contains eighteen poems. Published at 2*s.* 6*d.* Number of copies not known.

JESU DULCIS MEMORIA (167);
TWO ODES OF HORACE (165 and 166)

A105   Jesu dulcis memoria: an unpublished translation by Gerard Manley Hopkins, S.J. *Letters and Notices*, vol. 55, Sept. 1947, pp. 205–6.

> See notes in P4, p. 323. *Letters and Notices* is a private domestic publication of the English Jesuits.

A106   *'Iesu, Dulcis Memoria', 'Odi profanum volgus', 'Persicos Odi'. *America*, vol. 77, no. 23, 26 Sept. 1947, pp. 633–5.

A107   Two translations by Gerard Manley Hopkins: new English versions of two odes of Horace. *Tablet*, vol. 190, no. 5601, 27 Sept. 1947, p. 199.

> The texts of 'Odi profanum volgus' and 'Persicos odi': textual notes in P4, p. 322.

A108   The 'Iesu Dulcis Memoria' translated by Gerard Manley Hopkins S.J. *Month*, vol. 184, no. 963, Oct. 1947, pp. 182–3.

> See notes in P4, p. 323.

IL MYSTICO (77); TWO FRAGMENTS (78 and 79)

A109   Blakiston, J. M. G. An unpublished Hopkins letter. *Times Literary Supplement*, 25 Sept. 1948, p. 548.

A letter to E. H. Coleridge, dated 3 Sept. 1862, containing 'Il Mystico', 'A Windy Day in Summer', and 'A Fragment of Anything You Like'. This letter (printed in FL2, pp. 5–14) is the only source for these verses. Textual notes in P4, p. 297.

POEMS OF GMH (THIRD EDITION, 1948)

A110 POEMS OF/Gerard Manley Hopkins/[ornamental rule]/ THIRD EDITION/*The First Edition/with Preface and Notes/by/* ROBERT BRIDGES/*Enlarged and Edited/with Notes/and a/Biographical Introduction/by/*W. H. GARDNER/GEOFFREY CUMBERLEGE/ OXFORD UNIVERSITY PRESS/*London New York Toronto/*1948

[a]⁸, b⁶, B–S⁸, T¹⁰. 160 leaves, comprising one blank leaf; p. [i] half-title: POEMS OF/GERARD MANLEY HOPKINS; p. [ii] publisher's notice; p. [iii] title; p. [iv] bibliographical and printer's notices; p. v. ACKNOWLEDGEMENTS; p. [vi] blank; pp. vii–xi CONTENTS; p. [xii] blank; pp. xiii–xxvi INTRODUCTION/TO THE THIRD EDITION; p. [1] fly-title: *Poems of/*GERARD MANLEY HOPKINS; p. [2] blank; p. [3] dedication; p. [4] Robert Bridges's sonnet 'Our generation already is overpast . . .'; pp. 5–10 AUTHOR'S PREFACE; p. [11] fly-title: EARLY POEMS/(1860–1875?); p. [12] blank; pp. 13–52 text; p. [53] fly-title: POEMS/(1876–1889); p. [54] blank; pp. 55–114 text; p. [115] fly-title: UNFINISHED POEMS/ FRAGMENTS/LIGHT VERSE/ETC./(1864–1889); p. [116] blank; pp. 117–73 text; p. [174] blank; p. [175] fly-title: TRANSLA-TIONS/LATIN AND/WELSH POEMS/ETC.; p. [176] blank; pp. 177–200 text; p. [201] fly-title: EDITORS' NOTES; pp. 202–79 text of Editor's Notes; pp. 280–5 APPENDIX/*The Convent Threshold/By* CHRISTINA ROSSETTI; pp. 286–7 INDEX OF TITLES, ETC.; pp. 288–92 INDEX OF FIRST LINES

18·2 × 12·1 cm. Bulk 2·2 × 2·6 cm. White wove paper, all edges trimmed. White wove endpapers. Bound in dark-blue cloth, lettered in gold on spine: [ornamental rule]/POEMS/OF/GERARD/MANLEY/ HOPKINS/[rule]/*Third/Edition/*[ornamental rule]/OXFORD

Notes. This much enlarged edition breaks away completely from the arrangement and numbering of the first edition and second edition, though the heart of the book—the poems written 1876–89—remains

very much as Bridges left it. Nearly all the new material is taken from
G M H's notebooks, diaries, and miscellaneous papers; and the editor
acknowledges his debt to the researches of Humphry House and
Father Anthony Bischoff. In all, this edition contains 141 numbered
items. Published in 1948, and reprinted in 1949, 1950, and 1952. The
fifth impression in 1956 was revised and included additional poems:
see A146.

Reviews:

A111   L., R. J. Poet and priest. *New Haven Register*, 28 Aug. 1948, p. 6.
       G M H's poems are '. . . not easy to read, not easy to understand, but
       in all of them there is . . . intensity and brilliance combined with a
       wealth of technical invention . . .'

A112   Anon. in *Guardian* (The Church Newspaper), 3 Sept. 1948,
       p. 429.

A113   *Meagher, Edward F. in *Commonweal*, vol. 48, no. 21, 3 Sept.
       1948, p. 505.
       Review of A110 and H116.

A114   McDonald, Gerald. in *Library Journal*, vol. 73, no. 16, 15
       Sept. 1948, p. 1277.
       A brief review with nothing original to say.

A115   McKenzie, Gordon. Great and odd poet and some of his great
       and odd poetry. *San Francisco Chronicle*, 26 Sept. 1948, p. 19.
       Review of A110 and H116.

A116   Pick, John. Revolutionary traditionalist. *America*, vol. 80, no. 1,
       9 Oct. 1948, p. 19.
       Review of A110 and H116. G M H was both a revolutionary and a
       traditionalist, because he found the matter of his poetry in the tra-
       dition of Christian sacramentalism and its form in traditional sprung
       rhythm.

A117   Anon. Hopkins and Habington. *Scotsman*, 28 Oct. 1948, p. 7.
       '. . . we need not make the mistake of calling him a great poet, and we
       may concede that he is always likely to stand a little outside the main
       tradition of English poetry, by reason of his metrical excesses and his
       almost Germanic love of composites . . .'

A118   Anon. in *Durham University Journal*, vol. 10, no. 1, Dec. 1948,
       p. 40.

A119   H., J. J. in *Studies* (Dublin), vol. 37, no. 148, Dec. 1948,
       pp. 494–7.
       Review of H120, H114, and A110. Much original critical comment.

A120   Turner, Luke. in *Blackfriars*, vol. 30, no. 346, Jan. 1949, p. 40.

A121   Clarke, Austin. Art and state. *Irish Times* (Dublin), 8 Jan. 1949,
p. 6.

A122   *Grace, William J. in *Books on Trial*, vol. 7, no. 7, Mar. 1949,
p. 258.

A123   Edridge, Ray. in *Downside Review*, vol. 67, no. 208, Apr. 1949,
pp. 231–2.

A124   Conley, John. Hopkins enshrined. *Poetry*, vol. 74, no. 5, Aug.
1949, pp. 292–300.
   Review of A110, H116, H118, H120, H137. Much original
   critical comment.

A125   Pick, John. in *Kenyon Review*, vol. 11, no. 1, Winter 1949,
pp. 155–9.
   Review of A110, H116, H120, H137. 'Hopkins considered inscape to be the aim of poetry, and this meant that every line must
   breathe the personality of the writer. Hence in his letters the emphasis
   on earnestness, sincerity, and honesty, and his denunciation of poetic
   diction . . .'

A126   La Drière, Craig. in *Journal of Aesthetics and Art Criticism*, vol.
9, no. 2, Dec. 1950, pp. 153–4.
   Review of A110, H116, H120, H137, with some original critical
   comment.

For another review, see M247.

POEMS OF GMH (PETER PAUPER PRESS, 1949)

A127   POEMS OF/GERARD MANLEY/HOPKINS/[ornament, in
brown]/Peter Pauper Press [type ornament] Mt. Vernon, New York

Unsigned: [1]–[7]⁸, 56 leaves, comprising one blank leaf; p. [1] title;
p. [2] copyright acknowledgement; pp. [3]–[4] The Contents; pp. [5]–
[8] Author's Note; pp. 9–108 text; p. [109] blank; p. [110] PUB-
LISHER'S NOTE

22·1 × 13·5 cm. Bulk 0·9 × 1·3 cm. White laid paper, all edges
trimmed, top edge stained brown. White laid endpapers. Bound in
paper boards, patterned in brown and white. White paper label on
spine, printed in black: [within a black border, with ornamental rules
at head and foot] *Gerard Manley Hopkins* · POEMS [this lettering reads
vertically down the label]

Issued in dark-brown slip case, with white label printed in black and brown.

Notes. This was a 'collector's' edition, published in 1949. Price $2. It contains all the major poems.

GLORY BE TO GOD FOR DAPPLED THINGS (PIED BEAUTY, 37)

A 128 *Glory be to God for Dappled Things. Denver, Printed by Theodore Jung at his Cloverleaf Press, 1950. unpaginated.

SELECTED POEMS OF GMH (REEVES, 1953)

A 129 SELECTED POEMS OF/GERARD MANLEY/HOPKINS/ *Edited with an Introduction/and Notes/by/*JAMES REEVES/[publisher's device]/WILLIAM HEINEMANN LTD/MELBOURNE :: LONDON :: TORONTO

[A]–G^8, H^{10}. 66 leaves, comprising p. [i] half-title: SELECTED POEMS OF/GERARD MANLEY HOPKINS; p. [ii] publisher's series note; p. [iii] title; p. [iv] copyright acknowledgement; publication date; publisher's and printer's notices; pp. v–vi CONTENTS; p. vii PREFACE; pp. viii–xxviii Introduction . . .; pp. 1–2 EARLY POEMS; pp. 3–76 POEMS, 1876–89; pp. 77–80 UNFINISHED POEMS; pp. 81–99 NOTES; p. 100 APPENDIX; pp. 101–3 INDEX OF TITLES AND FIRST LINES; p. [104] blank.

18·4 × 12·1 cm. Bulk 1 × 1·4 cm. White wove paper, all edges trimmed. White wove endpapers. Bound in dark blue cloth, lettered on spine in gold, vertically: *Gerard Manley Hopkins* [ornament] Selected Poems [ornament] *Heinemann*

Frontispiece portrait of GMH inserted.

Notes. This selection contains all the major poems, with a few examples of the early and unfinished poems. The text corresponds with A110, but all the accents marking stresses are omitted. Published in 1953, this book was reprinted in 1954, 1956, 1958, 1959, 1961 (twice), 1964,

1966, and 1967, and belongs to Heinemann's 'Poetry Bookshelf' series. The 1967 reprint was published as a paperback, with identical text but with a different title-page and without the frontispiece.

Reviews:

A130 Anon. Hopkins as poet and critic. *Times Literary Supplement*, 5 June 1953, p. 366.

> Review of A129 and B150. 'In Hopkins's prose we see a side of him which perhaps never finds full expression in his poetry: an ironic, flexible, and calmly penetrating habit of mind.'

A131 Richardson, Joanna. Poetry of stress. *Spectator*, vol. 191, no. 6531, 28 Aug. 1953, p. 226.

> Review of A129 and B150.

A132 Wintringham, Margaret. To understand Hopkins. *Time and Tide*, vol. 34, no. 36, 5 Sept. 1953, pp. 1153–4.

> Review of A129 and B150.

A133 Peschmann, Hermann. in *English*, vol. 9, no. 54, Autumn 1953, pp. 224–5.

> Review of A129 *and* B150.

A134 Fraser, G. S. Books in general. *New Statesman*, vol. 46, no. 1179, 10 Oct. 1953, pp. 424–5.

> Review of A129, A137, B150. Detailed critical discussion of GMH as poet.

A135 Bradbrook, M. C. in *Modern Language Review*, vol. 49, no. 3, July 1954, p. 370.

> Review of A129 and B150.

A136 *C., M. M. in *Dominicana*, vol. 42, no. 4, Dec. 1957, pp. 369–70.

For other reviews see B164, B165, B169, B173, M33, M255.

SELECTED POEMS OF GMH (GARDNER, 1953)

A137 POEMS AND PROSE OF/GERARD MANLEY HOPKINS/ [swelled rule]/SELECTED WITH AN INTRODUCTION/AND NOTES BY/W. H. GARDNER/PENGUIN BOOKS/MELBOURNE · LONDON · BALTIMORE

[A]–I¹⁶. 144 leaves, comprising p. [i] half-title: THE PENGUIN POETS/D15/GERARD MANLEY HOPKINS/[publisher's device];

p. [ii] blank; p. [iii] title; p. [iv] publisher's and printer's notices; p. [v] dedication; p. [vi] blank; p. [vii] ACKNOWLEDGEMENTS; p. [viii] blank; pp. [ix]–xii CONTENTS [and] ILLUSTRATIONS; pp. [xiii]–xxxvi INTRODUCTION; p. [1] fly-title: SECTION A/ [swelled rule]/POETRY; p. [2] blank; p. [3]–87 text; p. [88] blank; p. [89] fly-title: SECTION B/[swelled rule]/PROSE; p. [90] blank; pp. [91]–212 text; p. [213] fly-title: SECTION C/[swelled rule]/ EDITOR'S NOTES; p. [214] blank; pp. [215]–47 text of Editor's Notes; p. [248] SHORT BIBLIOGRAPHY; pp. [249]–50 INDEX OF FIRST LINES; pp. [251]–2 INDEX TO THE PROSE

18·1 × 11 cm. Bulk 1·4 cm. White wove paper, all edges trimmed. No endpapers. Bound in stiff paper, lettered in brown within green ornamental borders: [on front] THE PENGUIN POETS/*Gerard*/ *Manley*/*Hopkins*/[swelled rule, in green]/A SELECTION OF/HIS POEMS AND PROSE/BY W. H. GARDNER/[publisher's device, in green]/*Two Shillings and sixpence* [on back] [biography of editor].

Notes. This selection contains all the major poems, with a selection of early and unfinished poems; some representative passages of prose, and selected letters. Published in 1953, it was reprinted in 1954, 1958, 1960, 1961, 1962, 1963, 1964, 1966, and 1967. The last two impressions are of special interest. A slip pasted to the contents-page of the tenth impression (1967) reads as follows:

This new reprint incorporates, as did (prematurely) the 1966 reprint, some thirty improved readings which are among the many established, mainly by my fellow editor, Professor N. H. MacKenzie, for the new Fourth Edition of *Poems of Gerard Manley Hopkins* (O.U.P., 1967). In acknowledging this debt I must warn readers that whenever new emendations in this Penguin reprint coincide with readings in the Oxford Fourth Edition, the text of the Fourth Edition is the *earlier*—the authoritative source.

For further details, see Professor Gardner's letter on this subject in *Times Literary Supplement* (1679).

Reviews:

A138 Dobrée, Bonamy. in *Universities Quarterly*, vol. 8, 1953–4, pp. 302, 304.

A139 Bolsover, Philip. Eye for the future. *Daily Worker* (London), 17 Sept. 1953, p. 2.

A brief review with comments on G M H's 'red' letter to Bridges

(LL I, pp. 27–8). 'Hopkins had an eye for coming events as well as a conscience. He saw Communism on the horizon—and he was both frightened and excited.'

A140 Anon. in *Listener*, vol. 50, no. 1283, 1 Oct. 1953, p. 557.

A141 Anon. Vocation and inspiration. *Times Literary Supplement*, 13 Nov. 1953, p. 730.

Stresses that G M H's vocation was integral to his poetry.

A142 Haley, Martin. Gerard Manley Hopkins among the Penguins. *Advocate* (Melbourne), 8 Apr. 1954, p. 9.

Much original comment. G M H was 'a highly individuated poet without an audience to hold him in check by giving him some idea of how ordinary well-educated men would read and understand or fail to understand his lines.'

For other reviews, see M 33, M 140, M 255, M 266.

SELECTED POEMS OF G M H (NONESUCH PRESS, 1954)

A143 GERARD MANLEY/HOPKINS/[ornamental rule]/SELEC-TED/POEMS/[woodcut within a frame of ornamental rules]/THE NONESUCH PRESS/66 Chandos Place London W C 2/1954 [title-page printed in red and brown]

A–G⁸, H⁴. 60 leaves, comprising two blank leaves; p. [i] title; p. [ii] printer's notice; pp. iii–v CONTENTS; p. [vi] blank; p. [vii] fly-title: THE POEMS; p. [viii] blank; pp. 1–100 text; pp. 101–4 INDEX OF FIRST LINES; p. [105] certificate: Of this edition 1100 copies have been printed . . . This is number . . .; p. [106] blank; one blank leaf.

16·2 × 11·8 cm. Bulk 1·2 × 0·9 cm. White laid paper, watermarked INGRES with device; top edge trimmed, other edges irregularly trimmed. White laid endpapers. Bound in brown paper boards, decorated with a pattern of leaves in lighter and darker shades of brown. Parchment spine, lettered in gold, vertically: [ornament] HOPKINS [ornament] SELECTED POEMS [ornament]

Notes. This selection contains most of the major poems. Published in 1954. 1,100 copies printed.

ST. THECLA (136)

A144   St. Thecla: an unpublished poem by Gerard Manley Hopkins. *Studies* (Dublin), vol. 45, Summer 1956, p. 187.

> Textual notes in P4, p. 309. A note printed with the poem states: 'I discovered the MS, written and corrected in Hopkins's own hand, in the course of a thorough search through papers and letters preserved in the Jesuit House, 35 Lower Leeson Street, Dublin. R.B.S.' The initials are those of Father R. Burke Savage.

A145   St. Thecla. *Month*, vol. 16 (n.s.), no. 1, July 1956, pp. 12–13.

> The poem is printed here without annotation or editorial comment.

POEMS OF GMH (THIRD EDITION, FIFTH IMPRESSION, REVISED, 1956)

A146   POEMS OF/Gerard Manley Hopkins/[ornamental rule]/ THIRD EDITION/*The First Edition/with Preface and Notes/by/* ROBERT BRIDGES/*Enlarged and Edited/with Notes/and a/Biographical Introduction/by/*W. H. GARDNER/GEOFFREY CUMBERLEGE/ OXFORD UNIVERSITY PRESS/*London New York Toronto*

> [A]–X⁸. 168 leaves, comprising one blank leaf, p. [i] half-title: POEMS OF/GERARD MANLEY HOPKINS; p. [ii] publisher's notice; p. [iii] title; p. [iv] copyright, bibliographical, and printer's notices; p. v ACKNOWLEDGEMENTS; p. [vi] FOREWORD TO FIFTH IMPRESSION; pp. vii–xi CONTENTS; p. [xii] blank; pp. xiii–xxvi INTRODUCTION/TO THE THIRD EDITION; p. [1] fly-title: *Poems of/*GERARD MANLEY HOPKINS; p. [2] blank; p. [3] dedication; p. [4] Robert Bridges's sonnet 'Our generation already is overpast . . .'; pp. 5–10 AUTHOR'S PREFACE; p. [11] fly-title: EARLY POEMS/(1860–1875?); p. [12] blank; pp. 13–52 text; p. [53] fly-title: POEMS/(1876–1889); p. [54] blank; pp. 55–114 text; p. [115] fly-title: UNFINISHED POEMS/ FRAGMENTS/LIGHT VERSE/ETC./(1864–1889); p. [116] blank; pp. 117–73 text; p. [174] blank; p. [175] fly-title: TRANSLATIONS/LATIN AND/WELSH POEMS/ETC.; p. [176] blank; pp. 177–200 text; p. [201] fly-title: EDITOR'S NOTES; pp. 202–79 text of Editor's Notes; pp. 280–91 ADDITIONAL POEMS AND FRAGMENTS; pp. 292–4 NOTES TO ADDITIONAL POEMS, ETC.; pp. 295–300 AP-PENDIX/*The Convent Threshold/By* CHRISTINA ROSSETTI;

pp. 301–2 INDEX OF TITLES, ETC.; pp. 303–7 INDEX OF FIRST LINES; p. [308] blank.

18·2 × 12·1 cm. Bulk 2 × 2·5 cm. White wove paper, all edges trimmed. White wove endpapers. Bound in dark-blue cloth, lettered in gold on spine: [ornamental rule]/POEMS/OF/GERARD/MANLEY/HOPKINS/[rule]/*Third/Edition*/[ornamental rule]/OXFORD

Notes. The additional poems and fragments were placed in an Appendix in order to preserve the numbering and arrangement of the third edition. These poems and fragments are arranged and numbered as follows:

1. Il Mystico
2. A Windy Day in Summer
3. A Fragment of Anything You Like
4. The Peacock's Eye
5. Miss Story's Character!
6. Io
7. The Elopement
8. St. Thecla
9. In Theclam Virginem

Nos. 1, 2, and 3 were first published in A109, and nos. 7 and 8 in A18 and A144 respectively. The others had not been previously published.

SELECTED POEMS OF GMH (VISTA BOOKS, 1960)

A147 [within an ornamental border] THE POCKET POETS/[swelled rule]/GERARD MANLEY/HOPKINS/[ornament]/[swelled rule]/LONDON : VISTA BOOKS

[A]–C⁸. 24 leaves, comprising p. [i] half-title: GERARD MANLEY HOPKINS/*THE POCKET POETS*; p. [2] publisher's series note; p. [3] title; p. [4] publisher's and printer's notices; p. [5] CONTENTS; p. [6] copyright acknowledgements; pp. 7–48 text.

18·3 × 10·5 cm. Bulk 0·5 cm. White laid paper, all edges trimmed. White wove endpapers. Bound in stiff paper, patterned in blue and grey, lettered in white on front: [within a black panel, bordered with white] *Hopkins*/[within a black panel, bordered with white] *POCKET POETS*; and in black on spine, vertically: Gerard Manley Hopkins/Vista Books

Notes. This selection contains thirty-five poems, comprising most of the mature shorter poems, and a few early and unfinished poems. Published in 1960, reprinted 1961, 1966. The 1966 reprint appeared under the Studio Vista imprint, with an unchanged text but a different binding and title-page.

SELECTED POEMS AND PROSE OF GMH (STOREY, 1967)

A148   NEW OXFORD ENGLISH SERIES/*General Editor:* A. NORMAN JEFFARES/HOPKINS/SELECTIONS/*Chosen and edited by*/GRAHAM STOREY/FELLOW OF TRINITY HALL, CAMBRIDGE/AND UNIVERSITY LECTURER IN ENGLISH/ OXFORD UNIVERSITY PRESS/1967

[A]–M⁸, N⁴, O⁸. 108 leaves, comprising p. [i] title; p. [ii] publisher's, copyright, and printer's notices; p. [iii] ACKNOWLEDGEMENTS; p. [iv] blank; pp. [v]–viii CONTENTS; pp. [1]–30 INTRODUCTION; pp. [31]–2 CHRONOLOGICAL TABLE/of Hopkins's Life; pp. [33]–4 SELECT BIBLIOGRAPHY; p. [35] NOTE ON THE TEXT; p. [36] blank; pp. [37]–175 text; p. [176] blank; pp. [177]–201 NOTES TO THE VERSE; pp. [202]–6 NOTES TO THE PROSE; one blank leaf.

18·5 × 12·2 cm. Bulk 1·5 × 1·9 cm. White wove paper, all edges trimmed. White wove endpapers, with publisher's series note on verso of front endpaper facing title-page. Bound in black cloth, lettered in white on front: HOPKINS/[portrait of GMH within oval-shaped ornamental border]/NEW OXFORD/ENGLISH SERIES; and in white on spine, vertically: STOREY [ornament] HOPKINS [ornament] OXFORD

Notes. This selection contains all the major poems, a few early and unfinished poems, some prose extracts and selected letters. The notes are brief but very useful. The text of the poems is based on P4.

Reviews:
A149   McChesney, Donald. in *New Blackfriars*, vol. 49, no. 569, Oct. 1967, pp. 54–5.
For other reviews, see A152, A154.

POEMS OF GMH (FOURTH EDITION, 1967)

A150   *The Poems of/Gerard Manley Hopkins/*[row of six type ornaments]/
FOURTH EDITION/*based on the First Edition of 1918/and enlarged to
incorporate all/known Poems and Fragments/*EDITED/*with additional
Notes, a/Foreword on the Revised Text, and a/new Biographical and Critical
Introduction/by/*W. H. GARDNER/and/N. H. MACKENZIE/LON-
DON/OXFORD UNIVERSITY PRESS/NEW YORK TORONTO/
1967

[A]–Z⁸, AA–BB⁸, CC⁶, DD⁸. 214 leaves, comprising p. [i] half-title:
POEMS OF/GERARD MANLEY HOPKINS; p. [ii] publisher's
notice; p. [iii] title; p. [iv] copyright, bibliographical, and printer's
notices; pp. v–vi ACKNOWLEDGEMENTS; pp. vii–xii CON-
TENTS; pp. xiii–xxxviii INTRODUCTION TO THE/FOURTH
EDITION; pp. xxxix–lxvi FOREWORD ON THE REVISED
TEXT/AND CHRONOLOGICAL REARRANGEMENT/OF
THE POEMS/BY NORMAN H. MACKENZIE; p. [1] fly-title:
EARLY POEMS/(1860–75?); p. [2] blank; pp. 3–40 text; p. 41
fly-title: POEMS/(1876–89); p. [42] blank; p. 43 dedication; p. 44
Robert Bridges's sonnet 'Our generation already is overpast . . .';
pp. 45–9 AUTHOR'S PREFACE; p. [50] blank; pp. 51–108 text;
p. 109 fly-title: UNFINISHED POEMS/FRAGMENTS/LIGHT
VERSE/&c/(1862–89); p. [110] blank; pp. 111–99 text; p. [200]
blank; p. [201] fly-title: TRANSLATIONS/LATIN AND/WELSH
POEMS/&c; p. [202] blank; pp. 203–27 text; p. [228] blank; p.
[229] fly-title: EDITORS' NOTES; p. [230] blank; pp. 231–43
PREFACE TO NOTES/BY W. H. GARDNER; pp. 244–343 text of
Editor's Notes; pp. 344–5 APPENDIX A/*St. Dorothea/(Lines for a
Picture)*; pp. 346–50 APPENDIX B/*The Convent Threshold/By*
CHRISTINA ROSSETTI; p. 351 APPENDIX C/ *The Nix/By*
RICHARD GARNETT; pp. 352–3 APPENDIX D/*Angelus ad
virginem*; p. [354] blank; pp. 355–6 INDEX OF TITLES, &c.;
pp. 357–62 INDEX OF FIRST LINES

21·5 × 14 cm. Bulk 2·7 × 3·3 cm. White wove paper, all edges
trimmed. Green wove endpapers. Bound in leaf-green cloth, lettered
in gold on spine: [within a red panel, bordered with gold rules at head
and foot] POEMS/of/GERARD/MANLEY/HOPKINS/[beneath
red panel] Fourth/Edition/Gardner/&/MacKenzie/Oxford

An illustration (reduced facsimile of G M H's headpiece drawing for 'A Vision of the Mermaids') is inserted facing p. 8.

Notes. This edition differs from all previous editions in one vital respect. It includes the *latest* verified versions of all the poems and fragments; resulting in nearly a hundred changes in the text, not counting minor changes in punctuation. The arrangement of the earlier editions has been forgotten in favour of strict chronological rearrangement in order of composition. The notes and introductions have also been thoroughly revised. This edition contains 183 items, many of them fragments and Latin poems not previously published. But despite the editors' claim to have incorporated all known poems and fragments, this edition does not include every scrap of verse written by G M H (see A 161). Until the Oxford English Texts edition now being prepared by Professor Mac-Kenzie is published, however, this edition remains the definitive one. Published in August 1967. Price 30*s*. Issued in green dust-jacket printed in black and grey.

Reviews of A 150

A 151 Grigson, Geoffrey. Poet to be read with the ears. *Country Life*, vol. 142, no. 3674, 3 Aug. 1967, pp. 286–7.

A 152 Levi, Peter. Understanding Hopkins. *Guardian* (formerly *Manchester Guardian*), 8 Sept. 1967, p. 5.
Review of A 150, A 148, and B 249. 'He was a great modern poet for the same reason as Hardy: because he was a profound and honest nineteenth century Englishman more sharply sensuous and more alive to the language than any of his established aquaintances. Bridges is all very well, but Hopkins is a great poet.'

A 153 Burgess, Anthony. Gash gold-vermilion. *Spectator*, vol. 219, no. 7265, 22 Sept. 1967, pp. 326–7.
This review includes an attack on Bridges as editor of G M H, and a perceptive comparison of G M H and Joyce: '. . . the kinship goes deeper than compressed syntax, a love of compound words, and a devotion to Anglo-Saxonisms. Musicians both, they were both concerned with bringing literature closer to music.'

A 154 Anon. Hopkins pickings. *Times Literary Supplement*, 5 Oct. 1967, p. 937.
Review of A 150 and A 148.

A 155 Payne, Mervyn. Greatness of a Jesuit poet. *Eastern Daily Press* (Norwich), 9 Oct. 1967, p. 10.

A156 MacCaig, Norman. Stress signs. *Listener*, vol. 78, no. 2013, 26 Oct. 1967, p. 545.

'It is interesting to see this poet, usually non-Latinate in spite of his classical education and his interest in Milton, infusing his use of that language with some of the vernacular qualities of his English poems . . .'

A157 Harmer, J. B. [Review of A150, B249, H265, H267] *Victorian Studies*, vol. 11, Mar. 1968, pp. 418–20.

A158 Whitehead, John. The authentic cadence. *Essays in Criticism*, vol. 18, no. 3, July 1968, pp. 329–36.

This review contains much original criticism, including explication of 'The Starlight Night' and 'The Windhover'.

A159 Kelly, Hugh. in *Studies* (Dublin), vol. 58, 1969, pp. 218–21.

General critical and biographical comment.

A160 White, Norman. in *Notes and Queries*, vol. 16 (n.s.), no. 6, June 1969, pp. 233–7.

Much original comment, showing expert knowledge of the Hopkins MSS.

FRAGMENTS OF POEMS BY GMH OMITTED FROM FOURTH EDITION

A161 White, Norman. Gerard Manley Hopkins. *Times Literary Supplement*, 22 Aug. 1968, p. 905.

Some fragments from the Hopkins MSS., with commentary. See ensuing correspondence: 1695, 1697, 1698, 1700, 1702, 1703, 1704, 1707.

SECTION B

PROSE

THIS section is a chronological list of the published prose writings of GMH. It includes all the prose known to the compiler to have been published before 1918, but from 1918 onwards only previously unpublished material is recorded. Books containing the first published version of any writings in prose by GMH, and all primary editions and selected editions are described in full. Later impressions are not described unless they differ significantly in form or content. Reviews in English of these books are listed following the entries for the books; reviews in foreign languages are in Section M, and cross-references to them have been provided.

LETTERS TO *NATURE*

B1   A curious halo. *Nature*, vol. 27, no. 681, 16 Nov. 1882, p. 53.
Signed 'Gerard Hopkins, Stonyhurst College', this letter comments on a letter from Father M. Dechevrens. It is concerned with the appearance of beams of shadow in the east at sunset, a natural phenomenon which GMH explains as a trick of perspective. (See also B2.) This letter was reprinted in LL2, p. 161.

B2   Shadow-beams in the east at sunset. *Nature*, vol. 29, no. 733, 15 Nov. 1883, p. 55.
Signed 'Gerard Hopkins', and dated 'Stonyhurst College, November 12th', this letter is again concerned with the natural phenomenon dealt with in B1. It was reprinted in LL2, pp. 161–2.

B3   The remarkable sunsets. *Nature*, vol. 29, no. 740, 3 Jan. 1884, pp. 222–3.
Signed 'Gerard Hopkins', and dated 'Stonyhurst College, Dec. 21, 1883', this letter is about the spectacular sunsets which followed the eruption of Krakatoa. For a comment on the letter by GMH, see LL1, p. 202. It was reprinted in LL2, pp. 162–6, and partially reprinted in B8, with comments. See also I557.

B3a   The red light round the sun—the sun blue or green at setting. *Nature*, vol. 30, no. 783, 30 Oct. 1884, p. 633.

Signed 'G.M.H.', and dated 'Dublin, October 19', this letter is about 'the colour now and for some time past seen round the sun', which G M H describes as '. . . sometimes rose, sometimes amber or buff'. G M H goes on to comment on the phenomena of green and blue sunsets, and argues that these colours are not uncommon just at the time of the sun's setting, though they were observed for long periods around sunset after the Krakatoa eruption.

BIOGRAPHICAL AND CRITICAL NOTE ON R. W. DIXON

B4   A MANUAL/OF/ENGLISH LITERATURE/HISTORICAL AND CRITICAL/*WITH AN APPENDIX ON ENGLISH METRES*/ BY/THOMAS ARNOLD, M.A./OF UNIV. COLL. OXFORD/ FELLOW OF THE ROYAL UNIVERSITY OF IRELAND, AND PROFESSOR OF ENGLISH/LANGUAGE AND LITERATURE IN THE UNIVERSITY COLLEGE/STEPHEN'S GREEN, DUBLIN/[in sans-serif] FIFTH EDITION, REVISED/LONDON/ LONGMANS, GREEN, AND CO./1885/*All rights reserved*

[A]⁶, B–Z⁸, AA–RR⁸, SS⁴, TT². 324 leaves, comprising p. [i] half-title: ENGLISH LITERATURE; p. [ii] printer's notice; p. [iii] title; p. [iv] blank; pp. [v]–vi PREFACE/TO/THE FIFTH EDITION.; pp. [vii]–xii CONTENTS.; pp. [1]–601 text; p. [602] blank; p. [603] fly-title: APPENDIX.; p. [604] blank; pp. [605]–16 text of Appendix; pp. [617]–32 INDEX.; pp. [633]–4 *LIST OF EXTRACTS.*; one unpaginated leaf, with publisher's advertisement on recto and verso.

19·5 × 12·2 cm. Bulk 3·7 × 4·3 cm. White wove paper, edges irregularly trimmed. Endpapers coated brown, on one side only. Bound in dark maroon cloth, lettered in gold on spine; [between ornamental rules at head and foot] MANUAL/OF/ENGLISH/LITERATURE/ [rule]/ARNOLD./LONGMANS & CO.; blind-stamped borders on front and back. Publisher's catalogue bound in between last leaf and endpaper in some copies.

Notes. G M H's note on Dixon appears as item 30, pp. 470–1. (See also footnote 1, p. 471: 'Notice by the Rev. G. Hopkins'.) It was reprinted in LL2, pp. 177–8. In the next edition of this book, however (6th edition, revised, 1888) it was compressed to less than a third of its original length, and the footnote acknowledging G M H's authorship was omitted—see p. 474. For GMH's own comments on the preparation and publication of this note, see LL1, pp. 198–9, 200–1; LL2, pp. 123–4.

COMMENTS ON SPECTRAL OR IMAGINED NUMBERS

B5   THE CARDINAL NUMBERS/WITH AN INTRODUCTORY CHAPTER ON/NUMBERS GENERALLY/BY/MANLEY HOPKINS/AUTHOR OF "A HISTORY OF THE HAWAIIAN ISLANDS,"/"A MANUAL OF INSURANCE," ETC./LONDON/ SAMPSON LOW, MARSTON, SEARLE, & RIVINGTON/St. 𝔇𝔲𝔫𝔰𝔱𝔞𝔫'𝔰 𝔥𝔬𝔲𝔰𝔢/FETTER LANE, FLEET STREET, E.C./1887/ [*All rights reserved*]

[A]⁴, B–F⁸, G⁴. 48 leaves, comprising p. [i] title; p. [ii] printer's notice; pp. [iii]–vi TO THE READER.; pp. [vii]–viii CONTENTS.; pp. [1]–73 text; p. [74] blank; pp. [75]–87 APPENDIX.; p. [88] printer's notice.

17·2 × 11 cm. Bulk 0·5 × 0·9 cm. White wove paper, all edges trimmed. White wove endpapers. Bound in dark maroon cloth over limp boards, blind-stamped with ornamental design on back and front, lettered in gold on front: THE/CARDINAL NUMBERS/ [rule]/MANLEY HOPKINS

Notes. Manley Hopkins acknowledges GMH's help on p. v: 'I have to express my thanks for valuable aid and useful criticism . . . to my near relative, the Rev. G. M. Hopkins, of University College, Dublin.' GMH's main contribution to the book is on pp. 20–1, where Manley Hopkins quotes at some length from a letter on spectral numbers written to him by GMH. He also quotes some of GMH's remarks on the Welsh method of reckoning or counting. The texts of GMH's contributions are given in LL1, Note AA, pp. 321–2. For GMH's own comments on this book see LL1, p. 294.

Review of B5

B6   Anon. 1, 2, 3, 4, 5, 6, 7, 8, 9, 10. *Saturday Review*, vol. 66, no. 1717, 22 Sept. 1888, pp. 351–2.

This review refers slightingly to GMH's contribution to the book, without naming him directly. For GMH's own wry comment, see LL1, p. 294.

LETTER TO THE *STONYHURST MAGAZINE* ON BAREFOOT FOOTBALL

B7 Football barefoot. *Stonyhurst Magazine*, vol. 3, no. 40, Nov. 1888, pp. 236–7.

Signed 'Gymnosophist', this letter is concerned with the Irish practice of playing football without boots. The authority for attributing it to G M H is Father John Gerard: see I462. For a carefully edited commentary on this letter, see I650.

LETTER TO *NATURE*

B8 Symons, G. J., *editor*. The eruption of Krakatoa, and subsequent phenomena: report of the Krakatoa Committee of the Royal Society. London, Trübner & Co., 1888. xvi, 494 pp.

See p. 172. Reprints part of G M H's letter to *Nature* on the sunsets following the Krakatoa eruption (B 3), with the comment: 'The above is merely an abstract of Mr. Hopkins's letter, to which he subjoins a very lucid description of the sunset of December 16, 1883.'

COMMENTS ON METRICAL EQUIVALENCE

B9 MILTON'S PROSODY/AN EXAMINATION OF THE RULES/OF THE BLANK VERSE in Milton's/later poems, with an Account of the/Versification of SAMSON AGONISTES,/and general notes by/ROBERT BRIDGES/[ornament]/OXFORD/AT THE CLARENDON PRESS/1893

[A]–K⁴(+K5). 41 leaves, comprising p. [1] half-title: MILTON'S PROSODY/*BRIDGES*; p. [2] certificate: *Only two hundred and fifty copies have been printed on Large Paper; of which/this is No.   ;* p. [3] title; p. [4] publisher's notice; pp. [5]–6 INTRODUCTION; p. 6 SYNOPSIS OF FIRST TRACT . . .; pp. [7]–45 text; p. [46] blank; pp. [47]–80 appendices; p. [81] blank; p. [82] printer's notice.

19·5 × 16 cm. Bulk 0·8 × 1·3 cm. White laid paper, top edge gilt, other edges untrimmed, watermarked W KING/ALTON MILL with device; white laid endpapers watermarked W KING/ALTON MILL with different device and wider chain-lines. Bound in dark-red cloth, lettered in gold on front: MILTON'S PROSODY/ROBERT BRIDGES/[ornament], and in gold on spine: [vertically] BRIDGES— MILTON'S PROSODY [horizontally at foot] 1893

Notes. See pp. 67–8: 'I used the term "metrical equivalence" as I found it. It only means that two short syllables are equivalent to one long syllable ... My friend, the late Father Gerard Hopkins, to whom I sent the MS. of my tract for criticism, blamed my omission of any statement of what he considered the truth on this point. He wrote thus to me:

"I cannot but hope that in your metrical paper you will somewhere distinctly state the principle of equivalence, and that it was quite unrecognised in Milton's, and still more in Shakespeare's time. All, but especially young students need to be made clearly to understand what metrical equivalence is, that it is in use in English now, and that it was not then,—and that it was Milton's artifices, as you explain them, that helped to introduce it."

In quoting this I consider that I have done my duty by the theory. I suppose that the statement represents fairly what some metrists hold, for it is the opinion of one who was learned and acute on all such questions.' The full text of the letter from which Bridges quoted here is in LL1, pp. 258–60 (Letter CLI). It is perhaps hardly surprising that Bridges omitted the sentence immediately following his extract: 'Now not to say this, when the context cries for it, is ... is ... I can find nothing to call it but blasted nonsense.'

A PRAYER

B10 A BOOK OF SIMPLE/PRAYERS./COLLECTED AND ARRANGED   BY/E.W./[ornament]/*SECOND   EDITION*./ READING:/MISS LANGLEY, 37 & 39, LONDON STREET./1893.

[A]–G8. 56 leaves, comprising p. [1] half-title: A BOOK OF SIMPLE PRAYERS.; p. [2] blank; p. [3] title; p. [4] printer's notice; p. [5] introductory note; p. [6] acknowledgements; pp. [7]–8 PREFACE TO THE SECOND/EDITION.; pp. [9]–11 CONTENTS.; pp. [12]– [13] text; p. [14] blank; p. [15] fly-title: FIRST WEEK.; p. [16] blank; pp. [17]–30 text; p. [31] fly-title: SECOND WEEK.; p. [32] blank; pp. [33]–45 text; p. [46] blank; p. [47] fly-title: THIRD WEEK.; p. [48] blank; pp. [49]–58 text; p. [59] fly-title: FOURTH WEEK.; p. [60] blank; pp. [61]–70 text; p. [71] fly-title: PRAYERS THAT MAY BE USED IN/THE EVENING.; p. [72] blank;

pp. [73]–80 text; p. [81] fly-title: PRAYERS FOR SPECIAL DAYS AND/FOR VARIOUS OCCASIONS.; p. [82] blank; pp. [83]–109 text; p. [110] printer's notice with device; one blank leaf.

21·8 × 17 cm. Bulk 1·2 × 1·7 cm. White laid paper, watermarked VAN GELDER ZONEN with device, edges untrimmed. White laid endpapers. Bound in ivory-coloured paper boards; to simulate parchment; lettered in red on front cover: A BOOK OF/SIMPLE PRAYERS and in red on spine, vertically: A BOOK OF SIMPLE PRAYERS

Notes. The compiler of this book was Mrs. Elizabeth Waterhouse. G M H originally wrote the prayer for the first edition, but it was rejected: see LL1, p. 183. Mrs. Waterhouse has a few words to say about this matter in her Preface, pp. 7–8: 'The last prayer but one was kindly written for the first edition by the Rev. Gerard Manley Hopkins, of the Society of Jesus. At that time I thought it too explicitly dogmatic to conform to the purpose of this little book as suggested in the short preface, but gaining glimpses of the hope that the Truth may be inclusive of all sincere expressions of belief, and that as no words can fully set forth the things Eternal, nothing is narrow but contention and denial, and regarding with reverent affection the memory of the writer, now no longer with us, I am glad to be able to reconsider that decision.' The prayer appears on pp. 104–7. It is printed without G M H's name, but in the Contents (p. 11) it is entered as 'A Prayer ... *Father Hopkins* 104'. The text is identical with that printed from G M H's autograph as Appendix I in LL2, pp. 159–60. For G M H's own comments on the rejection of the prayer from the first edition, see LL1, p. 186.

LETTERS FROM G M H TO COVENTRY PATMORE

B11 (Volume 1)

Memoirs/and Correspondence of/[in red]Coventry Patmore/By/Basil Champneys/Vol. I/[ornament: panel from Patmore's monument at Lymington]/London/[in red] George Bell and Sons/1900

[a]⁸, b⁴, c², B–Z⁸, AA–BB⁸, CC⁶. 212 leaves, comprising p. [i] half-title: COVENTRY KERSEY DIGHTON/PATMORE. BY B. CHAMP-NEYS/[publisher's device]; p. [ii] blank; p. [iii] title; p. [iv] printer's notice; p. [v] *DEDICATION*; p. [vi] blank; pp. [vii]–xiv PRE-FACE; pp. [xv]–xx CONTENTS OF VOLUME I; p. [xxi] LIST

OF ILLUSTRATIONS TO VOL. I; p. [xxii] blank; pp. [xxiii]–
xxiv CHRONOLOGICAL ABSTRACT OF/C. PATMORE'S
LIFE; pp. [xxv]–xxvi THE PRINCIPAL EDITIONS/OF COVEN-
TRY PATMORE'S WRITINGS; p. [xxvii] CORRIGENDA ET
EXPLICANDA; p. [xxviii] blank; pp. [1]–396 text; with printer's
notice at foot of p. 396.

22·3 × 14·2 cm. Bulk 3·6 × 4·3 cm. White laid paper, watermarked
𝕮𝖍𝖎𝖘𝖜𝖎𝖈𝖐 𝕻𝖗𝖊𝖘𝖘 with device, edges untrimmed. White laid endpapers.
Bound in dark-red cloth, lettered in gold on spine: [within a frame of
gold   rules]   Coventry/Patmore/·/BASIL/CHAMPNEYS/[beneath
frame] VOL. I/[publisher's device]/GEO. BELL & SONS

Frontispiece portrait of Patmore, taken in 1891. Other illustrations are
inserted facing pp. 6, 34, 84, 88, 116, 118, 158, 210, 228, 232, 250,
262, 294, 306, 332, 336, 348, 350, 370, 380.

Notes. GMH is mentioned briefly on pp. 175 and 318, but the letters
from him (and important references to him by Patmore) are in the
second volume. See notes to next entry.

B11   (Volume 2)
Memoirs/and Correspondence of/[in red] Coventry Patmore/By/Basil
Champneys/Vol. II/[ornament: panel from Patmore's monument at
Lymington]/London/[in red] George Bell and Sons/1900

[a]⁴(+b1), B–Z⁸, AA–GG⁸, HH²(+HH1). 240 leaves, comprising
p. [i] half-title: COVENTRY KERSEY DIGHTON/PATMORE.
BY B. CHAMPNEYS/[publisher's device]; p. [ii] blank; p. [iii] title;
p. [iv] printer's notice; pp. [v]–viii CONTENTS OF VOLUME II;
p. [ix] LIST OF ILLUSTRATIONS TO VOL. II; p. [x] CORRI-
GENDA ET EXPLICANDA; p. [1] fly-title: RELIGION AND
PHILOSOPHY; p. [2] blank; pp. [3]–91 text; p. [92] blank; p. [93]
fly-title: FRAGMENTARY WRITINGS; p. [94] blank; pp. [95]–
112 text; p. [113] fly-title: LETTERS OF COVENTRY PAT-
MORE; p. [114] blank; pp. [115]–273 text; p. [274] blank; p. [275]
fly-title: LETTERS TO COVENTRY PATMORE; p. [276]
blank; pp. [277]–405 text; p. [406] blank; p. [407] fly-title: APPEN-
DICES; p. [408] blank; pp. [409]–45 text of Appendices; p. [446]
blank; p. [447] fly-title: INDEX; p. [448] blank; pp. [449]–68 Index;

p. [469] bibliographical list of Patmore's works in print; p. [470] printer's notice.

22·3 × 14·2 cm. Bulk 3·8 × 4·5 cm. White laid paper, watermarked 𝕮𝖍𝖎𝖘𝖜𝖎𝖈𝖐 𝕻𝖗𝖊𝖘𝖘 with device, edges untrimmed. White laid endpapers. Bound in dark-red cloth, lettered in gold on spine: [within a frame of gold rules] Coventry/Patmore/·/BASIL/CHAMPNEYS/[beneath frame] VOL. II/[publisher's device]/GEO. BELL & SONS

Frontispiece portrait of Patmore, from Sargent's portrait painted in 1894. Other illustrations are inserted facing pp. 32, 58, 82, 124, 138.

Notes. GMH is mentioned briefly on p. x and p. 40. See particularly, however, pp. 246–9 (Patmore's comments on GMH as a man and poet, in letters to Bridges) and pp. 345–55 (nine letters from GMH to Patmore). These letters from GMH are not all printed in full, but nothing of much importance is omitted. They are dated as follows: 23 Nov. 1883 (FL2, pp. 335–8); 3 Jan. 1884 (FL2, pp. 346–9); Easter Eve, 1885 (FL2, pp. 358–60); 14 May 1885 (FL2, p. 362); 21 Aug. 1885 (FL2, p. 365); 4 June 1886 (FL2, pp. 366–8); 20 Oct. 1887 (FL2, pp. 379–83); 6 May 1888 (FL2, pp. 385–90); Whitsunday, 1888 (FL2, pp. 392–3). Published October 1900, in a single edition of 1,000 sets. Price 32s. per set. 200 of this edition were bound up as a cheap reissue in October 1901, price 15s., bound in dark-green cloth with a different title-page. In 1907 the remaining copies were sold off.

Reviews of B11

B12   Anon. Coventry Patmore. *Times* (London), 22 Oct. 1900, p. 6.
       'The letters from Carlyle, from William Barnes, some of those from
       Ruskin, those from Mr. Holman Hunt and Mr. Aubrey de Vere,
       those from Father Hopkins—a man of delicate genius too early taken
       from us—and a few of those from the Tennysons, are really inte-
       resting, but of the rest a small proportion would have been sufficient.'
B13   Fisher, H. A. L. Coventry Patmore. *Speaker*, vol. 3 (n.s.), 10 Nov.
       1900, pp. 131–2.
       'A prose treatise called the *Sponsa Dei* . . . in 1887 . . . was destroyed
       by its author, for Father Gerard Hopkins, S.J., remarked, as he
       returned the MS., that it told secrets, and Patmore valued some
       things more highly than literary reputation.'

B14   Anon. Coventry Patmore. *Spectator*, vol. 85, no. 3780, 8 Dec. 1900, pp. 845–6.

'Among the varied contents of the second volume, not the least interesting are half a dozen letters from Father Gerard Hopkins, S.J., an Oxford man of remarkable intellect and some very remarkable, but too eccentric, poetical performance, who died in the prime of life.' This review goes on to praise G M H's criticism of Patmore's poems, and suggests that more of his letters should have been published.

B15   [Symons, Arthur]. Coventry Patmore. *Saturday Review*, vol. 90, no. 2356, 22 Dec. 1900, pp. 795–6.

'Patmore was not altogether a good letter-writer. A letter . . . from the late James Dykes Campbell . . . contrasts brilliantly with Patmore's brief, sober statements. The letters of Father Hopkins are, in a very different way, profoundly interesting.'

EXTRACTS FROM G M H'S JOURNALS

B16   The diary of a devoted student of nature. *Letters and Notices*, vol. 28, no. 163, Apr. 1906, pp. 390–401.
Edited by J. G. MacLeod; see also B17–18.

B17   The diary of a devoted student of nature. *Letters and Notices*, vol. 29, no. 167, Apr. 1907, pp. 129–35.
Edited by J. G. MacLeod; see also B16, B18.

EXTRACTS FROM G M H'S JOURNALS

B18   The diary of a devoted student of nature. *Letters and Notices*, vol. 29, no. 169, Oct. 1907, pp. 270–81.
Edited by J. G. MacLeod; see also B16, B17. *Letters and Notices* is a private domestic publication of the Society of Jesus.

LETTER FROM G M H TO R. W. DIXON

B19   POEMS/BY THE LATE REV. DR./RICHARD WATSON DIXON/A SELECTION WITH PORTRAIT & A/MEMOIR/BY/ ROBERT BRIDGES/[ornament]/LONDON/SMITH, ELDER & CO., 15, WATERLOO PLACE/1909

a–c^8, B–N^8, O^2. 122 leaves, comprising one blank leaf; p. [i] half-title: SELECTED POEMS/OF/RICHARD WATSON DIXON/

D.D.; p. [ii] blank; p. [iii] title; p. [iv] printer's notice; pp. v–viii INDEX TO THE POEMS; pp. ix–xlvi MEMOIR; p. [1] fly-title: POEMS FROM CHRIST'S/COMPANY, 1861; p. [2] blank; pp. 3–56 text; p. [57] fly-title: FROM HISTORIC ODES,/ETC., 1864; p. [58] blank; pp. 59–74 text; p. [75] fly-title: FROM ODES AND/ECLOGUES, 1884; p. [76] blank; pp. 77–103 text; p. [104] blank; p. [105] fly-title: FROM LYRICAL POEMS,/1887; p. [106] blank; pp. 107–44 text; p. [145] fly-title: POSTHUMOUS POEMS; p. [146] blank; pp. 147–66 text; p. [167] fly-title: FROM MANO, 1883/SELECTION; p. [168] blank; pp. 169–81 text; p. [182] blank; pp. 183–96 NOTES

16·1 × 10·3 cm. Bulk 2 × 2·3 cm. White laid paper, watermarked 𝔄𝔟𝔟𝔢𝔶 𝔐𝔦𝔩𝔩𝔰/𝔊𝔯𝔢𝔢𝔫𝔣𝔦𝔢𝔩𝔡 with device, all edges trimmed. White laid endpapers, identical with text paper. Bound in blue cloth, lettered in gold on front: [within an ornamental border] Selected Poems/of/ R. W. Dixon/With a Memoir/by/Robert Bridges; and in gold on spine: [between ornamental rules at head and foot] Selected/Poems/of/R. W. Dixon/Smith/Elder & C⁰.

A frontispiece portrait of Dixon is inserted.

Notes. This book contains various references to G M H, and brief quotations from his criticism of Dixon's poetry: see pp. xviii, xxvi, xxviii, xxxi, xxxii, xxxiv, 192–3, 196. See particularly, however, pp. 189–92: full quotation of G M H's first letter to Dixon, dated 4 June 1878 (LL2, pp. 1–3). Published in February 1909. A slip giving the publisher's terms of supply to booksellers is tipped in at the front of some copies.

LETTER FROM G M H TO BRIDGES

B20 The Poems of/DIGBY MACKWORTH DOLBEN/edited/ with a Memoir/by/ROBERT BRIDGES/[ornament]/Henry Frowde/ Oxford University Press/London, New York, Toronto and Melbourne/ 1911

a–g⁸, B–I⁸(+K¹). 121 leaves, comprising p. [i] title; p. [ii] copyright notice; pp. [iii]–cxi MEMOIR; p. [cxii] blank; pp. [i]–115 text; p. [116] blank; p. [117] fly-title: NOTES; pp. [118]–27 text of Notes;

p. 128 NOTES TO THE MEMOIR; p. 129 THE ILLUSTRA-
TIONS; p. 130 printer's notice.

19·4 × 11·8 cm. Bulk 1·5 × 2 cm. White wove paper, edges irregularly
trimmed. White wove endpapers. Bound in light-blue paper boards,
with cream cloth spine. Cream paper label on spine, lettered in black:
[within a frame of black rules] Dolben/[ornament]/Poems/&/Memoir

Illustrations are inserted facing pp. i, xxxiii, lxxv, 1. These are sewn in,
not gummed.

Notes. This book contains various references to G M H—see pp. lxviii,
lxxxvi, xcvii, ciii—and two brief quotations from his letters to Bridges,
pp. lxxii–lxxiii, c–ci. See particularly, however, pp. cix–cx: quotation
of the entire first paragraph of G M H's letter to Bridges about Dolben's
death, dated 30 Aug. 1867 (LL1, pp. 16–17). Published in November
1911. A second edition was published in February 1915, with some
corrections and additions, and a different title-page. The references to
and quotations from G M H were unchanged. Some copies of this
edition were bound in blue cloth, others in red cloth.

Review:
B21 Anon. Digby Mackworth Dolben. *Times Literary Supplement,*
21 Dec. 1911, pp. 529–30.
    'Gerard Hopkins heard a report, too, that he [Dolben] was mobbed
    in the streets of Birmingham, where he appeared on his way to the
    Oratory barefoot and in the full habit of a Benedictine monk.'

EXTRACTS FROM G M H'S DIARIES

B22 Father Gerard Hopkins—IV, his prose. *Dublin Review,* vol. 167,
no. 334, July–Sept. 1920, pp. 58–66.
    Extracts from G M H's diaries, and from his letters to *Nature* (B 1–3).

PROSE EXTRACTS AND EARLY POEMS

B23 GERARD MANLEY/HOPKINS/[swelled rule]/*By* G. F.
LAHEY, *S.J.*/[swelled rule]/*OXFORD UNIVERSITY PRESS*/
LONDON: HUMPHREY MILFORD/*1930*

[A]⁶, B–L⁸, M⁶. 92 leaves, comprising one blank leaf; p. [i] half-title: GERARD MANLEY/HOPKINS; p. [ii] publisher's notice; p. [iii] title; p. [iv] printer's notice; p. [v] dedication; p. [vi] blank; pp. [vii]– viii PREFACE; p. [ix] CONTENTS; p. [x] quotation from Francis Thompson; pp. [1]–147 text; p. [148] APPENDIX I/BIOGRAPHI- CAL NOTE; pp. [149]–58 APPENDIX II/JUVENILE PROSE EXTRACTS; pp. [159]–69 APPENDIX III/PROSE EXTRACTS ON CLOUDS; p. [170] blank; pp. [171]–2 INDEX, with printer's notice at foot of p. 172.

19·3 × 12·7 cm. Bulk 1·3 × 1·7 cm. White wove paper, edges ir- regularly trimmed. White wove endpapers. Bound in dark-blue cloth, lettered in gold on front: GERARD MANLEY/HOPKINS/By G. F. LAHEY, S.J.; and in gold on spine: GERARD/MANLEY/HOP- KINS/*G. F. LAHEY*/ OXFORD

A frontispiece portrait of G M H is inserted.

Notes. This book is the pioneer biographical study (see G41). It is placed here because of the substantial number of prose extracts it contains; apart from those placed separately at the end, there are many prose quotations in the text. It also contains several early poems: one of these, 'Remembrance and Expectation', was not by G M H, as claimed, but by his sister (see P2, p. ix), and the text of some others is inaccurate (see P4, p. liv). Father Lahey was mistaken in thinking himself the first to publish 'Nondum'—see A29.

Reviews:

B24   Schneider, Isidor. A great poet. *Nation* (New York), vol. 130, no. 3380, 16 Apr. 1930, pp. 456–8.
       Review of A71 and B23.
B25   Abbott, C. Colleer. G. M. Hopkins. *Nation and Athenaeum*, vol. 47, no. 13, 28 June 1930, p. 411.
       'Gerard Hopkins is not everybody's poet, but those he wins must hold him in peculiar affection. For him they would willingly sacrifice many a more trumpeted writer.'
B26   O'Brien, Justin. in *Bookman* (New York), vol. 71, no. 4, July 1930, p. 447.
       Some general critical comment. The book is '. . . the first satisfactory introduction to the work of an unjustly ignored poet'.

B27   Anon. *in Times Literary Supplement*, 17 July 1930, p. 593.
'Hopkins was one of the major poets of the second half of the nineteenth century . . .'

B28   Anon. A Victorian who has come into fashion. *New York Times Book Review*, vol. 79, no. 26482, 27 July 1930, p. 12.

GMH '. . . has recently been the object of a revival based more upon the tendencies which he represents than upon the specific qualities of his work.' See reply by S. J. Kunitz (I32).

B29   *Sykes, Gerald. in *New York Evening Post*, 9 Aug. 1930, pp. 5–6.

B30   Underhill, Evelyn. Gerard Hopkins. *Spectator*, vol. 145, no. 5332, 6 Sept. 1930, p. 318.

'Most lovers of English verse at least know something of Gerard Hopkins' work . . .'

B31   Kent, Muriel. Gerard Manley Hopkins, poet and prosodist. *Bookman* (London), vol. 81, no. 486, Mar. 1932, pp. 312–13.

'Today, forty years after Gerard Manley Hopkins's early death, it seems possible that he will be widely recognised as a genius of a very rare order . . .'

For other reviews see A76, A77, A78, A80, A84, A88, A89, A91, A93, A95.

LETTERS OF GMH TO ROBERT BRIDGES, 1935

B32   The Letters/of/GERARD MANLEY HOPKINS/to/ROBERT BRIDGES/Edited with notes &/an Introduction/by/CLAUDE COLLEER ABBOTT/PROFESSOR OF ENGLISH LANGUAGE AND/ LITERATURE IN THE UNIVERSITY OF/DURHAM/[ornament]/LONDON/OXFORD UNIVERSITY PRESS/1935

[a]–f⁴, B–Z⁴, Aa–Rr⁴, Ss⁶. 186 leaves, comprising p. [i] half-title: The Letters of/GERARD MANLEY HOPKINS/to/ROBERT BRIDGES; p. [ii] blank; p. [iii] title; p. [iv] printer's and publisher's notices; pp. v–x PREFACE; p. xi CONTENTS; p. xii LIST OF ILLUSTRATIONS; pp. xiii–xiv LIST OF LETTERS/TO ROBERT BRIDGES; pp. xv–xlvii INTRODUCTION; p. [xlviii] blank; pp. 1–306 text; pp. 307–22 ADDITIONAL NOTES/ VOLUME I; p. [323] printer's notice; p. [324] blank.

22·2 × 13·9 cm. Bulk 3 × 3·5 cm. White laid paper, top edge stained brown, other edges trimmed. White wove endpapers. Bound in light-brown cloth, lettered in gold on spine: [between gold rules at head and foot] The Letters/of/GERARD MANLEY/HOPKINS/to/ROBERT BRIDGES/[ornament]/ABBOTT/OXFORD

Frontispiece portrait of G M H, photographed in 1863. Other illustrations are inserted facing pp. 8, 20, 118, 262, 274, 284.

Notes. This book and its companion volume (B 33) were issued as a set, and not sold separately. An errata slip giving three corrections for this volume and two for B 33 is tipped in. All copies seen by the compiler contain this slip, but its position varies. A second impression of both volumes, with minor revisions, was published in 1955, printed lithographically. This impression was again issued as a set, with slightly different title-pages and bound in a darker and smoother brown cloth.

LETTERS OF G M H TO R. W. DIXON, 1935

B 33 The Correspondence/of/GERARD MANLEY HOPKINS/and /RICHARD WATSON DIXON/Edited with notes &/an Introduction/ by/CLAUDE COLLEER ABBOTT/PROFESSOR OF ENGLISH LANGUAGE AND/LITERATURE IN THE UNIVERSITY OF/DURHAM/[ornament]/LONDON/OXFORD UNIVERSITY PRESS/1935

[a]–d⁴, B–Z⁴, Aa–Bb⁴. 112 leaves, comprising p. [i] half-title: The Correspondence of/GERARD MANLEY HOPKINS/and/RICH-ARD WATSON DIXON; p. [ii] blank; p. [iii] title; p. [iv] printer's and publisher's notices; pp. v–vii PREFACE; p. [viii] blank; p. ix CONTENTS; p. x LIST OF ILLUSTRATIONS; pp. xi–xii LIST OF LETTERS/BETWEEN G.M.H. AND R.W.D.; pp. xiii–xxxi INTRODUCTION; p. xxxii blank; pp. 1–157 text; p. [158] blank; pp. 159–60 APPENDIX I/A PRAYER; p. 161–6 APPENDIX II/LETTERS CONTRIBUTED TO *NATURE* BY G.M.H.; pp. 167–70 APPENDIX III/G.M.H. AS ARTIST AND MUSI-CIAN; pp. 171–2 APPENDIX IV/POEMS BY R. W. DIXON COPIED BY G. M. HOPKINS; pp. 173–8 ADDITIONAL NOTES/VOLUME II; pp. 179–92 INDEX, with printer's notice at foot of p. 192.

22·2 × 13·9 cm. Bulk 1·7 × 2·2 cm. White laid paper, top edge stained brown, other edges trimmed. White wove endpapers. Bound in light-brown cloth, lettered in gold on spine: [between gold rules at head and foot] The Corresp^e./of/GERARD. [*sic*] M./HOPKINS/&/R. W. DIXON/[ornament]/ABBOTT/OXFORD

Frontispiece portrait of GMH, photographed in 1880. Other illustrations are inserted facing pp. 50, 132, 169.

Notes. See notes to B32. There is an error on the contents page of this volume: Appendix I (A Prayer) begins on p. 159, not on p. 158 as shown. This error persists in the second impression, 1955.

Reviews: (all reviews are of *both* B32 and B33).

B34   Carpenter, Maurice. in *Poetry Review*, vol. 26, 1935, p. 166.

B35   Dobrée, Bonamy. The Hopkins letters. *Spectator*, vol. 154, no. 5559, 11 Jan. 1935, p. 53.
   'The great value Hopkins has for us, and will have for future generations, is the amazingly high standards he set himself, and others, in poetry.'

B36   De Selincourt, Basil. Complete dedication. *Observer*, 20 Jan. 1935, p. 5.
   'Only too many novices have recently imitated Hopkins' . . . style, a style which, despite all his pains, has still more of effort in it than of accomplishment.'

B37   Stonier, G. W. Books in general. *New Statesman and Nation*, vol. 9 (n.s.), no. 205, 26 Jan. 1935, p. 108.
   Some biographical and critical comment.

B38   [House, Humphry]. Gerard Hopkins. *Times Literary Supplement*, 31 Jan. 1935, p. 59.
   A very perceptive review, much preoccupied with GMH's literary criticism. Reprinted in H180.

B39   Anon. in *Life and Letters*, vol. 11, no. 62, Feb. 1935, pp. 613–15. This review has been attributed to Dr. F. R. Leavis in at least two published sources (F1, F4). In a letter to the compiler, Dr. Leavis states that it was definitely not by him.

B40   Burdett, Osbert. Letters of Gerard Manley Hopkins. *Nineteenth Century*, vol. 117, no. 696, Feb. 1935, pp. 234–41.

B41   Keating, Joseph. Priest and poet: Gerard Manley Hopkins in his letters. *Month*, vol. 165, no. 848, Feb. 1935, pp. 125–36.
   This review includes a reproduction of the MS. of 'Rosa Mystica'.

B42   *Anon. in *Springfield Republican*, 24 Feb. 1935, p. 7.

B43 Marsden, M. in *Music and Letters*, vol. 16, no. 2, Mar. 1935, pp. 158–9.

Includes some expert discussion of G M H's musical abilities.

B44 Plowman, Max. in *Adelphi*, vol. 9, no. 6, Mar. 1935, pp. 356–61.

B45 Roberts, Michael. Reflections of Gerard Manley Hopkins. *London Mercury*, vol. 31, no. 185, Mar. 1935, pp. 480–1.

'. . . these two volumes contain better observations on poetry than any letters since Keats'.'

B46 Walker, M. E. Letters of Gerard Manley Hopkins. *New York Times Book Review*, 10 Mar. 1935, p. 2.

B47 Leslie, Shane. The exquisite doctor. *Saturday Review of Literature*, vol. 11, no. 35, 16 Mar. 1935, pp. 549–50.

B48 Deutsch, Babette. Gerard Manley Hopkins, poet and pioneer . . . *New York Herald Tribune Books*, 17 Mar. 1935, pp. 1–2.

'In his psychological insight and the delicacy of his analysis of poetry, whether his own or another's, he rivals Coleridge, and his effort to discriminate effects and affects anticipates the work of Coleridge's modern interpreter, I. A. Richards.'

B49 *Lynam, Thomas J. Self-portrait of a major poet. *America*, vol. 52, no. 24, 23 Mar. 1935, p. 574.

B50 Warren, C. Henry. in *Fortnightly Review*, vol. 137 (n.s.), Apr. 1935, pp. 503–4.

G M H is '. . . the one Victorian poet who should anticipate the modern poetic mind.'

B51 Phillipson, Wulstan. The letters of Gerard Manley Hopkins. *Downside Review*, vol. 53 (vol. 34 n.s.), no. 154, Apr. 1935, pp. 210–28.

This review includes notes on the reception of the letters by other critics.

B52 Read, Herbert. in *Criterion*, vol. 14, no. 56, Apr. 1935, pp. 478–82.

Strongly critical of Bridges, on rather uncertain grounds—suggests that G M H's friendship with him was founded on instinctive or even physical attraction. 'How otherwise could Hopkins have tolerated the conceit, the pedantry, the complete lack of perception that were the return for all his frankness, humility and grace?'

B53 Shewring, W. H. The letters of Father Hopkins. *Blackfriars*, vol. 16, no. 181, Apr. 1935, pp. 265–71.

Discussion of G M H's musical interests, his metrical theories, and his vocation as a Jesuit.

B54　*Leslie, Shane. Letters of Gerard Manley Hopkins. *Ave Maria*, vol. 41, no. 15, 13 Apr. 1935, pp. 456–8.

B55　Kunitz, Stanley J. The letters of Hopkins. *Wilson Bulletin for Librarians*, vol. 9, no. 9, May 1935, p. 491.

B56　Lewis, Cecil Day. Records of a great poet. *New Republic*, vol. 83, no. 1068, 22 May 1935, p. 52. See also M162.

B57　*Larsson, R. Letters of Gerard Manley Hopkins. *Commonweal*, vol. 22, 21 June 1935, pp. 219–21.

B58　Anon. Province news. *Letters and Notices*, vol. 50, no. 277, July 1935, pp. 169–70.

　　　A brief review. *Letters and Notices* is a private domestic publication of the English Jesuits.

B59　Downey, Harris. Gerard Manley Hopkins. *Virginia Quarterly Review*, vol. 11, no. 3, July 1935, pp. 458–61.

　　　'No poet in the history of English literature has reached an undisputed eminence with so slight a quantity of poetry as Gerard Manley Hopkins . . .'

B60　Zabel, M. D. Hopkins in his letters. *Poetry*, vol. 46, no. 4, July 1935, pp. 210–19.

B61　Walton, Eda Lou. Portrait of a poet. *Nation* (New York), vol. 141, no. 3655, 24 July 1935, pp. 109–11.

B62　Chew, Samuel C. Letters of Hopkins and Bradford. *Yale Review*, vol. 25, no. 1, Sept. 1935, pp. 209–12.

　　　GMH's letters '. . . contain some of the ripest and most acute literary criticism of the last half-century—it is scarcely too much to say, in the whole range of English literature.'

B63　Leahy, Maurice. Father Gerard Manley Hopkins, Jesuit and poet. *Irish Monthly*, vol. 63, no. 747, Sept. 1935, pp. 567–76.

　　　Written from a religious viewpoint, with little literary criticism.

B64　Leavis, F. R. The letters of Gerard Manley Hopkins. *Scrutiny*, vol. 4, no. 2, Sept. 1935, pp. 216–31.

　　　A widely influential and warmly appreciative review, reprinted in H160.

B65　Morrison, Theodore. Man of the month: Gerard Manley Hopkins. *Atlantic Monthly*, vol. 156, no. 3, Sept. 1935, pp. 6–8, supplement.

　　　Some remarks on GMH's influence on younger English poets. *Note* that this review appears in *Atlantic Bookshelf*, a supplement to the periodical with separate pagination.

B66　*Meagher, Margaret C. The letters of Gerard Manley Hopkins. *Catholic World*, vol. 142, no. 847, Oct. 1935, pp. 119–20.

B67   Clarke, Egerton. Gerard Hopkins: Jesuit. *Dublin Review*, vol. 198, no. 396, Jan.–Mar. 1936, pp. 127–41.

B68   Kelly, Hugh. Father Gerard Hopkins in his letters. *Studies*, vol. 25, no. 98, June 1936, pp. 239–52.

General critical and biographical comment.

For other reviews, see M20, M60.

Reviews of B32–3, *second impression 1955* (see notes to main entries for the books).

B69   *O'Gorman, Ned. The poet revealed to his friends. *Commonweal*, vol. 62, no. 16, 22 July 1955, pp. 403–4.

B70   *Anon. Of poetry and poets. *America*, vol. 93, 20 Aug. 1955, p. 496.

EXTRACTS FROM GMH'S NOTEBOOKS AND PAPERS

B71   H[ouse], H[umphry]. Early poems and extracts from the note-books and papers of Gerard Manley Hopkins. *Criterion*, vol. 15, no. 58, Oct. 1935, pp. 1–17.

Nine unpublished early poems (see A97), and four unpublished prose extracts, as follows: (1) Passage from Early Diary, September 1864, beginning 'The poetical language lowest . . .' (JP, p. 38); (2) Notes, 9 February 1868 (JP, pp. 125–6); (3) Extract from Lecture Notes on Rhetoric: ii, Poetry and Verse (JP, pp. 289–90); (4) An address based on the 'Foundation Exercise' of the Spiritual Exercises of St. Ignatius. All these items, including the poems, were published in House's edition of NP, and later in JP and SD.

SERMONS BY GMH

B72   A sermon on the Paraclete. *Tablet*, vol. 168, no. 5036, 14 Nov. 1936, pp. 665–8.

Preached at St. Francis Xavier's, Liverpool, on Sunday, 25 Apr. 1880. Text preceded by biographical and critical note. For full text see SD, pp. 68–75.

B73   God's first kingdom. *Tablet*, vol. 168, no. 5037, 21 Nov. 1936, pp. 703–4.

Preached at St. Francis Xavier's, Liverpool, on Sunday, 18 Jan. 1880. (The date is wrongly printed here as 17 Jan.) For full text see SD, pp. 58–62.

B74 Sermon on Matt. xii, 25: on the fall of God's first kingdom. *Tablet*, vol. 168, no. 5038, 28 Nov. 1936, pp. 739–40.

Preached at St. Francis Xavier's, Liverpool, on Sunday, 25 Jan. 1880. For full text see SD, pp. 62–7.

B75 The Immaculate Conception. *Tablet*, vol. 168, no. 5039, 5 Dec. 1936, p. 772.

Preached at St. Joseph's, Bedford Leigh, on 5 Dec. 1879. (Not at St. Joseph's, Bradford, as stated here.) For full text see SD, pp. 43–6.

B76 Sermon on Luke ii, 33: *Et erat pater ejus et mater mirantes . . .* *Tablet*, vol. 168, no. 5040, 12 Dec. 1936, pp. 830–1.

Preached at St. Joseph's, Bedford Leigh, on 23 Nov. 1879. For full text see SD, pp. 34–8.

B77 The Sacred Heart. *Tablet*, vol. 168, no. 5041, 19 Dec. 1936, pp. 864–5.

Preached at St. Francis Xavier's, Liverpool, on 26 June 1881. For full text see SD, pp. 100–4.

NOTEBOOKS AND PAPERS OF GMH (1937)

B78 THE NOTE-BOOKS/AND PAPERS/of/GERARD MAN-LEY HOPKINS/Edited with Notes and/a Preface/by/HUMPHRY HOUSE/[ornament: Hopkins family crest]/OXFORD UNIVERSITY PRESS/LONDON & NEW YORK/1937

[a]⁸, b², [A]–[B]⁸, C–Z⁸, Aa–Gg⁸, Hh⁶. 256 leaves, comprising p. [i] half-title: The NOTE-BOOKS and PAPERS/of/GERARD MAN-LEY HOPKINS; p. [ii] publisher's notice; p. [iii] title; p. [iv] printer's notice; p. [v] dedication; p. [vi] blank; pp. vii–viii CONTENTS: p. ix LIST OF ILLUSTRATIONS; p. [x] blank; pp. xi–xxxvi PREFACE; p. [1] fly-title: EARLY NOTE-BOOKS; p. [2] NOTE; pp. 3–102 text; p. [103] fly-title: JOURNAL; p. [104] blank; pp. 105–217 text; p. [218] blank; p. [219] fly-title: LECTURE NOTES: RHETORIC; p. [220] blank; pp. 221–51 text; p. [252] blank; p. [253] fly-title: SERMONS ETC.; p. [254] blank; pp. 255–305 text; p. [306] blank; p. [307] fly-title: COMMENTS ON THE SPIRITUAL EXERCISES/OF ST. IGNATIUS LOYOLA; p. [308] blank; pp. 309–51 text; p. [352] blank; p. [353] fly-title: NOTES; p. [354] blank; pp. 355–420 text of Notes; p. [421] fly-title: APPENDIXES; p. [422] blank; pp. 423–8 APPENDIX I/

Catalogue of the Manuscripts; pp. 429–34 APPENDIX II/*List of Sermons in 'Fr. Humphrey's book'*; pp. 435–40 APPENDIX III/. . .; pp. 441–4 APPENDIX IV/*The Convent Threshold*/*By* CHRISTINA ROSSETTI; pp. 445–7 APPENDIX V/*The Organisation of the Society of Jesus*; pp. [448]–[450] maps; pp. 451–2 INDEX I/*First Lines and Titles of Early Poems and Fragments*; pp. 453–66 INDEX II/ *Names and Places*; pp. 467–[474] INDEX III/*Words and Subjects*; p. [475] printer's notice; p. [476] blank.

21·7 × 13·9 cm. Bulk 3·5 × 4·2 cm. White laid paper, top edge stained blue, other edges trimmed. White wove endpapers. Bound in dark-blue cloth, lettered in gold on spine: [double rule]/THE NOTE-BOOKS/AND PAPERS/of/GERARD MANLEY/HOPKINS/[ornament]/HOUSE/[double rule]/OXFORD/[double rule]

Frontispiece reproduction of G M H's drawing 'Dandelion, Hemlock and Ivy . . . 1862'. Other illustrations are inserted facing pp. 22, 32, 48, 64, 106, 120, 164, 180, 256, 304, 352. The maps on pp. 448–50 are as follows: p. 448 Stonyhurst District; p. 449 Isle of Man; p. 450 St. Bueno's District.

Notes. The contents of this book comprise nearly all the prose material which had then come to light, though the treatment of G M H's devotional writings was selective. Published in 1937, it was not re-issued in this form, but JP and SD (B208–9) together constitute the second edition, revised and enlarged.

Reviews:

B 79   Anon. Gerard Manley Hopkins's papers. *Times Literary Supplement*, 23 Jan. 1937, p. 57.

G M H's passion for the beautiful '. . . may . . . be called delimited. It was strenuous, even fierce, but within congenial boundaries.'

B 80   Stonier, G. W. The young Hopkins. *New Statesman and Nation*, vol. 13 (n.s.), no. 309, 23 Jan. 1937, pp. 124–6. See also M 166.

B 81   De Selincourt, Basil. Gerard Manley Hopkins: sidelights and memories. *Observer*, 24 Jan. 1937, p. 5.

B 82   *Grigson, Geoffrey. Gerard Hopkins: the genius who saw corn like a lion's mane. *Morning Post* (London), 26 Jan. 1937, p.

B 83   Keating, Joseph. Disjecta membra poetae. *Month*, vol. 169, no. 872, Feb. 1937, pp. 175–6.

B 84   Fausset, Hugh I'Anson. Private faith of a priest and poet. *Yorkshire Post*, 3 Feb. 1937, p. 6.

'It almost seems, indeed, as if his passion for the beautiful was so
fierce and strong that only by subduing it to minute details could he
control it . . .'

B85   Evans, B. Ifor. A poet's notebook. *Manchester Guardian*, 5 Feb.
1937, p. 7.

'To some of us he is the most original poet of his century, but wilful,
eccentric, and with a narrowness and hardness in his outlook that
limits his greatness.'

B86   Anon. The pursuit of wisdom. *Tablet*, vol. 169, no. 5048, 6 Feb.
1937, pp. 198–200.

This review contains much original criticism.

B87   *Anon. in *Springfield Republican*, 28 Feb. 1937, p. 7.

B88   Cox, R. G. in *Scrutiny*, vol. 5, no. 4, Mar. 1937, pp. 455–6.

Some acute remarks on GMH's descriptions of nature: 'At their
best these descriptions have an imaginative power which suggests the
imagery of the poems: often they seem to be a sort of exercise,
sometimes a training undergone simply for its own sake, as in the
more rigorously scientific observations.'

B89   Muir, Edwin. Hopkins's notebooks. *London Mercury*, vol. 35, no.
209, Mar. 1937, pp. 511–12.

B90   Dobrée, Bonamy. The Hopkins papers. *Spectator*, vol. 158, no.
5672, 12 Mar. 1937, pp. 479–80.

B91   Flanner, Hildegarde. Stations of the cross. *New Republic*, vol. 90,
no. 1165, 31 Mar. 1937, p. 243.

'His fame has been perhaps a trifle overspecialised and his influence
abused by those who are not equal to his own precepts.'

B92   Lewis, Cecil Day. Gerard Manley Hopkins, poet and Jesuit.
Left Review, vol. 3, no. 3, Apr. 1937, pp. 172–5.

'One has only to read the sermons printed in this volume to see what a
blight the trivial and ludicrous minutiae of Catholic doctrine had
cast upon the poet's intelligence.'

B93   *Feeney, Leonard. Hopkins without comment. *America*, vol. 57,
no. 2, 17 Apr. 1937, pp. 45–6.

B94   *Maude, Mother Mary. Notebooks with sketches of Gerard
Manley Hopkins. *Living Church*, vol. 96, no. 16, 17 Apr. 1937, pp.
495–6.

B95   Leavis, F. R. Hopkins canonised. *Cambridge Review*, vol. 58, no.
1428, 30 Apr. 1937, p. 364.

Little criticism of GMH; mainly discussion of the book *per se*, but
some of Dr. Leavis's comments provoked disagreement: see B112.

B96   Troy, William. Gloried from within. *Nation* (New York), vol. 144, no. 18, 1 May 1937, pp. 511–12.

B97   *Holmes, John. The essential soul of an English poet. *Boston Evening Transcript,* 15 May 1937, p. 1.

B98   Deutsch, Babette. Scholar, priest, and poet. *New York Herald Tribune Books,* 16 May 1937, p. 21.

'One would know him for an artist by the vividness with which he sees, the exactness with which he sets down, what to the ordinary eye is an ordinary sight . . .'

B99   Blackmur, R. P. Text and texture. *Virginia Quarterly Review,* vol. 13, no. 3, Summer 1937, pp. 449–53.

'Hopkins did not need to dedicate certain of his poems to the greater glory of God. The glory is in the incandescence of his language; and these notebooks show the mode and manner of making it shine . . .'

B100   Kelly, Bernard. Gerard Manley Tuncks. *Blackfriars,* vol. 18, no. 207, June 1937, pp. 424–9.

The underlying philosophy of G M H's thought and poetry is explored in this article-review.

B101   *Shuster, George N. A poet's by-paths. *Commonweal,* vol. 26, no. 6, 4 June 1937, p. 164.

B102   Walker, M. E. In the world of Gerard Manley Hopkins. *New York Times Book Review,* 27 June 1937, p. 6.

B103   MacNeice, Louis. in *Criterion,* vol. 16, no. 65, July 1937, pp. 698–700.

'. . . some poets tend to imitate the Hopkins letter while being miles away from the Hopkins spirit . . .'

B104   Moss, Ernest. in *Dublin Review,* vol. 201, no. 402, July 1937, pp. 165–7.

This review opens with the flat statement that 'Hopkins was the best poet of the nineteenth century . . .', and goes on to defend it passionately.

B105   Whitridge, Arnold. Poet's workshop. *Saturday Review of Literature,* vol. 16, no. 11, 10 July 1937, p. 20.

'Among all the English poets who have loved Nature there has been no more accurate observer . . .'

B106   Trueblood, Charles K. Esthetics of Gerard Hopkins. *Poetry,* vol. 50, no. 5, Aug. 1937, pp. 274–80.

This review develops into a rather unconvincing attempt to fit G M H's style into the framework of an aesthetic theory.

B107 *Kelly, Blanche M. in *Catholic World*, vol. 145, no. 870, Sept. 1937, pp. 750–1.

B108 Forster, Leonard. in *English Studies* (Amsterdam), vol. 19, no. 5, Oct. 1937, pp. 236–9.

'The sermons shew the personal peculiarities of their author as clearly as do those of Donne, and may indeed be found to be as important in their way.'

B109 Phillipson, Wulstan. The journals of G. M. Hopkins. *Downside Review*, vol. 55, no. 164, Oct. 1937, pp. 526–36.

This review contains much original critical comment. See also B112.

B110 *Friend-Pereira, F. J. in *New Review* (Calcutta), vol. 6, Nov. 1937, pp. 473–5.

B111 S., N. C. in *Oxford Magazine*, vol. 56, no. 16, 10 Mar. 1938, pp. 522–3.

'Extraneous causes have led to extravagant exaggeration of his stature and achievement as a poet . . . unfledged poets and unimaginative versifiers are making great play with his eccentricities.'

B112 Phillipson, Wulstan. Gerard Hopkins, priest. *Downside Review*, vol. 56, no. 167, July 1938, pp. 311–23.

Further detailed discussion, following B109, mainly concerned with the spiritual aspect of GMH's thought and work, and setting out to answer F. R. Leavis (B95).

For another review, see B136.

FURTHER LETTERS OF GMH, 1938

B113 Further Letters/of/GERARD MANLEY HOPKINS/including his Correspondence/with/COVENTRY PATMORE/Edited with Notes and/an Introduction/by/CLAUDE COLLEER ABBOTT/PROFESSOR OF ENGLISH LANGUAGE AND/LITERATURE IN THE UNIVERSITY OF/DURHAM/[ornament]/OXFORD UNIVERSITY PRESS/London New York Toronto/1938

[a]–b⁸, c⁴, B–T⁸, U⁶. 170 leaves, comprising one blank leaf, p. [i] half-title: Further Letters of/GERARD MANLEY HOPKINS/including his Correspondence with/COVENTRY PATMORE; p. [ii] blank; p. [iii] title; p. [iv] publisher's and printer's notices; pp. v–ix PREFACE; p. [x] blank; p. xi CONTENTS; p. [xii] blank; p. xiii LIST OF ILLUSTRATIONS; p. [xiv] blank; pp. xv–xviii LIST OF LETTERS; pp. xix–xxxviii INTRODUCTION; pp. 1–245 text;

p. [246] blank; pp. 247–9 APPENDIX I/*Letter from* C. N. LUX-
MOORE *to* ARTHUR HOPKINS; pp. 250–1 APPENDIX II/
Extracts from the Diary of W. A. COMYN MACFARLANE, 1866;
pp. 252–83 APPENDIX III/*Letters to* G.M.H. *from* [various]
correspondents; p. [284] blank; pp. 285–90 ADDITIONAL NOTES;
pp. 291–7 INDEX; p. [298] printer's notice; one blank leaf.

22 × 13·5 cm. Bulk 2·6 × 3·1 cm. White laid paper, top edge stained
brown, other edges trimmed. White wove endpapers. Bound in light-
brown cloth, lettered in gold on spine: [between gold rules at head and
foot] Further Letters/of/GERARD/MANLEY/HOPKINS/[orna-
ment]/ABBOTT/OXFORD

Frontispiece portrait of G M H, photographed *c.* 1856. Other illustrations are inserted facing pp. 1, 10, 32, 50, 92, 146, 246.

Notes. G M H's most important series of letters were those to Bridges and
Dixon (B 32–3). This book contains all further letters known at that
time. The correspondence with Patmore and the letters to A. W. M.
Baillie are the most important, and remained virtually unchanged in the
second edition (B 179). The book lacked the important series of family
letters discovered after the death of G M H's brother Lionel in 1952.

Reviews:

B 114   H[arrold], C[harles] F. in *Modern Philology*, vol. 35, no. 4, May
1938, p. 440.
A very brief review.

B 115   Anon. Gerard Manley Hopkins: a mind entirely religious. *Times
Literary Supplement*, 7 May 1938, p. 312.
Enthusiastic rather than critical: 'His intellectual subtlety is balanced
by a beautiful humility; his essential sadness lightened almost to
gaiety by a vein of riotous fun; his exquisite sensitiveness steadied by
penetrating good sense.' And so on.

B 116   Dobrée, Bonamy. More Hopkins letters. *Spectator*, vol. 160, no.
5733, 13 May 1938, p. 880.
'. . . the more one reads Hopkins the more complex does he become,
and the greater in stature.'

B 117   Stonier, G. W. More Hopkins letters. *New Statesman and Nation*,
vol. 15 (n.s.), no. 377, 14 May 1938, pp. 840–2.

B118 Anon. Gerard Manley Hopkins. *Tablet*, vol. 171, no. 5115, 21 May 1938, pp. 666–7.

B119 Anon. [Review of B113] *Month*, vol. 171, no. 888, June 1938, pp. 569–70.

B120 L'Estrange, H. K. in *Blackfriars*, vol. 19, no. 219, June 1938, pp. 465–7.

B121 Evans, B. Ifor. in *Manchester Guardian*, 24 June 1938, p. 7.

B122 *Anon. in *New Yorker*, vol. 14, no. 19, 25 June 1938, p. 67.

B123 MacManus, Francis. in *Irish Monthly*, vol. 66, no. 781, July 1938, pp. 508–10.

'He was a recreator of English words that the stream of usage had worn round and smoothly characterless.'

B124 *Pick, John. in *Commonweal*, vol. 28, no. 11, 8 July 1938, pp. 302–3.

B125 Fitts, Dudley. A poet's letters. *Saturday Review of Literature*, vol. 18, no. 11, 9 July 1938, p. 15.

'Even the fanatic admirer of Hopkins must be gravely tried by the sterile (and, as it happens, almost always unsound) scholarship of the bulk of the letters to Alexander Baillie . . .'

B126 Walker, M. E. The loneliness of the priest. *New York Times Book Review*, 10 July 1938, p. 9.

B127 Bogan, Louise. The hidden stream. *Nation* (New York), vol. 147, no. 5, 30 July 1938, pp. 111–12.

B128 *Holmes, John. The unity of Hopkins as letter-writer and poet. *Boston Evening Transcript*, 20 Aug. 1938, p. 1.

B129 Deutsch, Babette. Glimpses of a rare spirit. *New York Herald Tribune Books*, 21 Aug. 1938, p. 12.

Much original critical comment.

B130 Cox, R. G. Hopkins and Patmore. *Scrutiny*, vol. 7, no. 2, Sept. 1938, pp. 217–18.

'The correspondence relating to his conversion . . . brings home once more not only the depth and sincerity of his religious convictions, but also his independence and strength of character.'

B131 *Gordon, David. in *Catholic World*, vol. 147, Sept. 1938, p. 758.

B132 *Meagher, Margaret C. in *Catholic World*, vol. 147, Sept. 1938, pp. 758–9.

B133 *Maude, Mother Mary. A new collection of Gerard Manley Hopkins' letters. *Living Church*, vol. 99, no. 10, 7 Sept. 1938, p. 214.

B134 *Gordon, David. From Hopkins, poet, to Patmore, poet. *America*, vol. 59, no. 24, 17 Sept. 1938, pp. 573–4.

B135 Zabel, Morton Dauwen. The palace and the house. *New Republic*, vol. 97, no. 1252, 30 Nov. 1938, p. 106.

'. . . his acute and searching intelligence made a judgement on English poetry which must rank among the keenest appraisals . . . since Coleridge.'

B136 Gregory, Horace. Gerard Manley Hopkins. *Yale Review*, vol. 28, no. 2, Dec. 1938, pp. 415–18.

Review of B78 and B113. Much original comment.

B137 Quinn, Kerker. Portrait in letters. *Poetry*, vol. 53, no. 3, Dec. 1938, pp. 150–5.

B138 Finlay, Ida. Gerard Manley Hopkins: poet and priest. *Cornhill Magazine*, vol. 159, no. 952, Apr. 1939, pp. 467–78.

Little literary criticism, mainly biographical comment.

B139 Leishman, J. B. in *Review of English Studies*, vol. 15, no. 58, Apr. 1939, pp. 243–6.

Perceptive remarks on GMH's literary criticism: 'Partly because it was his nature and partly because of his theological training and creed, many of his objections to things in . . . other people's poetry have a plainness and a simple logic that often remind one of Johnson, with whom Hopkins had much in common.'

B140 Phillipson, Wulstan. Gerard Hopkins and Coventry Patmore. *Downside Review*, vol. 57, no. 171, July 1939, pp. 389–98.

Detailed biographical and critical comment.

B141 Blackmur, R. P. The mature intelligence of an artist. *Kenyon Review*, vol. 1, no. 1, Winter 1939, pp. 96–9.

Critical comment showing real understanding of GMH's achievement as a poet and his nature as a man.

For another review, see M22.

LETTER FROM GMH TO A. W. GARRETT

B142 Abbott, Claude Colleer. Gerard Manley Hopkins: a letter and drafts of early poems. *Durham University Journal*, vol. 1 (n.s.), no. 1, Jan. 1940, pp. 65–73.

A carefully annotated transcript of GMH's letter to Garrett dated 22 March 1872 (see FL2, pp. 55–7). Also discussion of three early poems: see A100.

SELECTIONS FROM THE NOTEBOOKS OF GMH
(WEISS, 1945)

B143 THE POETS OF THE YEAR/Selections from/the/Note-Books/of/Gerard Manley Hopkins/EDITED BY T. WEISS/NORFOLK · CONNECTICUT · MCMXLV/NEW DIRECTIONS [all lower-case on title-page is fancy type (Typo Upright)].

16 unsigned and unpaginated leaves, comprising p. [1] half-title: THE POETS OF THE YEAR/[ornament]/GERARD MANLEY HOPKINS; p. [2] blank; p. [3] title; p. [4] ACKNOWLEDGMENT, and copyright and publisher's notices; pp. [5]–8 The Apprenticeship of Gerard Manley Hopkins [Introduction, by T. Weiss]; pp. [9]–31 text; p. [32] publisher's series notes, and printer's notice [heading of p. 5 in fancy type (Typo Upright)].

21·6 × 15 cm. Bulk 0·3 × 0·8 cm. Cream wove paper, watermarked ARAR with device, all edges trimmed. Cream wove endpapers. Bound in cream paper boards, lettered in red on front: [ornamental rule]/ Selections from/the/Note-Books/of/Gerard Manley Hopkins/[ornamental rule] [this lettering in fancy type (Typo Upright)].

Notes. Published in 1945, price $1, this book contains miscellaneous extracts from GMH's previously published prose.

EXTRACTS FROM GMH'S JOURNAL, 1866–8

B144 [Bischoff, Anthony], *editor.* Journal of Fr. G. M. Hopkins, 1866. *Letters and Notices,* vol. 55, no. 295, May 1947, pp. 147–55.
This journal is the one discovered by Father Bischoff in February 1947, and here first published. These extracts cover 2 May 1866 to 5 July 1866, and the first extract is a facsimile. See further extracts —B145, B146, B147, and see also B148. *Letters and Notices* is a private domestic publication of the English Jesuits.

B145 [Bischoff, Anthony], *editor.* Journal of Fr. G. M. Hopkins, 1866–1867. *Letters and Notices,* vol. 55, Sept. 1947, pp. 223–35.
Extracts covering 6 July 1866 to 8 Sept. 1867. For further details see B144, and see also B146–8.

B146   [Bischoff, Anthony], *editor*. Journal of Fr. G. M. Hopkins, 1868.
Letters and Notices, vol. 56, Jan. 1948, pp. 18–29.
Extracts covering 18 Apr. 1868 to 14 July 1868, with reproductions
of sketches by GMH. For further details see B144, and see also
B145, B147–8.

B147   [Bischoff, Anthony], *editor*. Journal of Fr. G. M. Hopkins, 1868.
Letters and Notices, vol. 56, May 1948, pp. 100–4.
Extracts covering 15 to 17 July 1868. For further details see B144,
and see also B145–6, B148.

B148   Unpublished journal of Fr. G. M. Hopkins. *Month*, vol. 4 (n.s.),
no. 6, Dec. 1950, pp. 375–84.
Extracts covering May 1866 to July 1868, reprinted from B144–7.

LETTER FROM GMH TO E. H. COLERIDGE

B149   Blakiston, J. M. G. An unpublished Hopkins letter. *Times Literary
Supplement*, 25 Sept. 1948, p. 548.
A letter to E. H. Coleridge, dated 3 Sept. 1862. See FL2, pp. 5–14.
This letter contains extracts from 'Il Mystico': see A109.

A HOPKINS READER (PICK, 1953)

B150   A HOPKINS READER/[ornamental rule]/SELECTED AND
WITH AN INTRODUCTION BY/JOHN PICK/GEOFFREY
CUMBERLEGE/OXFORD UNIVERSITY PRESS/LONDON
NEW YORK TORONTO/1953

[a]⁸, b⁶, B–X⁸. 174 leaves, comprising p. [i] half-title: A HOPKINS
READER; p. [ii] blank; p. [iii] title; p. [iv] publisher's and printer's
notices; pp. [v]–viii TABLE OF CONTENTS; p. [ix] LIST OF
ILLUSTRATIONS; p. [x] blank; pp. [xi]–xxvii INTRODUC-
TION; p. [xxviii] blank; p. [1] fly-title: I/POEMS/[quotation]; p.
[2] blank; pp. [3]–31 text; p. [32] blank; p. [33] fly-title: II/OBSER-
VATION OF NATURE:/ INSCAPE/[quotation]; p. [34] blank;
pp. [35]–67 text; p. [68] blank; p. [69] fly-title: III/POETIC
THEORY/[quotation]; p. [70] blank; pp. [71]–124 text; p. [125] fly-
title: IV/PRACTICAL CRITICISM/[quotation]; p. [126] blank;
pp. [127]–69 text; p. [170] blank; p. [171] fly-title: V/THE OTHER
ARTS/[quotation]; p. [172] blank; pp. [173]–217 text; p. [218]

blank; p. [219] fly-title: VI/PERSONAL LETTERS/[quotation]; p. [220] blank; pp. [221]–56 text; p. [257] fly-title: VII/RELIGION/ [quotation]; p. [258] blank; pp. [259]–308 text; pp. [309]–12 NOTES; pp. [313]–17 INDEX; p. [318] printer's notice; one blank leaf.

21·6 × 13·7 cm. Bulk 2·2 × 2·7 cm. White wove paper, all edges trimmed. White wove endpapers. Bound in dark-red cloth, lettered in gold on spine: A/HOPKINS/READER/*Selected by*/JOHN PICK/ OXFORD

Illustrations are inserted facing pp. 36, 38, 58, 218.

Notes. Though this selection includes the more important poems, its chief value is as a comprehensive prose selection. Both in inclusiveness and in arrangement it outclasses any comparable work. Published in 1953, price 25*s*. A revised and enlarged edition was published in 1966 as a paperback by Image Books (Garden City, New York). The compiler has been unable to locate a copy of this book.

Reviews:

B151   Anon. Christian poet. *Time*, vol. 61, no. 21, 25 May 1953, p. 50.
B152   *Grady, Thomas J. in *Books on Trial*, vol. 11, no. 8, June 1953, p. 333.
B153   Evans, B. Ifor. in *Truth*, vol. 153, no. 4002, 5 June 1953, p. 689.
B154   Anon. Greatness and oddness. *Nation* (New York), vol. 176, no. 23, 6 June 1953, p. 486.
B155   Faussett, Hugh I'Anson. in *Manchester Guardian*, 16 June 1953, p. 4.
B156   Evans, B. Ifor. G. M. Hopkins. *Birmingham Post*, 23 June 1953, p. 3.
B157   Reeves, James. A poet's prose. *Listener*, vol. 49, no. 1269, 25 June 1953, pp. 1060, 1063.
B158   Gillett, Eric. in *National and English Review*, vol. 141, no. 845, July 1953, p. 50.
B159   *McLuhan, Marshall. in *Commonweal*, vol. 58, no. 13, 3 July 1953, pp. 326–7.
B160   *Ames, Ruth. in *Catholic World*, vol. 177, Aug. 1953, pp. 397–8.
B161   McDonald, Gerald D. in *Library Journal*, vol. 78, no. 14, Aug. 1953, p. 1334.

B162   H[alsband], R[obert]. A sprung cleric. *Saturday Review* (New York), vol. 36, no. 31, 1 Aug. 1953, p. 13.

B163   Gregory, Horace. The touch of timelessness. *New York Times Book Review*, 2 Aug. 1953, p. 5.

B164   Slevin, Gerard. Gerard Manley Hopkins. *Tablet*, vol. 202, no. 3907, 8 Aug. 1953, pp. 133–4.

> Review of B150 and A129. Includes some comments on the growth of Hopkins criticism.

B165   Meath, Gerard. in *Blackfriars*, vol. 34, no. 402, Sept. 1953, pp. 413–15.

> Some original critical comment, on both B150 and A129.

B166   Pridie, F. M. Gerard Manley Hopkins: priest and poet. *Westminster Cathedral Chronicle* (London), vol. 47, no. 9, Sept. 1953, pp. 147–8.

> 'A master of penumbral expression, he used language as the Greek dramatists used it, with profound recessions of meaning beyond the actual words.'

B167   *Moloney, Michael F. in *America*, vol. 89, no. 23, 5 Sept. 1953, pp. 555–7.

B168   *Anon. in *New Yorker*, vol. 29, no. 30, 12 Sept. 1953, pp. 135–6.

B169   Speaight, Robert. The price of poetry. *Dublin Review*, vol. 227, no. 462, Fourth Quarter 1953, pp. 371–80.

> Review of B150 and A129. Includes an attempt to compare GMH with Rimbaud.

B170   *Stauffer, Robert E. in *Voices*, no. 152, Sept.–Dec. 1953, pp. 55–7.

B171   Steuert, Hilary. in *Downside Review*, vol. 71, no. 226, Autumn 1953, pp. 459–61.

> A brief review.

B172   *Veetch, T. in *Australasian Catholic Record* (Sydney), vol. 30, no. 4, Oct. 1953, pp. 335–8.

B173   Gardner, W. H. Hopkins's harvest-home. *Month*, vol. 10 (n.s.), no. 5, Nov. 1953, pp. 304–8.

> Review of B150 and A129.

B174   *Thornton, Francis Beauchesne. in *Catholic Digest*, vol. 18, no. 1, Nov. 1953, pp. 105–6.

B175   *Hasley, Louis. in *Ave Maria*, vol. 78, no. 19, 7 Nov. 1953, p. 24.

B176   *Schoder, Raymond V. in *Thought*, vol. 28, no. 111, Winter 1953, pp. 619–21.

B177 McLuhan, Marshall. in *Queen's Quarterly*, vol. 61, no. 2, Summer 1954, pp. 268–70.

'As the favourite pupil of Pater, Hopkins is not only an authentic voice of the Pre-Raphaelites but as a poet he can be held to be their solitary artistic triumph.'

B178 Anon. in *Notes and Queries*, vol. 1 (n.s.), Sept. 1954, pp. 411–12.

'We have but to think of the greatest English poets to recognise that Hopkins cannot rank with them . . . to be difficult is not a virtue in the writing of English.'

For other reviews, see A130, A131, A132, A133, A134, A135, M33, M255, M266.

FURTHER LETTERS OF GMH (SECOND EDITION, 1956)

B179 FURTHER LETTERS OF/Gerard Manley Hopkins/IN-CLUDING HIS CORRESPONDENCE WITH/Coventry Patmore/[ornamental rule]/EDITED WITH NOTES AND/AN INTRODUC-TION BY/CLAUDE COLLEER ABBOTT/EMERITUS PRO-FESSOR OF ENGLISH LANGUAGE/AND LITERATURE IN THE UNIVERSITY/OF DURHAM/*SECOND EDITION/RE-VISED AND ENLARGED*/LONDON/OXFORD UNIVERSITY PRESS/NEW YORK TORONTO/1956

[a]–b[8], c[6], B–Z[8], Aa–Ff[8], Gg[10]. 256 leaves, comprising p. [i] half-title; FURTHER LETTERS OF/Gerard Manley Hopkins/INCLUDING HIS/CORRESPONDENCE WITH/Coventry Patmore; p. [ii] blank; p. [iii] title; p. [iv] publisher's, copyright, bibliographical and printer's notices; pp. v–ix PREFACE TO THE FIRST EDITION; p. [x] blank; pp. xi–xii PREFACE TO THE SECOND EDITION; p. xiii CONTENTS; p. xiv LIST OF ILLUSTRATIONS; pp. xv–xx LIST OF LETTERS; pp. xxi–xl INTRODUCTION TO THE/FIRST EDITION; pp. xli–xliii ADDENDUM TO THE INTRO-DUCTION/OF THE FIRST EDITION; p. [xliv] blank; pp. 1–393 text; pp. 394–6 APPENDIX I/*Letter from* C. N. LUXMOORE *to* ARTHUR HOPKINS; pp. 397–8 APPENDIX II/*Extracts from the Diary of* W. A. COMYN MACFARLANE, 1866; pp. 399–433 APPENDIX III/*Letters to* G.M.H. *from* [various] *correspondents*; pp. 434–6 APPENDIX IV . . .; pp. 437–51 ADDITIONAL NOTES; p. [452] blank; pp. 453–65 INDEX; p. [466] printer's notice; one blank leaf.

22 × 13·9 cm. Bulk 3·1 × 3·5 cm. White laid paper, top edge stained brown, other edges trimmed. White wove endpapers. Bound in light-brown cloth, lettered in gold on spine: [between gold rules at head and foot] Further Letters/of/GERARD/MANLEY/HOPKINS/[orna-ment]/ABBOTT/SECOND/EDITION/OXFORD

Frontispiece portrait of G M H, taken in the 1850s. Other illustrations are inserted facing pp. 1, 20, 39, 68, 91, 97, 144, 189, 240, 294.

Notes. The first edition (B 113) contained 99 letters. This edition contains 188. The largest and most important group of new letters are those to his family (mainly to his mother) discovered after the death of his brother Lionel in 1952, and here first published. Published in 1956, price 50s. Issued in cream dust-jacket printed in green and black.

Reviews of B 179:

B 180   Cockshut, A. O. J. A lonely vision. *Tablet*, vol. 208, no. 6081, 8 Dec. 1956, pp. 500–2.
'The greater a man's artistic gifts the fewer people are capable of satisfying the complex demands of friendship. Hopkins' religious vocation and the hard uncongenial work which gave him few oppor-tunities to travel, prevented him from finding those friends.'

B 181   Thomas, Gilbert. Round the shelves. *Birmingham Post*, 18 Dec. 1956, p. 3.
'Is not Hopkins, after all, too consciously mannered? Is there not truth in Herbert Palmer's description of him as "that ecstatic juggler and sentence smasher"? Not, of course, that this is Mr. Palmer's *whole* verdict.' The source of Mr. Palmer's remarks is unknown to the compiler.

B 182   Anon. Wrought in anguish. *Times* (London), 20 Dec. 1956, p. 11.
'It is not that Hopkins was narrow, or bigoted . . . on the evidence of his letters, it seems as if any human contact involving an emotion other than of the intellect was too much for him.'

B 183   Anon. Hopkins to his family. *Times Literary Supplement*, 21 Dec. 1956. p. 763.
A detailed and perceptive discussion: see reply by C. C. Abbott, B 187. See also I 504, I 506.

B 184   Hough, Graham. Hopkins and Patmore. *Spectator*, vol. 197, no. 6705, 28 Dec. 1956, pp. 936–7.

B185   Cockshut, A. O. J. Father Hopkins. *Manchester Guardian*, 1 Jan. 1957, p. 3.

B186   Gillett, Eric. Books new and old. *National and English Review*, vol. 148, Feb. 1957, pp. 85–8.

'He was not among the great letter-writers, but . . . he was, in every sense of the word, a good correspondent.'

B187   Abbott, Claude Colleer. 'Further Letters of G. M. Hopkins'. *Times Literary Supplement*, 1 Feb. 1957, p. 65.

Reply to B183, amplifying certain points about the history of the letters. Some further comments by the reviewer are appended. See also I504, I506.

B188   *D., N. K. in *San Francisco Chronicle*, 'This World' supplement, 24 Feb. 1957, p. 22.

B189   Kelly, Hugh. in *Studies* (Dublin), vol. 46, Spring 1957, pp. 121–3.

Little original criticism.

B190   Miller, Betty. in *Twentieth Century*, vol. 161, no. 961, Mar. 1957, pp. 306, 308.

B191   Spender, Stephen. in *London Magazine*, vol. 4, no. 3, Mar. 1957, pp. 58–9.

'One could compare both the gain and the loss in Hopkins of being outside the contemporary main literary stream with D. H. Lawrence in our own century. In Lawrence also, there is a great gain in idiomatic naturalness, but at the same time a loss which is the result of a willed isolation.'

B192   Armstrong, Robert. Lifting the veil. *Poetry Review*, vol. 48, no. 2, Apr.–June 1957, pp. 109–10.

A brief review with little original criticism.

B193   *Ames, Ruth. in *Catholic World*, vol. 175, May 1957, p. 155.

B194   Devlin, Christopher. The heart in hiding. *Month*, vol. 17 (n.s.), no. 5, May 1957, pp. 332–3.

A very perceptive and intelligent review.

B195   Allen, Louis. in *Durham University Journal*, vol. 18 (n.s.), no. 3, June 1957, pp. 136–7.

'Hopkins could be a prude, and—one imagines—something of a jingo too. One can guess at his insularity from Newman's note to him on Irish patriotism . . .'

B196   Anon. in *Quarterly Review*, vol. 295, no. 613, July 1957, pp. 363–4.

'What a pleasure it must have been to get a letter from him . . .'

B197   *Bischoff, D. A. in *Thought*, vol. 32, Autumn 1957, pp. 455–7.

B198   Pick, John. in *Victorian Studies*, vol. 1, no. 1, Sept. 1957, pp. 91–3.

Dr. Pick points out that the letters show '. . . the fact that no scholar has yet studied adequately the influence of Hopkins upon Patmore— nor, for that matter, upon Bridges.' In the compiler's opinion, and to the best of his knowledge, this remains true.

B199   Birrell, T. A. in *English Studies* (Amsterdam), vol. 38, no. 5, Oct. 1957, pp. 225–6.

'No poet of the Victorian age was less "aesthetic" than Hopkins. Neither Hellenism nor Mediaevalism had much attraction for him, and he had very little time for beauty as an abstract ideal.'

B200   Stevens, John. The Hopkins letters. *Cambridge Review*, vol. 79, no. 1916, 2 Nov. 1957, pp. 111–15.

Much original comment, especially on GMH's state of mind concerning his conversion to Roman Catholicism.

B201   Rillie, John A. M. in *Review of English Studies*, vol. 9 (n.s.), no. 35, 1958, pp. 334–6.

Mainly concerned with editorial questions and with the history of GMH's MS papers.

B202   Moore, Rosalie. The weather. *Poetry*, vol. 92, no. 2, May 1958, pp. 113–15.

'Much has been said about the sensitivity of the poet, most of it apologetic . . . let us say simply that Hopkins was a person who could not fail to see what he looked at . . .'

B203   Phillipson, Wulstan. More light on Hopkins. *Downside Review*, vol. 76, no. 246, Autumn 1958, pp. 402–10.

Detailed discussion and comment.

B204   Weyand, Norman. Opening some doors. *Renascence*, vol. 11, no. 1, Autumn 1958, pp. 53–6.

Review of B179 and K188. Some original critical comment.

For another review, see M256.

LETTERS FROM GMH TO HIS FATHER (SIEVEKING, 1957)

B205   THE EYE/OF THE BEHOLDER/*Lance Sieveking*/[ornament/*LONDON*/HULTON PRESS/1957

Unsigned: [1–19]⁸, [20]⁴. 156 leaves, comprising p. [1] half-title: THE EYE OF THE BEHOLDER; p. [2] bibliographical note on the author's other works; p. [3] title; p. [4] dedication and printer's notice; p. 5 CONTENTS; p. 6 ACKNOWLEDGEMENTS; pp. 7–8 LIST OF ILLUSTRATIONS; pp. 9–308 text; pp. 309–12 INDEX

22·8 × 14·7 cm. Bulk 2·4 × 3 cm. White laid paper, all edges trimmed. White wove endpapers, each with a 'Tree of First Encounters and Acquaintanceship' printed in black. Bound in maroon cloth, lettered in gold on spine [within an ornamental border] THE/EYE OF THE/BEHOLDER/BY/LANCE/SIEVEKING/[ornament, beneath border]/HULTON

Illustrations are inserted between pp. 2–3, 24–5, 56–7, 86–7, 112–13, 160–1, 176–7, 200–1, 208–9, 224–5, 272–3, 280–1, 288–9. These include two very rare portraits of GMH, facing pp. 273, 281; and a reproduction of one of the letters mentioned below, between pp. 280–1.

Notes. This is a collection of autobiographical reminiscences. Lance Sieveking's mother was GMH's cousin, and he writes with intimate knowledge of the Hopkins family. Besides important biographical information, he includes transcriptions of two letters from GMH to his father, not previously published. The first of these was written from Castlebar, County Mayo, and GMH absent-mindedly dated it with the year of his birth—5 July 1844. It was written on 5 July 1884 (see B206). The second was written from Stonyhurst, and dated 23 Dec. 1871. Both these letters were reprinted, with commentary, in B206.

LETTERS FROM GMH TO KATHARINE TYNAN

B206   Storey, Graham, *editor*. Six new letters of Gerard Manley Hopkins. *Month*, vol. 19 (n.s.), no. 5, May 1958, pp. 263–70.
Transcriptions, with commentary, of: (*a*) the two letters to Manley Hopkins published in B205, and (*b*) four letters to Katharine Tynan, dated 14 Nov. 1886, 2 June 1887, 8 July 1887, 15 Sept. 1888. These four letters form GMH's side of the letters from Miss Tynan in FL2. They are now in the University of Texas Library (see N9).

JOURNALS AND PAPERS OF GMH (1959)

B207   THE JOURNALS AND/PAPERS OF/GERARD MANLEY/
HOPKINS/*Edited by*/HUMPHRY HOUSE/SENIOR LECTURER
IN ENGLISH LITERATURE/AND FELLOW OF WADHAM
COLLEGE, OXFORD/*Completed by*/GRAHAM STOREY/FELLOW
OF TRINITY HALL, CAMBRIDGE/[ornament—Hopkins family
crest]/LONDON/OXFORD UNIVERSITY PRESS/NEW YORK
TORONTO/1959

[a]^8, b^{10}, B–Z^8, Aa–Ff^8, Gg–Hh^4, Ii–Oo^8, Pp^{10}. 308 leaves, comprising
one blank leaf, p. [i] half-title: THE JOURNALS AND/PAPERS
OF/GERARD MANLEY/HOPKINS; p. [ii] bibliographical note;
p. [iii] title; p. [iv] *nihil obstat* and *imprimatur*, publisher's, printer's and
copyright notices; pp. [v]–vi CONTENTS; pp. [vii]–viii LIST OF
ILLUSTRATIONS; pp. [ix]–xxxii PREFACE; p. [xxxiii] ABBRE-
VIATIONS; p. [xxxiv] blank; p. [1] fly-title: EARLY NOTE-
BOOKS; p. [2] NOTE; pp. [3]–130 text; p. [131] fly-title: JOUR-
NAL; p. [132] blank; pp. [133]–263 text; p. [264] blank; p. [265]
fly-title: LECTURE NOTES: RHETORIC; p. [266] blank; pp.
[267]–90 text; p. [291] fly-title: NOTES; p. [292] blank; pp. [293]–
451 text of Notes; p. [452] blank; pp. [453]–5 APPENDIX I/
Hopkins's Drawings; p. [456] blank; pp. [457]–97 APPENDIX II/
Gerard Manley Hopkins as Musician/By JOHN STEVENS; p. [498]
blank; pp. [499]–527 APPENDIX III/*Philological Notes*/By ALAN
WARD; p. [528] blank; pp. [529]–35 APPENDIX IV/*Catalogue of
the Manuscripts at Campion Hall, Oxford*; p. [536] blank; pp. [537]–9
APPENDIX V/*Hopkins's Resolutions and 'Slaughter of the innocents'*;
p. [540] blank; pp. [541]–3 APPENDIX VI/*The Organisation of the
Society of Jesus*; pp. [544]–[548] maps; pp. [549]–50 INDEX I/
First Lines of Early Poems and Fragments . . .; pp. [551]–68 INDEX
II/*Persons and Places* . . .; pp. [569]–79 INDEX III/*Words and
Subjects* . . .; p. [580] printer's notice.

21·9 × 13·9 cm. Bulk 3·6 × 4·4 cm. White wove paper, top edge
stained brown, other edges trimmed. White wove endpapers. Bound in
light-brown cloth, lettered in gold on spine: [between gold rules at head
and foot] The Journals/and Papers/of/GERARD MANLEY/HOP-
KINS/[ornament]/HOUSE/AND/STOREY/OXFORD

Frontispiece portrait of G M H taken in 1863. Other illustrations (reproductions of G M H's drawings, 29 figs. and 33 plates) are bound in between pp. 456–7: a 22-leaf gathering of coated paper. The maps on pp. 544–8 are as follows: p. 544 Oxford; p. 545 Bovey Tracey; p. 546 Stonyhurst District; p. 547 Isle of Man; p. 548 St. Beuno's District.

Notes. This volume and B 208 together constitute the second edition, revised and enlarged, of B 78. Of the new material published here, the most interesting and important is the new Journal, covering 2 May 1866 to 18 July 1868, discovered by Father Anthony Bischoff in February 1947. Extracts from this journal had already been published (see B 144–8), but it is here for the first time published in full. The contents also include five more undergraduate essays. Since the two volumes (B 207–8) were issued together, nearly all reviews deal with them together; and reviews of this volume will be found at B 209 onwards.

SERMONS AND DEVOTIONAL WRITINGS OF G M H (1959)

B 208   THE SERMONS AND/DEVOTIONAL WRITINGS OF/ GERARD MANLEY/HOPKINS/*Edited by*/CHRISTOPHER DEV-LIN, S.J./[ornament—Hopkins family crest]/LONDON/OXFORD UNIVERSITY PRESS/NEW YORK TORONTO/1959

[A–B]⁸, C–S⁸, T–Z⁸, Aa¹⁰. 194 leaves, comprising one blank leaf, p. [i] half-title: THE SERMONS AND/DEVOTIONAL WRIT-INGS OF/GERARD MANLEY/HOPKINS; p. [ii] bibliographical note; p. [iii] title; p. [iv] publisher's, printer's, and copyright notices; p. [v] dedication; p. [vi] *nihil obstat* and *imprimatur*; pp. [vii]–viii FOREWORD; pp. [ix]–xi CONTENTS; p. [xii] blank; pp. [xiii]–xiv INTRODUCTION; p. [1] fly-title: PART ONE/THE SER-MONS; p. [2] blank; pp. [3]–104 text; p. [105] fly-title: PART TWO/SPIRITUAL WRITINGS; p. [106] blank; pp. [107]–209 text; p. [210] blank; p. [211] fly-title: PART THREE/ISOLATED DISCOURSES AND/PRIVATE NOTES; p. [212] blank; pp. [213]–71 text; p. [272] blank; p. [273] fly-title: NOTES; p. [274] blank; pp. [275]–321 text of Notes; p. [322] blank; p. [323] fly-title: APPENDIXES; p. [324] blank; pp. [325]–37 APPENDIX I/ *Marie Lataste*; pp. [338]–51 APPENDIX II/*Scotus and Hopkins*;

pp. [352]–6 APPENDIX III/*Fall of the Angels according to Babylonian and Welsh Texts*; pp. [357]–63 INDEX I/PERSONS AND PLACES; pp. [364]–9 INDEX II/WORDS AND SUBJECTS; p. [370] INDEX III/POEMS QUOTED OR DISCUSSED IN THE TEXT; p. [371] printer's notice; p. [372] blank.

22 × 13·4 cm. Bulk 2·4 × 3 cm. White wove paper, top edge stained brown, other edges trimmed. White wove endpapers. Bound in light-brown cloth, lettered in gold on spine: [between gold rules at head and foot] The/Sermons and/Devotional/Writings of/GERARD/MANLEY /HOPKINS/[ornament]/DEVLIN/OXFORD

A map is printed on p. 227.

Notes. This volume and B207 together constitute the second edition, revised and enlarged of B78. Only a few sermons, and scattered extracts from the devotional writings, were included in B78; this book makes good the deficiency by bringing together all the known sermons, GMH's commentary on the Ignatian Spiritual Exercises, and miscellaneous religious notes and discourses.

Reviews: (all reviews are of *both* B207 and B208, except where stated)
B209   Anon. In the high aesthetic line. *Times* (London), 12 Feb. 1959, p. 13.
   'Few poets are better documented, few more remote. Hopkins the man hides inside his cassock; and when he emerges for a moment, it is usually in an uncharacteristic attitude.'
B210   Young, Kenneth. Ashamed to be a poet. *Daily Telegraph* (London), 13 Feb. 1959, p. 15.
   GMH '. . . showed there were other methods of loading every rift with ore than that inherited from Laforgue and Corbière via Pound and Eliot.'
B211   Bateman, David. A poet's notebook. *Western Mail* (Cardiff), 14 Feb. 1959, p. 6.
B212   Meath, Gerard. Gerard Manley Hopkins. *Tablet*, vol. 213, no. 6195, 14 Feb. 1959, pp. 154–5.
   'Just as Milton's belief in self-mastery is set off against the sensuality of some of his early Latin and Italian verse, so Hopkins' stern suppression of all vanity and self-esteem is set off against his passionate love of his poems and delight in inscapes. And . . . how free of self-

indulgence he was; the love of clouds, of grass, of glaciers, of stone arcading is never grasping.'

B213 Cronin, Anthony. Self-mortifier. *Sunday Times*, 15 Feb. 1959, p. 19.

B214 Heppenstall, Rayner. Too much editing. *Observer*, 15 Feb. 1959, p. 21.

Makes the remarkable assertion that 'Critics of poetry do not say much about Hopkins nowadays . . .' and suggests that there must have been a whole generation of readers who needed to be told who he was. 'His metrical theories turned out in the end to be unsound or un-fruitful . . . and yet to a handful of poems one still responds.'

B215 Thomas, Gilbert. Round the shelves. *Birmingham Post*, 17 Feb. 1959, p. 3.

'Hopkins was himself greater than anything he achieved. If he never quite discovered how to use his gifts, it was because those gifts were so varied and idiosyncratic . . .'

B216 Small, Christopher. Hopkins: pattern in the poet's eye. *Glasgow Herald*, 19 Feb. 1959, p. 5.

B217 Kermode, Frank. Hopkins and the moderns. *Manchester Guardian*, 27 Feb. 1959, p. 6.

B218 Robson, W. W. Choice of life. *Spectator*, vol. 202, no. 6818, 27 Feb. 1959, p. 300.

B219 Jones, John. The sad and difficult. *New Statesman*, vol. 57, no. 1460, 7 Mar. 1959, pp. 338–9.

B220 Nicholl, Donald. A ruthless scrutiny of the spirit. *Cambridge Review*, vol. 80, no. 1952, 7 Mar. 1959, pp. 405–9.

Much original critical comment.

B221 Russell, Peter. Why Hopkins wrote as he did. *Liverpool Daily Post*, 11 Mar. 1959, p. 10.

B222 Wain, John. Prose writings of a great poet-priest whose fame grows steadily. *New York Herald Tribune Book Review*, 15 Mar. 1959, p. 8.

Review of B207 only. 'Gerard Manley Hopkins is usually allowed to have been one of the five or six greatest poets to arise in the English-speaking world during the last hundred years . . .'

B223 Anon. Annotation in abundance. *Economist*, vol. 190, no. 6030, 21 Mar. 1959, Spring Book Supplement, p. 4.

Review of B207 only.

B224 Abbott, Claude Colleer. Priest and poet. *Listener*, vol. 61, no. 1563, 12 Mar. 1959, pp. 476, 479.

B225 Anon. Aspects of Hopkins's genius. *Scotsman*, 26 Mar. 1959, p. 20.

'The sensitiveness which marked [Hopkins's] response to nature was characteristic also of his relation with Society, and it was upon this rock that his career as a priest split.'

B226 Stephenson, A. A. Gerard Manley Hopkins: a poet utterly given to Christ. *Catholic Herald* (London), 26 Mar. 1959, p. 3.

This review attributes G M H's fits of depression to 'a tinge of practical Pelagianism'—possibly as good an explanation as any, but not substantiated here.

B227 Gillett, Eric. in *National and English Review*, vol. 152, no. 914, Apr. 1959, p. 150.

Review of B207 only. Brief.

B228 Robie, Burton A. in *Library Journal*, vol. 84, 1 Apr. 1959, p. 1133.

Review of B207 only. Brief.

B229 Morse, Samuel French. The image of a poet in his own words. *New York Times Book Review*, vol. 64, no. 14, 5 Apr. 1959, p. 4.

'No other English poet of the later nineteenth century has so deeply influenced the poets of the twentieth as Gerard Manley Hopkins.'

B230 Corke, Hilary. A housecarl in Loyola's menie. *Encounter*, vol. 12, no. 5, May 1959, pp. 63–7.

B231 Evans, Illtud. Fine, dull, beautiful. *Blackfriars*, vol. 40, no. 471, June 1959, pp. 270–3.

Much original critical comment.

B232 Stanford, Derek. in *English*, vol. 12, no. 71, Summer 1959, pp. 191–2.

Much preoccupied with the relationship of G M H's vocation to his poetry.

B233 Busby, Christopher. Time's Andromeda. *Dublin Review*, vol. 233, no. 480, Summer 1959, pp. 183–90.

B234 Kelly, John C. in *Studies* (Dublin), vol. 48, Summer 1959, pp. 226–30.

'Even when a man is, as Hopkins was, a major poet, to publish every extant scrap he wrote must seem faintly ridiculous.'

B235 Park, B. A. in *Books Abroad*, vol. 33, no. 4, Autumn 1959, p. 461. Review of B207 only. Brief.

B236 Anon. Rare ill-broker'd talent. *Times Literary Supplement*, 25 Sept. 1959, p. 544.

'Rarely has a poet attracted such a burden of documentation and commentary. But it is not so much the amount as the nature of the comment that is remarkable, for much of the editing . . . and criticism . . . is of a kind to make his fame a personal triumph.'

B237 Pick, John. in *Modern Philology*, vol. 57, no. 2, Nov. 1959, pp. 137–8.

Review of B208 only. G M H's sermons are '. . . in a sense, prose poems. In both his sermons and his poetry Hopkins was trying to translate theological truths into imagery that would touch the hearts of his auditors.'

B238 Westrup, J. A. in *Music and Letters*, vol. 41, no. 1, Jan. 1960, pp. 74–5.

Review of B207 only. Detailed criticism of G M H as a musician: 'There is something pathetic in [Hopkins's] pursuit of an art in which he had no competence . . .'

B239 Ong, Walter J. in *Victorian Studies*, vol. 3, no. 3, Mar. 1960, pp. 305–8.

G M H was a man who '. . . precisely because of his profound and uninhibited reaction to the intellectual and artistic forces of his own time finds himself projected as a living force into the second half of the twentieth century.'

B240 Hill, A. G. Victoriana with a difference. *Essays in Criticism*, vol. 10, no. 2, Apr. 1960, pp. 215–19.

'The rehabilitation of Hopkins as a Victorian has been a slow process. If the price we have to pay for this is to recognise that we no longer have to justify him as a "modern", then we should pay it gladly.'

B241 Phillipson, Wulstan. Hopkins again. *Downside Review*, no. 252, Summer 1960, pp. 213–17.

Some original critical comment.

B242 Ure, Peter. in *Review of English Studies*, vol. 11 (n.s.), no. 44, Nov. 1960, pp. 445–7.

Mainly concerned with editorial matters.

B243 Gardner, W. H. Anvil-ding and tongue that told: 1. The early journals and papers of Gerard Manley Hopkins. *Month*, vol. 25 (n.s.), no. 1, Jan. 1961, pp. 34–47.

Review of B207. See also next entry.

B244 Gardner, W. H. Anvil-ding and tongue that told: 2. The sermons and devotional writings of Gerard Manley Hopkins. *Month*, vol. 25 (n.s.), no. 2, Feb. 1961, pp. 82–95.

Review of B208. See also previous entry.

B245 *Litzinger, Boyd. in *Cithara*, vol. 1, Nov. 1961, pp. 48–50.

B246 Duncan-Jones, E. E. in *Modern Language Review*, vol. 57, no. 3, July 1962, pp. 431–3.

Some interesting suggestions about the meaning of an early fragment by GMH.

B247 Weyand, Norman. The vision and the writing. *Renascence*, vol. 14, no. 2, Winter 1962, pp. 106–9.

Review of B207–8 and H193. Includes a critical discussion of methods of interpreting GMH.

B248 Birrell, T. A. in *English Studies* (Amsterdam), vol. 44, no. 6, 1963, pp. 462–5.

Review of B207–8, H193, and G86. 'Hopkins was intensely clever, intensely sensitive, and intensely forthright. And he was no fool. He knew that he was thought to be odd and eccentric . . . [and] soon realised that his poetry would be considered as crazy . . .' Other comments are very critical of Bridges.

For other reviews, see M10, M47, M100, M259.

SCHOOL NOTES BY GMH ON THUCYDIDES, ETC. (BENDER, 1966)

B249 Gerard Manley Hopkins/THE CLASSICAL BACK-GROUND/AND CRITICAL RECEPTION/OF HIS WORK/*by Todd K. Bender/The Johns Hopkins Press/Baltimore*

Unsigned: [A–E]¹⁶, [F]¹². 92 leaves, comprising p. [i] half-title: *Gerard Manley Hopkins*; p. [ii] blank; p. [iii] title; p. [iv] copyright and printer's notices; p. [v] dedication; p. [vi] blank; pp. vii–viii *Preface*; p. ix *Contents*; p. [x] blank; pp. 1–4 *Introduction*; pp. 5–168 text, including one unpaginated leaf between pp. 54–5; pp. 169–72 *Index*, with publisher's notice at foot of p. 172.

21·3 × 13·5 cm. Bulk 1·3 × 1·9 cm. White wove paper, watermarked WARREN'S/OLDE STYLE; all edges trimmed. Blue wove end-papers. Bound in blue-grey cloth, lettered on spine in brown and black: [in brown] *Bender*/[in black, vertically] Gerard Manley Hopkins THE CLASSICAL/BACKGROUND AND CRITICAL RECEPTION OF HIS WORK/[in brown] JOHNS/HOPKINS

Two plates (maps drawn by GMH to illustrate the movements of Athenian ships described in Thucydides Bk. 2, chap. 90) are printed on the leaf between pp. 54–5. Plate I on recto of leaf, facing p. 54, Plate II on verso, facing p. 55.

Notes. This book includes a fairly long note by G M H, which may belong to his last days at school, on Thucydides, Bk. 2, chaps. 87 ff. It is taken from the note-book catalogued by Humphry House as B. II (see JP, p. 529), and is printed here, with comments, on pp. 52–6. See also pp. 57–8 for two short extracts from G M H's notes on other classical texts. Published in 1966, price $5.95. Issued in light-blue dust-jacket printed in black and brown.

Reviews: (see also A152, A157).

B250 Boyle, Robert. in *Journal of English and Germanic Philology*, vol. 66, 1967, pp. 609–13.
   Much original critical comment, mainly strong refutation of Bender's ideas and attitudes.

B251 Bostetter, Edward. in *Studies in English Literature* (Houston), vol. 7, no. 4, Autumn 1967, pp. 741–66.

B252 MacKenzie, Norman H. The classicism of Hopkins. *Queen's Quarterly*, vol. 74, no. 3, Autumn 1967, pp. 547–8.
   Some interesting comments on the texts of G M H's classical poems.

B253 Boyle, Robert. in *Thought*, vol. 42, no. 167, Winter 1967, pp. 624–6.

B254 Downes, David A. in *Victorian Poetry*, vol. 6, 1968, pp. 205–8.
   Much original criticism of G M H's poetic sensibility.

B255 Spector, Robert D. in *Books Abroad*, vol. 42, 1968, pp. 123–4.
   A brief review.

B256 Goode, John. in *New Statesman*, vol. 75, no. 1925, 2 Feb. 1968, pp. 144–5.

B257 Haller, John M. in *Comparative Literature Studies*, vol. 5, no. 1, Mar. 1968, pp. 92–3.

JOURNAL KEPT BY GMH AS PORTER (CHIEF NOVICE) AT MANRESA HOUSE, 11 Dec. 1869–19 Feb. 1870

B258 Hopkins the Jesuit/THE YEARS OF TRAINING/[double rule]/Alfred Thomas, S.J./LONDON/OXFORD UNIVERSITY PRESS/NEW YORK TORONTO/1969

[A]–I⁸, K–S⁸, T⁶. 150 leaves, comprising p. [i] half-title: Hopkins the

Jesuit; p. [ii] blank; p. [iii] title; p. [iv] publisher's, copyright, and printer's notices; p. [v] dedication; p. [vi] blank; p. [vii] CONTENTS; p. [viii] LIST OF ILLUSTRATIONS; pp. ix–x PREFACE; p. xi ACKNOWLEDGEMENTS; p. [xii] blank; p. xiii ABBREVIATIONS; pp. xiv–xv CHRONOLOGICAL TABLE/OF HOPKINS'S LIFE; p. [xvi] three quotations from GMH's works; pp. [1]–210 text; pp. [211]–13 APPENDIX 1/Manley Hopkins and the Roman Catholic Priesthood; pp. [214]–45 APPENDIX 2/Refectory reading 1868–74, 1881–2; pp. [246]–56 APPENDIX 3/St. Beuno's Debating Club; pp. [257]–63 BIBLIOGRAPHY; p. [264] blank; pp. [265]–83 INDEX; p. [284] printer's notice.

21·6 × 14 cm. Bulk 2 × 2·5 cm. White wove paper, all edges trimmed. White wove endpapers. Bound in emerald-green cloth, lettered in gold on spine: [within a dark-green panel, edged with gold] HOPKINS/THE/JESUIT/*The Years of/Training*/ALFRED/THOMAS/ [beneath panel, at foot of spine] OXFORD

Frontispiece portrait of GMH, photographed in 1880. Other illustrations are inserted between pp. 80–1 and 96–7. The illustration facing p. 81 is a facsimile of two pages from the Porter's Journal mentioned below.

Notes. During his noviceship at Manresa House, Roehampton, GMH was Porter, or chief novice, from 11 Dec. 1869 until 19 Feb. 1870. Throughout his tenure of this office it was his duty to write up the Porter's Journal, a day-to-day diary showing the events, activities, and comings and goings in the community. This Porter's Journal, discovered by Father Thomas, contains 24 pages in GMH's handwriting. These pages are here first published (pp. 67–82), meticulously transcribed and edited. Published in July 1969, price 65*s*. Issued in dust-jacket printed in green and purple, lettered in purple and white.

Reviews:
B259 Bergonzi, Bernard. Sacramental poet. *Observer*, 10 Aug. 1969, p. 25.
    The only unfavourable review. Also deals with H298.
B260 Grigson, Geoffrey. A kind of martyrdom. *New Statesman*, vol. 78, no. 2005, 15 Aug. 1969, pp. 214–15.
    Review of B258 and H298. Contains some original criticism;

especially on the validity of Father Thomas's assertion that G M H the poet, as well as G M H the priest, was formed by his Jesuit training.

B261   *M., M. M. Poet among the Jesuits. *Kentish Gazette*, 22 Aug. 1969, p.

B262   Hanshell, Deryck. More than violets. *Tablet*, vol. 223, no. 6745, 30 Aug. 1969, pp. 857–8.

B263   Anon. in *British Book News*, Sept. 1969, pp. 726–7. Brief but enthusiastic. No original criticism.

B264   Sewell, Gordon. Poet and priest. *Southern Evening Echo*, 5 Sept. 1969, p. 10.

B265   Moffatt, Ronald. Poetic details. *Month*, vol. 42 (n.s.), no. 4, Oct. 1969, pp. 220–1.

    Some comments on the relationship between G M H's vocation and his poetry.

B266   Anon. Behind the scenes of Hopkins's training. *Times Literary Supplement*, 18 Dec. 1969, p. 1455.

    Review of B258 and H298.

B267   Dunne, Tom. World without event. *Library Review*, vol. 22, no. 4, Winter 1969, pp. 216–17.

LETTER FROM G M H TO THE ARCHBISHOP OF LIVER-POOL

B268   Sherwood, H. C. A letter of G. M. Hopkins. *Times Literary Supplement*, 4 Sept. 1969, p. 984.

    A letter from G M H to the Archbishop of Liverpool, dated 12 Aug. 1881, not previously published. Full text with commentary. For further comments see I714. See also N7.

LETTERS FROM G M H TO M. F. COX

B269   [Troddyn, P. M.] Gerard Manley Hopkins: two unpublished letters on Anglo–Irish relations. *Studies* (Dublin), vol. 59, no. 233, Spring 1970, pp. 19–25.

    Two letters from G M H to Dr. Michael F. Cox, an examiner for the Royal University of Ireland. Dated 26 Mar. 1887 and 31 Mar. 1887, the letters are printed with notes and commentary. In both letters G M H comments on a book lent to him by Dr. Cox: *Arts and Industries in Ireland*, by S[arah] A[tkinson] (1882).

SECTION C

ANTHOLOGIES

THIS section is a selective chronological list of anthologies containing work by G M H. G M H is now represented in a very large number of anthologies, but many of them contain only a few of his 'popular' poems, or a few short extracts from his prose, and a comprehensive list would therefore serve no useful purpose. The selection given here includes the more important anthologies, and also attempts to show the wide range of different *types* of anthology in which his work is to be found. Anthologies published before 1918 are placed in Sections A and B.

1925

C1 Leslie, Shane. An anthology of Catholic poets. London, Burns, Oates & Washbourne Ltd., 1925. xv, 371 pp.
  See pp. 12–13 (introductory comment) and pp. 282–9. Seven poems by G M H included.

1927

C2 Squire, J. C., *editor*. The Cambridge book of lesser poets. Cambridge, Cambridge University Press, 1927. viii, 470 pp.
  See p. 443. One poem by G M H included: 'Heaven-Haven', wrongly titled 'I Have Desired to Go'.

1928

C3 Marchant, Sir James. The Madonna: an anthology. London, Longmans, Green and Co., 1928. xxxix, 207 pp.
  See pp. 78–82. One poem by G M H included: 'Mary Mother of Divine Grace, Compared to the Air We Breathe'.

1929

C4　Monro, Harold, *editor*. Twentieth century poetry. London, Chatto and Windus, 1929. 255 pp.

　　See pp. 27, 76, 129, 131, 137. Five poems by G M H included. This anthology was a popular and important one in its day, and probably helped the growth of G M H's reputation.

1936

C5　Roberts, Michael, *editor*. The Faber book of modern verse. London, Faber and Faber, 1936. xvi, 352 pp.

　　See pp. 39–60. Thirteen poems by G M H included: this number reflects the intense interest in his life and work prevailing in the 1930s. The book has since become a classic of its kind.

C6　Yeats, W. B., *editor*. The Oxford book of modern verse. Oxford, Clarendon Press, 1936. xlvii, 450 pp.

　　Seven poems by G M H included. See also the comments on G M H in the introduction, p. v, xxxix–xl. Yeats's grudging but interesting remarks are amplified in H204. That both Yeats and Eliot should lack enthusiasm for G M H seems to the compiler one of the more interesting perversities of literature.

1938

C7　Murphy, Gwendolen. The modern poet: an anthology. London, Sidgwick & Jackson, Ltd., 1938. xx, 208 pp.

　　See pp. xvi–xvii, 1–4. Five poems by G M H included.

1939

C8　Quiller-Couch, Sir Arthur, *editor*. The Oxford book of English verse, 1250–1918. Oxford, Clarendon Press, 1939. xxviii, 1172 pp.

　　See pp. 1010–13. Four poems by G M H included. This new edition is the first in which his work appears, despite the frequent impressions of the original 1900 edition. But Quiller-Couch included one poem by G M H in the first edition of his *Oxford book of Victorian verse*, 1912 (see A28).

1940

C9　Cecil, David, *editor*. The Oxford book of Christian verse. Oxford, Clarendon Press, 1940. xxxiii, 560 pp.
　　See pp. xxx–xxxi (brief critical comment) and pp. 492–503. Nine poems by G M H included.

1947

C10　Williams, Oscar, *editor*. A little treasury of modern poetry, English and American. London, Routledge & Kegan Paul Ltd., 1947. 640 pp. Fifteen poems by G M H included. See also introduction, pp. 31–2, brief but perceptive critical comment.

1950

C11　Grigson, Geoffrey, *editor*. The Victorians: an anthology. London, Routledge & Kegan Paul Ltd., 1950. xi, 336 pp.
　　See nos. 131, 157, 203, 204, 217, 235 (ii), 248. Six poems and one prose extract by G M H included.

1951

C12　Rothenstein, Elizabeth, *editor*. The Virgin and the Child: an anthology of paintings and poems. London, Collins, 1951. 95 pp.
　　See pp. 12, 32, 72, 88. Selections from G M H's poems about the Virgin Mary, coupled with appropriate paintings.

1952

C13　Auden, W. H., *and* Pearson, Norman Holmes, *editors*. Poets of the English language, [Vol.] V, Tennyson to Yeats. London, Eyre & Spottiswoode, 1952. xlvii, 624 pp.
　　See pp. 498–516. Nine poems included.

1955

C14　Grigson, Geoffrey. English drawing from Samuel Cooper to Gwen John. London, Thames and Hudson, 1955. xv, 186 pp.
　　See pp. 132–3, 167–8. Four drawings by G M H included, with critical and biographical comment.

1957

C15   Chapin, John, *editor*. The book of Catholic quotations. London, John Calder, 1957. x, 1073 pp.
   Twenty-four entries refer to G M H's work.

1958

C16   Hampden, John. Great poems, from Shakespeare to Manley Hopkins. London, University of London Press Ltd., 1958. 256 pp.
   See pp. 215–18. Three poems by G MH included, with explanatory notes on pp. 244–6.

C17   Jeffares, A. Norman, *and* Davies, M. Bryn. The scientific background: a prose anthology. London, Sir Isaac Pitman & Sons, Ltd., 1958. xii, 306 pp.
   See pp. 80–3, 292–3. An extract from one of G M H's letters to *Nature* (B 1–3) with questions on it, e.g. '2. Note any sentence which illustrates the almost painful precision of the writer.'

C18   Warburg, Jeremy. The industrial muse: the Industrial Revolution in English poetry. London, Oxford University Press, 1958. xxxv, 169 pp.
   See pp. 68–70. Two poems by G M H included, to illustrate his attitude to nineteenth-century industrialism.

1959

C19   Sitwell, Edith, *editor*. The Atlantic book of British and American poetry. London, Victor Gollancz Ltd., 1959. 2 vols., paginated continuously: xlii, 597 pp., and pp. 598–1092.
   See pp. 757–72. Brief but excellent critical introduction, followed by seven of G M H's poems, including 'The Wreck of the Deutschland' in full.

1962

C20   Brown, E. K., *and* Bailey, J. O., *editors*. Victorian poetry. 2nd edition, New York, Ronald Press Company, 1962. xlv, 911 pp.
   See particularly pp. 696–703, 891–6. Fifteen poems by G M H included, with notes.

1963

C21 Grigson, Geoffrey, *editor*. O rare mankind! a short collection of great prose. London, Phoenix House, 1963. 168 pp.
> *See* pp. 137–8. Four extracts from G M H's prose included.

1964

C22 Hayward, John. The Oxford book of nineteenth-century English verse. Oxford, Clarendon Press, 1964. xxxv, 969 pp.
> *See* pp. 852–71. Eleven poems by G M H included.

1965

C23 Brett, R. C. Poems of faith and doubt: the Victorian age. London, Edward Arnold, 1965. 191 pp.
> *See* pp. 171–88. Three poems by G M H included, annotated and with introductory notes.

C24 Mottram, R. K. The lyric mood: an anthology of lyric poetry. London, Oxford University Press, 1965. xiv, 288 pp.
> *See* pp. 35, 36, 95, 109, 193, 196, 205. Seven poems by G M H included. See also brief notes, pp. 251–2, 259, 260, 268.

1966

C25 Hoffman, Daniel G., *and* Hynes, Samuel, *editors*. English literary criticism, Romantic and Victorian. London, Peter Owen, 1966.
> *See* pp. 274–80. Two extracts from G M H's criticism.

C26 Johnson, E. D. H. The poetry of earth: a collection of English nature writings. London, Gollancz, 1966. xxii, 423 pp.
> *See* pp. 321–44. A short critical introduction to G M H's life and work, followed by a selection of extracts from his journals. Some poor reproductions of his drawings are included.

1967

C27 Piper, H. W. The beginnings of modern poetry. Melbourne, Oxford University Press, 1967. xviii, 161 pp.

See p. xv (brief introductory comment) and pp. 33–45. Sixteen poems and two prose passages by G M H included.

1968

C28 Simpson, Louis. An introduction to poetry. London, Macmillan, 1968. xvii, 418 pp.

See pp. 247–50. Five poems by G M H included.

1969

C29 MacBeth, George, *editor*. The Penguin book of Victorian verse: a critical anthology. Harmondsworth, Middlesex, Penguin Books, 1969. 440 pp.

See pp. 306–13. Six poems by G M H included, with brief critical introduction.

1970

C30 Freer, Allen, *and* Andrew, John, *editors*. Cambridge book of English verse, 1900–39. Cambridge, Cambridge University Press, 1970. xi, 205 pp.

See pp. 1–11, 137–45. Fourteen poems by G M H included, with introduction and explanatory notes.

SECTION D

TRANSLATIONS

THIS section is a list of translations of GMH's work, arranged alphabetically by language and chronologically within each language group. Cross-references to Section M have been provided, since some of the critical essays in that section include translations.

ENGLISH

D1 Knox, Ronald. Nativity hymn by Gerard Manley Hopkins, S.J., now first translated by Ronald Knox. *Tablet*, vol. 168, no. 5042, 26 Dec. 1936, pp. 897–8.
The Latin text of 'Ad Matrem Virginem' (178) with English verse translation.

D2 *Boyle, Robert R. A Christmas poem by Father Gerard Hopkins S.J., translated from the Latin by R. Boyle. *Queen's Work*, vol. 50, no. 3, Dec. 1957, pp. 18–19.

FRENCH *See also* M23, M31

D3 Roditi, Edouard. Poèms de Gerard Manley Hopkins. *Mesures* (Paris), no. 1, 15 Jan. 1935, pp. 91–102.
Translations into French of four poems: numbers 38, 44, 36, 70. Brief introductory note.

D4 Landier, Germain. Lettres de Gerard Manley Hopkins. *Mesures* (Paris), no. 1, 15 Jan. 1935, pp. 103–9.
Translations into French of three letters to Bridges, dated 13 May 1878, 10 Feb. 1888, and (in a footnote, p. 109) 2 Aug. 1871.

D5 *Leyris, Pierre. Putride pâture. *Dieu Vivant* (Paris), no. 3, 1945, pp. 51–9.

D6   *Leyris, Pierre. Deux lettres. *Dieu Vivant* (Paris), no. 11, 1948, pp. 27–42.

D7   *Mambrino, J. La Sainte Vierge comparée à l'air que nous respirons. *Christus* (Paris), vol. 1, no. 3, July 1954, pp. 7–15.

D8   Leyris, Pierre. Reliquiae: vers, proses, dessins de G. M. Hopkins, réunis et traduits. Paris, Éditions du Seuil, 1957. 174 pp.

A fine selection from G M H's poems and prose, brilliantly translated into French. See also D9. For reviews, see I519, M37, M39, M41, M42, M43, M48, M257.

D9   Leyris, Pierre. Le Naufrage du Deutschland. Paris, Éditions du Seuil, 1964. 70 pp.

'The Wreck of the Deutschland' translated into French. (See also D8.) The sustained excellence of this translation can hardly be exaggerated. For reviews, see M53, M54.

GERMAN   *See also* M59

D10   Behn, Irene. Gerard Manley Hopkins: Gedichte. Übertragung, Einführung und Erläuterung von Irene Behn. Hamburg, Claassen & Goverts, [1948]. 138 pp.

D11   *Clemen, Wolfgang, *and* Clemen, Ursula. Gerard Manley Hopkins: Gedichte, Schriften, Briefe. Munich, Kösel-Verlag, 1954. 744 pp. For reviews, see M77, M80, M82.

D12   *Clemen, Ursula, *and* Enzensberger, Christian. Von Hopkins bis Dylan Thomas: Englische Gedichte und Deutsch Prosaübertragungen; herausgegeben und übertragen von Ursula Clemen und Christian Enzensberger. Frankfurt and Hamburg, Fischer Bucherei, 1961. 200 pp.

ITALIAN   *See also* M117, M128

D13   *Escobar, Mario. Rosa Mystica. *Frontespizio*, vol. 11, no. 10, Oct. 1936, p. 23.

D14 Guidi, Augusto. Poesie di G. M. Hopkins con testo a fronte. Bologna, Gaunda, [1942]. 195 pp.
See also D15, D18.

D15 Guidi, Augusto. Gerard Manley Hopkins: Il Naufragio del Deutschland, La Fine dell'Euridice. Testo inglese premessa e traduzione . . . Brescia, Morcelliana, [1947]. 56 pp. For review, see M132.

D16 *Anon. Il Mistero Dei Magi. *L'Illustrazione Italiana* (Milan), June 1961, pp. 34–7.

D17 Anderson, Robin. La Santa Vergine paragonata all'aria che respiriamo, di Gerardo Manley Hopkins. *L'Osservatore Romano*, 25 Dec. 1965, p.

D18 Guidi, Augusto. Gerard Manley Hopkins: poesie e prose scelte dal diario, dalle prediche e dalla corrispondenza, introduzione e versioni di Augusto Guidi. Parma, Gaunda, 1965. xxxi, 314 pp. (Collana Fenice, 15.)
A generous selection from the poems and prose, translated into Italian with facing English texts. Introduction and notes included.

JAPANESE *See* M164–5, M167, M174, M180, M227

PORTUGUESE

D19 Kim, Tomaz. Um poema de Gerard Manley Hopkins. *Diario de Noticias* (Lisbon), 25 Oct. 1955, p. 7.
A translation into Portuguese of one poem: 'I wake and feel the fell of dark . . .' (67).

SCOTS

D20 Robertson, Edith Anne. Translations into the Scots tongue of poems by Gerard Manley Hopkins. Aberdeen, Aberdeen University Press, 1968. 47 pp.
Twenty-seven poems translated into Scots, with facing English texts.

SPANISH *See also* M 241, M 251

D 21 *Martinez, Angel. Gerard Manley Hopkins (Poemas). *El Pez y la Serpiente* (Rivista de Cultura, Managua, Nicaragua), no. 6, 1965, pp. 153–73.
 Translations into Spanish. See also D 22.

D 22 *Martinez, Angel. G. M. Hopkins: Halcon del viento; traducción de Angel Martínez. Mexico, Librería de M. Porrúa, 1959. unpaginated. (Cuadernos del Unicorno, 20.)

SECTION E

DUBIA

THE two entries in this section are complete transcripts of the originals. In the compiler's opinion both were probably written by G MH, and they are included in the hope that they may link up with evidence discovered by other researchers.

E 1   *Church Times*, 7 Oct. 1865, unpaginated.

THE SURPLICE DISPUTES.

Sir,—Your correspondent "A. B." has got so wrong a version of the rhyme he quotes, that I venture to send the original if you can find a place for it.

Yours truly,

G. H.

From "Oxford College Rhymes," Vol. II.

ON THE SURPLICE DISPUTES.

A very pretty public stir
Is making down at Exeter,
    About the surplice fashion:
And many unkind words and rude
Have been exchanged about the feud,
    And much untoward passion.

For me—I neither know nor care
Whether a parson ought to wear
    A black dress or a white dress:
—Filled with a trouble of my own—
A wife who preaches in her gown,
    And lectures in her night-dress!

Notes. Professor Cohen (F 14, part 1, p. 1) attributes this letter to G MH. The compiler, however, has no definite evidence to show that it was written by him. Inquiries to the editor of the *Church Times* have been inconclusive. In JP, p. 37, there is a single cryptic reference to the *Church Times* by G M H, but because of its date this probably relates (in the compiler's opinion) to G M H's concern over the 'excesses' (as he called them) of some contributors to the paper: see his letters to Baillie, FL2, pp. 220, 226. But there is no doubt that G M H read the *Church Times* during this period of his life, or that this is exactly the kind of comic rhyme which would have appealed to him. And he had a passion for accuracy and 'getting things right'. The circumstantial evidence for his authorship is strong enough.

E 2   *Notes and Queries*, vol. 9 (3rd series), no. 234, 23 June 1866, p. 522.

CONCILIUM CALCHUTENSE (3rd S. ix. 295, 419)

A.E.S. seeks information as to the locality where this Council was held. In a paper by the Rev. J. H. Blunt, read on April 25 at the British Archaeological Association, occurs the following:—

"The earliest record by which we can positively identify the parish of Chelsea is a charter of Edward the Confessor, in which the manor there called *Chilchelle*, or *Chilchede* (for I think the reading is doubtful), is confirmed in the possession of Westminster Abbey . . . In Domesday it would appear that the scribe was puzzled how to spell the name, and

for safety's sake he has bracketed two names, thus $\left\{ \begin{array}{l} Cercehede \\ Chelched \end{array} \right\}$.

Henry of Huntingdon writes it, anno 1110, *Cealcyde*. In the Taxation of Pope Nicholas, 1291, it is spelt *Chelchethe*. In manorial records, *temp.* Edward II., it is *Chelcheya* and *Chelchuthe* . . . Leland, 1658, writes *Chilseya*, vulgo Chelsey."

Mr. Blunt adds, that the church was originally built of chalk (as may still be seen in the chancel), and that a "hythe," or dock, existed close to it until twenty years ago.

G.M.H.

Notes. On the evidence of style and subject-matter the compiler is inclined to believe that this contribution was written by G M H, but there is again no proof. The editor of *Notes and Queries* has no record of its authorship. There is a marked file in the Library of the University of Newcastle Upon Tyne, but the annotations do not cover this volume. The compiler has been unable to discover anything in G M H's published writings which links up in any way with the note, except his great interest in the development and relationships of words and names.

PART TWO

WRITINGS ABOUT HOPKINS IN ENGLISH

SECTION F

BIBLIOGRAPHIES

THIS section is a selection of the most useful bibliographies for Hopkins studies, divided into two groups, retrospective and current. The entries in the first group are arranged chronologically by date of publication, and those in the second group chronologically by date of publication of the first part in the continuing series.

1940

F 1   Library of Congress (Division of Bibliography) Gerard Manley Hopkins, 1844–1889: a bibliographical list. 1940. 12 pp.

Includes works by and about G M H. Completely superseded by F 4 and later bibliographies. No. 8, 'Out of Captivity' is wrongly attributed to G M H; it is by his nephew, Gerard Hopkins. This error is repeated in F 16 (no. 36).

1949

F 2   Weyand, Norman. A chronological Hopkins bibliography. *in his* Immortal diamond . . . London, Sheed & Ward, 1949. pp. 393–441.

Covers writings by G M H and writings about him up to 1946. Largely but not entirely duplicated by F 4. For further details of this book, see H 137.

1950

F 3   Charney, Maurice. A bibliographical study of Hopkins criticism, 1918–1949. *Thought*, vol. 25, no. 97, June 1950, pp. 297–326.

Detailed evaluative study of Hopkins criticism, followed by a carefully selected bibliography of 117 items.

F4   Mary Patricia, Sister. Forty years of criticism: a chronological checklist of criticism of the works of Gerard Manley Hopkins from 1909 to 1949. *Bulletin of Bibliography* (Boston), vol. 20, 1950, pp. 38–44, 63–7.

> Supplements and largely duplicates F2. Includes a brief list of published editions of G M H's work.

1951

F5   Bischoff, D. Anthony. The manuscripts of Gerard Manley Hopkins. *Thought*, vol. 26, no. 103, Winter 1951–2, pp. 551–80.

> A scholarly survey of the history of the Hopkins MSS., and a detailed catalogue of them, giving descriptions and locations. See also Humphry House's catalogue of the Campion Hall MSS. (JP, pp. 529–35).

1957

F6   Sutcliffe, Edmund F. Bibliography of the English Province of the Society of Jesus, 1773–1953. London, Manresa Press, 1957. xii, 247 pp.

> *See* pp. 206–8. The entry for G M H (no. 208) includes work by and about him, and contains 63 items.

1959

F7   Mellown, Elgin W. Gerard Manley Hopkins and his public, 1889–1918. *Modern Philology*, vol. 57, no. 2, Nov. 1959, pp. 94–9.

> A useful examination of references to G M H found prior to 1919. See also F9, J173.

1963

F8   Ritz, Jean-Georges. Bibliographie. *in his* Le poète Gérard Manley Hopkins . . . Paris, Didier, 1963. pp. 673–709.

> Written substantially in English. Detailed but occasionally inaccurate. Includes work by and about G M H; comprehensively up to 1956, then very selectively up to 1961.

1965

F9 Mellown, Elgin W. The reception of Gerard Manley Hopkins' poems, 1919–1930. *Modern Philology*, vol. 63, no. 1, Aug. 1965, pp. 38–51.

A useful discussion of the reviews of the first edition of GMH's work, including identification of some of the anonymous reviewers. See also F7, J173.

1966

F10 Sotheby & Co., Ltd., London. Catalogue of nineteenth century and modern first editions, presentation copies, autograph letters and literary manuscripts . . . 12–13 July 1966. London, Sotheby & Co., 1966. 147 pp.

See p. 20, lots 115, 116; pp. 123–8, lots 673–99. Descriptions of first editions and MSS. by GMH put up for sale by John Hayward and Lady Pooley. Most of this material was sold to a New York dealer for very high prices, and subsequently sold by him to the University of Texas Library for still higher prices.

1967

F11 Cohen, Edward H. A comprehensive Hopkins bibliography, 1863–1918. *Bulletin of Bibliography*, vol. 25, no. 4, Sept.–Dec. 1967, pp. 79–81.

A useful list of published work by and about GMH up to 1918. Incorporated in and superseded by F14. See also F12.

1968

F12 Cohen, Edward H. Bibliografia italiana: Gerard Manley Hopkins. *Rivista di Letterature Moderne e Comparate*, vol. 21, 1968, pp. 128–30. A useful bibliography of Italian criticism of GMH, with short introduction. Written in English. Incorporated in and superseded by F14. See also F11.

F13 Pick, John. Gerard Manley Hopkins. *in* Faverty, Frederic E., *editor*. The Victorian poets: a guide to research. *2nd edition*. Cambridge (Mass.), Harvard University Press, 1968. pp. 317–51.

Completely revised and expanded from the first edition (1956). Provides an excellent general survey of Hopkins scholarship, including a critical discussion of the history of Hopkins criticism, down to about 1966.

1969

F14   Cohen, Edward H. Works and criticism of Gerard Manley Hopkins: a comprehensive bibliography. Washington, D.C., Catholic University of America Press, 1969. xv, 217 pp.

Part 1 is a list of G M H's published works and contains 79 entries. Part 2 is a list of criticism of G M H's works, and contains 1,522 entries. Chronological arrangement in both sections. No annotations, except for a few isolated entries. This was the first comprehensive bibliography of G M H. It is very accurate, and contains no superfluous or worthless entries, but no attempt was made to give full descriptions of primary works.

F15   Storey, Graham. Gerard Manley Hopkins. *in* Watson, George, *editor*. The new Cambridge bibliography of English literature. Vol. 3, 1800–1900. Cambridge, Cambridge University Press, 1969. cols. 581–93.

Completely supersedes W. H. Gardner's entry for G M H in *The Cambridge bibliography of English literature*.

1970

F16   Seelhammer, Ruth. Hopkins collected at Gonzaga. Chicago, Loyola University Press, 1970. xiv, 272 pp.

A catalogue of the Hopkins collection at Gonzaga University (see N13). Part 1, *Works by Hopkins*, contains 106 entries; Part 2, *Association items*, contains 795 entries; Part 3, *Writings on Hopkins*, contains 2,400 entries. Alphabetical arrangement in all sections. No annotations. Includes a very substantial amount of material which is of only peripheral interest in Hopkins studies. The lack of annotation makes this a disadvantage, since it is often difficult to discriminate between important and unimportant entries.

1971

F 16a Enozawa, Kazuyoshi. Writings on Gerard Manley Hopkins in Japan, 1930–1970. Tokyo, compiled for the English Literary Society of Japan, 1971. xii, 34 pp.

This bibliography is in three parts: an alphabetical list of entries arranged under author's names, a chronological list of the same entries, and a classified list grouping them under such headings as translations, theses, essays and studies, and so on. It contains 122 entries, covering 1930–70. Names of authors are given in romanized Japanese symbols, as are Japanese titles. English translations of Japanese titles are given. There are a few brief but helpful annotations. This is certainly the most comprehensive and useful guide to Japanese Hopkins studies ever produced. The work was undertaken by Mr. Enozawa at the compiler's request: the compiler is pleased to acknowledge his indebtedness to the excellent results.

CURRENT BIBLIOGRAPHIES

F 17 English Association. The year's work in English studies. 1921–

F 18 Modern Humanities Research Association. Annual bibliography of English language and literature. 1921–

F 19 Modern Language Association of America. Annual bibliography in *P.M.L.A.*

From 1919 to 1956 this bibliography included work by American scholars only. From 1956 onwards it has been general in scope.

F 20 *Archivum Historicum Societatis Iesu* (Rome), 1932–

This multi-lingual Jesuit journal is published twice a year, and the second issue for each year contains an extensive bibliography of current writings about the Society of Jesus and its members. The entry for G M H is of primary value to bibliographers, since it frequently contains obscure material overlooked by other sources of reference.

F 21 *Modern Philology*, 1933–57.
See F 24.

F 22 Catholic Library Association. The Catholic periodical index: a cumulative author and subject index to a selected list of Catholic periodicals, 1930/33– New York, Published for the Catholic Library Association by the H. W. Wilson Company, 1939–

1930/33 forms the first volume in the cumulated series, and supersedes the two annual volumes for 1930 and 1931. See also F23.

F23 The guide to Catholic literature, 1888– Michigan and Detroit, Walter Romig, 1940–

From volume 6 onwards this guide has been published by the Catholic Library Association, and is almost entirely duplicated by the corresponding volumes of F22, at least so far as GMH is concerned.

F24 *Victorian Studies*, 1958–

The annual Victorian bibliographies in *Modern Philology*, 1933–57 (F21) have been continued in *Victorian Studies* since 1958. GMH's annual entries can be more conveniently consulted (up to the 1964 entry) in the following reprints from these two periodicals:

1. Templeman, William D., *editor*. Bibliographies of studies in Victorian literature for the thirteen years 1932–44. Urbana, University of Illinois Press, 1945.
2. Wright, Austin, *editor*. Bibliographies of studies in Victorian literature for the ten years 1945–54. Urbana, University of Illinois Press, 1956.
3. Slack, Robert C., *editor*. Bibliographies of studies in Victorian literature for the ten years 1955–64. Urbana, University of Illinois Press, 1967.

F25 *Abstracts of English studies*, 1959–

Abstracts a wide range of periodicals, and regularly includes references to GMH. The abstracts are brief but useful. Cumulative indexes.

F26 *The Hopkins Research Bulletin*, 1970–

Published annually by the Hopkins Society, this bulletin includes (besides notes on research in progress) a Hopkins bibliography and notes on recent publications. The bibliography in the first issue (Spring, 1970) covered writings on GMH published during 1968. It is intended in future issues to narrow this time-lag and bring the bibliography as nearly up-to-date as possible before going to press.

SECTION G

BIOGRAPHY

THIS section is a chronological list of writings dealing wholly or in part with GMH's life, or with specific periods and incidents in his life.

1869

G 1   Catalogus Provinciae Angliae Societatis Iesu. Roehampton, Manresa Press, 1869–

This annual Province catalogue lists GMH from 1869 onwards, showing where he was stationed each year, and in what position. It is a valuable source of information about his Jesuit contemporaries.

1879

G 2   Anon. Marriage at St. Joseph's Catholic Church. *Leigh Chronicle* (Leigh, Lancashire), 25 Oct. 1879, p. 4.

'The marriage of Mr. John Fairclough, of Leigh, to Miss Maggie Unsworth, daughter of Mr. Wm. Unsworth, Bond-street, Leigh, was solemnised at St. Joseph's Catholic Church, Bedford, on Tuesday morning by the Rev. Father Fanning, assisted by Fathers Hopkins, Kavanagh, and Wright . . .' This was probably the wedding which inspired GMH to write 'At the Wedding March': 'Tuesday morning' was 21 Oct. 1879, which is the date on MS. A of the poem (see P4, p. 278), and the Marriage Registers of St. Joseph's Church show that no other wedding was celebrated on that day.

1882

G 3   Anon. Mission services at Maryport. *Maryport Advertiser and Weekly News*, 24 Mar. 1882, p. 5.

'During the past fortnight mission services have been conducted at Our Lady and St. Patrick's Church, Maryport, by the Revs. Fathers

Hopkins and Waterton [*sic*: G MH shared his duties with Father Alfred White; see G 101, pp. 199–200] . . . On Sunday evening last . . . the Rev. Father Hopkins preached an appropriate and eloquent sermon.' For G M H's own comments, see LL 1, pp. 140–1, 143.

G 4   Anon. Hexham and Newcastle [Diocese]. *Tablet*, vol. 27 (n.s.), no. 698, 1 Apr. 1882, p. 512.

'Maryport.—A very successful mission has been preached in this Church during the last fortnight by the *Revv. Fathers White and Hopkins, S.J.* . . .'

G 5   [Geldart, Martin]. A son of Belial: autobiographical sketches, by Nitram Tradleg. London, Trübner & Co., 1882, viii, 250 pp.

Reminiscences of Balliol life by one of G M H's contemporaries. G M H is mentioned several times, thinly disguised as 'Gerontius Manley', and he certainly recognized himself in the copy lent to him by Geldart: see FL2, pp. 254–5.

1884

G 6   Gorman, W. Gordon. Converts to Rome: a list of over three thousand Protestants who have become Roman Catholics since the commencement of the nineteenth century. London, W. Swan Sonnenschein & Co., 1884. 80 pp.

See p. 29. A brief entry for 'Gerard R. [*sic*] Hopkins'.

G 7   Mackinnon, Hamilton, *editor*. The Marcus Clarke memorial volume . . . Melbourne, Cameron Laing and Co., 1884. xii, 322 pp.

See pp. 15–16. At Highgate School, Clarke had '. . . only two friends, with whom he was on terms of great intimacy. They were brothers, Cyril and Gerald [*sic*] Hopkins, and they appear, judging from jottings and sketches of theirs in his scrap album, to have been talented both as versifiers and pen and ink sketchers . . .'

1888

G 8   Foster, Joseph. Hopkins, Gerard Manley. *in his* Alumnae Oxoni-

enses: the Members of the University of Oxford, 1715–1886 . . . Vol.
2. London, Joseph Foster, 21, Boundary Road, N.W., 1888. p. 688.
A brief entry giving basic facts.

1889

G9   *Anon. Gerard Manley Hopkins. *Freeman's Journal* (Dublin),
10 June 1889, p. 5.
A notice of G M H's death.

G10   Anon. [Notice of G M H's death] *Nation* (Dublin), vol. 47, no. 24,
15 June 1889, p. 8.
See also p. 12, deaths column: a brief formal announcement containing two errors. G M H's name is misspelt, and he is said to have died
in the '44th year of his age'—he died in his 45th year.

1889

G11   Anon. Obituary: Gerard Manley Hopkins. *Cholmeleian, or Highgate School Magazine*, vol. 16, no. 67, Oct. 1889, p. 179.
No mention is made of G M H's poetry.

1890

G12   Anon. Father Gerard Hopkins. *Letters and Notices*, vol. 20, no.
99, Mar. 1890, pp. 173–9.
Notice of G M H's death. No mention of his poetry; the emphasis
is entirely on his personal and priestly qualities. *Letters and Notices* is
a private domestic publication of the English Jesuits.

1892

G13   Boase, Frederic. Modern English biography . . . Vol. 1. Truro,
Netherton and Worth, 1892. vi pp., 1710 cols.
See col. 1533. Reprints facts from G9.

1894

G 14 Dowden, Edward. The poetry of Robert Bridges. *Fortnightly Review*, vol. 56 (n.s.), 1 July 1894, pp. 44–60.

'Father Gerard Hopkins, an English priest of the Society of Jesus, died young, and one of his good deeds remains to the present time unrecorded ... Father Hopkins was a lover of literature, and himself a poet. Perhaps he did in many quarters missionary work on behalf of the poetry of his favourite, Robert Bridges. He certainly left, a good many years since, at my door two volumes by Mr. Bridges, and with them a note begging that I would make no acknowledgment of the gift. I did not acknowledge it then; but, with sorrow for a fine spirit lost, I acknowledge it now.' For G M H's comments, see LL1, pp. 244, 247–8, 303–4. This essay was reprinted in G 16.

G 15 Oxford honours, 1220–1894, being an alphabetical register of distinctions conferred by the University of Oxford from the earliest times. Oxford, Clarendon Press, 1894. 282 pp.

See p. 126. A brief entry in which G M H's name is again misspelt.

1895

G 16 Dowden, Edward. The poetry of Robert Bridges. *in his* New studies in literature. London, Kegan Paul, Trench, Trübner & Co., Ltd., 1895. pp. 61–89.

Reprint of G 14. This book would bring Dowden's reference to G M H before a wider audience.

1896

G 17 Clarke, R. F. The training of a Jesuit. *Nineteenth Century*, vol. 40, no. 234, Aug. 1896, pp. 211–25.

G M H is not mentioned, but this account of Jesuit training is so nearly contemporary (Clarke became a Jesuit three years after G M H) that it probably presents a very true picture of how G M H spent his noviceship.

G 18 Skeat, Walter W. A student's pastime ... Oxford, Clarendon Press, 1896. lxxviii, 410 pp.

See pp. ix–xi. G M H is again not mentioned, but the book provides

some valuable insights on G M H's schooldays, since Skeat entered
Highgate School a few years before G M H. 'Our headmaster
[Dyne] had one somewhat uncommon idea ... instead of invariably
requiring us to turn English poetry into Latin verse, he sometimes
gave us pieces of Latin poetry to turn into English verse, a change
which was delightful and refreshing.' Evidently, G M H began
practising poetry early.

1900

G 19   St. Joseph's Church, Leigh, Lancashire. St. Joseph's, Leigh,
Lancashire: handbook souvenir, Grand Bazaar, May 1900. Leigh,
Collins and Darwell, 1900. 107 pp.
   See p. 17. 'Fr. Hopkins, S.J., succeeded Fr. Hagen [in November
   1879] and left in December 1879.'

1902

G 20   *Russell, Matthew. Poets I have known, V. Katharine Tynan.
Donahoe's Magazine, vol. 47, no. 4, Apr. 1902, pp. 389–406.
Reprinted in G 21.

1903

G 21   Russell, Matthew. Poets I have known; no. 5—Katharine Tynan.
Irish Monthly, vol. 31, no. 359, May 1903, pp. 250–67.
Biographical information on the G M H–Tynan–Russell friendship.
G M H is described as a '... gifted but somewhat impracticable man
(on whom the brilliant little group of Pre-Raphaelites counted at one
time as their future literary interpreter.)'

1905

G 22   Gosse, Edmund. Coventry Patmore. London, Hodder & Stoughton, 1905. viii, 252 pp.
   See p. 169. Gosse's remark here was largely responsible for the wide-
   spread and long-lasting belief that G M H (referred to as 'a remarkable man of imperfect genius') was wholly and deliberately responsible for Patmore's burning of *Sponsa Dei*. G M H has been ably

defended against this charge by Professor Abbott: see FL2, pp. xxxiii–ix.

1906

G23   Champneys, Basil. Coventry Patmore. *in* Patmore, Coventry. Poems. London, George Bell and Sons, 1906, pp. xxxv–vi.
Comment on Patmore's burning of *Sponsa Dei*. 'The suppression is ostensibly due to his reliance on the judgement of his priestly adviser . . .'

1909

G24   Keating, Joseph. Impressions of Father Gerard Hopkins, S.J. 1. *Month*, vol. 114, no. 541, July 1909, pp. 59–68.
A pioneer biographical essay, illustrating by quotation from their letters the impressions made by GMH upon Newman, H. P. Liddon, and others.

G25   Keating, Joseph. Impressions of Father Gerard Hopkins, S.J. 2. *Month*, vol. 114, no. 542, Aug. 1909, pp. 151–60.
The impression made by GMH on R. W. Dixon, illustrated by Dixon's letters. Quotes a letter from GMH to Dixon.

G26   Keating, Joseph. Impressions of Father Gerard Hopkins, S.J. 3. *Month*, vol. 114, no. 543, Sept. 1909, pp. 246–58.
The impressions made by GMH on Coventry Patmore and Dr. R. Stewart.

1910

G27   Anon. Manresa House, Roehampton. *Letters and Notices*, vol. 30, no. 179, Apr. 1910, p. 391.
A note on 'some distinguished novices', including GMH as 'Father *Gerard Hopkins*, styled by Dr. Pusey "the star of Balliol." ' See also G28. *Letters and Notices* is a private domestic publication of the English Jesuits.

G 28   Anon. Manresa House, Roehampton. *Letters and Notices*, vol. 30, no. 180, July 1910, p. 468.

Mentions G M H, together with some of his contemporaries, as having been trained by Father Fitzsimon.

1912

G 29   Lechmere, W. L. Oxford, 1863–1867. *Oxford and Cambridge Review*, no. 19, May 1912, pp. 96–8.

Describes a meeting between G M H and Lechmere at Oxford, and includes a description of G M H's personal appearance.

G 30   Tynan, Katharine. Father Matthew Russell, S.J., dearest of friends. *Irish Monthly*, vol. 40, no. 472, Oct. 1912, pp. 551–8.

See p. 555. 'I remember him [Russell] coming into Mr. Yeats's studio on Stephen's Green with Father Gerard Hopkins, when Mr. Yeats was painting me, more than once, I think. He had had some difficulty in coaxing the other poet from his seclusion. I remember he was quite proud of bringing Father Hopkins and me together, for Father Hopkins could not always be trusted to make friends.'

1913

G 31   Tynan, Katharine. Twenty-five years: reminiscences. London, Smith, Elder & Co., 1913. viii, 355 pp.

See pp. 299–300. 'One of these Sunday mornings at St. Aloysius's I heard the prayers of the congregation asked for the repose of the soul of Father Gerard Hopkins, my first intimation of his illness, of his death.'

1916

G 32   Tynan, Katharine. The middle years. London, Constable and Company, Ltd., 1916. 415 pp.

See pp. 349–50. 'An Irish Jesuit told me that Father Gerard Hopkins, also a poet, had told him that Coventry Patmore submitted to him, for his opinion, a chapter of *Sponsa Dei* . . .' The version of this episode which follows presents the whole thing as a misunderstanding, caused by G M H thinking that the chapter which had been given to him was the complete book.

1919

G 33   Harting, E. M. Gerard Hopkins and Digby Dolben. *Month*,
vol. 133, no. 658, Apr. 1919, pp. 285–9.
A biographical note about Dolben, with comments on his possible
influence on G M H.

G 34   B[arraud], C[lement] [William]. Reminiscences of Father
Gerard Hopkins. *Month*, vol. 134, no. 662, Aug. 1919, pp. 158–9.
An interesting character-sketch by a contemporary. Less than enthusi-
astic about G M H's poems.

1920

G 35   'Plures'. Father Gerard Hopkins: his character. *Dublin Review*,
vol. 167, no. 334, July–Sept. 1920, pp. 47–58.
Biographical character-sketch; very indignant about Bridges's
'Preface to Notes' in P1.

1921

G 36   Paget, Stephen, *editor*. Henry Scott Holland . . . memoir and
letters. London, John Murray, 1921. xii, 336 pp.
See pp. 29 ff. Correspondence between T. H. Green and Holland
about G M H's entry into the Jesuit Order. The following quotation
is from Green's letter dated 29 Dec. 1868: 'I am glad that you and
Nettleship saw Hopkins. A step such as he has taken, tho' I can't
quite admit it to be heroic, must needs be painful, and its pain should
not be aggravated—as it is pretty sure to be—by separation from old
friends. I never had his intimacy, but always liked him very much.'

1923

G 37   Anon. Appreciation of Bishop Frederick Hopkins. *Letters and
Notices*, vol. 38, no. 230, July 1923, p. 376.
'We were ordained together, nineteen priests in all . . . September
23rd, 1877. Among us was the poet, Gerard Hopkins—"the gentle
Hop." we called him in contradistinction to "the genteel Hop.",
for Frederick never lost his "bedside manner" . . .'

1924

G 38   Tynan, Katharine. Father Matthew Russell, S.J. *in her* Memories. London, Eveleigh Nash and Grayson, Limited, 1924. pp. 145–60.
See particularly pp. 155–6. Biographical details about G M H's life in Dublin.

1929

G 39   Bridges, Robert. The testament of beauty. Oxford, Clarendon Press, 1929. 192 pp.
See Book IV, lines 433–8.
The background to the incident referred to here by Bridges can be partly gleaned from LL1, pp. 145, 152.

1930

G 40   *Fathers of the Society of Jesus, *editors*. A page of Irish history: story of University College, Dublin, 1883–1909. Dublin, The Talbot Press Limited, 1930, pp. 105–6, *et passim*.

G 41   Lahey, G. F. Gerard Manley Hopkins. London, Oxford University Press, 1930. 172 pp.
The first biography. Intensely sympathetic towards G M H, but slight in substance and not always accurate. For full description, and reviews, see B 23.

1932

G 42   Patmore, Francis J. Coventry Patmore: a son's recollections. *English Review*, vol. 54, Feb. 1932, pp. 135–41.
Detailed comments on G M H's part in Patmore's burning of *Sponsa Dei*. The author's close relationship to Patmore makes this version of the affair especially interesting.

G 43   Bridges, Robert. Three friends . . . London, Oxford University Press, 1932. 243 pp.
Memoirs of D. M. Dolben (first published in B 20), R. W. Dixon (first published in B 19), and Henry Bradley.

1933

G 44   Scott, Michael M. Gerard Manley Hopkins, S.J. *Irish Monthly*,
vol. 61, no. 725, Nov. 1933, pp. 715–20.
Short biographical essay, containing nothing very original.

1935

G 45   Hopkins, Lionel C. Gerard Hopkins's birthday. *Times Literary
Supplement*, 14 Mar. 1935, p. 160.
A letter from G M H's brother, confirming his date of birth as 28
July 1844; in reply to Max Plowman, *Times Literary Supplement*,
28 Feb. 1935, p. 124.

G 46   Keating, Joseph. Fr. Gerard Hopkins and the Spiritual Exercises.
Month, vol. 166, no. 855, Sept. 1935, pp. 268–70.
This article sets out to rectify a false impression which Father Keating
believed to be current about the effect of G M H's training upon his
development. No literary criticism is attempted.

G 47   Crehan, J. H. Poetry and the religious life: the case of Gerard
Manley Hopkins, S.J. *Month*, vol. 166, no. 858, Dec. 1935, pp. 493–
503.
A defence of G M H's vocation against those critics who considered
it his personal tragedy. No literary criticism.

1937

G 48   Hope, Felix. A modern Lycidas: Digby Mackworth Dolben,
1848–1867. *Month*, vol. 170, no. 877, July 1937, pp. 33–40.
A biographical essay on Dolben: G M H *passim*.

1938

G 49   D'Arcy, Martin C. Gerard Manley Hopkins: *in* Williamson,
Claude, *editor*. Great Catholics. London, Nicholson and Watson, 1938,
pp. 438–46.
An exceptionally perceptive and understanding essay on G M H's
spiritual life and character.

1940

G 50   Pick, John. The growth of a poet: Gerard Manley Hopkins S.J. *Month*, vol. 175, no. 907, Jan. 1940, pp. 39–46.

A biographical essay demonstrating the spiritual foundation of G M H's poetry.

1942

G 51   Sieveking, Lance. Gerard Manley Hopkins. *Poetry Review*, vol. 33, no. 5, Sept.–Oct. 1942, pp. 323–5.

Biographical reminiscences. Members of Sieveking's family knew G M H, and Sieveking's mother was G M H's cousin. See also G 80, B 205.

1944

G 52   Hanson, W. G. Gerard Manley Hopkins and Richard Watson Dixon. *London Quarterly and Holborn Review*, vol. 169, Jan. 1944, pp. 63–7.

Biographical notes on G M H and Dixon.

G 53   Price, Fanny. G. M. Hopkins on Robert Bridges. *Notes and Queries*, vol. 186, no. 2, 15 Jan. 1944, p. 49.

An attempt to illustrate the quality of the friendship between G M H and Bridges.

G 54   Hopkins, Gerard. Gerard Manley Hopkins. *Times Literary Supplement*, 24 June 1944, p. 309.

A letter from G M H's nephew, confirming the date of G M H's birth as 28 July 1844.

G 55   *Ruggles, Eleanor. Gerard Manley Hopkins: a life. New York, W. W. Norton & Company, Inc., 1944, viii, 305 pp.

For annotation see G 64. For reviews, see I 244, I 246, I 247, I 248, I 250, I 251, I 252, I 253, I 254, I 263, I 267, I 268, I 279, I 280, I 284, I 293, I 297, I 300. See also the following reviews:

Reviews:

G 56   Engle, Paul. *in Chicago Sunday Tribune Books*, 30 July 1944, p. 11.

G 57   Currier, Isabel. *in Boston Traveler*, 2 Aug. 1944, p.

G 58   Kennedy, Leo, *in Chicago Sun Book Week*, 13 Aug. 1944, p. 9.

G 59   [O'Brien, Robert David.] *in Boston Globe*, 16 Aug. 1944, p. 15.

G 60   Furness, Clifton Joseph. *in Atlantic Monthly*, vol. 174, no. 4, Oct. 1944, pp. 131–3.

G 61   Warren, Austin. *in Kenyon Review*, vol. 6, no. 4, Autumn 1944, pp. 587–9.

G 62   Thompson, Edward. Robert Bridges, 1844–1930. London, Oxford University Press, 1944. vii, 131 pp.
See particularly pp. 86–9, 95. Biographical comment.

1947

G 63   Elliott, Brian. Gerard Hopkins and Marcus Clarke. *Southerly* (Sydney), vol. 8, no. 4, 1947, pp. 218–27.
Important biographical essay on the G M H–Clarke friendship at Highgate School. Quotes a letter from Clarke to G M H's brother Cyril, giving Clarke's views on G M H's conversion to Roman Catholicism. See also G 7.

G 64   Ruggles, Eleanor. Gerard Manley Hopkins: a life . . . London, John Lane the Bodley Head, 1947. 247 pp.
A short biography, enthusiastic but superficial. When facts were wanting the author tended to rely on her imagination. For reviews see I 326, I 327, I 328, I 329, I 330, I 339, M 134, M 245.

1948

G 65   Patmore, Derek. Coventry Patmore and Robert Bridges: some letters. *Fortnightly*, vol. 163 (n.s.), Mar. 1948, pp. 196–204.
Some references to G M H in letters exchanged by Patmore and Bridges.

1949

G 66 Doyle, Louis F. In the valley of the shadow of Hopkins. *Catholic World*, vol. 169, May 1949, pp. 102–8.

Hopkins was a religious poet of genius, but his character was much less attractive than the legend would have us believe. 'There is one feature of the *Letters* which cannot increase any Jesuit's esteem for the saintly Father Hopkins. They contain a great deal of personal agony endured by this sensitive soul in the sometimes uncongenial surroundings in which his work had to be done ... Now, quite simply, the typical Jesuit does not wash his bloody linen in public nor does he proclaim his own crucifixion ... It is not cricket.'

1950

G 67 Hawkes, Jacquetta. Gowland Hopkins and scientific imagination. *Listener*, vol. 43, no. 1097, 2 Feb. 1950, pp. 191–2.

A biographical article on Sir Frederick Gowland Hopkins, a cousin of G M H. G M H is mentioned *passim*, briefly, but some Hopkins family background information is provided.

1951

G 68 Pearson, W. H. G. M. Hopkins and Provost Fortescue. *Notes and Queries*, vol. 196, no. 20, 29 Sept. 1951, pp. 431–3.

Comments on the probable identity of 'Provost Fortescue' (JP, p. 71) and the meaning of G M H's cryptic comment. See also G 70, G 72, G 73.

G 69 Watkin, Aelred. Digby Mackworth Dolben and the Catholic Church: some fresh evidence. *Dublin Review*, vol. 225, no. 453, Third Quarter 1951, pp. 65–70.

An unpublished letter from Dolben to Dr. F. G. Lee, shedding light on Dolben's intention of becoming a Roman Catholic. G M H *passim*: see particularly footnote 3, p. 68.

1951

G 70 Brandreth, Henry R. T. Dr. Lee of Lambeth. London, S.P.C.K., 1951. ix, 197 pp.

J. H. Crehan considers that this book provides a clue to the meaning
of G M H's mysterious comment on 'provost Fortescue' (JP, p. 71).
Crehan's theory is discussed briefly in JP, pp. 338–9. See also G 68,
G 72, G 73.

G 71   De la Bedoyere, Michael. The life of Baron Von Hügel. London,
J. M. Dent & Sons, 1951. xviii, 366 pp.
   See p. 24. Brief mention of a possible visit to Baron von Hügel by
G M H, at Hampstead, in 1887.

1952

G 72   Micklewright, F. H. Amphlett. G. M. Hopkins and Provost
Fortescue. *Notes and Queries*, vol. 197, no. 8, 12 Apr. 1952, pp. 169–72.
   Follows up G 68, with more information. See also G 73, G 70.

G 73   Micklewright, F. H. Amphlett. G. M. Hopkins and Provost
Fortescue. *Notes and Queries*, vol. 197, no. 17, 16 Aug. 1952, pp. 365–
6.
   Further information, following up G 68 and G 72. See also G 70.

G 74   Gardner, Ralph. Two Jesuits. *Modern Churchman*, vol. 42, no. 4,
Dec. 1952, pp. 350–9.
   Biographical essays on G M H and George Tyrrell.

1953

G 75   Crehan, J. H. More light on Gerard Hopkins. *Month*, vol. 10
(n.s.), no. 4, Oct. 1953, pp. 205–14.
   An important biographical essay, dealing mainly with G M H's
friendship with Alexander Wood.

1954

G 76   Tai T'ung. The six scripts, or the principles of Chinese writing:
a translation by L. C. Hopkins, with a memoir of the translator by W.
Perceval Yetts. Cambridge, Cambridge University Press, 1954. xxvii,
84 pp.

Facsimile reprint of the first edition of 1881. The memoir contains various references to G M H and some information on the Hopkins family.

G 77 Tierney, Michael, *editor*. Struggle with fortune; a miscellany for the centenary of the Catholic University of Ireland, 1854–1954. Dublin, Browne & Nolan Ltd., [1954]. 237 pp.
See particularly pp. 32–3, 224. Biographical comment.

1955

G 78 Meadows, Denis. Obedient men. London, Longmans, 1955. viii, 308 pp.
An account of the author's ten years as a Jesuit before the 1914–18 War. G M H is mentioned several times, but the main interest of the book is in the accurate picture of Jesuit training it presents. G M H's experience would have been very similar.

1956

G 79 Oliver, E. J. Coventry Patmore. London, Sheed & Ward, 1956. 211 pp.
See particularly pp. 166–71. Biographical comment.

1957

G 80 Sieveking, Lance. Remembering Gerard Manley Hopkins. *Listener*, vol. 57, no. 1452, 24 Jan. 1957, pp. 151–2.
An important biographical essay drawing on the accounts of G M H's contemporaries and members of his family. See also G 51, G 81, G 82, B 205.

G 81 Baily, Bertha. Remembering Gerard Manley Hopkins. *Listener*, vol. 57, no. 1455, 14 Feb. 1957, p. 275.
A letter providing an addendum to G 80—some information on Edward Hodges Baily.

G 82 Sieveking, Lance. Gerard Manley Hopkins. *in his* The eye of the beholder. London, Hulton Press, 1957, pp. 275–85.

Very important and interesting biographical information, following G 51, G 80. Includes two previously unpublished letters from G M H to his father. For full description see B 205.

1958

G 83   Green, David Bonnell. A new letter of Robert Bridges to Coventry Patmore. *Modern Philology*, vol. 55, no. 3, Feb. 1958, pp. 198–9.
The letter, dated 19 Oct. 1885, begins with a rather plaintive reference to G M H: 'He [G M H] will have told you that my wife has been unfortunately laid up more or less all the summer—which he made an excuse for not coming to see me, whereas it sh^d have been his reason for coming . . .'

G 84   Elliott, Brian. Marcus Clarke. Oxford, Clarendon Press, 1958. xiv, 281 pp.
G M H *passim*. Several brief references which fill in the background to G M H's friendship with Clarke.

G 85   Korn, Alfons L. The Victorian visitors. Honolulu, University of Hawaii Press, 1958. 351 pp.
See particularly p. 207, also various references to G M H's father and the Hopkins family.

1960

G 86   Ritz, Jean-Georges. Robert Bridges and Gerard Hopkins, 1863– 1889: a literary friendship. London, Oxford University Press, 1960. xvii, 182 pp.
Bridges has been attacked for his attitude to G M H's religion, for suppressing publication of G M H's poems until 1918, and for destroying his own letters to G M H. This study examines the issues involved in a most fair-minded and sympathetic way.

Reviews:
G 87   Sewell, Brocard. in *Catholic Herald* (London), 3 June 1960, p. 3.

G 88   Cambon, Glauco. in *Poetry*, vol. 100, no. 1, Apr. 1962, pp. 53–4.
For other reviews, see I 559, I 560, I 562, I 563, I 565, I 566, I 569, I 570, I 571, I 574, I 577, I 595, I 598, B 248, M 105, M 151, M 261.

G 89   Untermeyer, Louis. Gerard Manley Hopkins. *in his* Lives of the
poets. London, W. H. Allen, 1960. pp. 590–600.
   A concise biographical summary.

1961

G 90   Downes, David A. The Hopkins enigma. *Thought*, vol. 36, no.
143, Winter 1961, pp. 571–94.
   'Hopkins is explained only in the tragicomic view of man, priest and
poet involved in a personal tragedy which is yet an enormous personal
victory.'

1962

G 91   Sambrook, James. A poet hidden: the life of Richard Watson
Dixon, 1833–1900. London, Athlone Press, 1962. ix, 134 pp.
   An important and interesting book which provides much biographical
information about Dixon's friendship with G M H. See also I608,
M 105.

1964

G 92   Thomas, Alfred. Hopkins, the Jesuits, and Barmouth. *Journal of
the Merioneth Historical and Record Society*, 1964, pp. 360–4.
   G M H's visits to Barmouth and Penmaen Pool during his holidays
as a Jesuit scholastic.

1965

G 93   Thomas, Alfred. A note on Gerard Manley Hopkins and his
superiors, 1868–77. *Irish Ecclesiastical Record* (Dublin), vol. 104
(5th series), Oct.–Nov. 1965, pp. 286–91.
   Notes on Fathers Weld, Fitzsimon, Gallwey, Whitty, Purbrick and
Jones, S.J., through whose hands G M H passed during his formative
years as a Jesuit.

G 94   Thomas, A[lfred]. G. M. Hopkins and 'tones'. *Notes and Queries*,
vol. 12 (n.s.), no. 11, Nov. 1965, pp. 429–30.

A 'tone' is a practice sermon preached by a Jesuit during his training. Notes are provided about the recorded occasions when G M H preached them.

1966

G 95   Thomas, Alfred. Hopkins, Welsh and Wales. *Transactions of the Honourable Society of Cymmrodorion*, session 1965, part 2, 1966, pp. 272–85.
Discussion of G M H's love of Wales and of his motives for learning Welsh.

G 96   Thomas, Alfred. Gerard Manley Hopkins: 'doomed to succeed by failure'. *Dublin Review*, vol. 240, no. 508, Summer 1966, pp. 161–75.
Hopkins's two vocations, priest and poet, presented through his own eyes and in his own words.

1967

G 97   *Thomas, Alfred. Father Gerard Manley Hopkins: the centenary of his entrance into the Society of Jesus. *in* The Jesuits: yearbook of the Society of Jesus, 1967–8. Rome, 1967, pp. 54–7.

1968

G 98   Anon. Gerard Manley Hopkins, 1844–1889. *To Our Friends* (Heythrop College), no. 60, Summer 1968, unpaginated.
Almost the whole issue is devoted to a brief illustrated biographical essay commemorating the centenary of G M H's entrance into the Society of Jesus.

G 99   O'Donovan, Patrick. The tragedy of Gerard Manley Hopkins. *Observer Magazine*, 18 Aug. 1968, pp. 29–30.
Brief biographical essay. 'He got no fame while alive and yet he was one of the greatest, some say the greatest, of the Victorian poets. And he was within a stone's throw of being a saint—by any standard, human or divine.'

1969

G 100   London Borough of Newham Library Service. An exhibition illustrating Stratford in the nineteenth century in connexion with the 125th anniversary of the birth of the Stratford-born poet Gerard Manley Hopkins: Stratford Reference Library, Water Lane, London, E.15., 18th–25th October, 1969. 7 pp.

> A duplicated typescript pamphlet, arranged in two sections; 'The Hopkins family and Stratford', and 'Stratford at the time of the Hopkins' residence'; this publication contains detailed biographical information not yet available elsewhere in published form.

G 101   Thomas, Alfred. Hopkins the Jesuit: the years of training. London, Oxford University Press, 1969. xv, 283 pp.

> An outstandingly important biographical study, limited in scope to the period of GMH's Jesuit training, but very thorough in its coverage of those years. Based on Jesuit archives. Contains a fully edited transcript of a previously unpublished journal kept by GMH as a Jesuit novice. For a full description and reviews, see B 258.

SECTION H

BOOKS AND PAMPHLETS

THIS section is a chronological list of books and pamphlets which are either full-length studies of G M H or include some criticism of his work. The reviews listed in this section are in the compiler's opinion merely appendages to the books concerned: other reviews are listed in Section I and Section M, and occasionally in other sections. Cross-references have been provided for the majority of these reviews.

1873

H1 *Clarke, Marcus. Holiday Peak, or Mount Might-ha-been. *in his* Holiday Peak and other tales. Melbourne, G. Robertson, 1873. pp. 8–10.

Fictitious account of a meeting with 'Gerard' (obviously G M H); then supposedly married, and a painter. See B23, p. 4. Clarke seems to have remembered G M H in another story besides this: in his novel *Chidiock Tichbourne* there is a character called Gerrard, and one called Hopkins.

1885

H2 Dixon, Richard Watson. The history of the Church of England from the abolition of the Roman jurisdiction. Vol. III. . . . London, George Routledge and Sons, 1885. xxvi, 572 pp.

See footnote, pp. 418–19. G M H had provided Dixon with information about the first Jesuit mission in Ireland, and Dixon here acknowledges his debt to 'my gifted friend the Reverend Gerard Hopkins S.J.'. See LL2, pp. 128–9 for Dixon's letter to G M H about this. G M H was dubious about the adjective 'gifted': see LL1, pp. 223–4, and also I552.

1887

H 3   *Dixon, Richard Watson. Lyrical poems. Oxford, H. Daniel, 1887.
62 pp.
See the dedication: 'Dedicated to the Reverend Gerard Hopkins by
the Author'. For comments by Dixon and G M H, see LL2, pp. 131–
2, 138.

1896

H 4   Saintsbury, George. A history of nineteenth-century literature
(1780–1895). London, Macmillan and Co., 1896. xii, 477 pp.
See p. 294. 'The remarkable talents of Mr. Gerard Manley Hopkins,
which could never be mistaken by any one who knew him, and of
which some memorials remain in verse, were mainly lost to English
poetry by the fact of his passing the last twenty years of his life as a
Jesuit priest.' This is slightly inaccurate: G M H was a Jesuit from
1868 but not a priest until 1877.

H 5   Wright, Joseph, *editor*. The English dialect dictionary . . . Vol. I.
London, Oxford University Press, [1896]. xxiv, 864 pp.
See p. xii. A list of unprinted collections of dialect words, quoted in
the dictionary by the initials of their compilers, and entered here
under their compilers' names. G M H's collection is listed as 'Hopkins, Rev. G. M. [Ir.]'

1905

H 6   Coleridge, Mary E. *Preface to* Dixon, Richard Watson. The last
poems of Richard Watson Dixon . . . selected and edited by Robert
Bridges. London, Henry Frowde, 1905. p. v.
'A young Oxford student of brilliantly original powers loved the
poems of Richard Watson Dixon with such devotion that, when he
entered the ranks of the Jesuits and was forbidden to take any books
with him, he copied out almost all those in his possession.'

1906

H 7   Saintsbury, George. A history of English prosody, from the twelfth century to the present day. Vol. 1: From the origins to Spenser. London, Macmillan and Co., Limited, 1906. xvi, 428 pp.

> *See* p. 382. 'It has been held by some—for instance by my friend of long ago, the late Father Gerard Hopkins, in the letter quoted by Mr. Bridges in his 'Prosody of Milton'—while I am not certain whether Mr. Bridges does not to some extent hold it himself—that Equivalence and Substitution are modern things, that they did not exist in the period which this volume specially covers . . .' For further details see B9. The compiler has been unable to discover any documentary evidence of friendship between G M H and Saintsbury.

1910

H8   Saintsbury, George. A history of English prosody, from the twelfth century to the present day. Vol. 3: From Blake to Mr. Swinburne. London, Macmillan and Co., Limited, 1910. xiii, 562 pp.

> *See* p. 391. As a poet, G M H 'never got his notions into thorough writing-order. They belonged to the anti-foot and pro-stress division . . . He never published any, and it is quite clear that all were experiments.'

1912

H9   Brégy, Katherine. Gerard Hopkins. *in her* The poet's chantry. London, Herbert & Daniel, 1912. pp. 70–88.

> Reprinted from *Catholic World*, Jan. 1909 (see I1) this essay attracted some very favourable attention to G M H from reviewers. See I2a–I2e inclusive, and M15.

1913

H10   Warren, T. Herbert. Robert Bridges, Poet Laureate: readings from his poems . . . Oxford, Clarendon Press, 1913. 38 pp.

> *See* p. 16. A brief reference.

1914

H11   Young, F. E. Brett. Robert Bridges: a critical study. London, Martin Secker, 1914. 215 pp.

See pp. 142–3. 'The late Gerard Hopkins, S.J., was a writer with a very real poetic gift, whose metres were consciously elaborated from common syllabic types . . .' Further comment follows, together with a slightly inaccurate quotation of 'The Starlight Night'. This book was written by Francis Brett Young in collaboration with his brother Eric: for this information the compiler is indebted to Mr. Martin Secker.

1916

H12   MacDonagh, Thomas. Literature in Ireland: studies Irish and Anglo-Irish. London, T. Fisher Unwin, 1916. xiii, 248 pp.
    See p. 221. G M H is 'a rare and to some of us an exquisite poet'.

H13   Saintsbury, George. Lesser poets of the middle and later nineteenth century. *in* Ward, A. W. *and* Waller, A. R., *editors*. The Cambridge history of English literature, vol. 13. Cambridge, Cambridge University Press, 1916. xi, 611 pp.
    See pp. 207, 210–11. G M H 'developed partially acute, but not generally sound, notions on metre; and though, quite recently, broken-backed rhythms like his have been often attempted, the results have scarcely been delightful.'

1918

H14   Beeching, H. C. Richard Watson Dixon. *in* Ward, Thomas Humphry, *editor*. The English poets . . . Vol. 5, Browning to Rupert Brooke. London, Macmillan and Co., Limited, 1918. pp. 267–70.
    See p. 270. A brief, passing reference.

1919

H15   O'Neill, George. Gerard Hopkins. *in his* Essays on poetry. Dublin, The Talbot Press Ltd., 1919. pp. 117–38.
    A detailed evaluative essay, strongly critical of G M H's stylistic innovations. Some of the reviewers of this book were more enthusiastic about G M H than its author; but it is a closely argued and well-considered criticism. For the reviews, see I13–I17 inclusive.

1920

H 16   Murry, John Middleton. Gerard Manley Hopkins. *in his* Aspects
of literature. London, W. Collins & Co., Ltd., 1920. pp. 52–61.
Reprint of review in *Athenaeum*, June 1919 (see A62).

H 17   Underhill, Evelyn. The mystic as creative artist. *in her* The essen-
tials of mysticism, and other essays. London and Toronto, J. M. Dent &
Sons, Ltd., 1920. pp. 64–85.
See particularly pp. 71–2. Some elements of the mystical in G M H.

1921

H 18   Omond, T. S. English metrists . . . Oxford, Clarendon Press,
1921. viii, 336 pp.
See p. 263. 'I cannot believe that these poems deserve or will receive
attention from even the most determined seeker after novelties.'

1922

H 19   Shuster, George N. The Catholic spirit in modern English literature. New York, Macmillan, 1922. ix, 365 pp.
See pp. 115–21. General criticism with strong religious slant.

1923

H 20   *Monroe, Harriet, *and* Henderson, Alice Corbin. The new
poetry: an anthology of twentieth-century verse in English. New
edition. New York, The Macmillan Company, 1923. pp. xlv–xlviii.

1924

H 21   Kelshall, T. M. Robert Bridges (Poet Laureate). London,
Robert Scott, 1924. 93 pp.
See pp. 20–1. Comments on Bridges and G M H.

H 22   Maynard, Theodore. Our best poets, English and American.
London, Brentano's, Ltd., 1924. xxi, 233 pp.
See pp. 172–3. 'But then, everybody who tries to pack poetry tightly
suffers under some drawback—generally one that is much worse

than stiffness. Browning, and still more Father Gerard Hopkins, that extraordinary experimentalist, often pack so closely as to lose all intelligibility.'

H23 Welby, T. Earle. A popular history of English poetry. London, A. M. Philpot Ltd., 1924. ix, 282 pp.
See pp. 263–4. G M H 'aimed at using only the most suggestive words of the sentence as it forms in the mind, and at establishing a coincidence of grammatical, emotional and metrical stress to which poetry cannot continuously attain. He remains a fascinating failure.'

1926

H24 Fry, Roger, *and* Lowe, E. A. English handwriting . . . Oxford, Clarendon Press, 1926. (S.P.E. Tract No. 23.)
See plate 33, and pp. 90–1. Specimen of G M H's handwriting, with critical comments on its stylistic merits.

H25 Guiney, Louise Imogen. Letters . . . edited by Grace Guiney . . . Vol. 2. New York, Harper and Brothers, 1926. 270 pp.
See particularly pp. 239–40, 250–1. Discussion of G M H's talents with Father Geoffrey Bliss, S.J., and background information on Miss Guiney's criticism of G M H.

1929

H26 Richards, I. A. Poem VI *in his* Practical criticism . . . London, Routledge & Kegan Paul Ltd., 1929. pp. 81–90.
Analysis of 'Spring and Fall'; the results of field-work by Richards among his students at Cambridge. Students' comments on the poem are assessed, and their significance discussed.

1930

H27 Empson, William. Seven types of ambiguity. London, Chatto & Windus, 1930. 325 pp.
See particularly pp. 187–8, 284–6. Influential criticism, especially on 'The Windhover'.

1932

H 28   Gibbon, Monk. Seventeen sonnets. London, Joiner and Steele, 1932. 17 pp.
   See the dedication: 'These sonnets are dedicated to the memory of Gerard Manley Hopkins, the influence of whose work will be seen in some, if not in all.' See also p. 1: a sonnet, 'The Poetry of Gerard Manley Hopkins'.

H 29   Leavis, F. R. Gerard Manley Hopkins. *in his* New bearings in English poetry. London, Chatto & Windus, 1932. pp. 159–93.
   A widely influential essay, strongly appreciative. 'He is likely to prove, for our time and the future, the only influential poet of the Victorian age, and he seems to me the greatest.' See H 160.

H 30   Read, Herbert. Form in modern poetry. London, Sheed & Ward, 1932. xiii, 81 pp.
   See pp. 44–55. General critical comment. See 148.

1933

H 31   *Stonier, G. W. Gerard Manley Hopkins. *in his* Gog Magog and other critical essays. London, J. M. Dent & Sons, Ltd., 1933. pp. 43–63.

H 32   Drew, Elizabeth. Discovering poetry. London, Oxford University Press, 1933. xi, 224 pp.
   See pp. 82–5, 157–8, 110–11. General comment.

H 33   Elton, Oliver. The English muse: a sketch. London, G. Bell & Sons, Ltd., 1933. xiv, 464 pp.
   See pp. 399–400. 'Hopkins is deliberately and invincibly queer . . .

H 34   Evans, B. Ifor. English poetry in the later nineteenth century. London, Methuen, 1933. xxv, 404 pp.
   See pp. 210–18. General critical discussion.

H 35   Mégroz, R. L. Modern English poetry. London, Ivor Nicholson & Watson, 1933. ix, 267 pp.
   See pp. 18–19, 233–48. General critical comment.

H36   Phare, Elsie Elizabeth. The poetry of Gerard Manley Hopkins: a survey and commentary. Cambridge, Cambridge University Press, 1933. viii, 150 pp.
> Strongly influenced by I. A. Richards. Excellent on GMH's imagery, and on the form and meaning of certain poems, but the author's impatience towards GMH's religion sometimes distorts her judgements.

Reviews:

H37   Anon. in *Notes and Queries*, vol. 165, no. 21, 25 Nov. 1933, p. 378.

H38   Anon. in *Nation* (New York), vol. 138, no 3577, 24 Jan. 1934, p. 109.

H39   Walton, Eda Lou. in *New York Times Book Review*, 28 Jan. 1934, p. 2.

H40   Stonier, G. W. in *Fortnightly Review*, vol. 135, no. 807, Mar. 1934, p. 374.

H41   R[oberts], M[ichael]. in *Adelphi*, vol. 8, no. 11, Apr. 1934, pp. 76–7.

H42   R[idley], M. R. in *Oxford Magazine*, vol. 52, no. 20, 17 May 1934, pp. 714–5.
For other reviews, see I46, 59–61, 63–4, 66–73, M18.

H43   Read, Herbert. The poetry of Gerard Manley Hopkins. *in* Jones, Phyllis M., *editor*. English critical essays, twentieth century. London, Oxford University Press, 1933. pp. 351–74. (World's Classics.)
> A general critical essay. See also M163.

1934

H44   Bateson, F. W. English poetry and the English language. Oxford, Clarendon Press, 1934. vii, 129 pp.
> *See* pp. 118–20. GMH's linguistic experiments, and their significance when seen against the background of general developments in poetic language.

H45   Bennett, Joan. Four metaphysical poets. Cambridge, Cambridge University Press, 1934. 135 pp.
> *See particularly* pp. 70–1. A comparison of GMH with Herbert.

H46 *Brockington, A. Allen. Mysticism and poetry: on a basis of experience. London, Chapman & Hall, Ltd., 1934.

    See pp. 22–5, *et passim.*

H47 Bullough, Geoffrey. The trend of modern poetry. Edinburgh, Oliver & Boyd, 1934. vii, 181 pp.

    See pp. 23–5, 165–6. Brief discussion of G M H in the context of poetic modernism.

H48 De Selincourt, E. Oxford lectures on poetry. Oxford, Clarendon Press, 1934. 256 pp.

    See pp. 220, 225. 'Yet it was . . . Hopkins's brilliant, wayward verse that gave Bridges the initial stimulus towards metrical adventure; and where Hopkins failed, he, with his finer ear and infallible taste, achieved some of his most signal successes.'

H49 Eliot, T. S. After strange gods. London, Faber & Faber Limited, 1934. 68 pp.

    See pp. 47–8. Hopkins is a good poet, but much over-rated, and he is not truly a religious poet but merely a devotional poet. (See reply to this criticism in H201.) Brief comparison of G M H with George Meredith.

H50 Lewis, Cecil Day. A hope for poetry. Oxford, Basil Blackwell, 1934. 78 pp.

    See particularly pp. 6–12. Geoffrey Grigson refuted some of the points made here: see I74.

H51 McGuire, D. P. The poetry of Gerard Manley Hopkins: a lecture delivered to the Adelaide Branch of the English Association on September 22, 1933. Adelaide, F. W. Preece & Sons, 1934. 31 pp. (English Association, Adelaide Branch: Pamphlet No. 2.)

    An enthusiastic but well-reasoned discussion which deserves to be better known.

H52 Roberts, Michael. Critique of poetry. London, Jonathan Cape, 1934. 252 pp.

    See pp. 91, 134. Brief comment.

H 53   Sitwell, Edith. Gerard Manley Hopkins. *in her* Aspects of modern poetry. London, Duckworth, 1934. pp. 51–72.
   Critical essay including some astringent comments on imitators of G M H.

1935

H 54   Alexander, Calvert. Gerard Manley Hopkins. *in his* The Catholic literary revival. Milwaukee, Bruce Publishing Company, 1935. pp. 71–85.
   General comment, written from a religious viewpoint.

H 55   Doughty, Charles. Selected passages from *The Dawn in Britain* of Charles Doughty, arranged with an introduction by Barker Fairley. London, Duckworth, 1935. xxi, 110 pp.
   See pp. xiv–xv. G M H and Doughty are 'as natural a pair to name together as Wordsworth and Coleridge'.

H 56   Eliot, T. S. Introduction. *in* Moore, Marianne. Selected poems. London, Faber & Faber Limited, 1935. pp. 5–12.
   See p. 10. 'The tendency of some of the best contemporary poetry is of course to dispense with rhyme altogether, but some . . . have used it . . . to make a pattern directly in contrast with the sense and rhythm pattern, to give a greater intimacy. Some of the internal rhyming of Hopkins is to the point.'

H 57   Kelly, Bernard. The mind and poetry of Gerard Manley Hopkins, S.J. Ditchling, Pepler and Sewell, 1935. unpaginated. (Stones from the Brook, 2.)
   Written from a firmly Catholic viewpoint, but containing some very perceptive criticism. Edition limited to 300 copies: this book is now rare.

Reviews:
H 58   Anon. in *Month*, vol. 166, no. 853, July 1935, pp. 92–3.
H 59   P[hillipson], A. W. in *Downside Review*, vol. 53, no. 155, July 1935, pp. 407–8.
H 60   R[ead], H[erbert]. in *Criterion*, vol. 15, no. 58, Oct. 1935, p. 174.
For other reviews, see 194.

H 61   *Sargent, Daniel. Gerard Manley Hopkins. *in his* Four independents. London, Sheed & Ward, 1935. pp. 117–83.
Written within a Catholic framework.

Review :

H 62   K., N. in *Irish Ecclesiastical Record*, vol. 47 (5th series), Feb. 1936, pp. 215–16.
For another review, see I92.

H 63   Treneer, Anne. Charles M. Doughty: a study . . . London, Jonathan Cape, 1935. 350 pp.
See pp. 191, 328–31. Comparison of G M H and Doughty. For another attempt to bracket G M H and Doughty, see H 55, and for refutations see I103, I104, I107.

1936

H 64   Atkins, Elizabeth. Edna St. Vincent Millay and her times. Chicago, University of Chicago Press, 1936. xiii, 265 pp.
See particularly pp. 222–3. Suggested influence of G M H on Edna St. Vincent Millay.

H 65   Daiches, David. Gerard Manley Hopkins and the modern poets. *in his* New literary values. Edinburgh, Oliver & Boyd, 1936. pp. 23–51.
G M H's influence on modern poetry, with some very valuable discussion of his style in general and of the way in which his meaning emerges in the more difficult poems.

H 66   Eliot, T. S. Religion and literature. *in his* Essays ancient and modern. London, Faber & Faber Limited, 1936. pp. 93–112.
See pp. 96–8. Some comments on the nature and limitations of religious poetry, citing G M H as an example along with Vaughan, Southwell and Herbert.

H 67   *Kelly, Blanche Mary. The well of English. New York, Harper and Brothers, 1936. pp. 286–90.

H 68   Read, Herbert. Gerard Manley Hopkins. *in his* In defence of Shelley, and other essays. London, William Heinemann Ltd., 1936. pp. 113–44.

1937

H69   Bush, Douglas. Mythology and the Romantic tradition in English poetry. Cambridge, Mass.; Harvard University Press, 1937. xvi, 647 pp. (Harvard Studies in English, 18.)
> GMH *passim*.

H70   Groom, Bernard. The formation and use of compound epithets in English poetry from 1579. Oxford, Clarendon Press, 1937. (S.P.E. Tract No. 49.)
> *See* pp. 318–20. 'It is not necessary to pursue our survey beyond Hopkins. No writer, indubitably a poet, forms compound epithets with more audacity . . .'

H71   Horton, Philip. Hart Crane: the life of an American poet. New York, Norton, 1937. x, 352 pp.
> *See* pp. 229–30. Crane was enthusiastic about GMH, but not influenced stylistically by him.

H72   *Mansfield, Margery. Workers in fire: a book about poetry. New York, Longmans, Green and Co., 1937.
> *See* pp. 147–9, 161–5.

H73   *Weygant, Cornelius. The time of Yeats. New York, Appleton-Century Company, Inc., 1937.
> *See* pp. 386–8, *et passim*.

H74   Young, G. M. Daylight and champaign. London, Jonathan Cape, 1937. 312 pp.
> *See* pp. 197, 201–5. References to GMH in a reprint of I122.

1938

H75   MacNeice, Louis. Rhythm and rhyme. *in his* Modern poetry . . . London, Oxford University Press, 1938. pp. 114–35.
> *See particularly* pp. 123–5. 'Hopkins's influence on younger poets today has often been unfortunate. A close imitation of his manner is dangerous, because both his rhythms and his syntax were peculiarly appropriate to his own unusual circumstances . . .'

H76   Palmer, Herbert. Post-Victorian poetry. London, J. M. Dent & Sons, Ltd., 1938. xiii, 378 pp.
    See pp. 17, 40, *et passim.*

H77   Sitwell, Edith. Three eras of modern poetry: first lecture. *in* Trio: dissertations on some aspects of national genius, by Osbert, Edith and Sacheverell Sitwell. London, Macmillan & Co., 1938. pp. 97–139.
    See pp. 98–9. Brief, trenchant comments on G M H's influence on later poets. '. . . Hopkins was to influence technique alone, but that influence has been enormous—and all to the bad. For this we must not blame him, however, but the young persons who believe themselves to be descended from him technically . . . it is useless to try to form a technique from the outside.'

H78   *Slater, John Rothwell. Recent literature and religion. New York, Harper & Brothers, 1938.
    See pp. 185–9.

1939

H79   *Bailey, Ruth. A dialogue on modern poetry. London, Oxford University Press, 1939. pp. 42–4, 61–5, *et passim.*

H80   Henderson, Philip. Gerard Manley Hopkins. *in his* The poet and society. London, Secker & Warburg, 1939. pp. 103–31.
    Includes some comparison of G M H and Whitman. Very much preoccupied with the psychological implications of the priest–poet relationship in G M H.

H81   *Kenmare, Dallas. The passionate Christian: a paper on Gerard Manley Hopkins. *in his* The face of truth: collected writings on poetry and religion. Oxford, Shakespeare Head Press, 1939. pp. 92–100.

1940

H82   Daiches, David. Poetry and the modern world: a study of poetry in England between 1900 and 1939. Chicago, University of Chicago Press, 1940. x, 247 pp.
    See particularly pp. 24–35. General critical comment.

H83　*Daly, James J. Father Hopkins and the Society. *in his* The Jesuit in focus. Milwaukee, The Bruce Publishing Company, 1940. pp. 189–94.

H84　Evans, B. Ifor. Towards the twentieth century: Gerard Manley Hopkins and T. S. Eliot. *in his* Tradition and romanticism. London, Methuen, 1940. pp. 185–92.

H85　Southworth, James G. Gerard Manley Hopkins. *in his* Sowing the spring . . . Oxford, Basil Blackwell, 1940. pp. 15–32.
General critical comment.

H86　*Wells, Henry W. New poets from old: a study in literary genetics. New York, Columbia University Press, 1940. pp. 35–43.

H87　Withers, Percy. A buried life: personal recollections of A. E. Housman. London, Jonathan Cape, 1940. 133 pp.
See p. 59. Very brief comment; here given in full: '[Housman] greatly admired Bridges' essays in criticism, while so strongly resenting his opinions on many of our poets. His attitude towards Gerard Hopkins he looked on as a personal foible.'

1941

H88　Bullough, Geoffrey. The trend of modern poetry. *2nd edition.* Edinburgh, Oliver & Boyd, 1941. vii, 191 pp.
See particularly pp. 23–5, *et passim.*

H89　Matthiessen, F. O. American renaissance. New York, Oxford University Press, 1941. xxiv, 678 pp.
See pp. 584–92. Brilliantly perceptive comparison of GMH and Whitman.

H90　Winwar, Frances. Oscar Wilde and the Yellow 'Nineties. New York, Blue Ribbon Books, 1941. xviii, 381 pp.
See pp. 65–7, 145–7.

1942

H91　Pick, John. Gerard Manley Hopkins: priest and poet. London, Oxford University Press, 1942. x, 169 pp.

Biographical and critical study, emphasizing the importance of G M H's vocation in the development of his poetry. For those who seek detailed literary criticism, this book is of secondary importance, but as an introduction to Hopkins the *Jesuit* it is outstanding. A slightly revised second edition was issued in 1966—Oxford Paperbacks, No. 108.

Reviews:

H92   Turner, W. J. in *Spectator*, vol. 169, no. 5962, 2 Oct. 1942, p. 318.

H93   Conlay, Iris. in *Catholic Herald* (London), 16 Oct. 1942, p. 3.

H94   Turnell, Martin. in *Tablet*, vol. 180, no. 5345, 17 Oct. 1942, p. 192.

H95   Anon. in *Listener*, vol. 28, no. 722, 12 Nov. 1942, pp. 634–5.

H96   K., D. L. in *Month*, vol. 178, no. 930, Nov.–Dec. 1942, pp. 493–4.

H97   T., C. in *Poetry Review*, vol. 34, no. 1, Jan. 1943, pp. 33–42.

H98   Shuster, George N. in *Saturday Review of Literature*, vol. 26, no. 23, 5 June 1943, p. 31.

H99   Ashburner, Phoebe. in *Adelphi*, vol. 19, no. 4, July–Sept. 1943, p. 127.

H100   Deutsch, Babette. in *Nation* (New York), vol. 157, no. 9, 28 Aug. 1943, p. 247.

H101   Anon. in *Notes and Queries*, vol. 185, no. 8, 9 Oct. 1943, p. 240. For other reviews, see I 185–7, 189, 190, 192, 194–5, 197–8, 201–4, 206–8, 210–14, 217, M247.

H102   Scarfe, Francis. Auden and after: the liberation of poetry, 1930–1941. London, George Routledge & Sons, Ltd., 1942. xvi, 208 pp. *See particularly* p. 157. 'Hopkins . . . far from being a liberator, was a great but *thwarted* sensualist, a stuffed and stifled D. H. Lawrence of Jesuitry and Victorianism . . .'

1944

H103   Gardner, W. H. Gerard Manley Hopkins (1844–1889) a study of poetic idiosyncrasy in relation to poetic tradition. London, Martin Secker & Warburg, 1944. xvi, 304 pp. For annotation, see H116. For reviews, see I256, 269–77, 281, 283, 285–8, 291, 294, 296.

H104   Reid, J. C. Gerard Manley Hopkins; priest and poet: a centennial tribute. Wellington, Catholic Writers' Movement, 1944. 16 pp.
Written from a decidedly partisan religious viewpoint.

1945

H105   The Kenyon Critics. Gerard Manley Hopkins. Norfolk, Conn.; New Directions Books, 1945. viii, 144 pp.
Reprints of essays from *Kenyon Review*: see I233–6, 257–8.

Reviews:

H106   Kennedy, Leo. in *Chicago Sun Book Week*, 3 Feb. 1946, p. 2.

H107   Anon. in *United States Quarterly Book List*, vol. 2, no. 3, Sept. 1946, pp. 171–2.
For other reviews see I302–4, 306–8, 310–13, 318, 325.

1946

H108   Gordon, George. Gerard Manley Hopkins and Robert Bridges. *in his* The discipline of letters. Oxford, Clarendon Press, 1946. pp. 168–84.
This essay is concerned with 'the friendship, collaboration, and some of the experimental work for poetry generally' of the two men.

H109   Routh, H. V. English literature and ideas in the twentieth century . . . London, Methuen & Co., Ltd., 1946. viii, 204 pp.
See pp. 104, 106–8. General critical comment, reprinted with minor additions and revisions in the second and third editions (1948 and 1950).

H110   Suckling, Norman. Fauré. London, J. M. Dent and Sons Ltd., 1946. vii, 229 pp.
See pp. 54, 185–6. Comments on GMH's musical theories, and on his resistance to the ideas of the 'official' musicians of his time.

H111   Treece, Henry. Gerard Manley Hopkins and Dylan Thomas. *in his* How I see apocalypse. London, Lindsay Drummond, 1946. pp. 129–39.
Detailed discussion of GMH's influence on Thomas. See also H300.

1947

H112   Fausset, Hugh I'Anson. Poets and pundits: essays and addresses. London, Jonathan Cape, 1947. 319 pp.
> *See* pp. 96–113. A centenary tribute, and an essay on the conflict of priest and poet in GMH.

H113   Grierson, Herbert J. C. *and* Smith, J. C. A critical history of English poetry. *2nd edition*. London, Chatto & Windus, 1947. viii, 539 pp.
> *See* pp. 507–8. Brief general comment.

H114   *Holloway, Sister Marcella Marie. The prosodic theory of Gerard Manley Hopkins. Washington, Catholic University of America Press, 1947. 121 pp.

Review:

H115   Gleeson, William F. in *Thought*, vol. 23, no. 89, June 1948, pp. 342–3.
For other reviews, see A119, I358, I372.

1948

H116   Gardner, W. H. Gerard Manley Hopkins (1844–1889) a study of poetic idiosyncrasy in relation to poetic tradition. Vol. 1. *Second edition*. London, Martin Secker & Warburg, 1948. xvi, 304 pp.
> Together with the second volume (H128) this is the nearest approach to a definitive critical study yet written. Re-issued in 1958 by Oxford University Press. For reviews, see A113, A115–16, A124–6, I359, I360, I362, M6, M265.

H117   Graves, Robert. The white goddess: a historical grammar of poetic myth. London, Faber & Faber Limited, 1948. 430 pp.
> *See* pp. 372–3. GMH is instanced, with Skelton, Donne, and others, as proof of Graves's belief that 'it has become impossible to combine the once identical functions of priest and poet . . .' In GMH, the 'war between poet and priest was fought on a high mystical level;' but 'can . . . Hopkins be commended for humbly submitting his poetic ecstasies to the confession-box?'

H118   Srinivasa Iyengar, K. R. Gerard Manley Hopkins: the man and
the poet. Calcutta, Oxford University Press, 1948. 194 pp.

A rather superficial and unreliable study, which may have been
influential in India, but is of no particular importance now. For
reviews see A124, I354, I373, I380.

H119   *Mims, Edward. Gerard Manley Hopkins, Jesuit scholar. *in his*
The Christ of the poets. Nashville, Abingdon-Cokesbury Press, 1948.
pp. 204–11.

H120   Peters, W. A. M. Gerard Manley Hopkins: a critical essay
towards the understanding of his poetry. London, Oxford University
Press, 1948. xviii, 213 pp.

A very thorough and highly intelligent study, with emphasis on
GMH's theories of inscape and their effects on his poetry. In recent
years this book seems to have become more highly regarded among
Hopkins scholars than any other comparable one.

Reviews:

H121   Duncan-Jones, E. E. in *Birmingham Post*, 13 Apr. 1948, p. 2.

H122   Fausset, Hugh I'Anson. in *Manchester Guardian*, 13 Apr. 1948,
p. 3.

H123   Anon. in *Listener*, vol. 40, no. 1027, 30 Sept. 1948, pp. 495–6.

H124   Trethowan, Illtyd. in *Downside Review*, vol. 66, no. 206, Oct.
1948, p. 479.

H125   Templeman, W. D. in *Modern Philology*, vol. 46, no. 4, May
1949, p. 262.

For other reviews see A119, A124–6, I341, I343–4, I346–7, I349–
50, I353, I357–8, I361, I365–6, I368, I374, I394, M173, M247.

H126   Warren, Austin. Gerard Manley Hopkins. *in his* Rage for order.
Chicago, University of Chicago Press, 1948. pp. 52–65.

Reprint of essay from *Kenyon Review*: see I236.

1949

H127   Bowra, C. M. The creative experiment. London, Macmillan &
Co., Ltd., 1949. vii, 255 pp.

See pp. 4–5. Brief but unusual comment: because GMH aimed at
'conveying a sense of powers at work in nature', he is an example of
the 'Dionysian' type of poet defined by Nietzsche.

H128   Gardner, W. H. Gerard Manley Hopkins (1844–1889) a study of poetic idiosyncrasy in relation to poetic tradition. Vol. 2. London, Martin Secker & Warburg, 1949. xiv, 415 pp.

    Together with the first volume (H116) this book is the nearest approach to a definitive critical study yet written. Re-issued in 1958 by Oxford University Press.

Reviews:

H129   Fausset, Hugh I'Anson. in *Manchester Guardian*, 31 May 1949, p. 4.

H130   Anon. in *Listener*, vol. 42, no. 1068, 14 July 1949, p. 77.

H131   Nicholson, Norman. in *Fortnightly Review*, vol. 166 (n.s.), July 1949, pp. 65–6.

H132   Anon. in *Sunday Statesman* (Calcutta), 4 Sept. 1949, p. 13.

H133   Price, R. G. G. in *English Review Magazine*, vol. 3, no. 3, Sept. 1949, p. 212.

    For other reviews see I364, I385–90, I392–3, I395–7, I399–400, I403–4, I416, I428, I430–1, M6, M248, M265.

H134   Graves, Robert. The common asphodel. London, Hamish Hamilton, 1949. xi, 335 pp.

    See pp. 99–101. Comments on G M H as a modernist poet.

H135   Highet, Gilbert. The classical tradition. Oxford, Clarendon Press, 1949. xxxviii, 763 pp.

    See p. 254. A brief comment: when G M H wrote 'The Wreck of the Deutschland' and 'The Loss of the Eurydice' he was writing in the manner of Pindar.

H136   Patmore, Derek. The life and times of Coventry Patmore. London, Constable, 1949. xii, 250 pp.

    See particularly pp. 188–202. General comment on G M H's friendship with Patmore.

H137   Weyand, Norman, *editor*. Immortal diamond: studies in Gerard Manley Hopkins; edited by Norman Weyand, S.J., with the assistance of Raymond V. Schoder, S.J. London, Sheed & Ward, 1949. xxvi, 451 pp.

    An important but uneven book. Some of the essays are excellent, some only mediocre. The bibliography is given separate mention: see F2.

Contents:

H137a Carroll, Martin C. Gerard Manley Hopkins and the Society of Jesus. pp. 3–50.

H137b MacGillivray, Arthur. Hopkins and creative writing. pp. 51–72.

H137c Bonn, John Louis. Greco-Roman verse theory and Gerard Manley Hopkins. pp. 73–92.

H137d Ong, Walter J. Hopkins' sprung rhythm and the life of English poetry. pp. 93–174.

H137e Burns, Chester A. Gerard Manley Hopkins: poet of ascetic and aesthetic conflict. pp. 175–91.

H137f Schoder, Raymond V. An interpretive glossary of difficult words in the poems. pp. 192–221.

H137g McNamee, Maurice B. Hopkins, poet of nature and of the supernatural. pp. 222–51.

H137h Noon, William T. The three languages of poetry. pp. 252–74.

H137i Schoder, Raymond V. What does 'The Windhover' mean? pp. 275–306.

H137j Watson, Youree. 'The Loss of the Eurydice': a critical analysis. pp. 307–32.

H137k Boyle, Robert R. The thought-structure of 'The Wreck of the Deutschland'. pp. 333–50.

H137l Weyand, Norman. Appendix: the historical basis of 'The Wreck of the Deutschland' and 'The Loss of the Eurydice'. pp. 353–92.

H137m Weyand, Norman. A chronological Hopkins bibliography, pp. 393–436. See also F2.

Reviews:

H138 Halsband, Robert. in *Saturday Review of Literature*, vol. 32, no. 18, 30 Apr. 1949, p. 12.

H139 Kilcoyne, Francis P. in *Brooklyn Eagle* (Brooklyn, N.Y.), 11 May 1949, p. 18.

H140 Nims, John Frederick. in *Chicago Sunday Tribune*, 29 May 1949, part 4, p. 6.

H141 Chase, John W. in *New York Times Book Review*, 18 Sept. 1949, p. 12.

H142 Grisewood, Harman. in *Tablet*, vol. 194, no. 5715, 3 Dec. 1949, pp. 380–1.

H143 Anon. in *Scotsman*, 22 Dec. 1949, p. 9.

H144 Pepler, Conrad. in *Universe*, 10 Feb. 1950, p. 2.

H145   Haynes, Renee. in *Time and Tide*, vol. 31, no. 10, 11 Mar. 1950, p. 234.
For other reviews, see A124–6, I375–7, I379–80, I382–3, I401–2, I405–7, I412–13, I419, I421–2, I424, I428, I439, I450, M135.

H146   Baugh, Albert C., *editor*. A literary history of England. London, Routledge & Kegan Paul, 1950. xii, 1,673 pp.
See Book IV, pp. 1536–8. Reprinted with minor revisions in the second edition (1967). See also K107.

H147   Beck, George Andrew, *editor*. The English Catholics, 1850–1950 . . . London, Burns Oates, 1950. xix, 640 pp.
See pp. 456–7, 534–5.

H148   Heath-Stubbs, John. The darkling plain . . . London, Eyre and Spottiswoode, 1950. xvii, 221 pp.
See particularly pp. 140–7.

H149   Vines, Sherard. 100 years of English literature. London, Gerald Duckworth & Co., Ltd., 1950. 316 pp.
See particularly pp. 164–5. General comment.

1951

H150   Bartlett, Phyllis. Poems in process. New York, Oxford University Press, 1951. viii, 267 pp.
See particularly pp. 52–6, 82–4, 216–17. Critical comment.

H151   Churchill, R. C. English literature of the nineteenth century. London, University Tutorial Press, Ltd., 1951. vii, 270 pp.
See particularly pp. 210–16. General comment.

H152   *Digges, Sister Mary Laurentia. Gerard Manley Hopkins' sonnets of desolation: an analysis of meaning. Washington, The Catholic University of America Press, 1951. xi, 156 pp.

H153   Grigson, Geoffrey. The language of poetry. *in his* Essays from the air. London, Routledge & Kegan Paul, 1951. pp. 160–70.
See particularly pp. 167–8. General comment.

H154 Peschmann, Hermann. New directions in English poetry, 1920–45. *in* Literature and life; second volume: addresses to the English Association. London, George G. Harrap & Co., Ltd., 1951. pp. 146–67.

> *See* pp. 149–51. Brief but interesting comments on imitation of GMH by W. H. Auden.

H155 Pinto, Vivian de Sola. Hopkins and Bridges. *in his* Crisis in English poetry, 1880–1940. London, Hutchinson, 1951. pp. 59–84.

1952

H156 Bush, Douglas. English poetry. London, Methuen & Co., Ltd., 1952. ix, 222 pp.

> *See particularly* pp. 183–5. General comment.

H157 Davie, Donald. Hopkins as a decadent critic. *in his* Purity of diction in English verse. London, Chatto & Windus, 1952. pp. 160–82.

> An original view of Hopkins's criticism. See also I448.

H158 Durrell, Lawrence. Gerard Manley Hopkins. *in his* Key to modern poetry. London, Peter Nevill, 1952. pp. 164–77.

> Interesting and perceptive general comment. American edition published by University of Oklahoma Press (1952) as *A key to modern British poetry*, text identical with this edition.

H159 *Hart, Sister Mary Adorita. The Christocentric theme in Gerard Manley Hopkins' 'The Wreck of the Deutschland'. Washington, The Catholic University of America Press, 1952. viii, 178 pp.

H160 Leavis, F. R. The common pursuit. London, Chatto & Windus, 1952. viii, 307 pp.

> *See* pp. 44–72. Strongly appreciative and very influential criticism.

H161 Raiziss, Sona. The metaphysical passion. Philadelphia, University of Pennsylvania Press, 1952. xv, 327 pp.

> GMH *passim.*

H162 *Wilder, Amos Niven. Modern poetry and the Christian tradition: a study in the relation of Christianity to culture. New York, Charles Scribner's Sons, 1952. pp. 148–75, *et passim.*

1953

H163   Coombes, H. Literature and criticism. London, Chatto & Windus, 1953. 190 pp.
    See particularly pp. 61–2, 79–80, 145–7, 156–9. General comment.

H164   Crump, Geoffrey. Speaking poetry. London, Methuen & Co., Ltd., 1953. viii, 231 pp.
    See pp. 105–7, *et passim*. General comment; and some remarks on how G M H's poems should be spoken, with special reference to particular poems.

H165   Longaker, Mark, *and* Bolles, Edwin C. Contemporary English literature. New York, Appleton-Century-Crofts, Inc., 1953. xvii, 526 pp.
    See particularly pp. 86–8. Brief general comment.

H166   Morris, David. The poetry of Gerard Manley Hopkins and T. S. Eliot in the light of the Donne tradition. Bern, A. Francke, 1953. 144 pp. (Swiss Studies in English, 33.)
    Much stronger on Eliot than on G M H. Attempts to trace relationships between G M H and Donne, but produces no new evidence of *direct* influence. (G M H never mentioned Donne in any of his letters or papers.) See also I480.

H167   Read, Herbert. Inscape and gestalt: Hopkins. *in his* The true voice of feeling: studies in English romantic poetry. London, Faber & Faber, 1953. pp. 76–86.
    G M H's theories of poetic diction and their application to his poetry.

1954

H168   D'Arcy, M. C. The mind and heart of love. *2nd edition*. London, Faber & Faber Limited, 1954. 349 pp.
    See particularly pp. 166–70. Discussion of G M H's theories about the nature of the self, and their derivation from Duns Scotus.

H169   Hartman, Geoffrey H. Hopkins. *in his* The unmediated vision . . . New Haven, Yale University Press, 1954. pp. 49–67, 185–8.
    This essay centres on 'The Windhover', but sets the poem in the context of G M H's poetry as a whole.

Reviews:

H170 Anon. in *United States Quarterly Book Review*, vol. 11, no. 2, June 1955, pp. 207–8.

H171 Anon. in *Times Literary Supplement*, 22 July 1955, p. 414.

H172 Margoliouth, H. M. in *Review of English Studies*, vol. 7, no. 28, 1956, pp. 436–7.

H173 Townsend, Francis C. in *Journal of English and Germanic Philology*, vol. 55, 1956, pp. 166–8.

H174 Willcox, Stewart C. in *Books Abroad*, vol. 30, no. 4, Autumn 1956, p. 443.

H175 Maritain, Jacques. Creative intuition in art and poetry. London, The Harvill Press, 1954. xxxii, 423 pp.

GMH *passim*.

H176 Martz, Louis L. The poetry of meditation. New Haven, Yale University Press, 1954. xiii, 375 pp. (Yale Studies in English, 125.) *See* pp. 321–6, *et passim*. Perceptive and interesting comment.

1955

H177 Albert, Edward. A history of English literature. *3rd edition*. London, George G. Harrap & Co., Ltd., 1955. 624 pp. *See* pp. 527–31. General comment.

H178 Graves, Robert. The crowning privilege. London, Cassell, 1955. ix, 230 pp. *See* p. 135. 'Need I also dwell on the lesser idols now slowly mouldering: on sick, muddle-headed, sex-mad D. H. Lawrence who wrote sketches for poems, but nothing more; on poor, tortured Gerard Manley Hopkins?' This dismissal of GMH was challenged in a review of the book: see I486. Paperback reprint published by Penguin Books (Pelican A451, 1959).

H179 Grigson, Geoffrey. Gerard Manley Hopkins. London, Longmans, Green & Co., for the British Council and the National Book League, 1955. 34 pp. (Writers and their Work, No. 59.) Short general introduction, with special attention to GMH as a nature-poet. Includes some very perceptive comments on 'The Windhover'. Revised edition (1962) with minor additions. For reviews, see M34–5, M83, M144, I478–9.

H180   House, Humphry. Gerard Manley Hopkins, I, II, III. *in his*
All in due time. London, Rupert Hart-Davis, 1955. pp. 159–74.
    Reprints a centenary tribute and two reviews: see I231, B38, I66.

H181   Hudson, William Henry. An outline history of English literature.
London, G. Bell and Sons, Ltd., 1955. viii, 319 pp.
    See pp. 292–4, *et passim*. General comment.

H182   Tindall, William York. The literary symbol. New York, Columbia University Press, 1955. vii, 278 pp.
    An analysis of the place and uses of the symbol in literature, with
    frequent references to G M H.

H183   Ward, A. C. Illustrated history of English literature, volume
three: Blake to Bernard Shaw. London, Longmans Green and Co.,
1955. xi, 325 pp.
    See pp. 277–8. General comment.

1956

H184   *Chiari, Joseph. Symbolism from Poe to Mallarme. London,
Rockliff, 1956.
    See pp. 53–4, *et passim*.

H185   Deutsch, Babette. Poetry in our time. New York, Columbia
University Press, 1956. xvi, 411 pp.
    See particularly pp. 286–311. Examination of G M H's technique
    and influence on later poets, including a detailed analysis of 'The
    Windhover'.

H186   Melchiori, Giorgio. The tightrope walkers . . . London, Routledge & Kegan Paul, 1956. ix, 277 pp.
    See pp. 13–33, 224–9. Comparison of G M H's stylistic mannerisms
    with those of Henry James and Dylan Thomas.

H187   Oliver, E. J. Coventry Patmore. London, Sheed & Ward, 1956.
211 pp.
    See particularly pp. 166–70. General comment on G M H's friend-
    ship with Patmore.

H188   Treece, Henry. The debt to Hopkins. *in his* Dylan Thomas. *2nd edition.* London, Ernest Benn Limited, 1956. pp. 48–61.
Notes on G M H's influence on modern poetry, with detailed discussion of his influence on Thomas.

1957

H189   Miles, Josephine. Hopkins: the sweet and lovely language. *in her* Eras and modes in English poetry. Berkeley and Los Angeles, University of California Press, 1957. pp. 164–77.
A study of G M H's use of language, first published in 1944 (I235).

H190   Reid, J. C. The mind and art of Coventry Patmore. London, Routledge & Kegan Paul, 1957. viii, 358 pp.
See particularly pp. 229–35. An explanation of Patmore's limited understanding of G M H's poems.

H191   *Thwaite, Anthony. Essay on contemporary English poets; Hopkins to the present day. Tokyo, Kenkyuska, 1957. ix, 222 pp.
See pp. 14–29.

H192   Wain, John. Hopkins. *in his* Preliminary essays. London, Macmillan, 1957. pp. 103–14.
A general critical essay.

1958

H193   Heuser, Alan. The shaping vision of Gerard Manley Hopkins. London, Oxford University Press, 1958. viii, 128 pp.
The shaping vision of G M H's work is 'essentially primitive and ultimately mystical', but it 'receives continual theoretical exegesis by the curious mind of the poet, priest and scholar Hopkins.'

Reviews:
H194   Loughheed, W. C. in *Queen's Quarterly*, vol. 66, no. 1, Spring 1959, pp. 173–4.
H195   Park, B. A. in *Books Abroad*, vol. 33, no. 3, Summer 1959, p. 351.
H196   Anon. in *College English*, vol. 21, no. 2, Nov. 1959, pp. 113–14.
For other reviews, see I247, I523, I528–9, I530, I532, I533, I537–8, I541, I545, I553, I556, M50.

H 197   Lees, F. N. Gerard Manley Hopkins. *in* Ford, Boris, *editor*. The Pelican guide to English literature, vol. 6: from Dickens to Hardy. Harmondsworth, Penguin Books, 1958. pp. 371–84.
A very useful general introduction.

H 198   Meadows, Denis. A popular history of the Jesuits. New York, The Macmillan Company, 1958. xi, 160 pp.
See pp. 100, 136–7. Brief general comment.

H 199   Press, John. The chequer'd shade: reflections on obscurity in poetry. London, Oxford University Press, 1958. 229 pp.
Frequent references to G M H, including discussion of his own attitudes to the obscurities in his verse.

H 200   Wilson, John Burgess. English literature: a survey for students. London, Longmans, Green and Co., 1958. x, 340 pp.
See particularly pp. 253–5. Brief general comment.

1959

H 201   Buckley, Vincent. Poetry and morality . . . London, Chatto & Windus, 1959. 239 pp.
See particularly p. 145. Brief but impressive answer to T. S. Eliot's strictures on G M H (H 49).

H 202   Drew, Elizabeth. Poetry: a modern guide to its understanding and enjoyment. New York, W. W. Norton & Company Inc., 1959. 287 pp.
See pp. 21–2, 75–6, 107–9, 140–2, 248–52. Explications of various poems, the last, on 'The Windhover', being the most detailed.

H 203   Duncan, Joseph E. The revival of metaphysical poetry: the history of a style, 1800 to the present. Minneapolis, University of Minnesota Press, 1959. 227 pp.
See particularly pp. 91–102. The influence of the metaphysical poets, especially Donne and Crashaw, on G M H; and his interpretation of the metaphysical style. 'Hopkins approached the seventeenth-century conceit a little more closely than did any other nineteenth-century poet.'

H 204 Gibbon, Monk. The masterpiece and the man: Yeats as I knew him. London, Rupert Hart-Davis, 1959. 226 pp.

> *See* pp. 135–45. The influence of G M H on Monk Gibbon, and two previously unpublished letters from Yeats to Gibbon containing comments on G M H by Yeats.

H 205 *Mauriac, François. Faith and the writer. *in* Roggendorf, Joseph, *editor*. Catholicism in the cross-currents of the present. Tokyo, Sobunsha, 1959, pp. 379–90.

H 206 Walsh, William. G. M. Hopkins and a sense of the particular. *in his* The use of imagination. London, Chatto & Windus, 1959. pp. 121–36.

> 'In this chapter I want to discuss what is meant by a sense of the particular as the origin and conclusion of educational activity. I propose to do this by enquiring into the mind and practice of Gerard Manley Hopkins . . .'

1960

H 207 *Chiari, Joseph. Realism and imagination. London, Barrie & Rockliffe, 1960. 216 pp.

> *See* pp. 64–5, *et passim.*

H 208 Collins, A. S. English literature of the twentieth century. London, University Tutorial Press Ltd., 1960. vii, 410 pp.

> *See* pp. 56–62, *et passim.* General comment.

H 209 Daiches, David. A critical history of English literature. Volume 2. London, Secker & Warburg, 1960. iii, 537–1169 pp.

> *See* pp. 1042–8, *et passim.* General critical comment.

H 210 Downes, David A. Gerard Manley Hopkins: a study of his Ignatian spirit. London, Vision Press Limited, 1960. 195 pp.

> G M H expressed in poetic form the spiritual attitudes of the Society of Jesus: the Ignatian outlook is central to his art.

Review:

H 211 Heuser, Alan. in *Queens' Quarterly*, vol. 67, no. 3, Autumn 1960, p. 492.

For other reviews see I 567, I 575, I 632.

H 212   Mauriac, François. Mémoires intérieurs; translated from the
French by Gerard Hopkins. London, Eyre and Spottiswoode, 1960.
248 pp.

> *See* pp. 137–40. 'The poems of Hopkins . . . are obscure because
> they must be. Our probing eyes cannot reach to that secret point of
> junction where a soul and a spirit meet, nor see into that fold of the
> flesh where the splinter lies concealed.' This book was translated by
> G M H's nephew.

H 213   Rosenthal, M. L. The modern poets: a critical introduction.
New York, Oxford University Press, 1960. xii, 288 pp.

> *See particularly* pp. 24–6. Some comments on the integral religious
> faith in G M H's poetry ('It is less the faith itself than the *effort* that
> moves most of us so . . .') and a brief comparison of G M H with
> Hardy.

H 214   Sebeok, Thomas A., *editor*. Style in language. Massachusetts, The
Technology Press of Massachusetts Institute of Technology *and* John
Wiley & Sons, Inc., 1960. xvii, 470 pp.

> *See* pp. 358–69. An analysis of G M H's poetry from the linguistic
> viewpoint; with comments on his verse theories, particularly on his
> use of rhyme.

1961

H 215   Boyle, Robert. Metaphor in Hopkins. Chapel Hill, University of
North Carolina Press, 1961. xxiv, 231 pp.

> Father Boyle's basic thesis is that rhythm in G M H's poetry has meta-
> phorical significance. Includes a particularly important explication
> of 'The Windhover', with comments on other explications.

Reviews:

H 216   Robie, Burton A. in *Library Journal*, vol. 86, 15 Sept. 1961,
p. 2945.

H 217   Hemphill, George. in *College English*, vol. 23, no. 6, Mar. 1962,
p. 514.

H 218   Gibson, Walker. in *Victorian Studies*, vol. 5, no. 4, June 1962,
p. 353.

H 219   Stillinger, Jack. in *Studies in English Literature* (Houston), vol. 2,
Autumn 1962, p. 518.

H220 Keating, John E. in *Journal of English and Germanic Philology*, vol. 62, 1963, p. 413.
For other reviews see I590, I600–1, I605, I614, I616, I625.

H221 Churchill, R. C. Poetry since Hopkins. *in* Sampson, George. The concise Cambridge history of English literature . . . *2nd edition*. Cambridge, Cambridge University Press, 1961. pp. 947–54.
General critical and historical comment, reprinted with minor additions in the 3rd edition (1970).

H222 Heppenstall, Rayner. The fourfold tradition. London, Barrie & Rockliffe, 1961. 280 pp.
See p. 17. A very brief, but very acute remark on G M H's theory of sprung rhythm, which 'could not have been enunciated as it was if, in Hopkins's time, the mere structure of Anglo-Saxon verse had been understood.'

H223 Jennings, Elizabeth. The unity of incarnation: a study of Gerard Manley Hopkins. *in her* Every changing shape. London, Andre Deutsch, 1961. pp. 95–110.
'What is startling, and even shocking, in Hopkins's verse is not so much the audacity with language or the uninhibited play of imagery as the wholeness, the integration of the vision which these things embody.'

H224 Kranz, Gisbert. Gerard Manley Hopkins. *in his* Three centuries of Christian literature. London, Burns & Oates, 1961, pp. 118–26. (Faith and Fact Books, 119.)
An examination of G M H's love of nature and its spiritual significance for him. This book is a translation by J. R. Foster of the author's *Christliche Literatur der Neuzeit*, vol. 3, section 14.

H225 Reeves, James. A short history of English poetry, 1340–1940. London, Heinemann, 1961. xvi, 228 pp.
See pp. 199–203. General comment.

H226 Turnell, Martin. Modern literature and Christian faith. London, Darton, Longman and Todd, 1961. 69 pp.
See pp. 19–20. 'Hopkins was a great poet because his religion did enable him to resist the disintegrating forces of his time . . .'

1962

H227 Berry, Francis. Poetry and the physical voice. London, Routledge
& Kegan Paul, 1962. x, 205 pp.
See pp. 177–80. An interesting and unusual attempt to establish how
far G M H's poetry was influenced by the tone and timbre of his
own voice—G M H always wrote to be *heard* rather than read.

H228 Entwistle, William J. *and* Gillett, Eric. The literature of England,
AD 500–1960 . . . *4th edition*. London, Longmans, 1962. 303 pp.
See pp. 170–1. General comment. 'Much of the obscurity and un-
profitableness of the verse of the twenties and thirties must be brought
home to Hopkins.'

H229 Fairchild, Hoxie Neale. Religious trends in English poetry, Vol.
V; 1880–1920 . . . New York and London, Columbia University Press,
1962. xvii, 663 pp.
G M H *passim*.

H230 Phelps, Gilbert. A short history of English literature. London,
The Folio Society, 1962. 159 pp.
See p. 136. General comment.

H231 Tindall, William York. A reader's guide to Dylan Thomas.
London, Thames & Hudson, 1962. 317 pp.
Numerous brief comments suggesting G M H's influence in individual
poems by Thomas.

H232 Winters, Yvor. The poetry of Gerard Manley Hopkins. *in his*
The function of criticism. London, Routledge & Kegan Paul, 1962.
pp. 103–56.
A reprint of Winters's famous attack, first published in the *Hudson
Review* (I369).

1963

H233 Gardner, W. H. Gerard Manley Hopkins. *in* Spender, Stephen,
and Hall, Donald, *editors*. The concise encyclopaedia of English and
American poets and poetry. London, Hutchinson, 1963. pp. 151–4.
A general survey, well above the usual 'encyclopaedia-entry' standards.

H 234   Miller, J. Hillis. Gerard Manley Hopkins. *in his* The disappearance of God. Cambridge (Mass.), The Belknap Press of Harvard University Press, 1963. pp. 270–359.

This book considers G M H alongside Thomas de Quincey, Robert Browning, Emily Brontë and Matthew Arnold. All believed in God, but experienced difficulty in communicating with Him.

Reviews:

H 235   Culler, A. Dwight. in *Yale Review*, vol. 53, no. 3, Mar. 1964, pp. 440–3.

H 236   Mendel, Sydney. in *Dalhousie Review*, vol. 44, no. 1, Spring 1964, pp. 107–9.

H 237   White, John P. in *Blackfriars*, vol. 45, no. 528, June 1964, pp. 279–81.

H 238   Willy, Basil. in *Modern Language Review*, vol. 59, no. 3, July 1964, pp. 467–8.

H 239   Taylor, Griffin. in *Sewanee Review*, vol. 72, no. 4, Oct.–Dec. 1964, pp. 698–709.

H 240   Oldfield, Sybil. in *Victorian Studies*, vol. 8, Dec. 1964, pp. 195–6.

H 241   Spender, Stephen. The modern necessity. *in his* The struggle of the modern. London, Hamish Hamilton, 1963. pp. 98–109.

Comparison of G M H and D. H. Lawrence.

H 242   Vendler, Helen Hennessy. Yeats's *Vision* and the later plays. Cambridge (Mass.), Harvard University Press, 1963. ix, 286 pp.

See particularly p. 58. A brief but perceptive comparison of Hopkins's concept of 'haecceitas' and Yeats's 'Daimon' theory; thus contrasting the two poets' ideas of selfhood in inanimate things.

1964

H 243   Andreach, Robert J. Gerard Manley Hopkins. *in his* Studies in structure: the stages of the spiritual life in four modern authors. London, Burns & Oates, 1964. pp. 12–39.

G M H's spiritual development as reflected in his poems, viewed from a literary standpoint rather than a theological one.

Reviews:

H 244   Anon. in *Times Literary Supplement*, 5 Aug. 1965, p. 680.

H245   Meath, Gerard. in *Tablet*, vol. 219, no. 6540, 25 Sept. 1965, p. 1062.

H246   Boyle, Robert. in *James Joyce Quarterly*, vol. 3, no. 1, Fall 1965, pp. 77–81.

H247   Shaw, Priscilla W. in *Yale Review*, vol. 55, no. 2, Dec. 1965, pp. 310–12.

H248   Bowra, C. M. In general and particular. London, Weidenfeld & Nicolson, 1964. vii, 248 pp.
   See pp. 41–2. Brief comments on G M H's rise to posthumous fame, pointing out that this has been accelerated by the fine quality of the better Hopkins scholarship.

H249   Broadbent, J. B. Hopkins. *in his* Poetic love. London, Chatto & Windus, 1964. pp. 99–104.
   Comparison of G M H with Donne, and discussion of his poetry as religious *love* poetry. Very original and interesting.

H250   Evans, Ifor. A short history of English literature. *2nd edition.* London, MacGibbon & Kee, 1964. 234 pp.
   See pp. 66–7. Brief general comment.

H251   Fraser, G. S. The modern writer and his world. *New edition.* London, Andre Deutsch, 1964. 426 pp.
   See particularly pp. 294–7. General critical comment.

H252   Gross, Harvey. Gerard Manley Hopkins. *in his* Sound and form in modern poetry . . . Ann Arbor, The University of Michigan Press, 1964. pp. 88–96.
   A study of G M H's prosody, rhythm, and scansion.

H253   *Howarth, R. G. Robert Bridges and Gerard Manley Hopkins. *in his* A pot of gillyflowers: studies and notes. Capetown, University of Capetown, 1964. pp. 72–9.

H254   Legouis, Émile, *and* Cazamian, Louis. A history of English literature. *Revised edition.* London, J. M. Dent and Sons, Ltd., 1964. xxiii, 1469 pp.
   See p. 1441–3. Brief general comment.

1965

H255   Downes, David A. Victorian portraits: Hopkins and Pater. New York, Bookman Associates, 1965. 176 pp.

A study contrasting the two men and attempting to show what they had in common.

Reviews:

H256   Pick, John. in *Renascence*, vol. 18, no. 1, Autumn 1965, p. 53.

H257   DeLaura, David J. in *Victorian Studies*, vol. 9, no. 3, Mar. 1966, pp. 282–3.

H258   Lemon, Lee T. The partial critics. London, Oxford University Press, 1965. xi, 273 pp.

See particularly pp. 67–8.

H259   Preminger, Alex, *and others, editors*. Encyclopaedia of poetry and poetics. Princeton, N.J., Princeton University Press, 1965. xxiv, 906 pp.

Concise summaries of special topics important in Hopkins studies: see, for example, 'Sprung Rhythm', 'Counterpoint', 'Cynghanedd', and so on. G M H is often cited as an illustrative example.

H260   Scott, A. F. Current literary terms: a concise dictionary of their origin and use. London, Macmillan, 1965. vii, 324 pp.

G M H's work provides nine of the examples and definitions.

H261   Woodhouse, A. S. P. The poet and his faith: religion and poetry in England from Spenser to Eliot and Auden. Chicago, University of Chicago Press, 1965. xii, 304 pp.

See particularly pp. 241–9.

1966

H262   Bender, Todd K. Gerard Manley Hopkins: the classical background and critical reception of his work. Baltimore, Johns Hopkins Press, 1966. ix, 172 pp.

A discussion of the critical reception of G M H's work and an attempt to provide precedents for the structure and imagery of his verse in Greek and Latin writers. Prints a previously unpublished note on Thucydides by G M H, but as criticism this book is very uneven. For a full description and reviews, see B249.

H263   Crutwell, Patrick. The English sonnet. London, Longmans, Green & Co., 1966. 56 pp. (Writers and their Work, no. 191.)
See pp. 48–51. Brief comments on G M H's sonnets, showing how his practice reflected his theories.

H264   Fowler, Roger, *editor*. Essays on style and language. London, Routledge & Kegan Paul, 1966. ix, 188 pp.
See pp. 93–5, 149. Brief comments on G M H's use of rhythm, and on his linguistic style.

H265   Hartman, Geoffrey H. Hopkins: a collection of critical essays. Englewood Cliffs, N.J.; Prentice-Hall, Inc., 1966. vii, 182 pp. (Twentieth Century Views.)
An anthology of selected classics of Hopkins criticism and selected modern essays, including whole or partial reprints of I233, I527, H29, H89, H126, H137d, H169, H186, H232, H234.

Review :
H266   Bellas, Ralph A. in *Thought*, vol. 42, no. 164, Spring 1967, pp. 131–2.
For other reviews, see A157, I683.

H267   Hunter, Jim. Gerard Manley Hopkins. London, Evans Brothers Limited, 1966. 160 pp. (Literature in Perspective.)
A short general introduction. Hardback and paperback editions published simultaneously.

H268   Lees, Francis Noel. Gerard Manley Hopkins. New York, Columbia University Press, 1966. 48 pp. (Columbia Essays on Modern Writers, 21.)
An excellent introductory essay. Reviewed in I681.

H269   Moynihan, William T. The craft and art of Dylan Thomas. Ithaca, Cornell University Press, 1966. xvi, 304 pp.
See particularly pp. 87–8. 'Thomas's clauses tend to get detached from his sentences. This is not the case with Hopkins, where in the most headlong hectic rush of his language the proper subordination usually remains clear. (Obviously this is a stylistic distinction which has great semantic and thematic significance for the two poets.)'

H270 Press, John. The fire and the fountain: an essay on poetry. London, Methuen & Co. Ltd., 1966. 255 pp.

G M H *passim.*

H271 Stowell, H. E. An introduction to English literature. London, Longmans, 1966. xi, 192 pp.

See pp. 162–3. Brief general comment.

H272 Temple, Ruth Z., *and* Tucker, Martin. A library of literary criticism; modern British literature. Vol. 2, H.-P. New York, Ungar, 1966. xxxii, 510 pp.

See pp. 41–6. Seven passages of G M H criticism, covering 1926–63.

H273 Walcutt, Charles Child, *and* Whitesell, J. Edwin, *editors.* The Explicator cyclopaedia. Vol. 1. Modern poetry. Chicago, Quadrangle Books, 1966. xviii, 366 pp.

See pp. 157–74. A selection of critical articles on G M H from *Explicator.*

1967

H274 Baker, William E. The strange and the familiar: Hopkins and Yeats. *in his* Syntax in English poetry, 1870–1930. Berkeley and Los Angeles, University of California Press, 1967. pp. 84–94. (Perspectives in Criticism, 18.)

Detailed comparison of the two poets' use of syntactic innovation, through analysis of verse sentences chosen from their work.

H275 Boyle, Robert. Hopkins, Gerard Manley. *in* New Catholic encyclopaedia, vol. 7. New York, McGraw-Hill Book Company, 1967. pp. 144–7.

A short general survey, well above the usual 'encyclopaedia-entry' standards.

H276 Brophy, Brigid, *and others.* Gerard Manley Hopkins: poems. *in* Fifty works of English literature we could do without. London, Rapp & Carroll, 1967. pp. 97–8.

'Hopkins's is the poetry of a mental cripple. Sympathise as one might with his confusion, with the absurd struggle that went on within him between priest and poet, it is impossible not to end by feeling completely exasperated with the disastrous mess he made of his life.'

H277 Buckley, Jerome Hamilton. The triumph of time. Cambridge (Mass.), The Belknap Press of Harvard University Press, 1967. xi, 187 pp.
See particularly pp. 129–30, 139–40.

H278 *Milward, Peter. Christian themes in English literature. Tokyo, Kenkyusha, 1967. xvi, 269 pp.
See pp. 33–6, 84–7, 107–10, 135–6, 154–6.

1968

H279 Ball, Patricia M. The central self: a study in Romantic and Victorian imagination. London, The Athlone Press, 1968. 236 pp.
See pp. 223–6. 'Although he is theologically unique among the poets of his century, Hopkins, in the nature of his creative drive and his goals, is representative, not a maverick.'

H280 Buckley, Vincent. Poetry and the sacred. London, Chatto & Windus, 1968. 244 pp.
G M H *passim*.

H281 *Castle, Edgar. The poetry of Gerard Manley Hopkins. Adelaide, 1968. 57 pp.
An introduction for schools, with background material, discussion, and questions.

H282 Chapman, Raymond. The Victorian debate: English literature and society, 1832–1901. London, Weidenfeld & Nicholson, 1968. 377 pp.
See pp. 260, 266–9.

H283 Daiches, David. A study of literature for readers and critics. London, Andre Deutsch, 1968. 208 pp.
G M H *passim*.

H284 Donoghue, Denis. Hopkins, 'The World's body'. *in his* The ordinary universe. London, Faber & Faber, 1968. pp. 78–89.
'The special problem of Hopkins's poetry can be marked quite simply: what happens when the dapple is at an end? When a poet

invokes nature as the mediating term between Self and God, he faces an incipient ambiguity: is God naturalised, or is nature deified?'

H285   Earnshaw, H. G. Gerard Manley Hopkins. *in his* Modern writers: a guide to twentieth-century literature in the English language. Edinburgh, W. & R. Chambers, 1968. pp. 97–100.

H286   Fairchild, Hoxie Neale. Religious trends in English poetry. Vol. VI: 1920–65 . . . New York and London, Columbia University Press, 1968. xxi, 535 pp.
    G M H *passim.*

H287   Holland, Norman N. The dynamics of literary response. New York, Oxford University Press, 1968. xviii, 378 pp.
    See particularly pp. 237–8, 241. 'Hopkins uses religious ideas to transcend his anal images . . .'

H288   Hollis, Christopher. A history of the Jesuits. London, Weidenfeld & Nicholson, 1968. 284 pp.
    G M H *passim.*

H289   Inglis, Fred. An essential discipline: an introduction to literary criticism. London, Methuen Educational Ltd., 1968. xiv, 272 pp.
    See pp. 104–6. 'Certainly, there is much more genuinely creative genius in Hopkins's work than in any contemporaries' . . . But Hopkins's manner cannot be taken over piecemeal, for it abundantly demonstrates a new kind of danger to the poet: that of working too privately.'

H290   Jones, Glyn. The dragon has two tongues: essays on Anglo-Welsh writers and writing. London, J. M. Dent & Sons Ltd., 1968. ix, 221 pp.
    See particularly pp. 179–82. Discussion of G M H's possible influence on Dylan Thomas.

H291   Lester, John A., *Jr.* Journey through despair, 1880–1914: transformations in British literary culture. Princeton, Princeton University Press, 1968. xxiii, 211 pp.
    G M H *passim.*

H292   Levine, George, *and* Madden, William, *editors*. The art of
Victorian prose. New York, Oxford University Press, 1968. xxi,
378 pp.
   GMH *passim.*

H293   McChesney, Donald. A Hopkins commentary . . . London,
University of London Press, Ltd., 1968. viii, 195 pp.
   A detailed explanatory commentary on the main poems, 1876–89.

Reviews:
H294   Tucker, Bernard. in *Month*, vol. 41 (n.s.), no. 6, June 1969,
pp. 378–9.
H295   Dunne, Tom. in *Library Review*, vol. 22, no. 3, Autumn 1969,
pp. 165–6.
   For another review, see M230.

H296   MacKenzie, Norman H. Hopkins. Edinburgh, Oliver & Boyd,
1968. 128 pp. (Writers and Critics.)
   An excellent general introduction, with emphasis on textual questions.

Review:
H297   Dunne, Tom. in *Library Review*, vol. 21, no. 7, Autumn 1968,
pp. 372–3.
   For another review, see I694.

H298   Johnson, Wendell Stacy. Gerard Manley Hopkins: the poet as
Victorian. Ithaca, New York; Cornell University Press, 1968. viii,
178 pp.
   A study of GMH's poems in the context of the Victorian attitudes
which they reflect, with particular reference to Victorian concepts of
self and nature.
   For reviews, see B259, B260, B266.

H299   Schneider, Elisabeth W. The dragon in the gate: studies in the
poetry of G. M. Hopkins. Berkeley and Los Angeles, University of
California Press, 1968. xiv, 224 pp. (Perspectives in Criticism, 20.)
   Essays on central aspects of GMH's work.
   For a review, see I712.

H300   Thomas, Dylan. Poet in the making: the notebooks of Dylan Thomas, edited by Ralph Maud. London, J. M. Dent & Sons, Ltd., 1968. 364 pp.

> *See* pp. 15–16. A letter from Thomas to Henry Treece, in which Thomas disclaims any influence by GMH. 'I've never been conscious of Hopkins's influence . . .'

1969

H301   *Borrello, Alfred. A concordance of the poetry in English of Gerard Manley Hopkins. New Jersey, Scarecrow Press, 1969. 780 pp. Computer-programmed; based on P4.

H302   Grigson, Geoffrey. A passionate science. *in his* Poems and poets. London, Macmillan, 1969. pp. 124–46.

> An essay based on H179.

H303   Huddleston, Trevor. First annual Hopkins sermon; preached at St. John's Parish Church, Stratford, Essex, 18 October 1969, on the occasion of the celebration of the 125th anniversary of the birth of Gerard Manley Hopkins. London, The Hopkins Society, 1969. 6 pp.

H304   Milward, Peter. A commentary on the sonnets of Gerard Manley Hopkins. Tokyo, The Hokuseido Press, 1969. xii, 150 pp.

> A detailed commentary on 31 sonnets.

1970

H305   Chapple, J. A. V. Documentary and imaginative literature, 1880–1920. London, Blandford Press, 1970. 395 pp.

> *See particularly* pp. 370–6. General critical comment.

H306   *Dilligan, Robert J., *and* Bender, Todd K. A concordance to the English poetry of Gerard Manley Hopkins. Madison, University of Wisconsin Press, 1970. 321 pp.

> Computer-programmed; based on P4.

H307   Hardy, Barbara. Forms and feelings in the sonnets of Gerard Manley Hopkins. London, The Hopkins Society, 1970. 14 pp. (The Hopkins Society First Annual Lecture.)

Hopkins does not simply *name* feelings in his sonnets, he makes the reader *experience* them. The form and construction of the sonnets contribute to this effect; especially when the form is appropriate to the accumulation of feeling.

H308   Robson, W. W. Modern English literature. London, Oxford University Press, 1970. xv, 172 pp.

See pp. 60–3, 120–4. General critical comment.

H309   Mariani, Paul L. A commentary on the complete poems of Gerard Manley Hopkins. Ithaca and London, Cornell University Press, 1970. xxvii, 361 pp.

Includes all main poems and most fragments.

SECTION 1

PERIODICAL ARTICLES AND REVIEWS

THIS section is a chronological list of critical articles dealing with G M H wholly or in part. Reviews of books about him are included, unless they are merely appendages to the books concerned, when they are placed with the book in the appropriate section. All reviews of primary works and of books containing the first publication of work by G M H are also placed with the books, in Sections A and B. Critical articles dealing with a single poem by G M H are placed in Section K, but articles dealing with groups of poems are placed in this section.

1909

I1   Brégy, Katherine. Gerard Hopkins: an epitaph and an appreciation. *Catholic World*, vol. 88, no. 526, Jan. 1909, pp. 433–47.
One of the first substantial critical essays, but written from a firmly religious viewpoint. 'He was essentially a minor poet . . . but . . . he worked his narrow field with completeness and intensity.'

1910

I2   Brégy, Katherine. Coventry Patmore. *Catholic World*, vol. 90, no. 540, Mar. 1910, pp. 796–806.
See p. 803. A brief comment, here given in full: 'Father Gerard Hopkins (who knew the work [Patmore's *The Angel in the House*] in a later edition, which his own criticism had helped to perfect) declared that "to dip into it was like opening a basket of violets." '

1912

I2a   Anon. [Review of H9] *Nation* (London), vol. 11, no. 22, 31 Aug. 1912, p. 810.

Relegates G M H to passing mention after dealing with the other poets discussed in the book: 'The author pays her tribute also to Father Gerard Hopkins.'

I2b   Anon. 'As your own poets said'. *Tablet*, vol. 88 (n.s.), no. 3774, 7 Sept. 1912, p. 367.
Review of H9. Several references to G M H, e.g.: 'Robert Bridges' tribute to his young friend's "great personal charm" is borne out by the portrait which at once interprets and beautifies the text.'

I2c   Anon. Poets at prayer. *Academy and Literature*, vol. 83, no. 2107, 21 Sept. 1912, pp. 367–8.
Review of H9. Some very enthusiastic comments on G M H's poetry. 'Barnfloor and Winepress' is singled out for special praise: 'It is a standing reproach to English criticism that the author of these lines has hitherto received so small a meed of recognition, and it is little less than incredible that no collected edition of the poems of Hopkins has ever been published.'

I2d   Anon. Catholic poets. *Month*, vol. 120, no. 580, Oct. 1912, pp. 439–40.
Review of H9. 'But what of . . . Gerard Hopkins? Is it not an appalment for heaven and earth that so little is being done for him? Here is a writer emancipated from time and tradition. Here is a Prophet, a Martyr, and an Apostle who is at the same time a Poet—and which of us has the chance of reading him?'

I2e   O'N[eill,] G[eorge]. A poet's chantry. *Studies* (Dublin), vol. 1, no. 4, Dec. 1912, pp. 736–8.
Review of H9. Some quite detailed critical comment on G M H, with special reference to Miss Brégy's comparison of him with Crashaw. 'Crashaw was a master of melody. His *Music's Duel* is, perhaps, the most marvellous and delightful *tour de force* in English verse, and there are the more delicate sweetnesses of his "Nativity" and other odes . . . Compared to all this, Father Hopkins' is a tiny harp indeed, and one which was very rarely handled with deftness. It seems strange that judging ears should be excited to any rapture by what she gives us to hear of its notes. To most of us her specimens of this writer seem curiously cacophonous.'

1913

I3 Cornish, Blanche Warre. Digby Dolben. *Dublin Review*, vol. 152,
no. 304, Jan. 1913, pp. 111–31.
See p. 130. Brief comment on G M H and an extract from his letter
to Bridges about Dolben's death (LL1, pp. 16–17) presumably taken
from B20.

I4 Keating, Joseph. The poetry of Father Gerard Hopkins, S.J.
Month, vol. 121, no. 588, June 1913, pp. 643–4.
Includes notes on the MS. of 'Rosa Mystica', and comments on
'Winter with the Gulf Stream'.

1914

I5 Kilmer, Joyce. The poetry of Gerard Manley Hopkins. *Poetry*,
vol. 4, no. 6, Sept. 1914, pp. 241–5.
Critical and biographical essay.

1917

I6 Hone, J. M. Gerard Hopkins. *New Statesman*, vol. 9, no. 218,
9 June 1917, pp. 231–2.
Critical and biographical essay, containing interesting but inaccurate
biographical comment and a little rather unoriginal criticism. Makes
the unsubstantiated assertion that G M H contributed to *Punch*. To
the compiler this seems unlikely, though possible. See also I7 and I8.

I7 Caine, Hall. Gerard Hopkins. *New Statesman*, vol. 9, no. 220,
23 June 1917, p. 277.
A letter replying to Hone (I6) who had remarked on Caine's rejection of some sonnets by G M H from his anthology *Sonnets of three
centuries* (1881). For G M H's own comments on this rejection, see
LL1, pp. 127–8, 132, 162, and LL2, p. 47, 49. Caine here confirms
Professor Abbott's conjecture (LL1, p. 128, footnote 2) that the
rejection was advised by D. G. Rossetti. See also I534.

I8 'Dubliner'. Gerard Hopkins. *New Statesman*, vol. 9, no. 220, 23 June
1917, p. 277.

A letter pointing out that Hone (16) had wrongly inserted a comma between 'Wind-beat' and 'whitebeam' in quoting 'The Starlight Night'. Evidence of close and careful reading of G M H.

1918

I9   Young, E. Brett. The poetry of Gerard Hopkins. *To-day* (London), vol. 2, no. 11, Jan. 1918, pp. 191–6.

Biographical and critical essay, containing some of the most perceptive criticism published in England up to this time. 'Hopkins was both draughtsman and poet, and I think his few critics have failed to realise how far the verbal complexity is the outcome of a collision between the two arts . . . Phrases like "blear-all black," . . . show his impatience with a language that will not fit itself to niceties of colour and movement.'

I10   Hogan, Aloysius J. Father Hopkins' poetry. *America*, vol. 18, no. 19, 16 Feb. 1918, pp. 477–8.

'His excessive fondness for unusual words caused a certain obscurity to creep into his later poems . . .'

1919

I11   Trappes-Lomax, M[ichael]. The Literary Club. *Stonyhurst Magazine*, vol. 14, no. 220, Feb. 1919, p. 632.

'Mr. D'Arcy read a paper, the object of which was at first hard to discern, on the poetry of Father Gerard Manley Hopkins, S.J. He first gave the impression of defending a poet whom none desired to attack, but it eventually became apparent that he was extolling poems which none had read.' Further comment follows. Father M. C. D'Arcy has confirmed, in a letter to the compiler, that he was the 'Mr. D'Arcy' referred to here.

I12   [Kent, W. H.] Et caetera. *Tablet*, vol. 133, no. 4119, 19 Apr. 1919, p. 484.

Comments on the scarcity of P1 in the bookshops, and remarks on Bridges's 'Preface to Notes'. 'Spiritual barbed wire still separates [Bridges] from the poet he has edited . . . with such peculiar devotion.' The authorship of this entry has been confirmed by Mr. J. J. Dwyer, in a letter to the compiler.

1920

113   MacS., J. [Review of H15] *Irish Ecclesiastical Record* (Dublin),
vol. 15 (5th series), Jan. 1920, pp. 83–6.

'Few will disagree with what Father O'Neill writes concerning the
style of Gerard Hopkins ... He casts his words about, forgetting that
when using an uninflected language this cannot be done unduly
without involving the sense in obscurity.'

114   Anon. [Review of H15] *New Statesman*, vol. 14, no. 357, 14 Feb.
1920, p. 564.

'The rest of the book is occupied in discussing the poetry of Aubrey
de Vere, William Allingham, Thomas Boyd, Gerard Hopkins ... the
essay on Gerard Hopkins is the most interesting, and it could hardly
fail to be so, for Gerard Hopkins is far the most interesting poet of
the four.'

115   M., C. Some recent essays. *Bookman* (London), vol. 57, no. 342,
Mar. 1920, pp. 213–14.

Review of H15. 'The [essay on GMH] provides a complement to
the present Poet Laureate's edition of Father Hopkins's work that
simple justice required should be forthcoming from somewhere.'

116   Anon. [Review of H15] *Tablet*, vol. 136, no. 4171, 17 Apr. 1920,
p. 517.

'The most valuable paper in this collection is undoubtedly the last, on
Father Gerard Hopkins, S.J. . . .' More than half the review is
concerned with GMH.

117   Anon. [Review of H15] *Times Literary Supplement*, 13 May 1920,
p. 306.

'Of the essays on individual poets the most interesting is that on
Gerard Hopkins, a remarkable but (in point of expression) extra-
ordinarily perverse genius.'

1923

118   Porter, Alan. Difficult beauty. *Spectator*, vol. 130, no. 4933, 13
Jan. 1923, p. 66.

Perceptive critical essay; perhaps the first to stress that GMH's
obscurity is integral to his style and therefore repays close attention.

1924

I19   Gwynn, Aubrey. A daughter of Coventry Patmore. *Studies* (Dublin), vol. 13, no. 51, Sept. 1924, pp. 443–56.

Review of *A daughter of Coventry Patmore: Sister Mary Christina, S.H.C.J.*, by 'A Religious of the Society of the Holy Child Jesus' (1924). G M H is mentioned on p. 450. 'That Sister Mary Christina had a special vocation as a mystic is plain from her life. That she inherited those mystical tendencies from her father will be no news to those who have read Coventry Patmore's ... short "Autobiography", which he wrote in 1888 at the request of his Jesuit friend and fellow-poet, Father Gerard Hopkins.' This 'Autobiography' does not seem to have appeared in book form, but was printed in B11, vol. 2, pp. 41–56. It was certainly written before 1888, as G M H commented briefly on it in 1885 (see FL2, p. 365).

1925

I20   *Crowley, Austin. Gerard Hopkins. *Boston College Stylus*, vol. 38, no. 4, Jan. 1925, pp. 239–41.

I21   *Lawlor, William J. A Victorian Jesuit and his muse. *Georgetown College Journal*, vol. 53, no. 5, Mar. 1925, pp. 248–51.

1926

I22   Richards, I. A. Gerard Hopkins. *Dial* (New York), vol. 81, Sept. 1926, pp. 195–203.

'The more the poems are studied, the clearer it becomes that their oddities are always deliberate. They may be aberrations: they are not blemishes.' Some of G M H's poems are examined from this viewpoint. This essay is very important. Apart from its merits as criticism, its influence (because of Richards's status) was undoubtedly beneficial to G M H's reputation, especially in academic circles. See also I24.

1927

I23   Mirsky, D. S. [Review of *Charles M. Doughty*, by Barker Fairley.] *London Mercury*, vol. 16, no. 95, Sept. 1927, p. 547.

Brief comparison of GMH's metrical practice with Doughty's. Both poets were 'effective workers in destroying the "Spenserian" fluency of English verse.'

124 Richards, I. A. Gerard Hopkins. *Cambridge Review*, vol. 49, no. 1197, 28 Oct. 1927, pp. 49–51.
A shortened version of 122, probably no less influential. 'Few writers have dealt more directly with their experience or been more candid. Perhaps to do this must invite the charge of oddity . . . Like other writers he had to practise and perfect his craft. The little that has been written about him has already said too much about this aspect.'

125 'Pro Bono Publico'. Gerard Hopkins. *Cambridge Review*, vol. 49, no. 1198, 4 Nov. 1927, p. 75.
A letter, making the dogmatic but completely unsubstantiated assertion that a poem called 'The Kestrel' (quoted in full) was written by GMH, and should have been included in P1. 'Though this unaccountable omission may have been rectified elsewhere, I still find there are many students unaware of the existence of this significant poem.' A detailed explication of the poem follows. The editor remarks drily that 'As our ingenious correspondent gives no details of sources, we doubt the genuineness of the ascription.' This is the earliest, and also the most extreme, example of 'Hopkinsese' noted by the compiler.

1928

126 Brown, Alec. Gerard Hopkins and associative form. *Dublin Magazine*, vol. 3 (n.s.), no. 2, Apr.–June 1928, pp. 6–20.
'In the poetic art, extravagance, exaggeration of content is easier forgiven than extravagance and exaggeration of form. Hopkins erred on the wrong side.'

127 *Lahey, Gerald F. Gerard Manley Hopkins. *America*, vol. 39, no. 26, 6 Oct. 1928, pp. 619–20.

1929

128 N[orth], J[essica]. N[elson]. Quality in madness. *Poetry*, vol. 34, no. 5, Aug. 1929, pp. 270–3.

Critical note. 'Hopkins was born too early to be one of the modernists of today. He would otherwise have been the master of them all.'

129   Thomas, Dylan. Modern poetry. *Swansea Grammar School Magazine*, vol. 26, no. 3, Dec. 1929, pp. 82–4.

'The most important element that characterises our poetical modernity is freedom . . . of form, of structure, of imagery and of idea. It had its roots in the obscurity of Gerard Manley Hopkins' lyrics, where, though more often than not common metres were recognised, the language was violated and estranged by the efforts of compressing the already unfamiliar imagery.' This suggests something of Thomas's attitude to G M H's poems at a time when he might have been most receptive to their influence. Thomas himself denied being influenced by G M H at all: see H 300.

1930

130   *Barrett, Alfred. 'As the air we breathe.' *Ave Maria*, vol. 31 (n.s.), no. 10, 8 Mar. 1930, pp. 289–91.

131   Binsse, H. L. Gerard Manley Hopkins. *Saturday Review of Literature*, vol. 7, no. 3, 9 Aug. 1930, pp. 33–4.

Biographical and critical essay. 'The influence of Hopkins has had, and will have, an integrating effect on modern poetry . . .' See also the Oxford University Press advertisement on p. 46, entitled 'The Amen Corner'. This mentions the 'daily enquiries' about G M H's published works received by O.U.P., with the comment: 'Perhaps the enthusiasm of T. S. Eliot, Louis Untermeyer and the late Robert Bridges is bearing fruit.' The compiler has found no published comment on G M H by Eliot which could be called enthusiastic.

132   [Kunitz, Stanley J.] Dilly Tante observes. *Wilson Bulletin*, vol. 5, no. 1, Sept. 1930, p. 61.

'I know of no young poet of talent in this country today whose face is not turned to [Hopkins], though it will be many generations before a popular audience will even know his name.'

133   [Leahy, Maurice.] The late Poet Laureate and Father Gerard Hopkins. *Carmina*, no. 2, Sept. 1930, p. 22.

A letter to Leahy from Bridges, concerning the publication of P 2.

134 *Burke, Molly M. Gerard Manley Hopkins. *Commonweal*, vol. 12, no. 19, 10 Sept. 1930, pp. 459–60.

135 Z[abel], M. D. Gerard Manley Hopkins: poetry as experiment and unity. *Poetry*, vol. 37, no. 3, Dec. 1930, pp. 152–61.
Critical essay. 'The difficulties in his verse will probably never disappear, but as long as they confront readers they will elicit the creative effort . . . which remains the first demand of absolute art.'

136 [entry deleted]

1931

137 *Coblentz, Catherine Cate. A Catholic poet comes into his own. *Ave Maria*, vol. 33 (n.s.), no. 6, 7 Feb. 1931, pp. 161–3.

138 Hope, Felix. Gerard Manley Hopkins. *Irish Ecclesiastical Record* (Dublin), vol. 37 (5th series), June 1931, pp. 561–70.
This critical essay is a collection of unacknowledged extracts from other critics' work, but it brings conveniently together a number of valuable insights on G M H.

1932

139 Winters, Yvor. An appreciation of Robert Bridges. *Hound and Horn*, vol. 5, no. 2, Jan.–Mar. 1932, pp. 321–7.
'The qualities that have won Hopkins almost immediate recognition during the past few years are, I fear, the very reasons for his limitations and his definite inferiority to Bridges.' This theme is developed briefly but emphatically.

140 D'Arcy, M. C. Gerard Manley Hopkins, S.J. *Archivum Historicum Societatis Iesu*, vol. 1, no. 1, Jan.–May 1932, pp. 118–22.
'Somewhat to their surprise . . . the English public are being told by the best critics of the day . . . that a Jesuit who died over forty years ago must be regarded as one of England's great poets.' This article is outstandingly perceptive.

141 Roberts, Michael. Notes on English poets. *Poetry*, vol. 39, no. 5, Feb. 1932, pp. 271–9.
Some comments on G M H's influence on twentieth-century poets.

142   Haugh, Irene. Gerald [*sic*] Manley Hopkins. *Irish Monthly*, vol. 60, no. 706, Apr. 1932, pp. 220–7.
General critical essay, with little attention to technique. Biased in GMH's favour by religious outlook.

143   Gary, Franklin. [Review of H29] *Symposium*, vol. 3, no. 4, Oct. 1932, pp. 521–34.
GMH *passim*.

144   James, Stanley B. The triumph of the poet. *Irish Monthly*, vol. 60, no. 713, Nov. 1932, pp. 678–83.
A rather feeble essay on the relationship between religion and poetry, written from a Catholic viewpoint. GMH *passim*.

145   *Burke, Francis. The muse called grace. *Measure*, vol. 1, no. 1, Christmas 1932, pp. 27–31. (See I55.)

1933

146   Anon. Donne and Hopkins. *Poetry Review*, vol. 24, 1933, pp. 464–5.
Brief review of H36 and of an edition of Donne's poems, with some comments on the two poets' affinities with each other.

147   Read, Herbert. Poetry and belief in Gerard Manley Hopkins. *New Verse*, no. 1, Jan. 1933, pp. 11–15.
The effect of GMH's religious belief on the nature of his poetry. 'True originality is due to a conflict between sensibility and belief: both exist in the personality, but in counter-action.'

148   Anon. Poetry in the present. *Times Literary Supplement*, 9 Feb. 1933, pp. 81–2.
Review of H30, with comments on Herbert Read's attitudes to GMH.

149   Tierney, Michael. Gerard Hopkins's metres. *Times Literary Supplement*, 16 Feb. 1933, p. 108.
A letter suggesting some sources for GMH's metrical theories. See also I50–3.

150 Read, Herbert. Gerard Hopkins's metres. *Times Literary Supplement*, 23 Feb. 1933, p. 127.
   Comment on GMH's metrical theories. See also 149, 151–3.

151 Stanier, R. S. Gerard Hopkins's metres. *Times Literary Supplement*, 23 Feb. 1933, p. 127.
   Comment on GMH's metrical theories. See also 149, 150, 152, 153.

152 House, Humphry. Gerard Hopkins's metres. *Times Literary Supplement*, 2 Mar. 1933, p. 147.
   Comment on GMH's metrical theories. See also 149–51, 153.

153 Tierney, Michael. Gerard Hopkins's metres. *Times Literary Supplement*, 9 Mar. 1933, p. 167.
   Final word in the correspondence. See also 149–52.

154 Phillipson, Wulstan. Gerard Manley Hopkins. *Downside Review*, vol. 51 (vol. 32 n.s.), no. 146, Apr. 1933, pp. 326–48.
   Biographical and critical essay, with notes on the state of GMH's reputation *circa* 1930.

155 Evans, Richard X. The poetry of Gerard Manley Hopkins. *Measure* (Georgetown University), Summer 1933, pp. 25–9.
   A critical essay written from a firmly Catholic viewpoint. *Measure* was the journal of the Gerard Manley Hopkins Poetry Society, founded at Georgetown University, Washington, D.C., in December 1932. Only three issues appeared. This is the only article in them specifically concerned with GMH.

156 K., B. [Review of *Canons of giant art*, by Sacheverell Sitwell.] *Blackfriars*, vol. 14, no. 161, Aug. 1933, pp. 712–13.
   Includes a brief comparison of GMH and Sacheverell Sitwell. 'It is interesting to compare Mr. Sitwell with a poet like Gerard Manley Hopkins, whose metrical innovations arose from the desire of a discipline more flexible, but more tense and vital than common iambics will give . . .'

157 Kelly, Bernard. The joy of chastity in the poetry of Gerard Manley Hopkins. *Blackfriars*, vol. 14, no. 163, Oct. 1933, pp. 833–6.

GMH's chastity was not only a self-imposed discipline, but is fundamental to a proper understanding of his work.

158   *Lahey, Gerald F. Gerard Manley Hopkins. *Commonweal*, vol. 18, no. 25, 20 Oct. 1933, pp. 581–4.

159   Plomer, William. Gerard Manley Hopkins. *Spectator*, vol. 151, no. 5499, 17 Nov. 1933, p. 712.
      Review of H 36. 'There are readers who will differ sharply from Miss Phare when she calls "The Wreck of the Deutschland" shallow . . .'

160   Clarke, Austin. Father Hopkins and James Joyce. *Observer*, 26 Nov. 1933, p. 9.
      Review of H 36. 'His work, apart from its moments of freedom, so often seems that of a marvellous amateur rather than a complete poet.'

161   Browne, Wynyard. Introduction to Hopkins. *Bookman* (London), vol. 85, no. 507, Dec. 1933, pp. 228–9.
      Review of H 36. 'Although Hopkins was probably the most important poet of the nineteenth century, until Dr. Bridges's comparatively recent edition of his poems he remained almost unknown. Since then he has been a primary influence on the best of the younger English poets and an object of awe and argument in the universities.'

162   Scott, Michael M. Gerard Manley Hopkins, S.J.: II. *Irish Monthly*, vol. 61, no. 726, Dec. 1933, pp. 786–92.
      A general critical essay. For the first (biographical) part, see G 44.

1934

163   *Cock, Albert A. [Review of H 36] *Wessex*, vol. 3, 1934, pp. 95–7.

164   Anon. [Review of H 36] *Month*, vol. 163, no. 835, Jan. 1934, p. 93.
      'Her defence is an able piece of writing . . . nevertheless, except for those who, like Miss Phare, have time and wit enough to unravel the thread of his inspiration, we fear that "the strangeness of his vocabulary and the involutions of his syntax" will continue to frighten off possible readers.'

165 Pound, Ezra. Mr. Housman at Little Bethel. *Criterion*, vol. 13, no. 51, Jan. 1934, pp. 216–24.
A review of Housman's *The name and nature of poetry*, with two brief references to G M H's poetic method.

166 [House, Humphry.] Gerard Manley Hopkins. *Times Literary Supplement*, 25 Jan. 1934, p. 57.
Review of H 36. Interesting and original critical comment. Reprinted in H 180.

167 Deutsch, Babette. Gerard Manley Hopkins. *New York Herald Tribune Books*, 28 Jan. 1934, p. 2.
Review of H 36. 'In dealing with Hopkins' work the question of belief is so fundamental that one could wish that his critics would state frankly their own position.'

168 Fairley, Barker. A survey and commentary. *Canadian Forum*, vol. 14, no. 161, Feb. 1934, pp. 186–7.
Review of H 36. 'The approach to Hopkins through English poetry is not enough, he must be approached also as a modernist through all the modernist channels in art and letters . . .'

169 Benét, William Rose. Round about Parnassus. *Saturday Review of Literature*, vol. 10, no. 32, 24 Feb. 1934, p. 508.
Short note on H 36. 'Miss Phare considers Hopkins a major poet. I do not. He was a fine eccentric poet for the few, but there is certainly a lack of proportion in canonising him . . .'

170 Tierney, Michael. [Review of H 36] *Studies* (Dublin), vol. 23, no. 89, Mar. 1934, pp. 180–1.
'Hopkins has been a very powerful influence on the "modern" school of current English poetry, and his doctrine of "inscape" has a close resemblance to their "poetic logic".'

171 Auden, W. H. [Review of H 36] *Criterion*, vol. 13, no. 52, Apr. 1934, pp. 497–500.
An attack not on G M H, but on the system of criticism represented by Miss Phare.

172   *Downey, Harris. A pioneer of poetry. *Commonweal*, vol. 19, no. 24, 13 Apr. 1934, pp. 667–8.
      Review of H 36.

173   *Meagher, Margaret C. [Review of H 36] *Catholic World*, vol. 139, no. 832, July 1934, p. 499.

1935

174   Grigson, Geoffrey. [Review of H 50] *Criterion*, vol. 14, no. 55, Jan. 1935, pp. 326–9.
      See pp. 328–9. Refutation of two comments on G M H by C. Day Lewis: See H 50.

175   Young, G. M. Tunes ancient and modern. *Life and Letters*, vol. 11, no. 62, Feb. 1935, pp. 544–54.
      G M H *passim*. 'Hopkins's principles and practice were a challenge to the Muse on two points: the paeon and the collision of stress. The result is that his counterpoint tears through the tune altogether: his rhythm is sprung until it founders . . .'

176   Gallagher, Donald A. The originality of Gerard Manley Hopkins. *Fleur de Lis* (St. Louis University), vol. 34, no. 2, Mar. 1935, pp. 34–44.
      Biographical and critical essay, written from a strongly Catholic viewpoint.

177   Abbott, Claude Colleer. Gerard Manley Hopkins. *Times Literary Supplement*, 21 Mar. 1935, p. 176.
      A request for information for FL, giving an interesting list of possible correspondents of G M H.

178   Anon. This number. *New Verse*, no. 14, Apr. 1935, p. 2.
      A note on the purpose of the special Hopkins number. 'It is time to begin on the real difficulties in Hopkins . . . this number, in some degree, is intended as such a beginning.'

179   Brémond, André. Art and inspiration. *New Verse*, no. 14, Apr. 1935, pp. 5–12.

This essay investigates the nature of the inspiration in G M H's poetry in relation to the artistic working-out of the poems.

180 Devlin, Christopher. Hopkins and Duns Scotus. *New Verse*, no. 14, Apr. 1935, pp. 12–15.

A brief but valuable account of the Scotist theory of knowledge and its influence on G M H. See also I113

181 Griffith, Ll. Wyn. The Welsh influence. *New Verse*, no. 14, Apr. 1935, pp. 27–9.

'Many Welsh poets have written in English, but none has dared to carry into another language . . . characteristics of Welsh diction: it has been left to Hopkins to acknowledge in this form his debt to Wales.'

182 Grigson, Geoffrey. 1. Blood or bran. *New Verse*, no. 14, Apr. 1935, pp. 21–3.

Traces an interest in bloodshed in G M H's poems.

183 Grigson, Geoffrey. 2. Hopkins and Hopkinsese. *New Verse*, no. 14, Apr. 1935, pp. 24–6.

G M H's use of language. 'His language may be rich and thick, but in his best work he does spread his meaning without making it weak.'

184 House, Humphry. A note on Hopkins's religious life. *New Verse*, no. 14, Apr. 1935, pp. 3–5.

Brief explanation of G M H's religious observances as a practising Jesuit priest.

185 MacNeice, Louis. A comment. *New Verse*, no. 14, Apr. 1935, pp. 26–7.

'Hopkins was a poet of many assets, in particular a sharp eye, a precise mind, and an intense religious feeling. It is a pity . . . that he should be thought of primarily as a Jesuit, or . . . a metrical experimenter.'

186 Madge, Charles. What is all this juice? *New Verse*, no. 14, Apr. 1935, pp. 17–21.

An examination of G M H's nature-imagery. 'These images make their appeal straight to the salivary glands . . . Hopkins is fond of an edible and potable nature.'

187   Roberts, Michael. A Hopkins number. *Spectator*, vol. 154, no. 5577, 17 May 1935, p. 844.
A review of *New Verse*, no. 14.

188   *Emerson, Dorothy. Gerard Manley Hopkins. *Scholastic*, vol. 26, 25 May 1935, p. 10.

189   Fairley, Barker. Charles Doughty and modern poetry. *London Mercury*, vol. 32, no. 188, June 1935, pp. 128–37.
Some comparison of G M H with Doughty.

190   T[urnell], G. M. Homage to Gerard Manley Hopkins. *Colosseum*, vol. 2, no. 6, June 1935, pp. 156–8.
Review of *New Verse*, no. 14, with much original critical comment written from a Catholic viewpoint. 'It sometimes strikes one as terrifying to think that we live in a civilization which produced almost contemporaneously the experiences represented by Hopkins and Baudelaire; but are not their similarities after all at least as great as their differences?'

191   *James, Stanley B. The sacrifice of song. *Catholic World*, vol. 141, June 1935, pp. 290–5.

192   Walker, M. E. Four independent men of letters within a tradition. *New York Times Book Review*, 7 July 1935, p. 2.
Review of H 61. Remarks of G M H that 'A nature so sensible to his surroundings could not but suffer a great deal when faced with just the ordinary business of existence.'

193   *Maynard, Theodore. When the pie was opened. *Commonweal*, vol. 22, no. 14, 2 Aug. 1935, pp. 339–41.

194   Vann, Gerald. [Review of H 57] *Colosseum*, vol. 2, no. 7, Sept. 1935, pp. 233–4.
Brief; but has this to say: '. . . is not the whole point of the Hopkins story precisely the tension, the division, if not springing altogether from within, at least coming from without, to the frustration of unity, a tension of such importance as makes this a test case in the discussion of Catholic disorder?'

I95   Roggen, F. N. Gerard Manley Hopkins. *Studies in English Literature* (Tokyo), vol. 15, no. 4, Oct. 1935, pp. 517–34.

This critical essay plagiarised the article by André Brémond in *Études* (M19). Most of it is an English translation of Brémond's French, without acknowledgement. This fact has also been noted by Mellown (J173).

I96   Kelly, Bernard. Hopkins in the nineteen thirties. *G.K.'s Weekly*, vol. 22, no. 552, 10 Oct. 1935, pp. 23–4.

An essay on G M H's style, concerned not so much with matters of technique as with his poetic sensibility in general. 'If there had been about him just one trace of mental sloth, one scrap of ability to put up with the second-rate, the highly accentuated spiritual conflicts of his later poetry might never have arisen. And he might have filled as many volumes as Swinburne and done as much harm.' An animated correspondence followed: see I97–102.

I97   Bennett, Victor. [Letter to the editor] *G.K.'s Weekly*, vol. 22, no. 554, 24 Oct. 1935, p. 70.

Reply to Kelly (I96). Denies that the 'tendencies' in G M H's work were relevant to 1930s poetry. 'Fr. Hopkins is the missing link between Keats and Mr. Joyce.' See also I99–101.

I98   Young, B. A. [Letter to the editor] *G.K.'s Weekly*, vol. 22, no. 554, 24 Oct. 1935, p. 70.

Reply to Kelly (I96). Strong but unreasoned criticism of G M H's poetry. 'I wish Mr. Bernard Kelly could convince me of the greatness of Gerard Manley Hopkins. The twentieth century, which worships oddness for its own sake, accept [*sic*] him as a major prophet; his own, a saner generation, ignored him.' See also I99–101.

I99   Kelly, Bernard. [Letter to the editor] *G.K.'s Weekly*, vol. 22, no. 555, 31 Oct. 1935, p. 86.

Reply to Bennett (I97) and Young (I98). 'Hopkins was a poet, a real live man, not a phase of poetic tendency . . .' See also I102.

I100   Topliss, John. [Letter to the editor] *G.K.'s Weekly*, vol. 22, no. 555, 31 Oct. 1935, p. 86.

A defence of G M H against Bennett (I97) and Young (I98).

1101   Power, Ellen M. [Letter to the editor] *G.K.'s Weekly*, vol. 22, no. 558, 21 Nov. 1935, p. 134.

A defence of GMH against Bennett (197) and Young (198).

1102   Young, B. A. [Letter to the editor] *G.K.'s Weekly*, vol. 22, no. 558, 21 Nov. 1935, p. 134.

Final rejoinder to Kelly (196, 199) unrepentant in condemning GMH. '. . . since Hopkins has proved to be artistically a mule, it is perhaps not worth much time to try and appreciate his veiled glories.'

1103   Anon. Dead Doughty. *New Verse*, no. 17, Oct.–Nov. 1935, pp. 21–2.

Review of H55 and H63. 'The professors are digging up Charles Doughty. But it won't do. They are trying to level him with Hopkins . . . But there was something which Hopkins named "the roll, the rise, the carol, the creation": search Doughty for it, and you will find the limp, the squawk, the gravel, the antique; and a vast amount of awkward bathos.'

1104   Anon. Doughty as an influence today: an over-simple creed. *Times Literary Supplement*, 9 Nov. 1935, p. 716.

Review of H55 and H63, protesting against the levelling of GMH and Doughty. 'The similarity between Doughty's poetic style and Hopkins's is appearance only, an illusion seen from the outside. Try to express Hopkins's experience—even the simplest—on Doughty's instrument, and the strings would break.'

1105   Anon. Four literary converts. *Times Literary Supplement*, 30 Nov. 1935, p. 799.

Review of H61. A brief but emphatic defence of Bridges against Sargent's charge that he did not realize the importance of GMH's work.

1106   Devlin, Christopher. The Ignatian inspiration of Gerard Hopkins. *Blackfriars*, vol. 16, no. 189, Dec. 1935, pp. 887–900.

Sets out the thesis (defended most ably) that the Spiritual Exercises of St. Ignatius formed the very stuff, and not merely the accidental channel, of GMH's poetry. The volume number on the title-page of this issue of *Blackfriars* is misprinted XIV.

I 107   Leavis, Frank Raymond. Doughty and Hopkins. *Scrutiny*, vol. 4, no. 3, Dec. 1935, pp. 316–17.

A reasoned protest against recent attempts to level G M H and Doughty.

1936

I 108   *Basil, Sister M. Gerard Manley Hopkins. *Burnished Gold* (College of St. Francis, Joliet, Illinois), vol. 1, 1936, pp. 62–7.

I 109   Downey, Harris. Gerard Hopkins: a study of influences. *Southern Review*, vol. 1, no. 4, 1936, pp. 837–45.

G M H did not introduce anything entirely new into the English tradition, but he has been more influential than most experimenters because of the unusually fine quality of his work.

I 110   Turnell, G. M. Two notes on modern poetry: I. Hopkins to W. H. Auden. *Colosseum*, vol. 3, no. 10, 1936, pp. 120–5.

Review of C 5. Much original critical comment on G M H, including a brief comparison of him with Langland.

I 111   Fletcher, John Gould. Gerard Manley Hopkins: priest or poet? *American Review*, vol. 6, no. 3, Jan. 1936, pp. 331–46.

Stresses the conflicting demands of G M H's poetic genius and his Jesuit vocation, and concludes that this conflict was not beneficial to his poetry as a whole. Refers to G M H's 'growing acceptance among men of letters as one of the great English classics for all time'. See also I 119.

I 112   Leahy, Maurice. A priest-poet: Father Gerard Manley Hopkins, S.J. *Irish Ecclesiastical Record* (Dublin), vol. 47 (5th series), Apr. 1936, pp. 355–68.

A biographical and critical essay, including comment on G M H by Fathers M. C. D'Arcy, Geoffrey Bliss, and Joseph Keating.

I 113   Gardner, W. H. A note on Hopkins and Duns Scotus. *Scrutiny*, vol. 5, no. 1, June 1936, pp. 61–70.

Explores the relationship between G M H's Scotism and his poetry. Supplements Christopher Devlin's *New Verse* article (I 80).

1114   *Ginneken, J. Van. Barbarous in beauty. *Onze Taaltuin* (Rotterdam), vol. 5, no. 3, July 1936, pp. 65–73.

1115   Morley, C. 'The Wreck of the Deutschland'. *Saturday Review of Literature*, vol. 14, no. 16, 15 Aug. 1936, p. 12.
No criticism of the poem (the comment is only made in passing) but the following astonishing statement seems worth recording: 'The scraps of Hopkins that I have seen, whether verse or prose, give me the feeling of a sort of 19th century Jeremy Taylor.'

1116   *James, Stanley B. The Blessed Sacrament in English literature: Father Gerard Manley Hopkins, S.J. *Sentinel of the Blessed Sacrament* (New York), vol. 39, no. 9, Sept. 1936, pp. 467–70.

1117   *Feeney, Leonard. Father Hopkins and Professor Abbott. *America*, vol. 56, no. 3, 24 Oct. 1936, p. 68.

1118   *Barrett, Alfred. Critics, communists, and Gerard Manley Hopkins. *America*, vol. 56, no. 4, 31 Oct. 1936, pp. 90–1.
See also 1121.

1119   *Shaw, James Gerard. Mr. Fletcher on Hopkins. *Commonweal*, vol. 25, no. 3, 13 Nov. 1936, pp. 69–71.
A letter replying to J. G. Fletcher (1111).

1120   Anon. Gerard Manley Hopkins. *Tablet*, vol. 168, no. 5036, 14 Nov. 1936, p. 665.
A brief general note.

1121   Anon. Father G. M. Hopkins, communist. *Month*, vol. 168, no. 870, Dec. 1936, pp. 487–8.
A note on GMH's 'red' letter to Bridges (LL1, pp. 27–8), supplementing Barrett (1118). 'Father Hopkins was not a Communist but a Catholic seer, who was aghast, as well he might be, at man's inhumanity to man, embodied in the accepted industrial system of his time . . .'

1122   Young, G. M. Forty years of verse. *London Mercury*, vol. 35, no. 206, Dec. 1936, pp. 112–22.
Review of C6. Young deplores the fashion for imitating GMH, and

concludes that his influence on metrical experiment has been pernicious. He is also very critical of G M H's use of rhythm; making charges refuted by C. K. Ogden (I123).

I123 Ogden, C. K. Sprung rhythm. *Psyche* (Orthological Institute), vol. 16, 1936, pp. 5–50.
A detailed and witty examination of G M H's theory and practice of sprung rhythm, including a strong refutation of G. M. Young's strictures (I122).

1937

I124 Binyon, Laurence. [Review of C6] *English*, vol. 1, no. 4, 1937, pp. 339–40.
Some comments on sprung rhythm. 'Bridges took the idea from Hopkins and wrote many poems in this stress-metre before 1890. His example spread, and the result was a great broadening of the conception of rhythm in verse, so that critics of the nineties would have been outraged by what had become common form by 1918.'

I125 *Shields, John. The poetry of Gerard Manley Hopkins. *Georgetown University French Review*, vol. 5, 1937, pp. 29–44.

I126 *Kelly, Blanche Mary. Immortal diamond. *Catholic World*, vol. 144, no. 867, Jan. 1937, pp. 481–2.
An excerpt from her *The well of English* (1936). See H67.

I127 *Thornton, Francis Beauchesne. Gerard Manley Hopkins: major poet or major craftsman? *America*, vol. 56, no. 16, 23 Jan. 1937, pp. 379–80.
Some correspondence followed: see I128, I130, I131.

I128 *Feeney, Leonard. A further comment. *America*, vol. 56, no. 16, 23 Jan. 1937, p. 380.
Supplements Thornton (I127).

I129 *Berchmans, Sister Louise. Superb? Absurd? *America*, vol. 56, no. 18, 6 Feb. 1937, p. 425.
A letter about G M H.

I130   *Gordon, David. Superb? Absurd? *America*, vol. 56, no. 18, 6 Feb. 1937, p. 425.

A reply to Thornton (I127).

I131   *Thornton, Francis Beauchesne. Hopkins again. *America*, vol. 56, no. 20, 20 Feb. 1937, p. 475.

A letter about G M H. See also I127, I128, I130.

I132   Abbott, C. C. Gerard Manley Hopkins. *Times Literary Supplement*, 13 Mar. 1937, p. 188.

A request for information about the letter from G M H to Patmore dated 7 Nov. 1886. See also I133.

I133   Abbott, Claude Colleer. Gerard Manley Hopkins: letters. *Notes and Queries*, vol. 172, no. 12, 20 Mar. 1937, p. 210.

A request for letters written by G M H for publication in FL, with special reference to the letter to Patmore dated 7 Nov. 1886.

I134   *Cock, Albert A. Robert Bridges' Testament of Beauty; with some references to Gerard Manley Hopkins. *France-Grande Bretagne* (Paris), Apr. 1937, pp. 92–6.

I135   MacManus, Francis. Gerard Manley Hopkins, S.J., part I— return of a Victorian. *Irish Monthly*, vol. 65, no. 767, May 1937, pp. 327–35.

A survey of some critical attitudes to G M H from 1918. See also I136.

I136   MacManus, Francis. Gerard Manley Hopkins, S.J., part II—the poet who knew too much. *Irish Monthly*, vol. 65, no. 768, June 1937, pp. 389–99.

An essay on G M H's poetic method. See also I135.

I137   Gardner, W. H. The religious problem in G. M. Hopkins. *Scrutiny*, vol. 6, no. 1, June 1937, pp. 32–42.

A thoughtful discussion of the following question: 'How far, and in what manner, was the personality of Hopkins the poet stultified, or assisted, by the character of Father Hopkins, S.J.?'

I138   Waterhouse, John F. Gerard Manley Hopkins and music. *Music and Letters*, vol. 18, no. 3, July 1937, pp. 227–35.

Detailed and specialized critical comment on G M H's musical theory and practice.

I139 *Feeney, Thomas B. Gerard Manley Hopkins, priest and poet. *Boston Pilot*, 3 July 1937, pp. 1, 6.

I140 *Simons, John W. Hopkins in his sermons. *Commonweal*, vol. 26, no. 24, 24 Sept. 1937, pp. 491–3.

1938

I141 Srinivasa Iyengar, K. R. Gerard Manley Hopkins. *New Review* (Calcutta), vol. 7, no. 37, Jan. 1938, pp. 1–11.
General critical essay. See also I142, I143.

I142 Srinivasa Iyengar, K. R. Gerard Manley Hopkins. *New Review* (Calcutta), vol. 7, no. 38, Feb. 1938, pp. 115–25.
General critical essay. See also I141, I143.

I143 Srinivasa Iyengar, K. R. Gerard Manley Hopkins. *New Review* (Calcutta), vol. 7, no. 39, Mar. 1938, pp. 264–73.

I144 *Daly, James J. Father Hopkins and the Society of Jesus. *Thought*, vol. 13, no. 48, Mar. 1938, pp. 9–13.
Reprinted in his *The Jesuit in focus* (1940). See H83.

I145 Heywood, Terence. Hopkins and Bridges on trees. *Poetry Review*, vol. 29, May 1938, pp. 213–18.
Discusses G M H in the light of the following question: 'Are we likely to learn anything about a poet from his attitude towards trees?' The results are interesting if not always convincing.

I146 Coogan, Marjorie D. Dare-gale skylark. *Fonthill Dial* (College of Mount St. Vincent, New York), vol. 19, no. 4, June 1938, pp. 12–19.
General biographical and critical essay, influenced by religious outlook but still valuable as criticism, at least in parts.

I147 *Angus, Anne Margaret. *Gerard Manley Hopkins. Canadian Poetry Magazine*, vol. 3, no. 1, June 1938, pp. 9–14.

1148   MacColl, D. S. Patmore and Hopkins: sense and nonsense in English prosody. *London Mercury*, vol. 38, no. 225, July 1938, pp. 217–24.

'It is high time that the bubble so assiduously blown around Hopkins' mistaken views on prosody should be pricked.' Occasioned by the publication of FL, this essay stoutly maintains that Patmore was the only English poet who ever really understood the subject of prosody. (Mr. MacColl's own understanding of it seems to the compiler's limited knowledge less than perfect.) GMH is praised as a critic; but dismissed as a poet, in terms a little too shrill to be convincing.

1149   Walker, Ralph S. An introduction to the poetry of Gerard Manley Hopkins. *Aberdeen University Review*, vol. 25, no. 75, July 1938, pp. 232–43.

Unpretentious but excellent general essay. 'He is not just a poet's poet for the less successful modern poets, as we are sometimes led to believe: nor is he just a literary critic's poet, though endless theories have been spun about him. He is a poet to read and enjoy.'

1150   Williamson, C. C. H. Gerard Manley Hopkins. *Pax* (Prinknash), vol. 28, no. 201, July 1938, pp. 87–91.

General critical essay. GMH '. . . was clumsy with rhyme and metre . . . He always seems to have been ashamed of this clumsiness and he obviously invented his theory of "sprung rhythm" to explain away his clumsiness and his consequent (it wasn't at all his membership in the Society of Jesus) hesitation in putting pen to paper.' See also 1151.

1151   Williamson, C. C. H. Gerard Manley Hopkins. *Pax* (Prinknash), vol. 28, no. 202, Aug. 1938, pp. 107–10.

Continuation and conclusion of 1150.

1152   *Gordon, David. The prose of Gerard Manley Hopkins. *America*, vol. 59, no. 15, 16 July 1938, pp. 355–6.

1153   Hughes, Emily. The innovators. *Irish Monthly*, vol. 66, no. 786, Dec. 1938, pp. 820–4.

Similarities exist—from the viewpoint of their originality—between GMH as a poet and Debussy as a musician. Reprinted in condensed form in *Catholic Digest*, vol. 3, Jan. 1939, pp. 77–8.

1939

1154 Etman, Nol. Haunting rhythm. *Tijdschrift voor Taal en Letteren* (Tilburg), vol. 27, 1939, pp. 94–101.

An essay on Hopkins's use of rhythm. His rhythms were spontaneous and natural, but he sometimes tried to force them into a system by reasoning them out after his poems were written.

1155 *Brégy, Katherine. Of poets and poetry. *Catholic World*, vol. 148, no. 887, Feb. 1939, pp. 522–30.

1156 Binyon, Laurence. Gerard Hopkins and his influence. *University of Toronto Quarterly*, vol. 8, no. 3, Apr. 1939, pp. 264–70.

Critical comment on G M H's technical achievement, and on his influence on other poets. 'Hopkins' range was narrow, his production small, but he has . . . peculiar, overpowering intensity. I think he often fails of his aim, but his intention is always that of an artist. No poet was ever more original.'

1157 [Murray, John]. Gerard Manley Hopkins. *Month*, vol. 173, no. 898, Apr. 1939, pp. 293–4.

A brief note on G M H's published works, and on the pioneer articles on him by Father Keating (G 24–6). The authorship of this note was confirmed by Father R. Moffatt, in a letter to the compiler.

1158 Heywood, Terence. On approaching Hopkins. *Poetry Review*, vol. 30, no. 5, May 1939, pp. 185–8.

How a newcomer should read the poems: a suggested (and very sensible) order of reading, with notes on some introductory criticism. See also 1159.

1159 Williams, Charles, *and* Heywood, Terence. Gerard Hopkins and Milton. *Poetry Review*, vol. 30, 1939, pp. 307–8.

A letter from Williams concerning Heywood's article (1158) with surrejoinder by Heywood.

1160 *Walsh, William T. Sabotage on Parnassus. *America*, vol. 61, 6 May 1939, pp. 91–2.

1161 Jones, Glyn. Hopkins and Welsh prosody. *Life and Letters Today*, vol. 21, no. 22, June 1939, pp. 50–4.

Discussion of G M H's possible debt to Welsh classical poetry.

I162   Heywood, Terence. Hopkins' ancestry: part 1. *Poetry*, vol. 54, no. 4, July 1939, pp. 209–18.
G M H's literary antecedents—the influences which helped to form his style. See also I163.

I163   Heywood, Terence. Hopkins' ancestry: part 2. *Poetry*, vol. 54, no. 5, Aug. 1939, pp. 271–9.
Continuation and conclusion of I162. 'And so we find that Hopkins, like most revolutionaries, instead of breaking with tradition altogether, only went back to earlier traditions . . .'

I164   *Daly, J. J. One way of getting a Catholic literature. *Thought* vol. 14, no. 55, Dec. 1939, pp. 537–8.

1940

I165   Pick, John. The growth of a poet: Gerard Manley Hopkins, S.J. I. *Month*, vol. 175, no. 907, Jan. 1940, pp. 39–46.
An essay on the development of G M H's poetry, stressing the vital part played by his religious faith. See also I166.

I166   Pick, John. The growth of a poet: Gerard Manley Hopkins, S.J. II. *Month,* vol. 175, no. 908, Feb. 1940, pp. 106–13.
Continuation and conclusion of I165.

I167   Heywood, Terence. Gerard Manley Hopkins: his literary ancestry. *English*, vol. 3, no. 13, Spring 1940, pp. 16–24.
An analysis of G M H's literary antecedents in an attempt to establish the origins of his style. 'In the twenty-one years since the publication of his poems his influence has grown so steadily that today almost every young modern must admit (in the words of an early poem) "I have caught fire from this contagious sun".' See also I168.

I168   Howarth, R. G. [Letter to the editor] *English*, vol. 3, no. 15, 1940, p. 149.
Notes that Heywood (I167) attributes two lines from Dryden to Donne on p. 20.

I169   *[Lock, D. R.] Hopkins sets a poetic signpost. *Catholic World*, vol. 151, no. 902, May 1940, pp. 184–90.

I170 *Feeney, Leonard. By way of a summary of sorts. *America*, vol. 63, 4 May 1940, p. 104.

I171 *Barrett, Alfred. Image makers and image breakers. *Spirit*, vol. 7, no. 3, July 1940, pp. 84–7.

1941

I172 Dever, Joseph. Gerard Manley Tuncks! *Stylus* (Boston College), vol. 54, Mar. 1941, pp. 5–16.
· General critical comment; enthusiastic and idealistic, but never particularly original.

I173 *Speaight, Robert. Gerard Manley Hopkins, S.J. *Commonweal*, vol. 33, no. 23, 28 Mar. 1941, pp. 562–5.

I174 Matthai, A. P. Hopkins the Jesuit. *New Review* (Calcutta), vol. 13, no. 76, Apr. 1941, pp. 306–17.
Biographical and critical essay, with emphasis on G M H's vocation as a Jesuit.

I175 *Whitridge, Arnold. Gerard Manley Hopkins. *University Review*, vol. 7, no. 4, June 1941, pp. 247–56.

I176 *Kite, Elizabeth S. Conflict and vision in Hopkins. *America*, vol. 65, no. 15, 19 July 1941, pp. 411–12.

I177 Stanford, W. B. Gerard Manley Hopkins and Aeschylus. *Studies* (Dublin), vol. 30, no. 119, Sept. 1941, pp. 359–68.
Comparison of traits of style in order to demonstrate that G M H was influenced by Aeschylus.

I178 *Daly, James J. Conscience among the books. *America*, vol. 66, no. 3, 25 Oct. 1941, pp. 73–4.

1942

I179 Bell, David. The problem of translation. *Y Cymmrodor*, vol. 48, 1942, pp. 63–103.

Discussion of G M H's poetry in relation to the Welsh *cywydd*. 'It seems certain at least that there is nothing in English so close in form and imagery to the Welsh strict metres as the poetry of Hopkins.' This volume of *Y Cymmrodor* is published under the main title *Dafydd ap Gwilym: fifty poems translated . . . by H. Idris Bell and David Bell.*

1180   Pick, John. Gerard Manley Hopkins: the problem of religious poetry. *Stylus* (Boston College), vol. 55, Feb. 1942, pp. 14–21.

Emphasizes the spiritual element in G M H's poetry. This excellent essay seems to contain nothing which cannot be found in expanded form in Pick's book, published soon afterwards (H91).

1181   Taylor, Frajam. Rebellious will of Gerard Manley Hopkins. *Poetry*, vol. 59, no. 5, Feb. 1942, pp. 270–8.

A note on G M H and Nietzsche, suggesting that G M H 'found in Scotism an alembic through which he could transform a Nietzschean passion for world freedom into a manly submission to Christ.'

1182   Ghiselin, Brewster. Paeonic measures in English verse. *Modern Language Notes*, vol. 57, no. 5, May 1942, pp. 336–41.

Comments on G M H's theories of accentual verse, and on his use of paeonic measures in 'The Wreck of the Deutschland'.

1183   Anon. Prince of Celtic bards, singer of love and woodlands. *Times Literary Supplement*, 30 May 1942, p. 273.

Review of translated Welsh poetry, with brief comment on G M H. 'Even the . . . experiments of G. M. Hopkins in the "chiming of consonants" fall far short . . . of Welsh practice.'

1184   Tillemans, Th. Is Hopkins a modern poet? *English Studies* (Amsterdam), vol. 24, no. 3, June 1942, pp. 90–5.

This essay argues that G M H's position as the 'founder of modern poetry' is a false one, because '. . . his poems and his letters show that he lived in a mental sphere which is Victorian, not modern.' This was one of the first studies to react against the general tendency towards ignoring G M H's Victorianism. It is well worth reading.

1185   Anon. Gerard Manley Hopkins: a poet's conflict. *Times Literary Supplement*, 26 Sept. 1942, p. 474.

Review of H91. 'There could be no better proof that real style is inimitable than the verse of those who have tried to play the sedulous ape to Hopkins.'

1186 Stonier, G. W. Books in general. *New Statesman and Nation*, vol. 24, no. 605, 26 Sept. 1942, p. 207.

Review of H91. 'Hopkins had read Herbert closely, and . . . the two have much in common . . . they are of roughly equal stature in poetry . . .'

1187 Fausset, Hugh I'Anson. Priest and poet. *Manchester Guardian*, 7 Oct. 1942, p. 3.

Review of H91. 'Interest in Hopkins's poetry during the last twenty years has centred on his technical originality, and little attempt has been made to explore the spiritual background . . .'

1188 Lamb, A. L. F. Gerard Manley Hopkins. *Central Literary Magazine* (Birmingham), vol. 36, no. 1, Nov. 1942, pp. 50–5.

General introductory essay, aimed at 'providing some sort of key to those difficulties which make [G M H] distasteful to many readers.'

1189 Anon. [Review of H91] *Durham University Journal*, vol. 4 (n.s.), no. 1, Dec. 1942, pp. 34–5.

'Hopkins's priestly training influences, of course, everything he wrote after he entered the Novitiate; but the Society of Jesus counts for nothing, except negatively, in the story of Hopkins the poet.'

1190 Kelly, Hugh. Gerard Manley Hopkins: Jesuit-poet. *Studies* (Dublin), vol. 31, no. 124, Dec. 1942, pp. 438–44.

Review of H91. 'There is no English poet of the century who is so much of the *novus homo* in poetry as Hopkins. It would be difficult to indicate any feature he owes to his contemporaries or even his predecessors.'

1943

1191 Smith, Nowell. Thoughts on Laurence Binyon's poetry. *English*, vol. 4, no. 23, 1943, pp. 143–6.

Some brief comments on G M H's influence on Binyon and Bridges.

I192   P[hillipson], A. W. [Review of H91] *Downside Review*, vol. 61, no. 185, Jan. 1943, p. 44.

Suggests that Pick 'seems to owe much to six articles on Hopkins which appeared in the Downside Review . . .' These are presumably Phillipson's own articles: see index for his entries and those for Wulstan Phillipson.

I193   *Pick, John. The inspiration of Hopkins' poetry. *America*, vol. 68, no. 16, 23 Jan. 1943, pp. 437–8.

I194   D., M. [Review of H91] *Dublin Magazine*, vol. 18 (n.s.), no. 1, Jan.–Mar. 1943, pp. 63–4.

G M H's poetry '. . . has become fashionable at the moment, but must submit to the calmer judgement of the future. Acclamation is not literary criticism.'

I195   Little, Arthur. Hopkins and Scotus. *Irish Monthly*, vol. 71, no. 836, Feb. 1943, pp. 47–59.

Review of H91. Detailed discussion of G M H's Scotism and its philosophical implications.

I196   Lienhardt, R. G. Hopkins and Yeats. *Scrutiny*, vol. 11, no. 3, Spring 1943, pp. 220–4.

An attempt to define the differences between the two poets, built around a review of H91 and of a book on Yeats.

I197   Willy, Margaret. [Review of H91] *English*, vol. 4, no. 22, Spring 1943, pp. 131–2.

'In many recent critical studies Gerard Manley Hopkins the man of God has been neglected for the technician.'

I198   *Berryman, John. [Review of H91] *Harvard Advocate*, vol. 129, no. 3, Mar. 1943, pp. 31–2.

I199   *Barry, John J. Gerard Manley Hopkins. *Salesianum*, vol. 38, no. 2, Apr. 1943, pp. 55–66.

I200   Darby, Harold S. A Jesuit poet—Gerard Manley Hopkins. *London Quarterly and Holborn Review*, vol. 168, Apr. 1943, pp. 110–22.

'He was not what he thought himself "Time's Eunuch"; for he has permanently enriched not only our poetry, but our means of worship and spiritual understanding.'

1201 Stephenson, A. A. [Review of H91] *Dublin Review*, vol. 212, no. 425, Apr. 1943, pp. 170–4.

1202 *P., E. S. [Review of H91] *Springfield Republican*, 29 Apr. 1943, p. 8.

1203 *Hanlon, R. W. Gerard Manley Hopkins, priest and poet. *Catholic Book Club Newsletter*, vol. 30, no. 2, May 1943, pp. 1, 6. Review of H91. See also 1205.

1204 *Weyand, Norman. Hopkins: poet. *Books on Trial*, vol. 2, no. 1, May–June 1943, p. 273.

1205 *Pick, John. [Letter to the editor] *Catholic Book Club Newsletter*, vol. 30, no. 3, June 1943, pp. 1–2. Reply to Hanlon (1203).

1206 Baker, Carlos. The poetry of G. M. Hopkins. *New York Times Book Review*, 13 June 1943, p. 10. Review of H91. 'In the process of establishing Hopkins's reputation as a poet there has been a tendency to underrate him as a priest.'

1207 Abbott, Claude Colleer. [Review of H91] *Review of English Studies*, vol. 19, no. 75, July 1943, pp. 311–13.

1208 *Hopkins, J. G. E. [Review of H91] *Columbia*, vol. 22, no. 12, July 1943, p. 20.

1209 Lilly, Gweneth. The Welsh influence in the poetry of Gerard Manley Hopkins. *Modern Language Review*, vol. 38, no. 3, July 1943, pp. 192–205. A specialized essay comparing GMH's techniques with Welsh practice.

1210 *Meagher, Margaret C. [Review of H91] *Catholic World*, vol. 157, no. 940, July 1943, pp. 439–41.

1211 *Weyand, Norman. John Pick writes of great English poet; evaluates work of Gerard Manley Hopkins. *New World* (Chicago), 9 July 1943, p. 11.
Review of H91.

1212 *Carey, Charles M. [Review of H91] *Ave Maria*, vol. 58 (n.s.), no. 2, 10 July 1943, p. 58.

1213 *Gardiner, Harold C. Key to genius. *America*, vol. 69, no. 16, 24 July 1943, p. 439.
Review of Pick, H91.

1214 Eberhart, Richard. Heavenly-mindedness. *Poetry*, vol. 62, no. 6, Sept. 1943, pp. 347–50.
Review of H91.

1215 *Colligan, Geraldine. The mysticism of Hopkins. *Ave Maria*, vol. 58 (n.s.), no. 19, 6 Nov. 1943, pp. 591–3.

1216 *Parker, Mary. Gerard Manley Hopkins: poet of design. *Mount Mary Quarterly* (Mount Mary College, Milwaukee), vol. 19, no. 2, Winter 1943, pp. 21–34.

1217 *Lahey, G. F. [Review of H91] *Thought*, vol. 18, no. 71, Dec. 1943, pp. 721–2.

1944

1218 Abbott, Claude Colleer. Robert Bridges and Gerard Manley Hopkins: two English poets whose centenaries are celebrated this year. *British Book News*, 1944, pp. 17–22.
Centenary tributes.

1219 Leavis, F. R. Evaluations (IV): Gerard Manley Hopkins. *Scrutiny*, vol. 12, no. 2, Spring 1944, pp. 82–93.
'That Hopkins has a permanent place among the English poets may now be taken as established beyond challenge . . . it is now timely to ask just what that place is . . .' A very important and widely influential article.

I220 Mellers, W. H. Voice and dance in the sixteenth and seventeenth centuries. *Scrutiny*, vol. 12, no. 2, Spring 1944, pp. 119–35.
See pp. 126–7, footnote 3. Some criticism of music by GMH quoted, with brief comment.

I221 Harding, H. W. On first looking into Gerard Manley Hopkins. *Poetry Review*, vol. 35, no. 3/4, Mar.–Apr. 1944, p. 77.
'Not one of the great poets, I say, but unusual and assuredly no charlatan . . . a tortured soul . . . who came sometimes quite near to immortality.' See also I225.

I222 Anon. Gerard Manly [*sic*] Hopkins: the charge of obscurity. *New Zealand Tablet*, 12 Apr. 1944, pp. 17–19.
Too many people confuse obscurity with difficulty. GMH is certainly difficult, but not obscure to those who will make an effort to follow him.

I223 *Anderson, Mary Ann. Fruit of silence. *Mundelein College Review* (Chicago), vol. 14, no. 3, May 1944, pp. 249–54.

I224 *[Casalandra], Sister Estelle. The tragedy of Gerard Manley Hopkins. *Rosary*, vol. 95, no. 5, May 1944, pp. 21–4.

I225 O'Connor, Joseph Gerard. In defence of Gerard Manley Hopkins. *Poetry Review*, vol. 35, nos. 5/6, May–June 1944, p. 349.
Reply to Harding (I221).

I226 Kliger, Samuel. God's 'plentitude' in the poetry of Gerard Manley Hopkins. *Modern Language Notes*, vol. 59, no. 6, June 1944, pp. 408–10.
The theological theory of God's plentitude, and its presence in GMH's 'Pied Beauty'

I227 Churchill, R. C. Gerard Hopkins: a Christian socialist. *Tribune* (London), 9 June 1944, p. 15.
A centenary tribute, which emphasizes GMH's honesty in social matters. 'Hopkins's concern for the "dignity" of the workers was very like Cobbett's and Dickens's; very like, too, Mr. Shaw's . . .'

I228 Anon. Poet and priest: Gerard Hopkins, 1844–1889 . . . *Times Literary Supplement*, 10 June 1944, pp. 282, 284.

A centenary tribute. '. . . no English poet has perhaps more radiantly found the world of the spirit in the world of nature than he. His technical originality would need an article to itself.'

1229　Anon. Gerard Manley Hopkins. *Times Literary Supplement*, 10 June 1944, p. 283.

Leader-article. 'Outwardly, as a priest-poet, he bridged the gulf between poetry and religion which had gone on deepening since the Renaissance.'

1230　Anon. Glasgow in the 'Eighties. *Glasgow Herald*, 17 June 1944, p. 2.

Notes briefly that G M H was on the staff of St. Joseph's, Glasgow, during the autumn of 1881. 'His sermons read fairly well. They are very orderly, but they are inclined to suggest the classroom treatise or disputation.'

1231　House, Humphry. Gerard Manley Hopkins: poet-priest. *Listener*, vol. 31, no. 806, 22 June 1944, pp. 692–3.

'Hardly a poet who began writing between the wars was not directly influenced by Gerard Hopkins.'

1232　D'Arcy, M. C. Gerard Manley Hopkins. *Tablet*, vol. 183, no. 5433, 24 June 1944, p. 308.

A centenary tribute. 'Gerard Hopkins was born [in] 1844, but his centenary is being celebrated almost as if he were a contemporary poet.'

1233　McLuhan, Herbert Marshall. The analogical mirrors. *Kenyon Review*, vol. 6, no. 3, Summer 1944, pp. 322–32.

'Hopkins is not a nature mystic at all, nor a religious mystic, either, but an analogist. By stress and instress, by intensity and precision of perception, by analogical analysis and meditation he achieves all his effects.' Includes a detailed analysis of 'The Windhover'. Reprinted in H 105.

1234　Whitehall, Harold. Sprung rhythm. *Kenyon Review*, vol. 6, no. 3, Summer 1944, pp. 333–54.

The technique and origins of G M H's use of sprung rhythm. Reprinted in H 105. See also I 321.

I235 Miles, Josephine. The sweet and lovely language. *Kenyon Review*, vol. 6, no. 3, Summer 1944, pp. 355–68.

A study of the value and use of epithet and adjective in G M H's poetry. Reprinted in H105.

I236 Warren, Austin. Instress of inscape. *Kenyon Review*, vol. 6, no. 3, Summer 1944, pp. 369–82.

'The meaning of the poems hovers closely over the text, the linguistic surface of the poems. The rewarding experience of concern with them is . . . to stress the inscapes of our own language.' Reprinted in H105.

I237 Anon. Gerard Manley Hopkins 1844–1889. *Cholmeleian* (Highgate School), vol. 51, no. 306, July 1944, p. 741.

A centenary tribute. For continuation see I292.

I238 Hughes, Emily. Ripples on a pool. *Irish Monthly*, vol. 72, no. 853, July 1944, pp. 280–5.

G M H's technique as a poet, and his influence on later poets. 'Like a stone flung into a pool, his poems fell with a tiny noise into the year 1918 . . . but the ripples set up then are spreading still.'

I239 Ridler, Anne. Gerard Hopkins (1844–1889). *Periodical* (Oxford University Press), vol. 26, no. 210, July 1944, pp. 109–13.

A critical essay with emphasis on G M H's influence on later poets. Includes an interesting comparison of G M H with the French poet Louis Aragon.

I240 Turner, W. J. Gerard Manley Hopkins (1844 to 1889). *Spectator*, vol. 173, no. 6055, 14 July 1944, p. 32.

A centenary tribute. 'Hopkins' poetry, fine as it is, remains, in a sense, minor poetry. His range is very limited.'

I241 Winstedt, Sir Richard O. Gerard Manley Hopkins. *Guardian* (The Church Newspaper), 21 July 1944, p. 251.

A centenary tribute. Some correspondence ensued: see I243, I245, I249.

I242 Bliss, Geoffrey. The Hopkins centenary. *Month*, vol. 180, no. 940, July–Aug. 1944, pp. 233–40.

'It would be difficult to think of an instance parallel with that of

G M H in the contrast between the indifference his poetical work met with in his lifetime, and the extent of the interest taken in it today.'

I243   Davies, S.J. Gerard Manley Hopkins: 'to what serves mortal beauty?'. *Guardian* (The Church Newspaper), 4 Aug. 1944, p. 269. A reply to Winstedt (I241). Contends that G M H's spiritual life enriched his poetry and did not stifle it. See rejoinder by Winstedt, I245.

I244   Gregory, Horace. A biography of Gerard Hopkins . . . *New York Herald Tribune Weekly Book Review*, 6 Aug. 1944, p. 5. Review of G55. 'Today, some twenty-six years after his discovery, his poetry falls between the places reserved for the poetry of John Keats and that of the obscure, and still too little-known Thomas Lovell Beddoes.'

I245   Winstedt, Sir Richard O. Gerard Manley Hopkins. *Guardian* (The Church Newspaper), 11 Aug. 1944, p. 276. Rejoinder to Davies (I243). See also I249.

I246   *Anon. [Review of G55] *New Yorker*, vol. 20, no. 26, 12 Aug. 1944, p. 64.

I247   Anon. Poet's poet. *Time*, vol. 44, 14 Aug. 1944, pp. 99–104. Review of G55.

I248   Auden, W. H. A knight of the infinite. *New Republic*, vol. 111, no. 8, 21 Aug. 1944, pp. 223–4. Review of G55, with much sensitive and perceptive comment on the relationship between G M H's vocation and his poetry.

I249   Davies, S. J. Gerard Manley Hopkins. *Guardian* (The Church Newspaper), 25 Aug. 1944, p. 291. Final reply to Winstedt (I241, I245).

I250   *Pick, John. [Review of G55] *Commonweal*, vol. 40, no. 19, 25 Aug. 1944, pp. 447–8.

I251   *Bischoff, Anthony. Tussaud creation. *America*, vol. 71, no. 22, 2 Sept. 1944, pp. 539–40. Review of G55. See also I255, I265.

1252 Spencer, Theodore. Poet in search of 'Inscape'. *Saturday Review of Literature*, vol. 27, no. 36, 2 Sept. 1944, p. 20.
Review of G 55. 'Without the Jesuit discipline Hopkins, like several of his Oxford friends, might have gone to pieces or killed himself.'

1253 McLuhan, Herbert Marshall. Gerard Hopkins and his world. *New York Times Book Review*, 3 Sept. 1944, pp. 7, 14.
Review of G 55. 'The endlessly astonishing fact about Hopkins is the way in which he not only touches but escapes from his age.'

1254 *Weyand, Norman. Jesuit scholar lists tributes to famous poet: American author writes work on Gerard Hopkins. *New World* (Chicago), 15 Sept. 1944, p. 13.
Review of G 55.

1255 *Boyle, Robert. Gerard Manley Hopkins. *America*, vol. 71, no. 26, 30 Sept. 1944, p. 623.
Reply to Bischoff (1251).

1256 Lienhardt, R. G. Hopkins commemorated. *Scrutiny*, vol. 12, no. 4, Autumn 1944, pp. 296–301.
Review of H 103.

1257 Lowell, Robert. A note. *Kenyon Review*, vol. 6, no. 4, Autumn 1944, pp. 583–6.
Stresses the 'heroic sanctity' of G M H's life, with the comment that for him, life was 'a continuous substantial progress toward perfection'. Reprinted in H 105.

1258 Mizener, Arthur. Victorian Hopkins. *Kenyon Review*, vol. 6, no. 4, Autumn 1944, pp. 590–606.
G M H's social, moral, and political attitudes were typically Victorian, and the underlying sensibility of his poetry also. It is his originality and precision of thought that tends to obscure the fact. Reprinted in H 105.

1259 *MacGillivray, Arthur. [Review of H91] *Poet Lore*, vol. 50, no. 3, Autumn 1944, pp. 276–8.

1260 *Boyle, Robert R. The teaching of Hopkins. *Jesuit Educational Quarterly*, vol. 7, no. 2, Oct. 1944, pp. 91–5.

I261   Moore, Sebastian. Gerard Manley Hopkins. *Downside Review*, vol. 62, no. 190, Oct. 1944, pp. 184–95.

A centenary study, with particular reference to G M H's interest in Scotus.

I262   Turner, Vincent. Gerard Manley Hopkins, 1844–1944. *Dublin Review*, vol. 215, no. 431, Oct. 1944, pp. 144–59.

A centenary tribute, dealing very fairly and intelligently with the religious aspect of G M H's poetry and life.

I263   Deutsch, Babette. 'Fortune's football'. *Nation* (New York), vol. 159, no. 15, 7 Oct. 1944, pp. 415–17.

Review of G 55, with some original critical comment.

I264   *Ehmann, Benedict. Father Gerard M. Hopkins, S.J. *Catholic Courier* (Rochester, N.Y.), 12 Oct. 1944, p. 15.

I265   *Bischoff, Anthony. Postscript on Hopkins. *America*, vol. 72, no. 2, 14 Oct. 1944, p. 39.

Rejoinder to Boyle (I255). See also I251.

I266   *Shaw, James Gerard. Oddities and obscurities. *Canadian Register*, 28 Oct. 1944, p. 8.

I267   *Hughes, Riley. Life of Hopkins, sympathetic but inadequate. *Books on Trial*, vol. 3, no. 4, Oct.–Nov. 1944, p. 617.

Review of G 55.

I268   *Byles, Mary. [Review of G 55] *Catholic World*, vol. 160, Nov. 1944, p. 184.

I269   Stonier, G.W. Hopkins. *New Statesman and Nation*, vol. 28, no. 715, 4 Nov. 1944, pp. 307–8.

Review of H 103. 'Hopkins will probably always divide readers into two classes; those who welcome him as a dazzling exception and those who put him beyond the pale.'

I270   Anon. Response to G. M. Hopkins: study in variations. *Times Literary Supplement*, 11 Nov. 1944, p. 550.

Review of H 103.

I271   MacCarthy, Desmond. Gerard Manley Hopkins. *Sunday Times*, 12 Nov. 1944, p. 3.
Review of H103. See also I274.

I272   Orwell, George. Poet and priest. *Observer*, 12 Nov. 1944, p. 3.
Review of H103. 'One ought to be able to say that "Felix Randal" is probably the best short poem in the English language, and at the same time that one objects to a phrase like "very-violet-sweet" and agrees with Bridges that to rhyme "communion" with "boon he on" is hideous.'

I273   Spender, Stephen. A Jesuit poet. *Tribune* (London), 17 Nov. 1944, pp. 15–16.
Review of H103. Some very acute comments are made on the nature and limitations of GMH's poetic achievement. 'The problem of Hopkins cannot be solved by simply stating that since everything he wrote can be elucidated into prose, therefore the way he wrote it is justified poetically. This runs counter to the fact that most great poets have attempted to write . . . with a syntax that does not obtrude itself upon the reader's consciousness . . . unless a forced utterance is absolutely necessary.'

I274   MacCarthy, Desmond. Gold and quartz. *Sunday Times*, 19 Nov. 1944, p. 3.
Further review of H103. See also I271.

I275   Smalley, T. Gerard Manley Hopkins: his place in the European poetic tradition. *Catholic Herald* (London), 24 Nov. 1944, p. 3.
Review of H103. 'It is interesting that in the poems of George Herbert . . . we find sentiments very similar to those of Hopkins in his "Terrible Sonnets". Yet Herbert had no Jesuit discipline to frustrate him.'

I276   Shewring, Walter. Gerard Manley Hopkins, 1844–1944. *Weekly Review*, vol. 40, no. 10, 30 Nov. 1944, pp. 115–16.
A centenary tribute, and review of H103. 'Hopkins has won his place as a poet—as a great poet, most critics agree . . . Hopkins is hailed as a master. Yet how misguidedly personal much of this enthusiasm has been! What efforts have been made . . . not to enter into a mind so different from their own, but to tug it into some familiar category.'

1277   H[ayes], J[ohn] J. Studies in poetry. *Studies* (Dublin), vol. 33, no. 132, Dec. 1944, pp. 558–61.
Review of H103. 'Close imitation of Hopkins has been frequent since 1930, but not very successful. It seems that in truth he is not very well understood: he is often scanned as free verse, whereas he always intended metre.'

1278   *Pick, John. The centenary of Gerard Manley Hopkins. *Thought*, vol. 19, no. 75, Dec. 1944, pp. 590–3.

1279   Sale, William M., *Jr*. Gerard Manley Hopkins: poet and convert. *Poetry*, vol. 65, no. 3, Dec. 1944, pp. 142–9.
Review of G55.

1280   *H., R. B. [Review of G55] *Orate Fratres*, vol. 19, no. 1, 3 Dec. 1944, pp. 47–8.

1281   Anon. [Review of H103] *Listener*, vol. 32, no. 832, 21 Dec. 1944, pp. 693–4.
'Gerard Hopkins came into his own late, but with this advantage— his poems . . . were all, on first publication, edited with the care given to an established classic.'

1945

1282   Hastings, M. D. The fallacies of argument concerning G. M. Hopkins. *Poetry Review*, vol. 36, no. 1, 1945, p. 67.
When two of GMH's own arguments on sprung rhythm are set side by side, they appear contradictory.

1283   Hastings, M. D. More comments on G. M. Hopkins. *Poetry Review*, vol. 36, no. 3, 1945, pp. 149–53.
A centenary tribute, followed by a highly unfavourable review of H103.

1284   Lowell, Robert. Hopkins and Baudelaire. *Sewanee Review*, vol. 53, 1945, pp. 136–40.
Review of G55, and of *Baudelaire: a criticism*, by Joseph D. Bennett; of interest because of a brief comparison of the two poets.

I285 Willy, Margaret. [Review of H103] *English*, vol. 5, no. 28, 1945, pp. 126–7.

I286 Anon. Gerard Manley Hopkins. *Tablet*, vol. 185, no. 5462, 13 Jan. 1945, p. 22.
Review of H103. 'Puzzlement and poetry are incompatible. A poet may take . . . license to make words mean what he chooses . . . only if that meaning is made plain to his readers.'

I287 D'Arcy, Martin C. Gerard Manley Hopkins. *Month*, vol. 181, no. 943, Jan–Feb. 1945, pp. 67–9.
Review of H103.

I288 Williams, Charles. Gerard Hopkins. *Time and Tide*, vol. 26, no. 5, 3 Feb. 1945. pp. 102–3.
Review of H103. Includes an account, from memory, of the first reception of G M H's poems.

I289 *Szlosek, J. F. Gerard Manley Hopkins, S.J. *Stylus* (Boston College), vol. 58, Spring 1945, pp. 54–6, 60.

I290 *Weiss, T. Gerard Manley Hopkins: realist on Parnassus. *Accent*, vol. 5, no. 3, Spring 1945, pp. 135–44.

I291 Gregory, Horace. Living poet, deadly critic. *Saturday Review of Literature*, vol. 28, no. 12, 24 Mar. 1945, pp. 38–9.
Review of H103.

I292 Anon. Gerard Manley Hopkins. *Cholmeleian* (Highgate School), vol. 51, no. 308, Mar. 1945, pp. 765–7.
A centenary tribute, continued from I237.

I293 Kirschbaum, Leo. [Review of G55] *Modern Language Notes*, vol. 60, no. 3, Mar. 1945, pp. 199–201.
'That Gerard Manley Hopkins belongs among the greatest English poets is now almost a truism.'

I294 P[hillipson], A. W. [Review of H103] *Downside Review*, vol. 63, no. 192, Apr. 1945, pp. 135–6.

I295   Howarth, R. G. Yeats and Hopkins. *Notes and Queries*, vol. 188, 19 May 1945, p. 202.

A note suggesting that Yeats was influenced by G M H, with illustrative examples. Yeats wrote to a friend: 'I shall write "sprung verse" only if I find it comes spontaneously—if a foot of four syllables seems natural I shall know I am in for it.' He disliked 'the constant uncertainty as to where the accent falls . . .'

I296   *Pick, John. [Review of H103] *Thought*, vol. 20, no. 77, June 1945, pp. 347–9.

I297   Harrold, Charles Frederick. [Review of G55] *Journal of English and Germanic Philology*, vol. 44, no. 4, Oct. 1945, pp. 434–6.

'Hopkins is one of the least striking among the world's religious personalities. His letters and papers yield comparatively little to the biographer: like Newman's, they contain little about the hidden "springs of action", no "confessions" or secrets.'

I298   *Noon, William T. Hopkins, Christian humanist. *America*, vol. 74, no. 3, 20 Oct. 1945, pp. 73–5.

I299   *Leahy, Maurice. Laureate and levite: Father Gerard Manley Hopkins, S.J., convert to the Church. *Epistle*, vol. 11, no. 1, Winter 1945, pp. 12–14.

I300   *Benham, Allen R. [Review of G55] *Interim*, vol. 1, no. 3, Winter 1945, pp. 42–4.

1946

I301   Thomas, M. G. Lloyd. Hopkins as critic. *Essays and Studies*, vol. 32, 1946, pp. 61–73.

A study of G M H's standards and practice in criticism.

I302   *Pick, John. Right directions in criticism. *America*, vol. 74, no. 20, 16 Feb. 1946, p. 539.

Review of H105.

I303   *Anon. [Review of H105] *New Yorker*, vol. 22, no. 2, 23 Feb. 1946, pp. 90–1.

I304   Mack, Maynard. Hopkins: his poetry and prose. *Yale Review*, vol. 35, no. 3, Mar. 1946, pp. 539–42.
Review of H105.

I305   *Pick, John. [Review of B143] *Thought*, vol. 21, no. 80, Mar. 1946, pp. 159–60.

I306   *Deutsch, Babette. [Review of H105] *New York Herald Tribune Weekly Book Review*, 17 Mar. 1946, p. 12.

I307   Schwartz, Delmore. The poetry of Hopkins. *Nation* (New York), vol. 162, no. 12, 23 Mar. 1946, p. 347.
Review of H105. 'Hopkins is a very good poet, but his goodness is of a special and limited kind . . . the reason for insisting on Hopkins's limitations is that he is often admired for the wrong reasons.'

I308   *Wyatt, E. V. R. [Review of H105] *Commonweal*, vol. 44, no. 1, 19 Apr. 1946, pp. 20–1.

I309   *Connolly, Francis X. Reaffirmations of poetic values. *Spirit*, vol. 13, no. 2, May 1946, pp. 52–7.

I310   *Meagher, Margaret C. [Review of H105] *Catholic World*, vol. 163, no. 974, May 1946, pp. 181–2.

I311   *Pick, John. [Review of H105] *Thought*, vol. 21, June 1946, pp. 323–4.

I312   *Duffy, John. [Review of H105] *Spirit*, vol. 13, no. 3, July 1946, pp. 88–91.

I313   *Grady, Thomas J. A great poet. *Books on Trial*, vol. 5, no. 2, July–Aug. 1946, p. 61.

I314   *Simons, John W. The credentials of the Catholic poet. *Spirit*, vol. 13, Nov. 1946, pp. 144–50.

I315   Devlin, Christopher. An essay on Scotus. *Month*, vol. 182, no. 954, Nov.–Dec. 1946, pp. 456–66.
An admirable explanation of Scotist philosophy; G M H *passim*.

1947

I316   Cohen, Selma Jeanne. The poetic theory of Gerard Manley Hopkins. *Philological Quarterly*, vol. 26, no. 1, Jan. 1947, pp. 1–20.
A study of G M H's poetic theory in relation to his professed beliefs, revealing a conception of poetry based on an essentially Christian view of art. See also I317.

I317   Mathison, John K. The poetic theory of Gerard Manley Hopkins. *Philological Quarterly*, vol. 26, no. 1, Jan. 1947, pp. 21–35.
Statements of G M H's poetic belief are scattered throughout his correspondence. This essay sets out to assemble a selection of them, to provide a cognate whole. See also I316.

I318   *Harding, John Paul. [Review of H105 and B143] *Liturgical Arts*, vol. 15, no. 2, Feb. 1947, p. 50.

I319   *Collins, James. Philosophical themes in G. M. Hopkins. *Thought*, vol. 22, no. 84, Mar. 1947, pp. 67–106.

I320   Anon. Newly discovered journals of Fr. G. M. Hopkins. *Letters and Notices*, vol. 55, no. 295, May 1947, pp. 103–4.
A short note on the discovery of new G M H MSS. by Father A. Bischoff. This periodical is a private domestic publication of the English Jesuits.

I321   Ghiselin, Brewster. Reading sprung rhythms. *Poetry*, vol. 70, no. 2, May 1947, pp. 86–93.
An emphatic refutation of Whitehall (H105 and I234) who argued that G M H's sprung rhythms, long regarded as accentual, are really dipodic.

I322   *Purcell, J. M. The poetry of Gerard Manley Hopkins. *Cronos* (Ohio State University), vol. 1, no. 2, Summer 1947, pp. 21–5.

I323   Shapiro, Karl. English prosody and modern poetry. *E.L.H.*, vol. 14, no. 2, June 1947, pp. 77–92.

Includes some very sensible and perceptive remarks on GMH as prosodist and poetic innovator, comparing him with Coleridge: 'Basically, both Hopkins and Coleridge stood for the prosody that sounds in the ear and therefore does not "scan" . . .'

I324 Howarth, R. G. Hopkins's earlier poems: the order of composition. *Notes and Queries*, vol. 192, no. 12, 14 June 1947, pp. 255–6.
An attempt to arrange the poems written before 1868 in order of composition.

I325 *Mowrer, Deane. [Review of H105] *New Mexico Quarterly Review*, vol. 17, no. 3, Autumn 1947, pp. 383–5.

I326 Lynd, Robert. Life and living. *Observer*, 30 Nov. 1947, p. 3.
Review of G64. 'Owing to the purity of his passion, language that would seem eccentric in a self-conscious stylist became with him lark-music.'

I327 Trower, Philip. The priest as artist. *Spectator*, vol. 179, no. 6234, 19 Dec. 1947, pp. 776, 778.
Review of G64.

1948

I328 Grisewood, Harman. A new life of Hopkins. *Dublin Review*, vol. 221, no. 442, First Quarter 1948, pp. 168–71.
Review of G64. Contains some critical comment.

I329 Anon. A great precursor. *Times Literary Supplement*, 3 Jan. 1948, p. 11.
Review of G64. 'Hopkins has exercised so great an influence over contemporary English and American poetry that any book which throws fresh light on [his] life is important.'

I330 Turner, Vincent. A two-dimensional portrait. *Tablet*, vol. 191, no. 5618, 24 Jan. 1948, p. 58.
Review of G64, pointing out some inaccuracies and misconceptions in the book.

I331 *Cunningham, Margaret. Hopkins and prosody. *Spheres* (Mount St. Agnes College, Baltimore), Spring 1948, pp. 10–13.

1332   *DeLargy, Peggy. Hopkins and prose. *Spheres* (Mount St. Agnes College, Baltimore), Spring 1948, pp. 7–9.

1333   *DeLargy, Peggy, *and* Cunningham, Margaret. Hopkins and analysis: 'Pied Beauty'. *Spheres* (Mount St. Agnes College, Baltimore), Spring 1948, pp. 5–6.

1334   *Eder, Betty. Bibliography. *Spheres* (Mount St. Agnes College, Baltimore), Spring 1948, pp. 26–35.

1335   *Evelyn, Sister Mary. Hopkins and theology. *Spheres* (Mount St. Agnes College, Baltimore), Spring 1948, pp. 22–4.

1336   *Hohman, Janet. Hopkins and history. *Spheres* (Mount St. Agnes College, Baltimore), Spring 1948, pp. 14–16.

1337   *Miller, Nancy Lou. Hopkins and science. *Spheres* (Mount St. Agnes College, Baltimore), Spring 1948, pp. 17–18.

1338   *Stanek, Rose Marie. Hopkins and philosophy. *Spheres* (Mount St. Agnes College, Baltimore), Spring 1948, pp. 19–21.

1339   K., H. [Review of G 64] *Studies* (Dublin), vol. 37, no. 145, Mar. 1948, pp. 111–12.

1340   Howarth, R. G. Hopkins: a correction. *Notes and Queries*, vol. 193, no. 7, 3 Apr. 1948, p. 150.
A correction to the published text of the 1871 Journal in NP.

1341   Raine, Kathleen. Gerard Manley Hopkins. *Time and Tide*, vol. 29, no. 17, 24 Apr. 1948, pp. 434–5.
Review of H 120. Much original critical comment, especially on GMH's theories of inscape.

1342   Kenmare, Dallas. Hid battlements: a short introduction to a study of English mystical and devotional poetry. *Poetry Review*, vol. 39, no. 2, Apr.–May 1948, pp. 199–207.
A brief comment on GMH, pointing out an affinity with Francis Thompson.

I343 *H., K. Hopkins interpreted. *John O'London's*, 14 May 1948.
Review of H120.

I344 MacCarthy, Desmond. Gerard Manley Hopkins. *Sunday Times*,
16 May 1948, p. 3.
Review of H120. 'The qualities for which Hopkins's poetry is
remarkable are precision, concreteness (that is why he so much preferred Saxon to Latin words) originality and a beautiful emotional
sincerity. His defects, often glaring, are due to his being ready to
sacrifice everything . . . in order to approach even a shade nearer to
exactness in expressing all he wanted to convey.'

I345 *Gleeson, William F. [Review of H114] *Thought*, vol. 23, June
1948, pp. 342–3.

I346 Morgan, William. A religious poet. *New English Review*, vol. 16,
no. 6, June 1948, pp. 570–2.
Review of H120.

I347 Clarke, Austin. Critic's circle. *Irish Times* (Dublin), 12 June
1948, p. 6.
Review, *inter alia*, of H120. 'Strange that scholasticism should express itself in this rich, sensuous, semi-pagan nature poetry. Newman
was more consistent . . .'

I348 Anon. The calligrapher's art. *Times Literary Supplement*, 19 June
1948, p. 352.
A brief comment on GMH's handwriting, with facsimile.

I349 Turner, Vincent. An essay in inscape. *Tablet*, vol. 192, no. 5641,
3 July 1948, p. 10.
Review of H120. 'Because of the intensity of his absorption in selves
Hopkins was more acutely nagged than are most artists by the problems of expressing inscape and instress in concepts that are universal
and images that words inevitably make general.'

I350 Anon. Duns Scotus and Hopkins. *Times Literary Supplement*,
10 July 1948, p. 386.
Review of H120. 'Hopkins has been absorbed by poets and lovers of
poetry; his vision has become part of our vision, and so . . . we tend
to take him for granted.' See also I351, I352.

I351   Sitwell, Edith. 'Duns Scotus and Hopkins'. *Times Literary Supplement*, 24 July 1948, p. 415.
　　　　A letter commenting on the review of H120 (I350).

I352   Cocking, J. M. 'Duns Scotus and Hopkins'. *Times Literary Supplement*, 31 July 1948, p. 429.
　　　　A further comment on I350.

I353   Sewell, Gordon. Hopkins, Scotus and poetic tradition. *Westminster Cathedral Chronicle*, vol. 42, no. 8, Aug. 1948, pp. 186–7.
　　　　Review of H120. Includes a lucid explanation of GMH's Scotism, in straightforward non-specialist terms.

I354   *Murphy, L.D.   G.M. Hopkins. *Sunday Hindu* (Madras), 1 Aug. 1948, p. 10.
　　　　Review of H118.

I355   *Turner, Vincent. Gerard Manley Hopkins. *Duckett's Register*, no. 36, Sept. 1948, pp. 1–3.

I356   *Doyle, Louis F. To M'sieu Jourdain. *America*, vol. 79, no. 24, 18 Sept. 1948, pp. 541–3.

I357   Grisewood, Harman. Language and imagery in Hopkins. *Dublin Review*, vol. 221, no. 444, Last Quarter 1948, pp. 163–5.
　　　　Review of H120.

I358   Haddakin, Lilian. [Review of H120 and H114] *Modern Language Review*, vol. 43, no. 4, Oct. 1948, pp. 534–5.
　　　　'Our knowledge that Hopkins wrote with great deliberation, and that he believed his meaning should be clear to careful readers, ought to make us wary of . . . attributing to him ideas or effects which he may equally well not have intended to convey.'

I359   *Pick, John. [Review of H116] *Catholic World*, vol. 168, Oct. 1948, pp. 90–1.

I360   *Anon. [Review of H116] *New Yorker*, vol. 24, no. 32, 2 Oct. 1948, p. 102.

I361   Bradbrook, M. C. [Review of H120] *Cambridge Review*, vol. 70, no. 1697, 16 Oct. 1948, p. 22.

Brief; but contains several very acute comments, e.g.—'Hopkins is a poet who must be understood in minute particulars or not at all.'

I362   Pearson, Norman Holmes. Two victories in the present tense. *Saturday Review of Literature*, vol. 31, no. 44, 30 Oct. 1948, pp. 26–7. Review of H116. Includes a brief comparison of G M H and Tennyson.

I363   Pietrkiewicz, Jerzy. Introducing Norwid. *Slavonic and East European Review*, vol. 27, no. 68, Dec. 1948, pp. 228–49. Discussion of parallels between G M H and the Polish poet Cyprian Norwid (1821–83).

1949

I364   Peschmann, Hermann. [Review of H128] *English*, vol. 7, no. 42, 1949, pp. 295–6.

I365   *Deutsch, Babette. Insight and inscape. *New York Herald Tribune Weekly Book Review*, 2 Jan. 1949, p. 11. Review of H120.

I366   Bett, Henry. Poet who tortured language. *British Weekly*, vol. 125, no. 3244, 13 Jan. 1949, p. 7. Review of H120. '. . . too often one feels that Hopkins has some of Donne's obscurities and perversities without his sombre passion and his startling insight.' This reviewer's generally low opinion of G M H was challenged: see I367.

I367   Owen, B. Evan. In defence of Hopkins. *British Weekly*, vol. 125, no. 3247, 3 Feb. 1949, p. 4. An unoriginal but enthusiastic defence of G M H against Bett (I366).

I368   Forster, Leonard. [Review of H120] *English Studies* (Amsterdam), vol. 30, no. 1, Feb. 1949, pp. 18–20.

I369   Winters, Yvor. The poetry of Gerard Manley Hopkins (1). *Hudson Review*, vol. 1, no. 4, Winter 1949, pp. 455–76.

A detailed, closely argued, and sustained attack on G M H as a poet. This is probably the most judicious and well-substantiated indictment of G M H ever written, but it does not seem to have been very influential. Continued in I370.

I370   Winters, Yvor. The poetry of Gerard Manley Hopkins (2). *Hudson Review*, vol. 2, no. 1, Spring 1949, pp. 61–93.
Continuation of the attack begun in the previous issue (I369). Includes a detailed but still very destructive examination of 'The Windhover'. The whole article was reprinted in H232. See also I380, I417, I585.

I371   Rothenstein, Elizabeth. The Pre-Raphaelites and ourselves. *Month*, vol. 1 (n.s.), no. 3, Mar. 1949, pp. 180–98.
Includes some discussion of G M H's affinities with the Pre-Raphaelites. Particular reference to Holman Hunt.

I372   Shapiro, Karl. [Review of H114] *Modern Language Notes*, vol. 64, no. 3, Mar. 1949, pp. 200–1.

I373   Gardner, W. H. Gerard Manley Hopkins. *Month*, vol. 1 (n.s.), no. 4, Apr. 1949, pp. 282–5.
Review of H118.

I374   Thomas, M. G. Lloyd. [Review of H120] *Cambridge Journal*, vol. 2, no. 7, Apr. 1949, pp. 438–40.
This review suggests a source for Dixon's phrase 'the terrible crystal' (see LL2, p. 80) in Ezekiel I:22. See also I493.

I375   *Rolfs, Alvin R. First of modern poets. *St. Louis Post-Dispatch*, 15 Apr. 1949, Section C, p. 2.
Review of H137.

I376   *Bischoff, D. A. Hopkins comes home. *America*, vol. 21, no. 2, 16 Apr. 1949, p. 86.
Review of H137. Reprinted in *Sheed and Ward's Own Trumpet*, vol. 20, Sept. 1949, p. 10.

I377   *Shuster, George N. [Review of H137] *New York Herald Tribune Weekly Book Review*, 17 Apr. 1949, p. 7.

1378   Leslie, Shane. Coventry Patmore. *Truth*, vol. 145, no. 3788, 29 Apr. 1949, p. 434.
Review of H136. Some comments on GMH's part in Patmore's burning of *Sponsa Dei*.

1379   Gribben, J. C. Hopkins: 'immortal diamond' in an appropriate setting. *Cincinnati Enquirer*, 30 Apr. 1949, p. 6.
Review of H137. GMH's technique was '. . . in a sense . . . not perfected. Had not the flame at the random grim forge waned so early, a different metal might have been tempered.'

1380   Bewley, Marius. Hopkins and his critics. *Partisan Review*, vol. 16, no. 5, May 1949, pp. 543–7.
Review of H118 and H137, with a strong defence of GMH against Yvor Winters (1369–70).

1381   Devlin, Christopher. Time's eunuch. *Month*, vol. 1 (n.s.), no. 5, May 1949, pp. 303–12.
The influence of Duns Scotus on GMH's poetry.

1382   *Scott, W. T. [Review of H137] *Providence Sunday Journal*, 8 May 1949, Section vi, p. 10.

1383   Shaw, James Gerard. New Hopkins studies written by Jesuits. *Ensign* (Kingston, Ontario), vol. 2, no. 29, 14 May 1949, p. 10.
Review of H137.

1384   Symes, Gordon. Hopkins, Herbert, and contemporary modes. *Hibbert Journal*, vol. 47, July 1949, pp. 389–94.
An attempt to establish *why* GMH's influence on later poets has been so strong. Comparison of GMH and Herbert also attempted. 'The influence of Hopkins has not ended with the so-called "political" poets of the thirties . . .'

1385   *Anon. [Review of H128] *Sunday News of India* (Bombay), 3 July 1949, p.

1386   MacCarthy, Desmond. Poetic idiosyncrasy. *Sunday Times*, 3 July 1949, p. 3.
Review of H128. 'I have always been astonished at Mr. Eliot's lower

estimate of [Hopkins's] religious poems. True, Hopkins was not so well acquainted with the *ténèbres qui puent* or *miasmes morbides* as Baudelaire, but I agree with Dr. Gardner that this is hardly the ultimate test of a religious poet.'

1387   Muir, Edwin. Modern criticism. *Observer*, 10 July 1949, p. 7. Review of H128.

1388   Tiller, Terence. Major or minor? *Tribune* (London), 15 July 1949, p. 17.
Review of H128. '. . . as with Blake, we are faced in Hopkins with a sort of nervous and defiant self-confidence: "*This* is how it should be: all the others are wrong; I *know*." This is the attitude not of a great, but merely of a thwarted, mind, if it is persisted in when the speaker is demonstrably wrong—as, unhappily, Hopkins often was.'

1389   Treneer, Anne. Beauty past change. *Time and Tide*, vol. 30, no. 29, 16 July 1949, pp. 726–7.
Review of H128. Some original critical comment.

1390   Clarke, Austin. The devil in the house. *Irish Times* (Dublin), 23 July 1949, p. 4.
Review of H136 and H128. Some comments on GMH's relationship with Patmore.

1391   Sargent, Daniel. The charm and the strangeness: Gerard Manley Hopkins. *Atlantic Monthly*, vol. 184, no. 2, Aug. 1949, pp. 73–7.
Critical essay. GMH is not merely a religious poet for the few, but 'as much for all men as Dante'—his strangeness is part of his charm.

1392   Grisewood, Harman. The genius of Hopkins. *Tablet*, vol. 194, no. 5699, 13 Aug. 1949, p. 104.
Review of H128. 'There are limits to what an artist can do in solitude, meeting with nothing to reciprocate his own mode of thought and style. Few can have explored these limits more thoroughly than did Hopkins, or with an equal fortitude.'

1393   House, Humphry. Manley Hopkins: an interpretation. *Britain Today*, no. 161, Sept. 1949, pp. 42–3.
Review of H128. 'What is remarkable . . . is to realise that Hopkins

can *stand* interpretation on this scale. With Shelley, say, or Tennyson or Swinburne, the concentration of poetic effect is not such that work of this kind would be worth while. Hopkins himself knew this; he knew that he was attempting something that the most representative poetry of his own century had missed . . .'

I394 Pick, John. [Review of H120] *Thought,* vol. 24, no. 94, Sept. 1949, pp. 534–6.
Contains much original criticism, especially regarding G M H's theories of inscape.

I395 Pearson, Norman Holmes. Priest and professional poet. *Saturday Review of Literature,* vol. 32, no. 38, 17 Sept. 1949, pp. 16–17.
Review of H128.

I396 Anon. Rare masterly beauties. *Times Literary Supplement,* 23 Sept. 1949, p. 616.
Review of H128. 'If he belongs, after all, to the main tradition it is . . . through . . . a feeling for nature, for the soul, and for man's mortal being, that makes him rank, at his best, with the best of Wordsworth.'

I397 Peters, W. A. M. Gerard Manley Hopkins. *Month,* vol. 2 (n.s.), no. 4, Oct. 1949, pp. 269–73.
Review of H128.

I398 Stobie, Margaret R. Patmore's theory and Hopkins' practice. *University of Toronto Quarterly,* vol. 19, no. 1, Oct. 1949, pp. 64–80.
A discussion of the relationship between the metrical theories of Patmore and Hopkins.

I399 Miles, Josephine. Hopkins as poet. *Yale Review,* vol. 39, no. 2, Dec. 1949, pp. 368–70.
Review of H128. 'Always Hopkins is clearly individual, and always he is seen to be working with strong consciousness of his responsibilities not only to God and nature but to poetic craft.'

I400 *Pick, John. [Review of H128] *Catholic World,* vol. 170, Dec. 1949, pp. 238–9.

I401 Devlin, Christopher. In the living tradition. *Catholic Herald* (London), 2 Dec. 1949, p. 6.

Review of H137. 'Eliot often excels where Hopkins fails—in the meditative pause that instils intuition, rather than in the dramatic arrest by which Hopkins excites muscular accompaniment of his meaning.'

1402   *Bethel, S. L. Gerard Manley Hopkins: priest and poet. *Church of England Newspaper*, 9 Dec. 1949, p.
       Review of H137.

1403   *Wollaston, Arthur. Gerard Manley Hopkins: Catholic and poet. *Egyptian Gazette* (Cairo), 12 Dec. 1949, p.
       Review of H128.

1404   Fisher, Phil J. Three poetic minds. *Methodist Recorder*, 15 Dec. 1949, p. 9.
       Review of H128.

1405   Anon. [Review of H137] *Times Literary Supplement*, 16 Dec. 1949, p. 830.

1406   Clarke, Austin. Apollo's men. *Irish Times* (Dublin), 24 Dec. 1949, p. 6.
       Review of H137, *inter alia*. 'Gerard Manley Hopkins is one of the great religious poets of all time, declares Mr. John Pick ... This claim reminds us of the extravagant but short-lived praise which greeted Francis Thompson a generation ago.'

1407   Spender, Stephen. [Review of H137] *Universities Quarterly*, vol. 4, 1949–50, pp. 293–5.
       Some discussion of the relation of G M H's vocation to his poetry.

                                    1950

1408   Baker, James V. The lark in English poetry. *Prarie Schooner*, vol. 24, 1950, pp. 70–9.
       'Hopkins merits our gratitude for having rescued the lark from Meredith's expansiveness and Henley's sentimentalism; he restores it [*sic*] the symbolism of spiritual life and aspiration which was the meaning it had for Shelley.'

1409 *Freeman, James C. Immortal diamond: Gerard Manley Hopkins. *Journal of Bible and Religion*, vol. 18, 1950, pp. 42–4.

1410 *Hookens, W. Gerard Manley Hopkins. *New Review* (Calcutta), vol. 31, 1950, pp. 132–3.

1411 Treneer, Anne. The criticism of Gerard Manley Hopkins. *Penguin New Writing*, no. 40, 1950, pp. 98–115.
A perceptive and intelligent examination of G M H's literary criticism, with some discussion of his own poetic practice.

1412 Routh, H. V. [Review of H137] *Adelphi*, vol. 26, no. 2, Jan.–Mar. 1950, pp. 210–11.

1413 *Anon. Poetry and praise. *Standard* (Dublin), 27 Jan. 1950, p. 3. Review of H137.

1414 Devlin, Christopher. The image and the word—I. *Month*, vol. 3 (n.s.), no. 2, Feb. 1950, pp. 114–27.
An expert and scholarly discussion of what G M H found in Duns Scotus, and the extent of Scotist influence in his thought and work. Continued in 1415.

1415 Devlin, Christopher. The image and the word—II. *Month*, vol. 3 (n.s.), no. 3, Mar. 1950, pp. 191–202.
Continuation and conclusion of 1414. Father Devlin's final position is that for G M H Scotus provided a solution to the old dilemma between Beauty and Truth which could be both grasped by intuition and justified by reason. See also 1438.

1416 *Anon. [Review of H128] *New Yorker*, vol. 25, no. 52, 18 Feb. 1950, pp. 90–1.

1417 Johnston, J. H. A reply to Yvor Winters. *Renascence*, vol. 2, no. 2, Spring 1950, pp. 117–25.
A detailed refutation of 1369–70.

1418 Coogan, Marjorie D. Inscape and instress: further analogies with Scotus. *P.M.L.A.*, vol. 65, no. 2, Mar. 1950, pp. 66–74.
'Hopkins' ideas of inscape and instress were clear and distinct and

already the center of his aesthetic life long before he knew Scotus' commentary on the *Sentences*.'

1419   Gardner, W. H. Facets of Hopkins. *Month*, vol. 3 (n.s.), no. 3, Mar. 1950, pp. 217–21.
Review of H137.

1420   *Sewell, Elizabeth. Humour and Hopkins. *Duckett's Register*, vol. 5, Mar. 1950, pp. 41–2.

1421   Anon. [Review of H137] *Listener*, vol. 43, no. 1102, 9 Mar. 1950, pp. 443–4.
'When one thinks of what might have been done for Hopkins and poetry by a little encouragement from his superiors it is difficult to stomach the sententious self-congratulation that now seems to be encouraged within his Society.'

1422   *Clark, Eleanor Grace. [Review of H137] *Catholic World*, vol. 171, Apr. 1950, pp. 78–9.

1423   *Pick, John. [Review of H120] *Thomist*, vol. 13, no. 2, Apr. 1950, pp. 289–96.

1424   Heppenstall, Rayner. Hopkins the Jesuit. *New Statesman and Nation*, vol. 39, no. 995, 1 Apr. 1950, pp. 377–8.
Review of H137.

1425   Anon. [Review of H105] *Listener*, vol. 43, no. 1107, 13 Apr. 1950, p. 664.
'It is time that critics and would-be critics of Gerard Hopkins realised that it is better to say nothing if one has nothing to say . . . so fashionable is Hopkins as a critical practice-ground that his involuntary bibliography already reaches astonishing dimensions . . .'

1426   Read, Herbert. Americans on Hopkins. *Tribune* (London), 21 Apr. 1950, p. 19.
Review of H105. Some comments on the 'New Criticism' as represented by the Kenyon Critics, and discussion of the validity of their approach to GMH.

1427   Corr, Gerard M. Our Lady's praise in Gerard Manley Hopkins. *Clergy Review*, vol. 33 (n.s.), no. 5, May 1950, pp. 289–94.
G M H's devotion to the Blessed Virgin as expressed in his poems.

1428   Every, George. The two vocations. *Poetry London*, vol. 5, no. 18, May 1950, pp. 22–4.
Review-article dealing with H 128 and H 137, including a short but sensible survey of the main critical attitudes to G M H from Bridges onwards.

1429   *Stanford, William Bell. Gerard Manley Hopkins. *Sheed and Ward's Own Trumpet*, vol. 23, May 1950, p. 8.

1430   *Tyne, James L. [Review of H 128] *Thought*, vol. 25, no. 97, June 1950, pp. 352–3.

1431   Thwaites, Michael. G. M. Hopkins: forerunner of the moderns. *Melbourne Age* (Melbourne), 24 June 1950, p.
Review of H 128. Much general comment on G M H as a poet, but nothing very original.

1432   Jarrett-Kerr, Martin. Poetry under religious discipline: a sixth-form broadcast on Gerard Manley Hopkins. *British Weekly*, vol. 128, no. 3320, 29 June 1950, pp. 1, 8, 11.
Text of a schools broadcast. An enthusiastic assessment with a strong religious slant. See also 1433, 1436.

1433   Anon. Poet's travail. *British Weekly*, vol. 128, no. 3320, 29 June 1950, p. 1.
Editorial comment on 1432. 'If we ourselves had sought for a Christian poet of modern times to commend to upper forms of schools, we should have preferred Hopkins' friend Robert Bridges.'

1434   Owen, B. Evan. Gerard Manley Hopkins. *Fortnightly*, vol. 168 (n.s.), July 1950, pp. 38–42.
An examination of critical attitudes to G M H.

1435   Welland, D. S. R. Half-rhyme in Wilfred Owen: its derivation and use. *Review of English Studies*, vol. 1, no. 3, July 1950, pp. 226–41.
Includes some comments on G M H's use of 'half-rhyme', or vowel

dissonance. G M H *may* have influenced Owen's use of this device, but there is little positive evidence.

1436 Fyfe, Jean. The poets. *British Weekly*, vol. 128, no. 3322, 13 July 1950, p. 11.
A letter in praise of 1432.

1437 Devlin, Christopher. Hopkins and tradition. *Month*, vol. 4 (n.s.), no. 3, Aug. 1950, p. 141.
Review of H105.

1438 Gardner, W. H. [Reply to Devlin] *Month*, vol. 4 (n.s.), no. 3, Sept. 1950, pp. 210–13.
A reply to 1414–15, raising further points about G M H and Scotus. A rejoinder from Father Devlin is appended, pp. 213–15.

1439 *Gleeson, William F. [Review of H137] *Thought*, vol. 25, no. 98, Sept. 1950, pp. 528–30.

1440 Howarth, R. G. Hopkins and Sir Thomas More. *Notes and Queries*, vol. 195, no. 20, 30 Sept. 1950, p. 438.
'Heaven-Haven' may be an echo of George Herbert, not of More as suggested in K41.

1951

1441 Reeves, James. The study of poetry; with notes on Gerard Manley Hopkins. *Use of English*, vol. 2, no. 3, Spring 1951, pp. 130–6.
Suggestions, written from the practical teaching viewpoint, about introducing G M H to sixth-formers.

1442 Raymond, William O. 'The mind's internal heaven' in poetry. *University of Toronto Quarterly*, vol. 20, no. 3, Apr. 1951, pp. 215–32.
An examination of the relationship between the sensuous and the imaginative elements in poetry. G M H *passim*.

1443 Cohen, J. M. The road not taken: a study in the poetry of Robert Bridges. *Cambridge Journal*, vol. 4, no. 9, June 1951, pp. 555–64.
Includes some brief comments on G M H's influence on Bridges's poetry.

1444 Cohen, J. M. Prophet without responsibility: a study in Coventry Patmore's poetry. *Essays in Criticism*, vol. 1, no. 3, July 1951, pp. 283–97.

GMH *passim*. Some comments on GMH's attitudes to Patmore's poetry.

1445 Patmore, Derek. Three poets discuss new verse forms: the correspondence of Gerard Manley Hopkins, Robert Bridges, and Coventry Patmore. *Month*, vol. 6 (n.s.), no. 2, Aug. 1951, pp. 69–78.

This article is based on previously unpublished letters of Bridges and Patmore.

1446 Anon. Did not live to see his work in print: Oxford tribute to Gerard Manley Hopkins. *Oxford Mail*, 23 Aug. 1951, p. 2.

A report of a lecture on GMH given at St. Peter's Hall, Oxford, on 22 Aug. 1951 by Father Vincent Turner.

1447 Burns, P. D. Gerard Manley Hopkins. *Ampleforth Journal*, vol. 56, part 3, Sept. 1951, pp. 180–8.

A general biographical and critical essay.

1448 Davie, Donald A. Hopkins, the decadent critic. *Cambridge Journal*, vol. 4, no. 12, Sept. 1951, pp. 725–39.

'It is as a critic that Hopkins is most surprisingly and most obviously impressive, for it is in his criticism that he is most plainly ahead of his time.' Reprinted in H157.

1449 Winters, Yvor. The audible reading of poetry. *Hudson Review*, vol. 4, no. 3, Autumn 1951, pp. 433–47.

An essay on how poetry should be read aloud, with numerous references to GMH. As usual, Winters is very critical of GMH's poetry. 'Hopkins ... apparently failed to realise that his own dramatic and musical deformations of language were not based on universal principles but were purely private. As a result one can often be only dumbfounded when he indicates his intentions by metrical signs, and one often can be only baffled when he fails to do so.'

1450 Thomas, M. G. Lloyd. [Review of H137] *Review of English Studies*, vol. 2 (n.s.), no. 8, Oct. 1951, pp. 397–9.

1451   *Futrell, John Carroll. Gerard Manley Hopkins and God's 'Poem of Beauty'. *Catholic World*, vol. 174, Feb. 1952, pp. 352–8.

1452   Gardner, W. H. The achievement of Coventry Patmore. *Month*, vol. 7 (n.s.), no. 2, Feb. 1952, pp. 89–97.
GMH *passim*. Continued in 1453.

1453   Gardner, W. H. The achievement of Coventry Patmore. *Month*, vol. 7 (n.s.), no. 4, Apr. 1952, pp. 220–30.
GMH *passim*. Continuation and conclusion of 1452.

1454   Pitchford, Lois W. Curtal sonnets of Gerard Manley Hopkins. *Modern Languages Notes*, vol. 67, no. 3, Mar. 1952, pp. 165–9.
'Pied Beauty', 'Peace', and 'Ashboughs' are all carefully modified forms of the Petrarchan sonnet.

1455   Taylor, E. K. Gerard Manley Hopkins: a poet for priests. *Clergy Review*, vol. 37 (n.s.), no. 7, July 1952, pp. 394–404.
An essay on the spiritual and Scotist elements in GMH's work.

1456   Healy, Sister M. Aquinas. Milton and Hopkins. *University of Toronto Quarterly*, vol. 22, no. 1, Oct. 1952, pp. 18–25.
This essay deals with Hopkins's own view of Milton as man, as a thinker, and as an artist.

1457   Jeremy, Sister Mary. Hopkins and St. Gertrude. *Times Literary Supplement*, 14 Nov. 1952, p. 743.
GMH was influenced by the *Revelations of St. Gertrude*, especially in writing 'To him who ever thought with love of me . . .'

1458   Buckler, William E. *Once a Week* under Samuel Lucas, 1859–65. *P.M.L.A.*, vol. 67, no. 7, Dec. 1952, pp. 924–41.
Lucas published 'Winter With the Gulf Stream' in 1863, and is thus the first editor known to have recognized GMH's merits. He was friendly with GMH's father, and also published work by him. See footnote 32, p. 934: 'The ledgers for *Once a Week* accredit 24 contributions to the Hopkinses between 3 Dec. 1859 and 29 Oct. 1864. The first 9 contributions are entered in the ledger under the father's name, the remaining 15 under the name of the son.' Further

comment follows, including details of the signature under which each contribution was published. Mr. Buckler considers that all of them except 'Winter With the Gulf Stream' were by Manley Hopkins and not by GMH. The compiler has examined the contributions, and agrees with this opinion.

1953

1459 Connolly, Cyril. The bard of Boar's Hill. *Sunday Times*, 11 Jan. 1953, p. 5.
Review of an edition of Robert Bridges's *Poetical Works*. Remarks, of Bridges, that '. . . it was perhaps sufficient that he should carry round unwittingly the time-bomb that would destroy him, the manuscript of Hopkins.
"And thy lov'd legacy, Gerard, hath lain
Coy in my home . . ."
Famous last words?'

1460 Lewis, Cecil Day. Some influences on modern poetry. *Listener*, vol. 49, no. 1248, 29 Jan. 1953, pp. 185–7.
Some comments on GMH's influence on modern poetry. 'Hopkins' influence is potent and dangerous . . . there is a danger, because this style is so infectious, of merely copying his . . . mannerisms without possessing a structure of thought or an imaginative tension capable of carrying them.'

1461 *Anon. The axe and the stone: a note on poetry and criticism. *Blue Guitar*, vol. 1, no. 4, Apr. 1953, unpaginated.

1462 Anon. A letter of Gerard Hopkins. *Stonyhurst Magazine*, vol. 31, no. 378, Apr. 1953, pp. 168–9.
Reprints the letter 'Football barefoot' (B7) citing Father John Gerard as the authority for attributing it to GMH.

1463 *Van Doren, Mark. The plain case of Gerard Manley Hopkins. *Griffin*, vol. 2, July 1953, pp. 23–6.

1464 Anon. Purchase of manuscripts of Gerard Manley Hopkins. *Bodleian Library Record*, vol. 4, no. 6, Dec. 1953, p. 290.

1954

1465 *Bhattacherje, M. M. Gerard Manley Hopkins. *Pictorial Poetry* (Hoshiarpur), 1954, pp. 118–46.

This publication is a Research Bulletin (Arts) of the University of Punjab.

1466 Holloway, John. Poetry and plain language: the verse of C. M. Doughty. *Essays in Criticism*, vol. 4, no. 1, Jan. 1954, pp. 58–70.

Some comments on G M H's objections to Doughty's use of archaic language, examining the relationship between Doughty's practice and G M H's argument.

1467 Templeman, William Darby. Hopkins and Whitman: evidence of influence and echoes. *Philological Quarterly*, vol. 33, no. 1, Jan. 1954, pp. 48–65.

Attempts to present 'evidence of actual and of possible influence by Whitman upon Hopkins'.

1468 Garlick, Raymond. The endless breviary: aspects of the work of Dylan Thomas. *Month*, vol. 11 (n.s.), no. 3, Mar. 1954, pp. 143–53.

Some comments, *passim*, about G M H's influence on Thomas.

1469 *Boyle, Robert R. The nature of metaphor. *Modern Schoolman*, vol. 31, May 1954, pp. 257–80.

1470 Anon. Pied beauty in Spanish. *Times Literary Supplement*, 13 Aug. 1954, p. 509.

Review of M 251. Includes detailed discussion of the problems involved in translating G M H into Romance languages.

1471 Wickham, John F. Mariology in G. M. Hopkins. *Month*, vol. 12 (n.s.), no. 3, Sept. 1954, pp. 161–72.

An examination of G M H's attitudes to the Blessed Virgin in terms of traditional Catholic teaching.

1472 Pick, John. Hopkins' imagery: the relation of his journal to his poetry. *Renascence*, vol. 7, no. 1, Autumn 1954, pp. 30–8.

During G M H's seven years of poetic silence after joining the Jesuit noviceship in 1868, his journal was a sketch-pad on which images later used in his poems were worked out.

1473 Amis, Kingsley. Communication and the Victorian poet. *Essays in Criticism*, vol. 4, no. 4, Oct. 1954, pp. 386–99.

Includes some brief comments on G M H's unsatisfied, frustrated need to communicate through his poetry.

1474 *Goldhurst, Richard. Translation *sine qua non*: Bowra and Hopkins. *Classical Journal*, vol. 50, no. 1, Oct. 1954, pp. 5–11.

1955

1475 *Harriott, John F. X. Hopkins the Victorian. *Interim* (Manresa House, Roehampton), no. 2, Easter Term 1955, pp. 4–10.

1476 Moore, Geoffrey. Dylan Thomas. *Kenyon Review*, vol. 17, no. 2, Spring 1955, pp. 258–77.

Includes some comments on the use made of Welsh verse-technique by G M H and Thomas.

1477 Vigée, Claude. Metamorphoses of modern poetry. *Comparative Literature*, vol. 7, no. 2, Spring 1955, pp. 97–120.

Includes some brief but quite brilliant comments on G M H, notably a comparison of him with Mallarmé. Linguistically speaking, Hopkins and Mallarmé were faced with similar problems, and solved them in similar ways.

1478 Anon. Passionate science. *Times Literary Supplement*, 18 Mar. 1955, p. 165.

Leading article dealing with H 179.

1479 Devlin, Christopher. Nature in Hopkins. *New Statesman and Nation*, vol. 49, no. 1255, 26 Mar. 1955, p. 447.

Review of H 179.

1480 Sharrock, Roger. [Review of H 166] *Modern Language Review*, vol. 50, no. 2, Apr. 1955, pp. 242–3.

1481 Graves, Robert. Gerard Manley Hopkins. *Times Literary Supplement*, 29 Apr. 1955, p. 209.

A letter calling attention to the discussion of G M H in K 54.

1482   *Bischoff, Anthony. Hopkins. *Jubilee*, vol. 3, no. 1, May 1955, pp. 20–9.

1483   Grigson, Geoffrey. English drawing through three centuries. *Listener*, vol. 53, no. 1368, 19 May 1955, pp. 884–6.
Includes some comments on G M H's views on the art of drawing, and their relation to his theories of inscape. No criticism of G M H's own drawings.

1484   Pinto, V. de S. Hopkins and *The Trewnesse of the Christian Religion*. *Times Literary Supplement*, 10 June 1955, p. 317.
G M H's coinage of the word 'inscape' may have been taken from 'inshape' used in *The Trewnesse of the Christian Religion*, translated by Sir Philip Sidney from the French of Philippe de Mornay (1587).

1485   Anon. Difficult poetry. *Times Literary Supplement*, 24 June 1955, p. 349.
Editorial comment on the elucidation of difficult poetry, prompted by the controversy over 'The Windhover' (K 116–26).

1486   Anon. Convention and misrule. *Times Literary Supplement*, 23 Sept. 1955, p. 556.
Review of H 178, refuting Graves's rather contemptuous dismissal of G M H. See also I 490.

1487   Bowen, Robert O. Hopkins and Welsh prosody. *Renascence*, vol. 8, no. 2, Winter 1955, pp. 71–4, 87.
The Welsh influence on G M H is not as extensive as some critics have claimed. He had already developed independently (before encountering the Welsh forms) a type of *cynghanned* of his own.

1488   Donoghue, Denis. Technique in Hopkins. *Studies* (Dublin), vol. 44, Winter 1955, pp. 446–56.
Hopkins's example has often been misunderstood, leading to inept imitation. His technical peculiarities do not always achieve their aim. Some of the poems are examined here in an attempt to 'find where the metre pulls loose from the sense'.

1489   Miller, J. Hillis. The creation of the self in Gerard Manley Hopkins. *E.L.H.*, vol. 22, no. 4, Dec. 1955, pp. 293–319.

An attempt to isolate the pervasive imaginative structure in G M H's work as a whole.

1490 Blunden, Edmund. Convention and misrule. *Times Literary Supplement*, 2 Dec. 1955, p. 723.
A letter commenting on a comparison of G M H and Robert Graves made in 1486.

1956

1491 Tillotson, Geoffrey. Hopkins and Ruskin. *Times Literary Supplement*, 6 Jan. 1956, p. 7.
A letter suggesting some possible influences of Ruskin on G M H.

1492 *Baird, Sister Mary Julian. Blake, Hopkins and Thomas Merton. *Catholic World*, vol. 183, Apr. 1956, pp. 46–9.

1493 Duncan-Jones, E.E. R.W. Dixon's 'terrible crystal'. *Notes and Queries*, vol. 3 (n.s.), no. 6, June 1956, p. 267.
An explanation of the source and meaning of the phrase. See also 1374.

1494 *Romualdez, Antonio V. That being indoors dwells. *Heights* (Manila), vol. 5, no. 1, July 1956, pp. 59–61.

1495 *Mapa, Dionisio L. Hopkins and pragmatism. *Heights* (Manila), vol. 5, no. 1, July 1956, pp. 63–5.

1496 *Paterno, Roberto. The 'in-between' being. *Heights* (Manila), vol. 5, no. 1, July 1956, pp. 67–71.

1497 *Dualan, Jesús P. Hope and desolation. *Heights* (Manila), vol. 5, no. 1, July 1956, pp. 73–4.

1498 *Ayala, Antonio V. The problem of suffering. *Heights* (Manila), vol. 5, no. 1, July 1956, pp. 75–9.

1499 *Severine, Rodolfo. Echoes. *Heights* (Manila), vol. 5, no. 1, July 1956, pp. 81–4.

I500   *Wilcox, Stewart C. [Review of H169] *Books Abroad*, vol. 30, Autumn 1956, p. 443.

I501   D'Arcy, M. C. The tactics of meditation. *Listener*, vol. 61, no. 1433, 13 Sept. 1956, pp. 386–7.
A most valuable explanation of the Spiritual Exercises of St. Ignatius, with a brief reference to their effect on G M H.

I502   Schoeck, R. J. Influence and originality in the poetry of Hopkins. *Renascence*, vol. 9, no. 2, Winter 1956, pp. 77–84.
A discussion of the Welsh and Anglo-Saxon strains in G M H's work.

1957

I503   *Prasad, Shree Krishna. G. M. Hopkins: the pioneer-artist of the psychic life in modern English poetry. *Sri Aurobindo Circle* (Bombay), no. 13, 1957, pp. 104–16.

I504   Gardner, W. H. Hopkins's 'spiritual diaries'. *Times Literary Supplement*, 29 Mar. 1957, p. 193.
A letter suggesting evidence for the destruction of G M H's private spiritual diary by his sisters. See also I506.

I505   *Guzie, Tad W. Are modern poets morbid? *Catholic World*, vol. 185, Apr. 1957, pp. 27–32.

I506   Bischoff, A. Hopkins's spiritual diaries. *Times Literary Supplement*, 7 June 1957, p. 349.
A reply to I504, pointing out that on existing evidence nobody can be sure if G M H's spiritual diary still exists or ever existed.

I507   Coanda, Richard. Hopkins and Donne: 'mystic' and metaphysical. *Renascence*, vol. 9, no. 4, Summer 1957, pp. 180–7.

I508   Harrison, Thomas P. The birds of Gerard Manley Hopkins. *Studies in Philology*, vol. 54, no. 3, July 1957, pp. 448–63.
Discussion of G M H's references to birds in his poems and prose.

I509   *Bischoff, D. A. A forgotten Hopkins poem. *America*, vol. 97, no. 18, 3 Aug. 1957, pp. 464–5.

The poem, 'Persephone', is by Digby Mackworth Dolben, not by
G M H. This error is confirmed by Father Bischoff in a note appended
by him to the copy of this article in the Hopkins Collection at Gonzaga University.

I510   Buckley, Vincent. Notes on religious poetry. *Encounter*, vol. 9,
no. 3, Sept. 1957, pp. 54–63.
G M H *passim*.

I511   Kelly, Hugh. [Review of K188] *Studies* (Dublin), vol. 46,
Winter 1957, pp. 491–2.
Some critical comment, written from a religious viewpoint.

I512   Peel, J. H. B. Echoes in the booming voice. *New York Times Book
Review*, 20 Oct. 1957, pp. 40–1.
A comparison of G M H and Dylan Thomas. This article provoked
a large number of replies, and a selection from them was published in
the issue for 10 Nov. 1957, p. 34.

I513   Nowell-Smith, Simon. Bridges, Hopkins, and Dr. Daniel. *Times
Literary Supplement*, 13 Dec. 1957, p. 764.
Evidence of Bridges's desire to print a collection of Hopkins's poems
before 1918 is to be found in his letters to the printer C. H. O.
Daniel.

I514   Armstrong, Thomas. G. M. Hopkins as a musician. *Oxford Mail*,
16 Dec. 1957, p. 6.
A brief essay drawing attention to the acute insights in G M H's
criticism of music, but stressing the lack of any real musical creative-
ness in his own compositions.

1958

I515   *Sarma, G. V. L. N. The growth of poetic sensibility in G. M.
Hopkins. *Journal of the University of Gauhati*, 1958, pp. 73–94.

I516   Gibson, Walker. Sound and sense in G. M. Hopkins. *Modern
Language Notes*, vol. 73, no. 2, Feb. 1958, pp. 95–100.
This essay suggests a connection between G M H's use of assonance,

internal rhyme, and similar effects, and the sense of what he was trying to say in his poems.

1517   *Bischoff, A. Gerard Manley Hopkins. *Victorian Newsletter*, no. 13, Spring 1958, pp. 23–4.

1518   Buckler, William E. [Review of F13] *Comparative Literature*, vol. 10, no. 2, Spring 1958, pp. 159–62.
Includes a summary of research topics recommended for students of G M H in the 1st edition.

1519   Anon. Hopkins in French. *Times Literary Supplement*, 4 Apr. 1958, p. 184.
Review of D8, with lengthy comment on the problems of rendering G M H in French.

1520   H., D. Hopkins poems as song cycle: Cheltenham music. *Daily Telegraph*, 15 July 1958, p. 10.
Brief review of a Cheltenham Festival performance of Grace Williams's song cycle of G M H poems.

1521   Bradbury, Ernest. Song cycle of poems by Gerard Manley Hopkins. *Yorkshire Post*, 16 July 1958, p. 5.
Review of a performance of Grace Williams's song cycle. 'The poems of Gerard Manley Hopkins . . . are not such as would seem . . . to be made for music—at least not the intrusive kind that a composer, rather than a reciter, can supply.'

1522   Aprahamian, Felix. New spice at the spa. *Sunday Times*, 20 July 1958, p. 8.
Brief comment on a Cheltenham Festival performance of Grace Williams's song cycle which 'allowed the text to make its own impetuous effect in relief against the silken texture of the background'.

1523   Anon. The wrong approach? *Times Literary Supplement*, 17 Oct. 1958, p. 594.
Review of H193. Remarks that G M H '. . . has some affinity . . . with certain French poets like Claudel and Péguy, but there have been few English poets at all like him.'

1524   Storey, Graham. The Notebooks and Papers of Gerard Manley
Hopkins: a new edition. *Month*, vol. 20 (n.s.), no. 5, Nov. 1958, pp.
273–81.
Notes on the forthcoming JP and SD.

1525   Kelly, John C. Gerard Manley Hopkins: piety versus poetry.
Studies (Dublin), vol. 47, Winter 1958, pp. 421–30.
'The honest and self-critical admirer of Hopkins' poems must ask
himself on what his appreciation is based. Does he admire the poems
because they are by a Catholic priest . . . or because of their intrinsic
value as poetry?'

1959

1526   Conran, Anthony. The English poet in Wales: 1. The alien corn.
Anglo-Welsh Review, vol. 10, no. 25 [1959] pp. 28–35.
Includes discussion of G M H's debt to Welsh poetry.

1527   Wain, John. Gerard Manley Hopkins: an idiom of desperation.
Proceedings of the British Academy, vol. 45, 1959, pp. 173–97.
'Hopkins . . . was a completely successful poet; his work, despite its
occasional eccentricities, was right in all its major decisions; he is the
needle that points to the true North.' Reprinted in **Venture*, vol. 2,
no. 3–4, Sept.–Dec. 1961, pp. 145–73.

1528   Turner, Vincent. An American study of Gerard Manley Hopkins.
Month, vol. 21 (n.s.), no. 1, Jan. 1959, pp. 54–5.
Review of H193.

1529   *Pick, John. [Review of H193] *America*, vol. 100, no. 14,
10 Jan. 1959, pp. 431–2.

1530   Graham, Cuthbert. [Review of H193] *Aberdeen University
Review*, vol. 38, no. 120, Spring 1959, pp. 63–4.
'The truth is perhaps that poets of Hopkins' calibre can develop only
on the lines of their own personal vision—however heterodox and
eccentric that may seem to the rest of the world.'

1531   Marcotte, Paul. Gerard Manley Hopkins: mortal without glitter.

Inscape (Hopkins Club, Dept. of English, University of Ottawa), Issue One, Spring 1959, pp. 4–17.

A biographical and critical essay, written from a firmly Catholic viewpoint, but full of sharp insights into the nature of GMH's achievement.

I532   Stanford, Derek. [Review of H193] *English*, vol. 12, no. 70, Spring 1959, pp. 146–8.

I533   Hardy, John Edward. After the new criticism. *Yale Review*, vol. 48, no. 3, Mar. 1959, pp. 410–13.
Review of H193.

I534   Mellown, Elgin W. Hopkins, Hall Caine, and D. G. Rossetti. *Notes and Queries*, vol. 6 (n.s.), no. 3, Mar. 1959, pp. 109–10.
The background to Hall Caine's rejection of GMH from his anthology *Sonnets of three centuries* (1881). See also I7.

I535   Pryce-Jones, Alan. The rococo spirit. *Listener*, vol. 61, no. 1564, 19 Mar. 1959, pp. 506–8.
An essay on the rococo style in art and architecture, with a brief but unusual reference to GMH: 'It has always seemed to me that one of the reasons for the late discovery of Gerard Manley Hopkins was that he possessed a much greater appeal for the ornament-starved reader of 1930 than for the saturated Victorian world in which he actually wrote. There remains, among the freshness and beauty of Hopkins's poetry, a certain smell of macassar-oil . . .'

I536   *Sumner, C. Gerard Manley Hopkins: twenty-five poems written 1860–75. *Centre Mariel Canadien* (Nicolet, Quebec), Tract no. 98, April 1959, pp. 5–40.

I537   *McDonnell, Thomas P. [Review of H193] *Catholic World*, vol. 189, May 1959, pp. 174–5.

I538   Pick, John. [Review of H193] *Modern Philology*, vol. 56, no. 4, May 1959, pp. 282–3.

I539   *Hayes, Richard. So flagrant a mortal ecstasy. *American Record Guide*, vol. 25, June 1959, pp. 738–9.

Review of a gramophone record: 'The poetry of Gerard Manley Hopkins read by Cyril Cusack.'

1540   Anon. The mind of G. M. Hopkins. *Letters and Notices*, vol. 64, no. 318, July 1959, pp. 104–9.
  A selection of extracts from reviews of JP and SD. *Letters and Notices* is a private domestic publication of the English Jesuits.

1541   Gardner, W. H. [Review of H193] *Modern Language Review*, vol. 54, no. 3, July 1959, pp. 424–5.
  Remarks that Heuser's '. . . final ranking of Hopkins with the great poets of the nineteenth century testifies to the truth of those high evaluations of this poet which began to appear in the early 1930's'.

1542   Story, Graham. [*sic*] Hopkins. *Encounter*, vol. 13, no. 1, July 1959, pp. 86–7.
  A letter explaining the omission of GMH's self-examination notes (i.e. confession notes) from JP. A rejoinder by Hilary Corke is appended.

1543   Baum, Paull F. Sprung rhythm. *P.M.L.A.*, vol. 74, no. 4, part 1, Sept. 1959, pp. 418–25.
  'If one may risk a definition: "sprung rhythm" is the name Hopkins gave to his own blend of the freedom of prose and the ordered patterns of verse.'

1544   Rathmell, J. C. A. Explorations and recoveries: I—Hopkins, Ruskin and the 'Sidney Psalter'. *London Magazine*, vol. 6, no. 9, Sept. 1959, pp. 51–66.
  Hopkins knew, and was directly indebted to, the *Sidney Psalter*; a collection of metrical psalm translations by Sir Philip Sidney and his sister. See also 1551.

1545   Jennings, Elizabeth. [Review of H193] *London Magazine*, vol. 6, no. 9, Sept. 1959, pp. 75–8.

1546   Stephenson, A.A. G.M. Hopkins and John Donne. *Downside Review*, vol. 77, no. 249, Summer–Autumn 1959, pp. 300–20.
  A comparative study.

I547   *Johnson, W. Stacey. The imagery of Gerard Manley Hopkins: fire, light and the Incarnation. *Victorian Newsletter*, no. 16, Fall 1959, pp. 18–23.

I548   Nowell-Smith, Simon. Housman inscriptions. *Times Literary Supplement*, 6 Nov. 1959, p. 643.
   The Latin dedication in P1 is by A. E. Housman, not by Bridges.

I549   *Bowen, Robert O. Scotism in Gerard Manley Hopkins. *History of Ideas Newsletter*, vol. 5, no. 1, Winter 1959, pp. 11–14.

I550   Howarth, R. G. An unconscious prophet of Hopkins. *Notes and Queries*, vol. 6 (n.s.), no. 11, Dec. 1959, pp. 443–4.
   Suggests a Cambridge scholar, Edwin Guest, as a forerunner of G M H's metrical ideas.

I551   Mesterton, Erik. [Letter to the editor] *London Magazine*, vol. 6, no. 12, Dec. 1959, p. 60.
   An addendum to I544, drawing attention to a reprinting of the *Sidney Psalter* in Albert Feuillerat's standard edition of Sidney. A comment by J. C. A. Rathmell is appended.

I552   Pearson, W.H. G.M. Hopkins and 'Gifted Hopkins'. *Notes and Queries*, vol. 6 (n.s.), no. 11, Dec. 1959, pp. 452–3.
   Some notes on a possible reference to G M H in *Saturday Review*, 14 Oct. 1882. See also H2, L2.

1960

I553   Merchant, W. Moelwyn. The vision of G. M. Hopkins. *Church Quarterly Review*, vol. 161, 1960, pp. 124–5.
   Review of H193.

I554   O'Brien, A. P. Structure complex of Hopkins's words. *Indian Journal of English Studies* (Calcutta), vol. 1, no. 1, 1960, pp. 48–55.
   G M H's use of words: compound words, asyntactical formations, polyphonic combinations, and so on.

I555   Boyle, Robert. Hopkins' imagery: the thread for the maze. *Thought*, vol. 35, no. 136, Spring 1960, pp. 57–90.

A critical essay on G M H's imagery, with emphasis on its religious aspects.

1556   Moore, Carlisle. [Review of H193] *Comparative Literature*, vol. 12, no. 2, Spring 1960, pp. 172–5.
'Throughout his arduous career Hopkins was amazingly true to his own poetic voice. When it could not bespeak his vocation, he was silent.'

1557   Altick, Richard D. Four Victorian poets and an exploding island. *Victorian Studies*, vol. 3, no. 3, Mar. 1960, pp. 249–60.
The Krakatoa eruption of 1883 seen through the eyes of G M H, Bridges, Tennyson, and Swinburne.

1558   *Wayman, Dorothy G. Mary and two poets. *Cord: a Franciscan Spiritual Review*, vol. 10, no. 4, Apr. 1960, pp. 121–4.

1559   Anon. A strong fire of love. *Times Literary Supplement*, 6 May 1960, p. 288.
Review of G 86. 'M. Ritz has no difficulty in showing that the two poets had "no great sympathy with each other's conception of poetry". What they had in abundance was sympathy with each other's need for encouragement and affection.'

1560   Reeves, James. Fire and clay. *New Statesman*, vol. 59, no. 1522, 14 May 1960, p. 724.
Review of G 86.

1561   Mortimer, Raymond. The emergence of a great poet. *Sunday Times*, 15 May 1960, p. 26.
Review of G 86. 'Bridges was exceptionally prejudiced even in his criticism of the old poets: he hated Donne . . . If he had not loved Hopkins, he would probably not have looked twice at his verse.'

1562   Melchiori, Giorgio. [Review of H166] *English Studies* (Amsterdam), vol. 41, no. 3, June 1960, pp. 211–13.

1563   Abbott, Claude Colleer. [Review of G 86] *Listener*, vol. 63, no. 1630, 23 June 1960, pp. 1107–8.
A few corrections are offered on minor points of fact.

I564   Jennings, Elizabeth. The unity of incarnation: a study of Gerard Manley Hopkins. *Dublin Review*, vol. 234, no. 484, Summer 1960, pp. 170–84.

A critical essay on G M H's work in general, showing exceptional sympathy and feeling for the poems.

I565   Meath, Gerard. Bridges and Hopkins. *Tablet*, vol. 214, no. 6271, 30 July 1960, pp. 721–2.

Review of G 86. Some comments on the complexities of the G M H–Bridges friendship.

I566   Stanford, Derek. Christian humanist: recent works on Hopkins. *Month*, vol. 24 (n.s.), no. 3, Sept. 1960, pp. 158–64.

Review mainly of G 86. Very much concerned with the G M H–Bridges friendship.

I567   Clark, L. D. [Review of H 210] *Arizona Quarterly*, vol. 16, no. 3, Autumn 1960, pp. 282–3.

Some sensible comment on G M H's vocation and its effect on his poetry. 'We may say that Hopkins without the Society of Jesus would have sent Victorian poetry to an early grave, or we may just as well say that without his chosen spiritual career . . . he would have preceded the Decadents in the practice of falling off bar-stools.'

I568   Mooney, Stephen. Hopkins and counterpoint. *Victorian Newsletter*, no. 18, Fall 1960, pp. 21–2.

Some notes on G M H's use of counterpoint in sprung rhythm.

I569   Pinto, V. de S. A dynamic friendship. *Critical Quarterly*, vol. 2, no. 3, Fall 1960, pp. 281–2.

Review of G 86.

I570   Reid, J. C. [Review of G 86] *Victorian Studies*, vol. 4, no. 2, Dec. 1960, pp. 182–3.

I571   Cary-Elwes, Columba. [Review of G 86] *Critic*, vol. 19, Dec. 1960–Jan. 1961, p. 57.

Sensible comment on the question of Bridges's destruction of his letters to G M H. 'In any case, he had a perfect right to destroy them. We have no claim on them . . .'

I572   *Joshi, B. N. Hopkins and T. S. Eliot: a study in linguistic innovation. *Osmania Journal of English Studies* (Osmania University,
Hyderabad), vol. 1, 1961, pp. 13–16.

I573   Onesta, P. A. The self in Hopkins. *English Studies in Africa*,
vol. 4, 1961, pp. 174–81.
The importance of the self to Hopkins is the dependence of the self
on God. His poetry is here examined from this viewpoint.

I574   Ure, Peter. [Review of G86] *Review of English Studies*, vol. 12,
no. 47, 1961, pp. 317–18.

I575   *Boyle, Robert R. [Review of H210] *Thought*, vol. 36, Spring
1961, pp. 135–7.

I576   Nist, John. Gerard Manley Hopkins and textural intensity: a
linguistic analysis. *College English*, vol. 22, no. 7, Apr. 1961, pp. 497–
500.
See also the small correction by Ong (I589).

I577   Hartman, Geoffrey H. [Review of G86] *Modern Philology*,
vol. 58, no. 4, May 1961, pp. 290–2.

I578   Nowell-Smith, Simon. Bridges's debt to Hopkins. *Times Literary
Supplement*, 12 May 1961, p. 293.
A letter about the influence of G M H on Bridges. Some correspond-
ence followed: see I579–80, I582–3.

I579   Ritz, Jean-Georges. Bridges's debt to Hopkins. *Times Literary
Supplement*, 30 June 1961, p. 408.
A reply to I578.

I580   Tillotson, Geoffrey. Bridges's debt to Hopkins. *Times Literary
Supplement*, 30 June 1961, p. 408.
A reply to I578.

I581   Donoghue, Denis. In the scene of being. *Hudson Review*, vol. 14,
no. 2, Summer 1961, pp. 232–46.

Includes some brief but highly intelligent comments on G M H. 'A limitation of language is a limitation of perception. Hopkins did not hold hard to the distinction between an active sense of Being . . . and a habit of projecting one's own excitements upon a natural scene.'

I582   Gardner, W. H. Bridges's debt to Hopkins. *Times Literary Supplement*, 18 Aug. 1961, p. 549.
Another contribution to the correspondence begun by I578–80. See also I583.

I583   MacKenzie, Norman. Bridges's debt to Hopkins. *Times Literary Supplement*, 1 Sept. 1961, p. 588.
Final contribution to the correspondence: see I578–80, I582.

I584   Brown, T. J. English literary autographs, XXXIX: Gerard Manley Hopkins, 1844–1889. *Book Collector*, vol. 10, no. 3, Autumn 1961, p. 321.
Notes on the evolution of G M H's handwriting, with plates showing three specimens.

I585   McDonnell, Thomas P. Hopkins as a sacramental poet: a reply to Yvor Winters. *Renascence*, vol. 14, no. 1, Autumn 1961, pp. 25–33, 41.
An answer to Winters's strictures: see particularly I369–70.

I586   Nowell-Smith, Simon. Some uncollected authors, XXIX: Richard Watson Dixon. *Book Collector*, vol. 10, no. 3, Autumn 1961, pp. 322–8.
G M H *passim*. Bibliographical information on Dixon, with checklist of first editions.

I587   Strange, G. Robert. Recent Studies in nineteenth-century English literature. *Studies in English Literature* (Houston), vol. 1, no. 4, Autumn 1961, pp. 149–66.
Includes a brief review of G 86.

I588   Sutherland, Donald. Hopkins again. *Prairie Schooner*, vol. 35, no. 3, Fall 1961, pp. 197–242.
A general critical essay, deliberately controversial and provocative in tone. Extremely clever in both the best and the worst senses of the word.

I589   Ong, Walter J. Hopkins: not for burning. *College English*, vol. 23, no. 1, Oct. 1961, p. 60.

A correction to Nist (I576). GMH did not burn his poems on receiving ordination, but on entering the Jesuit order.

I590   *Teeling, John. Admirable criticism. *America*, vol. 106, no. 2, 14 Oct. 1961, pp. 50–1.

Review of H215.

1962

I591   Davies, A. Talfan. William Barnes, Gerard Manley Hopkins, Dylan Thomas: the influence of Welsh prosody on modern English poetry. *Actes du IIIe Congrès de l'Association Internationale de Littérature Comparée*, 1962. pp. 90–122.

I592   *Flinn, S. Scotus and Hopkins: Christian metaphysics and poetic creativity. *Duns Scotus Philosophical Association Convention Report*, vol. 26, 1962, pp. 50–94.

I593   Norris, Carolyn Brimely. 'Fused images' in the sermons of Gerard Manley Hopkins. *Tennessee Studies in Literature*, vol. 7, 1962, pp. 127–33.

'Fused images'—words and phrases carrying a double meaning—can be identified in Hopkins's sermons and are similar to those in his poetry.

I594   Ryals, Clyde de L. The poet as critic: appraisals of Tennyson by his contemporaries. *Tennessee Studies in Literature*, vol. 7, 1962, pp. 113–25.

Critical estimates of Tennyson by GMH constitute 'as telling a criticism . . . as was made in the nineteenth century'. In the context of the other Victorian estimates given here this is probably true.

I595   Scarfe, Francis. [Review of G 86] *Études Anglaises*, vol. 15, no. 1, Jan.–Mar. 1962, pp. 85–6.

Some comments on the complex relationship between GMH and Bridges.

I596   Kermode, Frank. Characteristicks. *New Statesman*, vol. 63, no. 1618, 16 Mar. 1962, p. 382.

Review of H232. Some comments on Winters's criticism of G MH.

I597   Anon. Appeals to reason. *Times Literary Supplement*, 30 Mar. 1962, p. 219.

Review of H232. Includes a strong defence of GMH against Winters's criticism. See also I599.

I598   Bradbrook, M. C. [Review of G86] *Modern Language Review*, vol. 57, no. 2, Apr. 1962, pp. 254–5.

'Bridges's writing was almost at the opposite pole from that of Hopkins; he constructed a beautiful shell of words, a protective screen between the vulnerable self and the world. Hopkins exposed himself in his writings with terrible clarity.'

I599   Gomme, A. H. 'The function of criticism' *Times Literary Supplement*, 13 Apr. 1962, p. 249.

Reply to I597, with rejoinder from the reviewer appended, mainly discussing the presence or absence of a 'clear skeleton-sense' in 'The Windhover'.

I600   Stallknecht, Newton P. On metaphor. *Yale Review*, vol. 51, no. 4, June 1962, pp. 637–42.

Includes review of H215. '. . . it would seem that Hopkins anticipated MacLeish's famous dictum "a poem should not mean but be" except that he clearly recognised that the being of the poem is composed of meanings integrated with the sound of the spoken words.'

I601   *Heuser, Alan. [Review of H215] *Queen's Quarterly*, vol. 69, no. 2, Summer 1962, p. 323.

I602   Burnshaw, Stanley. The three revolutions of modern poetry. *Sewanee Review*, vol. 70, no. 3, July–Sept. 1962, pp. 418–50.

Includes some brief but acute comments on GMH's innovations and experiments in technique.

I603   *Dent, Alan. The milk of paradise. *John O'London's Weekly*, 2 Aug. 1962, p.

Review of a gramophone record: 'The poetry of Gerard Manley Hopkins read by Cyril Cusack.'

1604 Wooton, Carl. The terrible fire of Gerard Manley Hopkins. *Texas Studies in Literature and Language*, vol. 4, no. 3, Autumn 1962, pp. 367–75.

A study of G M H's use of fire in his imagery.

1605 Gardner, W. H. [Review of H215] *Modern Language Review*, vol. 57, no. 4, Oct. 1962, pp. 600–1.

1606 *Litzinger, Boyd. Gerard Manley Hopkins: the wild vicissitudes of taste. *Critic*, vol. 21, no. 2, Oct.–Nov. 1962, pp. 36, 39–40.

1607 Stanford, Derek. Coleridge: the pathological sage. *Month*, vol. 28 (n.s.), no. 5, Nov. 1962, pp. 276–80.

Includes a brief comparison between G M H and Coleridge. '. . . both men found themselves tortured by "dry seasons" of the spirit and the imagination. Hopkins lived out these dessicated spells, while recording his agony in his journals [*sic*] by means of routine and discipline. Coleridge, on the other hand, resorted to opium, and the valid joy of poetry receded the further.'

1608 Ritz, Jean-Georges. [Review of G91] *Victorian Studies*, vol. 6, no. 2, Dec. 1962, pp. 185–6.

G M H *passim*: comments on his relationship with Dixon.

1963

1609 *Byrne, Virginia C. The creator and the maker in the aesthetics of Gerard Manley Hopkins. *McNeese Review*, vol. 14, 1963, pp. 60–73.

1610 *Singh, Yashoda N. Gerard Manley Hopkins: a problem of prosody. *English Miscellany* (St. Stephen's College, Delhi), no. 2, 1963, pp. 49–56.

1611 Norris, Carolyn Brimely. Gerard Manley Hopkins in his sermons and poetry. *Notes and Queries*, vol. 10 (n.s.), no. 1, Jan. 1963, p. 27.

Some examples of similarities in language and imagery between G M H's sermons and poems.

1612 *Hess, M. Whitcomb. Hopkins and the metaphor in poetry. *Spirit*, vol. 30, no. 1, Mar. 1963, pp. 21–4.

Review of H215.

1613   Abraham, John. The Hopkins aesthetic. *Continuum* (Chicago), vol. 1, no. 1, Spring 1963, pp. 32–9.

A very specialized and abstract discussion of G M H's theories of inscape and his Scotism. 'As the most minimal essential of the Hopkins aesthetic, inscape . . . may be defined as distinctive design manifest in the harmonious relationship of common nature and individuating traits of the object contemplated.' See also 1626, for continuation.

1614   *Kreuzer, James R. [Review of H215] *Criticism*, vol. 5, no. 2, Spring 1963, pp. 191–2.

1615   Fulweiler, Howard. Mermen and mermaids: a note on an 'alien vision' in the poetry of Tennyson, Arnold, and Hopkins. *Victorian Newsletter*, no. 23, Spring 1963, pp. 16–17.

A discussion of the use made by the three poets of mermen and mermaids as subject-matter.

1616   Rose, E. J. [Review of H215] *Dalhousie Review*, vol. 43, no. 1, Spring 1963, pp. 110–11.

'Until Hopkins criticism frankly accepts the fact that Hopkins is a Romantic poet, it will never get beyond its present self . . .'

1617   Pick, John. A literary friendship. *Renascence*, vol. 15, no. 3, Spring 1963, pp. 157–61.

Review of G 86.

1618   Anon. Fr. G. M. Hopkins in the National Portrait Gallery. *Letters and Notices*, vol. 68, no. 330, Mar. 1963, p. 5.

A brief note, here given in full: 'Among the additions made to the National Portrait Gallery during the year 1962 is a water-colour drawing of Gerard Manley Hopkins at the age of 15, delicately stippled by his aunt, Anne Eleanor Hopkins, in 1859.' This portrait is reproduced in L 33 and 1687.

1619   Miller, J. Hillis. The theme of the disappearance of God in Victorian poetry. *Victorian Studies*, vol. 6, no. 3, Mar. 1963, pp. 205–27.

'Hopkins . . . has beyond all his contemporaries the most shattering experience of the disappearance of God. He too believes in God, but is unable to reach him.'

1620   Milward, Peter. The underthought of Shakespeare in Hopkins. *Studies in English Literature* (Tokyo), vol. 39, no. 1, Mar. 1963, pp. 1–9.

Hopkins knew Shakespeare so thoroughly that imagery from the plays often forms an 'underthought' to G M H's 'overthought'—it is not conscious imitation, but subconscious influence.

1621   Davie, Donald. Spender struggling. *New Statesman*, vol. 65, no. 1672, 29 Mar. 1963, p. 465.

Review of H 241. G M H *passim*; see also I 624.

1622   Graves, William L. Gerard Manley Hopkins as composer: an interpretive postscript. *Victorian Poetry*, vol. 1, no. 2, Apr. 1963, pp. 146–55.

1623   Hines, Leo. Pindaric imagery in G. M. Hopkins. *Month*, vol. 29 (n.s.), no. 5, May 1963, pp. 294–307.

1624   Spender, Stephen. Shook foil. *New Statesman*, vol. 65, no. 1679, 17 May 1963, p. 745.

A letter answering Davie (I 621). A brief surrejoinder by Davie is appended.

1625   Pick, John. Metaphor a key. *Renascence*, vol. 15, no. 4, Summer 1963, pp. 219–20.

Review of H 215.

1626   Abraham, John. The Hopkins aesthetic, II. *Continuum* (Chicago), vol. 1, no. 3, Autumn 1963, pp. 355–60.

Continuation of I 613. In G M H's Scotism, 'the role of common nature in the individuating process and in the apprehension of inscape' was an important basic concept, and had definite functions in his poetry.

1627   Visser, G. J. James Joyce's prose and Welsh cynghanedd. *Neophilologus*, vol. 47, no. 4, Oct. 1963, pp. 305–19.

Suggests that the Welsh strain in G M H's verse may have influenced Joyce.

1628   Boyle, Robert. [Review of K 200] *Journal of English and Germanic Philology*, vol. 63, 1964, pp. 536–8.
Includes some original criticism, with comments on G M H's affinities with Scotus.

1629   Litzinger, Boyd. [Review of H 234] *Journal of English and Germanic Philology*, vol. 63, 1964, pp. 818–20.
'If Miller is right in saying that "Hopkins has, beyond all his contemporaries, the most shattering experience of the disappearance of God" . . . we must also add that it was probably the most fruitful in terms of spiritual development.'

1630   MacKenzie, Norman H. Hopkins among the Victorians: form in art and nature. *English Studies Today*, 3rd series, 1964, pp. 155–68.
A lecture read at the 5th Conference of the International Association of Professors of English, held in August 1962.

1631   Olson, Signe. Meaning and obscurity: Gerard Manley Hopkins. *Discourse* (Moorhead, Minnesota), vol. 7, no. 2, Spring 1964, pp. 188–99.
A detailed discussion of obscurity in G M H's style. G M H 'saw meaning only as supporting and employing the "shape which is contemplated for its own sake" '—most of his obscurity results from this.

1632   Pick, John. Manresa. *Renascence*, vol. 16, no. 3, Spring 1964, pp. 163–5.
Review of H 210.

1633   *Thompson, A. K. Gerard Manley Hopkins. *Opinion* (Adelaide), vol. 8, Aug. 1964, pp. 16–28.

1634   Doughty, M. M. C. Hades or heaven-haven? *Stella Maris*, no. 445, Sept. 1964, pp. 502–5.
An essay stressing the place of G M H's spiritual outlook in his poetry. Written from a strongly Catholic viewpoint.

1635   Hafley, James. Hopkins: 'a little sickness in the air'. *Arizona Quarterly*, vol. 20, no. 3, Autumn 1964, pp. 215–22.

There are two pervasive deficiencies in G M H's poetry. Firstly, the personality of the 'first-person speaker' in the poems, always yearning and straining for 'something lovely, fresh, sweet and dear' (G M H's favourite adjectives); secondly, the didactic moralizing related to G M H's guilt at this yearning for what he feels he cannot have.

1636   Litzinger, Boyd. The pattern of ascent in Hopkins. *Victorian Poetry*, vol. 2, no. 1, Winter 1964, pp. 43–7.
An analysis of three poems: 'Pied Beauty', 'As kingfishers catch fire' and 'That nature is a Heraclitean fire . . .' designed to show an orderly pattern in G M H's praise of God.

1637   McNamara, Peter L. Motivation and meaning in the 'terrible sonnets'. *Renascence*, vol. 16, no. 2, Winter 1964, pp. 78–80, 94.

1638   Sergeant, Howard. The innovations of Gerard Manley Hopkins. *Aryan Path*, vol. 35, no. 12, Dec. 1964, pp. 540–5.
A general biographical and critical essay.

1965

1639   Lees, F. N. [Review of K 200] *Notes and Queries*, vol. 12 (n.s.), no. 2, Feb. 1965, pp. 74–5.

1640   Sergeant, Howard. Poetry and the sense of tradition. *Aryan Path*, vol. 36, no. 2, Feb. 1965, pp. 78–82.
Some brief but acute comments included on G M H as innovator: his sprung rhythm was in the tradition of Langland, Skelton, and Milton.

1641   Ochshorn, Myron. Hopkins the critic. *Yale Review*, vol. 54, no. 3, Mar. 1965, pp. 346–67.
'Hopkins, like Arnold, is one of our classics, and deserves a place alongside him as one of the two foremost literary critics of the Victorian Age.'

1642   MacKenzie, Norman H. Hopkins MSS—old losses and new finds. *Times Literary Supplement*, 18 Mar. 1965, p. 220.
A letter from the editor of the forthcoming Oxford English Texts edition of G M H's poems, discussing recently made discoveries in the field of G M H's MSS.

1643   Nassar, Eugene Paul. Hopkins, 'figura', and grace: God's better beauty. *Renascence*, vol. 17, no. 2, Spring 1965, pp. 128–30, 136.

An essay on some aspects of the philosophical background to G M H's work, written from a Catholic viewpoint.

1644   Warburg, Jeremy. Idiosyncratic style. *Review of English Literature*, vol. 6, no. 2, Apr. 1965, pp. 56–65.

Some comments on G M H's style are included, with emphasis on his use of compound words. 'Perhaps no other poet has used compounds more often in so short a space, none with more potent originality.'

1645   *Davies, Phillips George. A discovery of death. *CEA Critic* (Skidmore College, N.Y.), vol. 27, May 1965, pp. 7–8.

1646   Mackenzie, Norman H. Gerard and Grace Hopkins: some new links. *Month*, vol. 33 (n.s.), no. 6, June 1965, pp. 347–50.

Some recently discovered letters from G M H to his sister Grace, apparently asking her to set 'Spring' and 'In the Valley of the Elwy' to music. Provides an exact date for 'In the Valley of the Elwy'. Includes some comment on G M H's musical theories.

1647   Schneider, Elisabeth W. Sprung rhythm: a chapter in the evolution of nineteenth-century verse. *P.M.L.A.*, vol. 80, no. 3, June 1965, pp. 237–53.

A very thorough and perceptive discussion of the sources and the nature of sprung rhythm, and of G M H's use of it.

1648   Thomas, A[lfred]. G. M. Hopkins and the Silver Jubilee album. *Library*, vol. 20 (5th series), no. 2, June 1965, pp. 148–52.

An excellent bibliographical description of the album presented to the Bishop of Shrewsbury by the Jesuits of St. Beuno's in 1876, with textual notes on the three poems contributed to it by G M H.

1649   Towner, Annemarie Ewing. Welsh bardic meters and English poetry. *Massachusetts Review*, vol. 6, no. 3, Spring–Summer 1965, pp. 614–24.

Includes some comments on the influence of Welsh poetry on G M H's work, with particular reference to *cynghanedd*.

1650 [Thomas, Alfred], *editor.* An uncollected letter of Gerard Manley Hopkins. *Dublin Review*, vol. 239, no. 505, Autumn 1965, pp. 289–92.
A letter first published in *Stonyhurst Magazine*, Nov. 1888 (B7) about barefoot football as played in Ireland. It is printed here with thorough explanatory notes and glosses.

1651 *Honora, Sister. Positively speaking: Gerard Manley Hopkins. *Delta Epsilon Sigma Bulletin*, vol. 10, no. 3, Oct. 1965, pp. 69–77.

1652 Bowen, Paul. Music last week. *Listener*, vol. 74, no. 1910, 4 Nov. 1965, p. 733.
Review of a radio performance of Rubbra's 'Inscape' (L34).

1653 *Boyle, Robert R. [Review of H243] *Thought*, vol. 40, Winter 1965, pp. 598–600.

1654 Chevigny, Bell Gale. Instress and devotion in the poetry of Gerard Manley Hopkins. *Victorian Studies*, vol. 9, no. 2, Dec. 1965, pp. 141–53.
An interesting and original discussion of G M H's struggle to reconcile the conflicting demands of art and devotion.

1966

1655 Guiget, Jean. [Review of M51] *Anglia*, vol. 84, no. 2, 1966, pp. 248–50.

1656 Hecht, Anthony. On the methods and ambitions of poetry. *Hudson Review*, vol. 18, 1965–6, pp. 481–505.
See pp. 491–2. Some comments on the history of G M H's 'inscape' and Scotus's 'haecceitas', and on the application of the concept to poetry.

1657 Hoffman, Frederick J. The religious crisis in modern literature. *Comparative Literature Studies*, vol. 3, no. 3, 1966, pp. 263–71.
G M H *passim.*

1658 Webster, E. M. Rubbra's 'Inscape' at Stroud Festival. *Musical Opinion* (London), vol. 89, no. 1060, Jan. 1966, p. 215.

Quite detailed criticism of L34. 'The total impression was one of impassioned involvement with the poet's belief in the diversity and wonder of creation, and a despairing desire to see beauty remain whole and unspoilt. But, somehow, the music could not match those exacting words . . .'

1659   Thomas, Alfred. A Hopkins fragment replaced. *Times Literary Supplement*, 20 Jan. 1966, p. 48.
Letter LXXVIII in FL2 is the conclusion of Letter LXXXIV. See also 1660.

1660   MacKenzie, Norman H. A Hopkins fragment. *Times Literary Supplement*, 10 Feb. 1966, p. 110.
Further evidence in support of Father Thomas's conclusion in 1659. The watermark on the two pieces of paper matches up perfectly.

1661   Ciardi, John. Four poets and one actor. *Saturday Review*, vol. 49, 12 Feb. 1966, p. 49.
Review of a gramophone record: 'Poems of Gerard Manley Hopkins read by Richard Gray.' 'The essence of Hopkins, as I read him, is in the interplay of gentleness and violence . . . The language and rhythms of the poems must often respond to both forces at once.'

1662   Vickers, Brian. Hopkins and Newman. *Times Literary Supplement*, 3 Mar. 1966, p. 178.
A letter suggesting that the phrase 'I can no more' in 'Carrion Comfort' may be an echo from Newman. See also 1666.

1663   Hufstader, Anslem. The experience of nature in Hopkins' journals and poems. *Downside Review*, vol. 84, no. 275, Apr. 1966, pp. 127–49.
'Between the most exact descriptions of nature in the journals and the great religious poems runs a strong continuity of visual experience . . . we must understand the experience in order to understand the poems.'

1664   *King, Donald R. The vision of 'being' in Hopkins' poetry and Ruskin's *Modern Painters* I. *Discourse*, vol. 4, no. 3, Summer 1966, pp. 316–24.

1665 Drew, David. New music at York. *New Statesman*, vol. 72, no. 1843, 8 July 1966, pp. 62–3.

Review of a musical setting of some poems by G M H, composed by W. Mellers.

1666 Gardner, W. H. Hopkins and Newman. *Times Literary Supplement*, 15 Sept. 1966, p. 868.

A reply to Vickers (1662) suggesting *Anthony and Cleopatra* iv.xiii, 57–9 as a source of the phrase 'I can no more' in 'Carrion Comfort'.

1667 Fulweiler, Howard W. Gerard Manley Hopkins and the 'stanching, quenching ocean of a motionable mind'. *Victorian Newsletter*, no. 30, Fall 1966, pp. 6–13.

An essay on 'Hopkins' compelling interest in the sea, which so firmly relates him to the authors of "Ulysses", "Dover Beach", or "Out of the Cradle Endlessly Rocking".'

1668 Langbaum, Robert. Browning and the question of myth. *P.M.L.A.*, vol. 81, no. 7, Dec. 1966, pp. 575–84.

Includes a brief but perceptive comparison of G M H and Browning (p. 579). 'Both poets are obscure because they are trying to use words in such a way as to overcome the analytic effect of language . . . The difference between [them] is that Hopkins dislocates language in order to make his *image* more palpable . . .' G M H goes further than Browning in symbolizing and myth-making.

1967

1669 *Agrawala, D. C. Hopkins on Tennyson. *Banasthali Patrika*, vol. 9, 1967, pp. 39–44.

1670 C., P. [Review of H243] *Irish Ecclesiastical Record*, vol. 108 (5th series), 1967, pp. 70–2.

G M H *passim*. 'Hopkins and Eliot cover common ground in handling themes of spiritual awakening and purgation; Hopkins does not even attempt to explore . . . the further stages of illumination or mystical union and Eliot's attempts . . . do not come off.'

1671 *Gibson, Frances. The influence of Welsh prosody on the poetry of Hopkins. *Xavier University Studies* (New Orleans), vol. 6, no. 1, Feb. 1967, pp. 21–8.

1672   Rader, Louis. Hopkins' dark sonnets: another new expression. *Victorian Poetry*, vol. 5, no. 1, Spring 1967, pp. 13–20.

The 'dark sonnets' represent part of G M H's continuous efforts to find the best form of poetic expression. This article stresses their technical excellence.

1673   Sharples, Sister Marian. Hopkins and Joyce: a point of similarity. *Renascence*, vol. 19, no. 3, Spring 1967, pp. 156–60.

This essay traces an underlying thread of Scotism in Joyce.

1674   Stadlen, Peter. Manley Hopkins poems set by Rubbra. *Daily Telegraph*, 1 Apr. 1967, p. 13. Review of a performance of Rubbra's 'Inscape' (L34).

1675   Sonstroem, David. Making earnest of game: G. M. Hopkins and nonsense poetry. *Modern Language Quarterly*, vol. 28, no. 2, June 1967, pp. 192–206.

'In the poetry of Gerard Manley Hopkins, there is often a play with words and their sounds that comes very close to nonsense, a verbal play comparable to that of Lewis Carroll, Edward Lear, or Sir. W. S. Gilbert.' The comparison with Lear is worked out in special detail.

1676   Agrawala, D. C. Complexity in Hopkins's onomatopoeic coinages. *Literary Criterion* (Mysore), vol. 7, no. 4, Summer 1967, pp. 1–5.

'To the extent Hopkins is able to realise the inscape of speech, he lets his norm of current language in poetry be modified accordingly.'

1677   Hallgarth, Susan A. A study of Hopkins' use of nature. *Victorian Poetry*, vol. 5, no. 2, Summer 1967, pp. 79–92.

G M H's general view of nature examined, with discussion of his use of nature-imagery in specific poems.

1678   Burgess, Anthony. The democracy of prejudice. *Encounter*, vol. 29, no. 2, Aug. 1967, pp. 71–5.

Review of H276, refuting the dismissal of G M H as 'a mental cripple' with much reasoned critical argument.

1679   Gardner, W.H. G.M. Hopkins. *Times Literary Supplement*, 3 Aug. 1967, p. 707.

A letter on the relationship between the 1966 and 1967 impressions of A137 and the text of P4. See notes to A137.

1680 McCarthy, Adrian J. Toward a definition of Hopkins' 'inscape'. *University of Dayton Review*, vol. 4, no. 3, Autumn 1967, pp. 55–68. 'What Hopkins was trying to express was an intuition: he would take all the individualising features of an object and attempt to wrest from them the secret of its identity. Inscape thus came to mean both the individuating notes and the metaphysical reality lurking beneath them.'

1681 Maxwell, J. C. [Review of H 268] *Notes and Queries*, vol. 14 (n.s.), no. 10, Oct. 1967, pp. 398–9.

1682 Prendeville, Brendan. Visible thought. *British Journal of Aesthetics*, vol. 7, no. 4, Oct. 1967, pp. 339–49. 'The experiences . . . which Hopkins conveys to a reader are spatial ones, and "meaning" is in the structuring of them.' Comparisons are drawn between the aesthetic theory of G M H and of Wassily Kandinsky.

1683 Nist, John. [Review of H 265] *Western Humanities Review*, vol. 21, no. 1, Winter 1967, pp. 72–3. 'If there is one phrase to describe Hopkins' most characteristic poetry, perhaps it should be "neurotic orgasm"—a state much akin to the induced epilepsy of Vincent Van Gogh . . .'

1684 Agrawala, D.C. Hopkins on Shakespeare. *Rajasthan University Studies in English*, 1967–8, pp. 57–66. Discussion of G M H's appreciation and criticism of Shakespeare, with emphasis on his attitudes to Shakespeare's use of language and handling of the sonnet-form.

1968

1685 Kelly, T.J. Gerard Manley Hopkins. *Critical Review* (Melbourne), no. 11, 1968, pp. 48–59. An attack on G M H as a poet, strongly influenced by the views of Yvor Winters (I 369–70), and setting out to show that G M H's poetry is 'more radically flawed than even Winters recognised' by discussion of selected poems.

1686   Thomas, Alfred. Was Hopkins a Scotist before he read Scotus? *Studia Scholastico-Scotistica*, 4. *De Doctrina Ioannis Duns Scoti*; vol. iv: Scotismus Decursu Saeculorum (Rome), 1968, pp. 617–29.
G M H's experience of beauty and experience of religion (and his feelings about the relationship between the two) were developing on Scotist lines before he first read Scotus.

1687   Gardner, W. H. From fourth refusal to fourth edition: the posthumous fame of Fr. Gerard Manley Hopkins, S.J. *Stonyhurst Magazine*, vol. 35, no. 437, Feb. 1968, pp. 417–22.
A study of the neglect of G M H's poetry during his life and the growth of his posthumous publication, and acceptance as a major poet.

1688   Rawson, C. J. Some sources or parallels to poems by Ted Hughes. *Notes and Queries*, vol. 15 (n.s.), no. 2, Feb. 1968, pp. 62–3.
Some possible influences from G M H in Hughes's poem 'The Hawk in the Rain'.

1689   Wolfe, Patricia A. The paradox of self: a study of Hopkins' spiritual conflict in the 'terrible' sonnets. *Victorian Poetry*, vol. 6, no. 2, Summer 1968, pp. 85–103.
The central conflict of Hopkins's 'terrible' sonnets is a clash between the desire to reach spiritual fulfilment and the human reluctance to surrender personal identity. The poems represent successive stages in G M H's progress towards a resolution.

1690   Hobsbaum, Philip. Poet of deprivation. *Month*, vol. 40 (n.s.), nos. 1–2, July–Aug. 1968, pp. 46–9.
Hopkins's best work is to be found in the late sonnets written in Dublin between 1885 and 1889. Much of his earlier work has been overrated.

1691   L'Heureux, John. Images of Hopkins. *Month*, vol. 40 (n.s.), nos. 1–2, July–Aug. 1968, pp. 50–1.
A fellow-Jesuit's tribute. 'Not for his magnificent poetry but for his self, his hopelessly complex and involuted self, I reverence him.'

1692   McChesney, Donald. The meaning of 'inscape'. *Month*, vol. 40 (n.s.), nos. 1–2, July–Aug. 1968, pp. 52–63.

An attempt to establish 'the relationship between the inscapes Hopkins *saw* in nature and the inscapes he *created* in language.'

1693 Scott-Moncrieff, George. Scots. *Month*, vol. 40 (n.s.), nos. 1–2, July–Aug. 1968, p. 64.
Review of D20.

1694 Anon. Hopkins word by word. *Times Literary Supplement*, 22 Aug. 1968, p. 895.
Review of H296 and K218. 'Hopkins differs from Roman Catholic poets more or less contemporary with him . . . not merely in being a very, very much greater poet, but in . . . being much more fully and richly a product of all that was best in the general culture of his age.'

1695 Mackenzie, Norman H. Gerard Manley Hopkins. *Times Literary Supplement*, 26 Sept. 1968, p. 1090.
A reply to White (A161), taking issue with his interpretation of the MS. text in the fragments quoted. See also 1697–8, 1700, 1702–4, 1707.

1696 Milroy, James. Gerard Manley Hopkins. *Times Literary Supplement*, 26 Sept. 1968, p. 1090.
Suggests that by 'burl' ('The Wreck of the Deutschland', stanza 16) GMH meant *whirl*, with associations of strength and weight.

1697 Gardner, W. H. Gerard Manley Hopkins. *Times Literary Supplement*, 31 Oct. 1968, p. 1233.
A letter supporting MacKenzie (1695).

1698 White, Norman. Gerard Manley Hopkins. *Times Literary Supplement*, 31 Oct. 1968, p. 1233.
A surrejoinder to MacKenzie (1695) suggesting (*inter alia*) a correction of 'force' to 'forge' in line 3 of 'To his Watch'. See also 1700, 1702–4, 1707.

1699 Duncan-Jones, E.E. G.M. Hopkins's Bellisle. *Notes and Queries*, vol. 15 (n.s.), no. 11, Nov. 1968, p. 423.
'Bellisle' (P4, nos. 116 and 119) is in fact GMH's Oxford College, Balliol.

I700   MacKenzie, Norman H. Gerard Manley Hopkins. *Times Literary Supplement*, 21 Nov. 1968, p. 1311.

An emphatic rejection of White's reading of 'To his Watch' (I698). See also I702–4, I707.

I70I   Milward, Peter. Sacramental symbolism in Hopkins and Eliot. *Renascence*, vol. 20, no. 2, Winter 1968, pp. 104–11.

The Christian faith unites the work of G M H and Eliot, even though G M H's influence on him has been negligible.

I702   White, Norman. Gerard Manley Hopkins. *Times Literary Supplement*, 19 Dec. 1968, p. 1440.

A reply to MacKenzie (I700) defending the substitution of 'forge' for 'force' in 'To his Watch' (I698). See also I703–4, I707.

1969

I703   Alton, R. E. *and* Croft, P. J. Gerard Manley Hopkins. *Times Literary Supplement*, 23 Jan. 1969, p. 87.

Enthusiastic but slightly naïve confirmation of White's reading of 'To his Watch' (I698, I702).

I704   MacKenzie, Norman H. Gerard Manley Hopkins. *Times Literary Supplement*, 20 Feb. 1969, p. 186.

Final reply to White (A161, I698, I702), with discussion of some general problems involved in editing Hopkins's MSS.

I705   Petry, Charles. 'Society for poet' plan gets the go-ahead. *Evening News* (Bolton), 28 Feb. 1969, p. 6.

Report of an interview with the compiler, in which plans for the formation of the Hopkins Society are outlined and briefly discussed. See also I711.

I706   White, Norman *and* Dunne, Tom. A Hopkins discovery. *Library*, vol. 24 (5th series), no. 1, Mar. 1969, pp. 56–8.

A note on the printing of 'Thee, God, I come from . . .' in A21. The background to the poem's inclusion is given, with Bridges's comments (from a letter to Hopkins's mother). Comparisons are made with other printed versions of the poem. See also I716.

1707   Alton, R. E. *and* Croft, P. J. Gerard Manley Hopkins. *Times Literary Supplement*, 6 Mar. 1969, p. 242.
Restatement of support for White's reading of 'To his Watch' (1698, 1702).

1708   Masheck, J. D. C. Art by a poet: notes on published drawings by Gerard Manley Hopkins. *Hermathena* (Dublin), no. 108, Spring 1969, pp. 24–37.
Detailed criticism and evaluation of G M H's drawings, including notes on the influence of Ruskin and the Pre-Raphaelites.

1709   Murphy, Michael W. Violent imagery in the poetry of Gerard Manley Hopkins. *Victorian Poetry*, vol. 7, no. 1, Spring 1969, pp. 1–16.
Images of blood, death, torture, and punishment abound in G M H's work. This article discusses their importance in the poet's style and suggests reasons for his use of them.

1710   *Powell, Everett G. Recurrent patterns of word order in the poems of Gerard Manley Hopkins. *Computers and the Humanities*, vol. 3, no. 5, May 1969, p. 286.
See entry L 104 in the 'Directory of Scholars Active'. Professor Powell's scope for this project includes: 1. Concordance of G M H's poetry. 2. Frequency of appearance word-lists. 3. Lists resulting from searching for word-order patterns. 4. Lists according to morphological criteria.

1711   Petry, Charles. Poet's work will not be neglected. *Evening News* (Bolton), 16 May 1969, p. 6.
A report of a further interview with the compiler, outlining the progress made in the formation of the Hopkins Society. See also 1705.

1712   Johnson, Wendell Stacy. [Review of H 299] *Victorian Poetry*, vol. 7, no. 2, Summer 1969, pp. 169–71.

1713   Seelhammer, Ruth. Hopkins theses: a burgeoning wood. *Renascence*, vol. 21, no. 4, Summer 1969, pp. 210–12, 222.
A survey of over 150 theses on G M H, demonstrating the wide range of his appeal to scholarly investigators.

1714   Thomas, Alfred. G. M. Hopkins in Liverpool. *Times Literary Supplement*, 18 Sept. 1969, pp. 1026–7.
A letter giving further background information about B 268.

1715   *Schoder, Raymond V. [Review of K 218] *Thought*, vol. 44, no. 174, Autumn 1969, pp. 469–70.

1716   Uphill, Arthur. A Hopkins discovery. *Library*, vol. 24, no. 4, Dec. 1969, p. 346.
A letter pointing out the exact location of the 'Miles' text of 'Thee, God, I come from . . .' referred to by White and Dunne (1706).

1970

1717   [Dunne, Tom.] The Hopkins Society. *British Studies Monitor* (Bowdoin College), vol. 1, no. 1, Spring 1970, pp. 30–1.
A short account of the foundation, aims, and objects of the Hopkins Society, being an edited version of information sent by the compiler. See also the further note in the following issue (Summer 1970, pp. 36–7) in which the Society's first year is briefly reviewed.

1718   *The Hopkins Research Bulletin*, no. 1, Spring 1970, 27 pp.
To be published annually by the Hopkins Society. Contents include notes on research in progress, notes on recent publications, a Hopkins bibliography, Society news, and other items of interest.

1719   Dunne, Tom. Gerard Manley Hopkins: priest in the poet. *Katawakes* (Bradford), vol. 1, no. 2, Apr.–June 1970, pp. 19–24.
A general essay attempting to show that the three aspects of G M H— man, priest and poet—should be considered in relation to each other.

1720   Pick, John. [Review of F 14, F 16, and H 306] *Victorian Poetry*, vol. 8, no. 2, Summer 1970, pp. 176–9.
'Bibliographies are rather sterile in themselves . . . They are made for use . . .'

THESES AND DISSERTATIONS

THIS section is a chronological list of unpublished theses and dissertations dealing wholly or in part with GMH. Unpublished theses in foreign languages have been placed in this section rather than in Section M to avoid mixing published and unpublished material. Published theses in any language have been regarded as books, and placed in the appropriate section. Where a thesis is known by the compiler to have formed the basis of a subsequently published book, a cross-reference has been provided.

1916

J1 *Neenan, Sister Mary Pius. Some evidences of mysticism in English poetry of the nineteenth century. *M.A., Catholic University of America,* 1916.

1931

J2 *Lahey, G. F. The prosody of Gerard Manley Hopkins and Robert Bridges. *M.A., Fordham University,* 1931.

1932

J3 *Boner, Harold A. Gerard Manley Hopkins. *M.A., Columbia University,* 1932.

J4 *Caster, Sister Mary Casilda. Elements of mysticism in Hopkins. *M.A., De Paul University,* 1932.

1933

J5 *Frazier, Alexander. The prosody of Gerard Manley Hopkins. *M.A., University of Arizona,* 1933.

1934

J6 *Surtz, Edward L. The religious aspect of the poetry of Gerard Manley Hopkins. *M.A., Xavier University*, 1934.

1935

J7 *Junkersfeld, Sister Mary Julienne. The history and the critical reception of the poems of Gerard Manley Hopkins, S.J. *M.A., Loyola University*, 1935.

J8 *Ryan, Sister Mary Philip. Gerard Manley Hopkins: the physical basis of his poetical forms. *M.A., University of Detroit*, 1935.

J9 *Stritch, Thomas John. Matter and form in the poetry of Gerard Manley Hopkins. *M.A., University of Notre Dame*, 1935.

1936

J10 *Arnold, Jerome Louis. A study of imagery in the poetry of Gerard Manley Hopkins, S.J. *M.A., University of Western Ontario*, 1936.

J11 *Dohmann, Sister Ottilia. The poetic mind of Gerard M. Hopkins, S.J. *Ph.D., Fordham University*, 1936.

J12 *Rosten, Norman. The prosody of Gerard Manley Hopkins. *M.A., New York University*, 1936.

1937

J13 *Dicus, Sister Mary Vivian. An analysis of the literary importance of Gerard Manley Hopkins. *M.A., University of Wichita*, 1937.

J14 *Durant, Albert A. The concept of God in the poetry of Gerard Manley Hopkins. *M.A., Catholic University of America*, 1937.

J15 *McCrossan, Sister Joseph Marie. The magic baton of Gerard Manley Hopkins. *M.A., Villanova College*, 1937.

J16 *Noonan, James Joseph. Evidences of the supernatural in the poetry of Gerard Manley Hopkins, S.J. *M.A., Boston College*, 1937.

J17 *Sheetz, Sister Mary Johannina. Gerard Manley Hopkins: a modern Victorian. *M.A., Crieghton University*, 1937.

J18 *Willer, William Herman. The poetic evolution of Gerard Manley Hopkins. *M.A., University of Minnesota*, 1937.

J19 *Wilson, Howard Aaron. A study of Gerard Manley Hopkins' prosody. *M.A., Washington State College*, 1937.

1938

J20 *Cochrane, Josephine M. Gerard Manley Hopkins: his conception of Catholicism. *M.A., New York University*, 1938.

J21 *Hayes, George Michael. Gerard Manley Hopkins as a critic. *M.A., University of Wisconsin*, 1938.

J22 *MacKay, Ronald Dickie. Form in the poetry of Gerard Manley Hopkins. *M.A., University of Toronto*, 1938.

J23 *Pick, John. Religious thought and experience in the poetry of Gerard Manley Hopkins. *Ph.D., University of Wisconsin*, 1938.

1939

J24 *Burton, James Rector. The metrical theory of Gerard Manley Hopkins. *M.A., University of Texas*, 1939.

J25 *Coogan, Majorie D. The nature poetry of Gerard Manley Hopkins, S.J. *M.A., Catholic University of America*, 1939.

J26 *Durand, Anthony Joseph. The metrical theory of Gerard Manley Hopkins, *M.A., University of Western Ontario*, 1939.

J27 *Elliott, B. E. Gerard Manley Hopkins. *M.A., University of Western Australia*, 1939.

J28 *Heffernan, Miriam Margaret. Gerard Manley Hopkins as critic and theorist of English literature. *M.A., Columbia University*, 1939.

1940

J29   *Bardacke, Theodore Joseph. Gerard Manley Hopkins. *M.A., Syracuse University*, 1940.

J30   *Cox, Dorothy Scarborough. The mind of Gerard Manley Hopkins. *M.A., University of Texas*, 1940.

J31   *Fraunces, John Manning. The meaning and use of inscape. *M.A., Loyola University*, 1940.

J32   *Saint Milo, Sister. The sonnets of Gerard Manley Hopkins. *M.A., University of Montreal*, 1940.

J33   *Weiss, Theodore. Gerard Manley Hopkins: a study in romanticism. *M.A., Columbia University*, 1940.

1941

J34   *Bernstein, Melvin Herbert. Nature and pessimism in Gerard Manley Hopkins: a study in romantic agony. *M.A., New York University*, 1941.

J35   *Cooney, Mother Madeleine Sophie. A study of tone color in the poetry of Gerard Manley Hopkins, S.J. *M.A., Marquette University*, 1941.

J36   *Melody, Sister M. Winifred. Gerard Manley Hopkins: critic of English poetry. *M.A., University of Notre Dame*, 1941.

J37   *Ong, Walter J. Historical backgrounds of sprung rhythm in modern English verse: a preliminary survey. *M.A., St. Louis University*, 1941.

J38   *Ronninger, Karl. Versuch einer Systematischen Ordnung der Metrischen Theorien Gerard Manley Hopkins. *Ph.D., University of Vienna*, 1941.

J39   *Sylvester, Howard E. A study of Gerard Manley Hopkins. *M.A., University of New Mexico*, 1941.

1942

J40 *Engel, Monroe. Gerard Manley Hopkins: inscapist poet. *B.A., Harvard University*, 1942.

J41 *Farrell, Sister Mary Pius. The influence of the liturgy on the works of Gerard Manley Hopkins. *B.A., Manhattan College*, 1942.

J42 *Kerr, Sister Marguerite M. Gerard Manley Hopkins: aspects or his poetical theory and practice. *M.A., University of Detroit*, 1942.

J43 *Melchner, Sister Mary Roberta. Hopkins and the common man. *M.A., Boston College*, 1942.

J44 *O'Brien, Robert David. The critical mind of Gerard Manley Hopkins. *M.A., Boston College*, 1942.

J45 *Tobin, Sister Madeleine. The literary qualities in the prose of Gerard Manley Hopkins. *M.A., University of Notre Dame*, 1942.

J46 *Welch, Sister M. Charlotte. The unity of Gerard Manley Hopkins' achievement. *M.A., Loyola University*, 1942.

1943

J47 *Casalandra, Sister Estelle. Gerard Manley Hopkins: a study in spiritual progress. *M.A., Ohio State University*, 1943.

J48 *Gilman, William Henry. Gerard Manley Hopkins: the man. *M.A., George Washington University*, 1943.

J49 *Holloway, Sister Marcella Marie. Gerard Manley Hopkins in the light of critical opinion. *M.A., University of Missouri*, 1943.

J50 *Kearney, Sister Mary Michael. Gerard Manley Hopkins, S.J., as social worker and poet. *M.A., University of Vermont*, 1943.

J51 *Lanctot, Sister Agnes. The liturgical concept of life in Gerard Manley Hopkins and Paul Claudel. *M.A., University of Notre Dame*, 1943.

J52 *Mathison, John Kelly. The poetical relationship of Gerard Manley Hopkins, Coventry Patmore, and Francis Thompson. *Ph.D., Princeton University*, 1943.
    Abstracted in *Dissertation Abstracts*, vol. 12, no. 1, 1952, pp. 67–8.

J53 *Murphy, Sister Miriam Joseph. Gerard Manley Hopkins: critic of his contemporaries in the nineteenth century. *M.A., Pittsburgh University*, 1943.

J54 *Noon, William T. The art principles of Gerard Manley Hopkins, S.J. *M.A., Loyola University*, 1943.

J55 *Scott, Rebecca Kathryn. The individualism of Gerard Manley Hopkins. *M.A., University of Missouri*, 1943.

1944

J56 *Burke, Sister Pauline. The Wreck of the Deutschland. *M.A., Boston College*, 1944.

J57 *Grady, Thomas J. The poetic principles of Gerard Manley Hopkins. *M.A., Loyola University*, 1944.

J58 *Jaworski, Sister M. Cunegundis. The transcendent Victorianism of Gerard Manley Hopkins. *M.A., Creighton University*, 1944.

1945

J59 *Brown, Sister Margaret Eugene. Gerard Manley Hopkins: literary critic. *M.A., St. John's University*, 1945.

J60 *Delaney, Sister Anne Cyril. The Christocentricity of Gerard Manley Hopkins. *M.A., Boston College*, 1945.

J61 *Holloway, Roberta. Some effects of classical study in the work of Hopkins. *Ph.D., University of California*, 1945.

J62 *Macri, Clare Grace. Gerard Manley Hopkins and Robert Bridges. *M.A., Columbia University*, 1945.

1946

J63   *Carlson, Sister Marian Raphael. Gerard Manley Hopkins and his critics. *Ph.D., Loyola University*, 1946.

J64   *Cohen, Selma Jeanne. The poems of Gerard Manley Hopkins in relation to his religious thought. *Ph.D., University of Chicago*, 1946.

J65   *Curran, Mary Doyle. A commentary on the poetry of Gerard Manley Hopkins. *Ph.D., University of Iowa*, 1946.

J66   *Maguire, Alice Marie. A study of the poetry of Gerard Manley Hopkins. *M.A., Brown University*, 1946.

J67   *Mandelbaum, Allen. Of mind and metaphor: a study in Richard Crashaw and Gerard Manley Hopkins. *M.A., Columbia University*, 1946.

J68   *Minten, Sister Grace Ellen. The literary reputation of Gerard Manley Hopkins. *M.A., De Paul University*, 1946.

J69   *Moira, Sister. The poetic theory of Gerard Manley Hopkins and its relation to his own work. *M.A., Notre Dame University* (South Bend), 1946.

J70   *Molloy, Eugene Joseph. The true humanism of Gerard Manley Hopkins. *M.A., St. John's University*, 1946.

J71   *Spehar, Elizabeth Marie. Gerard Manley Hopkins as a literary critic. *M.A., University of Colorado*, 1946.

1947

J72   *Greene, Sister Moira. The poetic theory of Gerard Manley Hopkins. *M.A., University of Notre Dame*, 1947.

J73   *Mooney, Margaret Elizabeth. Gerard Manley Hopkins and Vincent Van Gogh. *M.A., Columbia University*, 1947.

J74   *Schwartz, Joseph Michael. Gerard Manley Hopkins as literary critic; with specific reference to the criticism of his significant contemporaries as seen in his correspondence. *M.A., Marquette University*, 1947.

J75   *Wiles, Sister M. Peter. An annotated edition of selected poems of Gerard Manley Hopkins. *M.A., Canisius College*, 1947.

1948

J76   *Fitzgerald, Sister Marie Christine. The influence of St. John of the Cross on several poets of the Victorian Era. *M.A., Catholic University of America*, 1948.

J77   *Hache, Mother Irene Marie. The place of the Incarnation in the poetry of Hopkins. *M.A., Boston College*, 1948.

J78   *Haven, Richard. The experience of Gerard Manley Hopkins: a contextualist approach to his poetry. *Honors Thesis, Harvard University*, 1948.

J79   *McNamara, Anne. A study of voice and address in the poetry of Gerard Manley Hopkins. *M.A., Catholic University of America*, 1948.

J80   *Moon, Nelson Ferdinand. Gerard Manley Hopkins' use of imagery. *M.A., University of Oklahoma*, 1948.

J81   *Roberts, Donald A. The technical influence of Gerard Manley Hopkins in modern British poetry. *M.A., Columbia University*, 1948.

J82   *Sharpe, Garold. Gerard Manley Hopkins: the Dublin years. *M.A., Columbia University*, 1948.

J83   *Sharper, Philip Jenkins. Evidences of the mystical state in the 'terrible sonnets' of Gerard Manley Hopkins. *M.A., Fordham University*, 1948.

J84   *Shea, Dennis Donald David. An organisation of Gerard Manley Hopkins' critical opinions. *M.A., Columbia University*, 1948.

J85 *Simpson, Ruth Winifrid. Gerard Manley Hopkins: religion and the creative process. *M.A., Duke University*, 1948.

J86 *Smith, Helen R. A study of the treatment of nature in the poetry of Gerard Manley Hopkins. *M.A., Ohio University*, 1948.

J87 *Wagner, Robert D. Gerard Manley Hopkins: the 'terrible sonnets' and other poems of desolation. *M.A., Columbia University*, 1948.

J88 *Watts, Janet Flowers. The sonnets of Gerard Manley Hopkins. *Honors Thesis, University of Oregon*, 1948.

J89 *Wecker, John Clement. A survey of the influence of a common religion upon four 19th-Century Catholic poets: Alice Meynell, Francis Thompson, Coventry Patmore and Gerard Manley Hopkins. *M.A., University of Southern California*, 1948.

J90 *Yoggerst, Sister M. Hilary. Gerard Manley Hopkins as a critic of Patmore's poetry. *M.A., Marquette University*, 1948.

1949

J91 *Brennan, Joseph Xavier. Gerard Manley Hopkins: a critical interpretation of his poetry. *M.A., Brown University*, 1949.

J92 *Foote, Timothy Gilson. To what serves mortal agony? A study of Hopkins' 'The Wreck of the Deutschland' in relation to 'Lycidas', and an analysis of the 'terrible sonnets' in relation to the Spiritual Exercises of St. Ignatius; the whole being related generally to Milton. *Honors Thesis, Harvard University*, 1949.

J93 *Foote, Timothy Gilson. 'The Wreck of the Deutschland': an elegy. *Bowdoin Prize entry for dissertations in English, Harvard University*, 1949.

J94 *Freeman, Beatrice D. The literary reputation of Gerard Manley Hopkins. *M.A., Columbia University*, 1949.

J95　*Heuser, Edward Alan. An investigation of the poetic imagery of Gerard Manley Hopkins. *M.A., McGill University*, 1949.

J96　*McDonough, Mary Lou. An investigation to determine the extent of the liturgical echoes in the English poems of Gerard Manley Hopkins. *M.A., Bowling Green State University*, 1949.

J97　*Maltman, Sister M. Nicholas. The odd words in the poetry of Gerard Manley Hopkins. *M.A., Catholic University of America*, 1949.

J98　*Nelson, Norman Kent. Gerard Manley Hopkins: analysis and interpretation of three representative sonnets. *M.A., Duke University*, 1949.

J99　*Orr, Paul Anthony. The artistic principles of Gerard Manley Hopkins. *M.A., McGill University*, 1949.

J100　*Peach, William W. Gerard Manley Hopkins: his outlook on external reality as it is revealed in his works. *B.A., University of Santa Clara*, 1949.

J101　*Ricker, Elizabeth Ann. The relation of Hopkins' theories of poetry to his applied criticisms. *M.A., Boston College*, 1949.

J102　*Torchiana, Donald Thornhill. Pater, Newman and the poetic development of G. M. Hopkins. *M.A., University of Iowa*, 1949.

1950

J103　*Akey, John. Liturgical imagery in the poetry of Gerard Manley Hopkins, Thomas Merton, and Robert Lowell. *M.A., University of Vermont*, 1950.

J104　*Blum, Sister Magdalen Louise. The imagery in the poetry of Gerard Manley Hopkins. *M.A., University of New Mexico*, 1950.

J105　*Brophy, James D., *Jr.* The early poems of Gerard Manley Hopkins and their place in Hopkins criticism. *M.A., Columbia University*, 1950.

J106 *Gleeson, William F., *Jr.* Gerard Manley Hopkins and the Society of Jesus. *M.A., Columbia University,* 1950.

J107 *Gormon, Patrick. The attitude to nature and the external world of Gerard Manley Hopkins. *M.A., University of Toronto,* 1950.

J108 *Griffin, Sister Mary Ignatia. Gerard Manley Hopkins' 'That Nature is a Heraclitean Fire and of the Comfort of the Resurrection,'— an analysis of meaning. *M.A., Catholic University of America,* 1950.

J109 *Heilsham, Ingeborg. Die Oxfordbewegung und ihr Einfluss auf die Englische Dichtung: Hopkins, Patmore, Thompson, Newman. *Ph.D., University of Vienna,* 1950.

J110 *Hoecker, Eric L. Hopkins, Joyce, and the development of the artist. *M.A., Columbia University,* 1950.

J111 *Mullaney, Stephen William. Religious elements in Hopkins' poetry. *M.A., University of Iowa,* 1950.

J112 *Scanlan, Sister Alissa Marie. A study of Gerard Manley Hopkins' dramatic fragment 'St. Winifred's Well'. *M.A., Catholic University of America,* 1950.

J113 *Wall, Sister Mary Aquin. The Christian synthesis of art and prudence as exemplified in Gerard Manley Hopkins. *M.A., Gonzaga University,* 1950.

1951

J114 *Bailey, Joseph G. The sonnet theory of Gerard Manley Hopkins. *M.A., Catholic University of America,* 1951.

J115 *Garvey, Mother Eugenia Marie. Gerard Manley Hopkins, S.J.; his criticism of the major writers in English literature. *M.A., Fordham University,* 1951.

J116 *Mlodzik, Sister Mary Nazaria. A study of the parallelism and evolution in the imagery of Gerard Manley Hopkins. *M.A., University of Detroit,* 1951.

J117   *Przywara, Sister Benice. 'The Wreck of the Deutschland': story and analysis. *M.A., Niagara University,* 1951.

J118   *Retinger, Sister Mary Anthony. Gerard Manley Hopkins as a critic of English literature. *M.A., De Paul University,* 1951.

J119   *Robinson, Brian L. Nature in the poetry of Gerard Manley Hopkins. *M.A., Columbia University,* 1951.

J120   *Ziemba, Walter J. Gerard Manley Hopkins' 'Tom's Garland' an analysis. *M.A., Catholic University of America,* 1951.

1952

J121   *Begley, J. B. The literary criticisms of Gerard ManleyHopkins. *M.A., University of Melbourne,* 1952.

J122   *Bischoff, Dolph Anthony. Gerard Manley Hopkins as literary critic. *Ph.D., Yale University,* 1952.

J123   *Keane, James F. An analysis of Gerard Manley Hopkins' sonnet 'Henry Purcell'. *M.A., Catholic University of America,* 1952.

J124   *McCarthy, Adrian James. The concept of inscape in the poetry of Gerard Manley Hopkins. *M.A., New York University,* 1952.

J125   *McCormick, Sister Mary James. Gerard Manley Hopkins' 'Spelt from Sibyl's Leaves': an analysis. *M.A., Catholic University of America,* 1952.

J126   *McDonald, Sister Mary Roy. Gerard Manley Hopkins as social critic. *M.A., Marquette University,* 1952.

J127   *Meuth, Georgeanna S. Gerard Manley Hopkins: creator and created. *M.A., Columbia University,* 1952.

J128   Pearson, W. H. A comparative study of Patmore, Hopkins and Francis Thompson . . . *Ph.D., University of London,* 1952.
   An evaluative comparison, including an attempt to establish whether these poets constitute a Catholic 'school' of poetry.

J129　*Sharp, Jean Margaret. A cycle of nine songs for soprano to poems of Gerard Manley Hopkins. *M.A., University of Washington,* 1952.

J130　*Wolking, Sister M. Theresa. Hopkins' 'The Blessed Virgin Compared to the Air We Breathe': a study in unity. *M.A., Catholic University of America,* 1952.

1953

J131　*Des Rochers, Sister Vitalis. Gerard Manley Hopkins' 'As Kingfishers catch fire, dragonflies draw flame': a study in artistic unity. *M.A., Catholic University of America,* 1953.

J132　*Gerken, John Diedrich. The date and sequence of the 'terrible sonnets' of Gerard M. Hopkins, S.J. *M.A., Loyola University,* 1953.

J133　*Gross, Robert Eugene. The criticism of Gerard Manley Hopkins' 'The Windhover'. *M.A., New York University,* 1953.

J134　*Heuser, Edward Alan. The development of aesthetic cognition in Gerard Manley Hopkins. *Ph.D., Harvard University,* 1953.

J135　McGaughran, Sister Ruth Marie. The poetry of Gerard Manley Hopkins embodies traditional aesthetics. *M.A., Xavier University,* 1953.

J136　*MacNeil, Stella Therese. The poetry of Thomas Merton considered in relation to that of Gerard Manley Hopkins and T. S. Eliot. *M.A., New York University,* 1953.

J137　*Marcotte, John Paul. A philosophical presentation of the aesthetic-poetics of Gerard Manley Hopkins as inferred from *Scape* and *Inscape,* with its significance as a new critique. *M.A., St. John's University,* 1953.

1954

J138　*Clines, Gerald Patrick. Gerard Manley Hopkins' ascetic–aesthetic conflict. *B.A., University of Santa Clara,* 1954.

J139   *Connellan, Sister Anne Miriam. An analysis of the qualitative structure of sound in 'The Wreck of the Deutschland' by Gerard Manley Hopkins. *M.A., Catholic University of America*, 1954.

J140   *Curran, John Patrick. 'Inscape' and 'instress' as related principles in the theory and practice of Gerard Manley Hopkins. *M.A., New York University*, 1954.

J141   *Fleming, Lenore Marie Moe. The influence of Duns Scotus on Gerard Manley Hopkins. *M.A., Loyola University*, 1954.

J142   *McBrien, William Augustine. Musical techniques in the versification of Gerard Manley Hopkins. *M.A., St. John's University*, 1954.

J143   *Patterson, Jean Kenny. The influence of Welsh alliteration upon the poetry of Gerard Manley Hopkins. *M.A., Fordham University*, 1954.

J144   *Turner, H. Paul. An indexed synthesis to the critical thought of Gerard Manley Hopkins. *M.A., De Paul University*, 1954.

1955

J145   *Anderson, Walter J. 'The golden echo': religion in the life and poetry of Gerard Manley Hopkins. *M.A., Trinity College*, 1955.

J146   *Boyle, Robert R. The nature and function of the mature imagery of Gerard Manley Hopkins. *Ph.D., Yale University*, 1955.

J147   *Burgan, Sister Mary Stella Maris. A study of Gerard Manley Hopkins' sonnet 'Andromeda'. *M.A., Catholic University of America*, 1955.

J148   *Byrne, Sister Mary Jean Catherine. A synthesis of the interpretations of 'The Windhover'. *M.A., Catholic University of America*, 1955.

J149   *Cassidy, Lawrence P. Gerard Manley Hopkins' ideas on beauty and truth as shown in his poems and letters. *M.A., De Paul University*, 1955.

J150   *Cole, David Bruce. 'Charged with the grandeur of God.' God's majesty, as expressed in the poetry of Gerard Manley Hopkins. *Honors Essay, Harvard University,* 1955.

J151   *Cunningham, Maureen Michaela. The poetry of Gerard Manley Hopkins, S.J. *M.A., University of Washington,* 1955.

J152   *Downes, David Anthony. The Ignatian spirit in Gerard Manley Hopkins. *Ph.D., University of Washington,* 1955.
    Abstracted in *Dissertation Abstracts,* vol. 16, no. 3, 1956, p. 535. See also H 210.

J153   *Eisenbraun, Meredith Visnow. A study of Gerard Manley Hopkins' sonnets with reference to his own commentary and to the formative influences in his life. *M.A., University of South Dakota,* 1955.

J154   *Faget, Sister Mary Ignatius. The concept of sake in Gerard Manley Hopkins. *M.A., Catholic University of America,* 1955.

J155   *Hazo, Samuel John. An analysis of 'inscape' in the poetry of Gerard Manley Hopkins. *M.A., Duquesne University,* 1955.

J156   *Kornacki, Wanda Charlotte. Thomistic principles of esthetics in the poetry of Gerard Manley Hopkins, Francis Thompson and Coventry Patmore. *M.A., De Paul University,* 1955.

J157   *Pennington, Frederic Adams. Gerard Manley Hopkins and Duns Scotus: the derivation of inscape and its poetical function. *M.A., Duke University,* 1955.

J158   *Rubenstein, Gladys. A study of Gerard Manley Hopkins' reputation as a poet. *M.A., Claremont College,* 1955.

J159   *Smith, Robert Francis. A comparative study of some nature poems of William Wordsworth and Gerard Manley Hopkins. *M.A., University of Notre Dame,* 1955.

1956

J160   *Andrews, Robert F. An explication of Gerard Manley Hopkins' 'On a Piece of Music'. *M.A., Catholic University of America,* 1956.

J161 *Conlon, Sister M. Brendan. The fire image in the poetry of Gerard Manley Hopkins. *M.A., Creighton University*, 1956.

J162 *De Verteuil, L. M. The language of Gerard Manley Hopkins. *M.A., National University of Ireland*, 1956.

J163 *Farrell, Melvin Lloyd. The significance of Christ in the poetry of Gerard Manley Hopkins. *M.A., University of Washington*, 1956.

J164 Lloyd-Jones, Richard. Common speech: a poetic effect for Hopkins, Browning and Arnold. *Ph.D., University of Iowa*, 1956.
Abstracted in *Dissertation Abstracts*, vol. 16, no. 5, May 1956, p. 957.

J165 *Paye, Sister Mary Paul. The logical structure of the sonnets of Gerard Manley Hopkins. *M.A., Catholic University of America*, 1956.

1957

J166 *Aronowitz, Herbert. The relationship of the Spiritual Exercises of St. Ignatius to the poetry of Gerard Manley Hopkins as evidenced in 'The Wreck of the Deutschland'. *B.A., Rutgers University*, 1957.

J167 *Connor, Sister Juanita Maria. The relationship of Gerard Manley Hopkins and his life of consecration. *M.A., Villanova University*, 1957.

J168 *Donovan, Mother Mary Inez. The aesthetics of Gerard Manley Hopkins, S.J. *M.A., University of Detroit*, 1957.

J169 *Gallo, Ernest Anthony. Gerard Manley Hopkins: linguistic innovator. *M.A., New York University*, 1957.

J170 *Schaumberg, Hans-Hubert. Gerard Manley Hopkins Naturauffassung (Eine Untersuchung der Tagebucher). *Ph.D., Georg-August-Universitat, Gottingen*, 1957.

J171 *Whelan, Rosalie C. The critical reception of the first and second editions of the poems of Gerard Manley Hopkins. *M.A., Marquette University*, 1957.

1958

J172 *Brinlee, Robert Washington. The religion and poetic theory of Gerard Manley Hopkins. *M.A., University of Tulsa*, 1958.

J173 Mellown, Elgin W. The reception of Gerard Manley Hopkins's poems, 1909–1957. *M.A., University of London*, 1958.
Traces the development of the public recognition and acceptance of G M H's work. See also F7, F9.

J174 *Northup, Eileen. Hopkins as a student of Pater. *M.A., University of Rhode Island*, 1958.

J175 *Swanzy, Annabeth. A study of Gerard Manley Hopkins' poetic theory and practice. *M.A., Louisiana State University*, 1958.

1959

J176 *Abraham, John August. Hopkins and Scotus: an analogy between inscape and individuation. *Ph.D., University of Wisconsin*, 1959.
Abstracted in *Dissertation Abstracts*, vol. 20, no. 6, Dec. 1959, pp. 2281–2.

J177 *Bell, Sister Ann Charles. Gerard Manley Hopkins and the mystical life. *M.A., Villanova University*, 1959.

J178 *Buggy, Sister James Marita. Growth of the literary reputation of Gerard Manley Hopkins. *M.A., Villanova University*, 1959.

J179 *Cascio, Joseph E., *Jr.* Gerard Manley Hopkins and the arts of literary criticism, painting, and music. *M.A., St. John's University*, 1959.

J180 *Lenz, Sister Mary Babylon. The meditative style in Gerard Manley Hopkins. *M.A., University of Notre Dame*, 1959.

J181 *Linane, Sister Francis Loretto. Intensification in G. M. Hopkins' 'The Leaden Echo and the Golden Echo'. *M.A., Catholic University of America*, 1959.

J182 *McBrien, William Augustine. Likeness in the themes and prosody of Gerard Manley Hopkins and Dylan Thomas. *Ph.D., St. John's University*, 1959.

J183 *Mann, John S. A study in the relation of structure to thought in the poetry of Gerard Manley Hopkins. *M.A., Columbia University*, 1959.

J184 *Shkolnick, Sylvia. Gerard Manley Hopkins: a study in the poetry of meditation. *M.A., Columbia University*, 1959.

J185 *Silverstein, Henry. On 'Tom's Garland'. *M.A., New York University*, 1959.

J186 *Young, Lillian. The 'maker' and his maker: a study in the conflict between the devotion to art and to God in Michelangelo, Donne and Hopkins as a background for their religious sonnets. *M.A., Cornell University*, 1959.

1960

J187 *Beauregard, David Napoleon. The aesthetic theory of Gerard Manley Hopkins. *M.A., Ohio State University*, 1960.

J188 *Byrne, Virginia Cartmel. Inscape in the aesthetic theory and poetic practice of Gerard Manley Hopkins. *M.A., College of the Holy Names* (Oakland, California), 1960.

J189 *Gunning, J. The intellectual and ascetical formation of Gerard Manley Hopkins. *M.A., University of Sheffield*, 1960.

J190 *Lacklamp, John Jerome. The influence of music on the life of Gerard Manley Hopkins. *M.A., Loyola University*, 1960.

J191 *Lawler, Donald L. Gerard Manley Hopkins: three patterns of his poetry. *M.A., Columbia University*, 1960.

J192 *Schreiber, Annette Claire. Hopkins' 'The Wreck of the Deutschland'; a study. *Ph.D., Cornell University*, 1960.

1961

J193 *Conlon, Michael J. A bibliography of the writings and ana of Gerard Manley Hopkins from January 1, 1947 to January 1, 1958. *M.A., University of Kentucky*, 1961.

J194 *Kelly, Richard Michael. The intellectual milieu of Gerard Manley Hopkins. *M.A., Duke University*, 1961.

J195 *Lenz, Mildred. A poet's view of reality: a study of the works of Gerard Manley Hopkins. *M.A., University of Kansas*, 1961.

J196 *McLaughlin, John Joseph. The influence of St. Paul on Gerard Manley Hopkins. *M.A., Boston College*, 1961.

J197 *Markert, Marilyn Rose. Gerard Manley Hopkins' use of sonnet form. *M.A., John Carroll University*, 1961.

J198 *Napier, Murray Patrick. A study from the sermons of Gerard Manley Hopkins. *M.A., McGill University*, 1961.

J199 *Norris, Carolyn Brimley. Rhetoric and poetic language in the sermons of Gerard Manley Hopkins. *M.A., University of Tennessee*, 1961.

J200 *Parker, Dorothy Elizabeth Hagman. Gerard Manley Hopkins and the critics. *Ph.D., University of Texas*, 1961.
　　Abstracted in *Dissertation Abstracts*, vol. 22, no. 1, July 1961, p. 263.

J201 *Pocs, John A. Nationalism in the poetry of Gerard Manley Hopkins. *M.A., Bowling Green State University*, 1961.

J202 *Rader, Louis. The dark sonnets of Gerard Manley Hopkins. *M.A., Cornell University*, 1961.

J203 *Riordan, Mary Marguerite. A study of the similarities in the works of Gerard Manley Hopkins and Walt Whitman. *M.A., San Francisco State College*, 1961.

J204 *Roeder, Raymond L., *Jr.* The sonnet tradition and Gerard Manley Hopkins. *Senior Thesis, University of Santa Clara*, 1961.

J205 *Turner, Edmond Glen. A study of dialect in the poetry of Gerard Manley Hopkins. *M.A., University of Idaho,* 1961.

1962

J206 *Ames, Charlotte. 'God's Grandeur': the image and effect. *M.A., Catholic University of America,* 1962.

J207 *Barnes, Roslyn Tennie. Gerard Manley Hopkins and Pierre Teilhard de Chardin: a formulation of mysticism for a scientific age. *M.A., University of Iowa,* 1962.

J208 *Bender, Todd Kay. Some derivative elements in the poetry of Gerard Manley Hopkins. *Ph.D., Stanford University,* 1962.
Abstracted in *Dissertation Abstracts,* vol. 23, no. 11, May 1963, p. 4352.

J209 *Berg, Sister Mary Gretchen. The prosodic structure of Robert Bridges' 'neo-Miltonic syllabics.' *Ph.D., Catholic University of America,* 1962.

J210 *Brennan, Norman Charles. An objective interpretation of three mature sonnets of Gerard Manley Hopkins. *M.A., Niagara University,* 1962.

J211 *Cleary, Helen Kae. In his own image: a study of Hopkins' poetic treatment of man. *M.A., Cornell University,* 1962.

J212 *Evarts, Prescott, *Jr.* Inscape and symbol in the poetry of Gerard Manley Hopkins. *M.A., Columbia University,* 1962.

J213 *Kernan, Sister M. Noel. A critique of poetry compiled from the prose writings of Gerard Manley Hopkins. *M.A., Duquesne University,* 1962.

J214 Speyrer, Anna Elizabeth (*née* Mitch). Bibliography of the Gerard Manley Hopkins collection in the Crosby Library, Gonzaga University. *M.A., Gonzaga University,* 1962.
Completely superseded by Seelhammer's published catalogue of the collection (see F16).

J215 *Westwater, Sister Agnes Martha. Sea imagery in Gerard Manley Hopkins' 'The Wreck of the Deutschland'. *M.A., St. John's University*, 1962.

J216 *Woodyard, Vivian Welch. A study of the vector in the poetry of Gerard Manley Hopkins. *Senior Thesis, University of California* (Riverside), 1962.

1963

J217 *Adams, Juliette Rose Marie. The theory of language in the poetics of Gerard Manley Hopkins. *M.A., University of Toronto*, 1963.

J218 *Andreach, Robert Joseph. The spiritual life in Hopkins, Joyce, Eliot, and Hart Crane. *Ph.D., New York University*, 1963.
Abstracted in *Dissertation Abstracts*, vol. 25, no. 1, July 1964, p. 467. See also H243.

J219 *Bloom, Lionel. The mystic pattern in the poetry of Gerard Manley Hopkins. *M.A., Columbia University*, 1963.

J220 *Colavecchio, Barbara Marie. The dominant symbols in Gerard Manley Hopkins' 'The Wreck of the Deutschland'. *M.A., University of Rhode Island*, 1963.

J221 *Collins, Winston Lee. Tennyson and Hopkins: intellectual and poetic affinities. *M.A., University of Toronto*, 1963.

J222 *D'Angelo, Frank Joseph. 'The Wreck of the Deutschland' and the pastoral tradition. *M.A., Tulane University*, 1963.

J223 De Souza, Frederick J. Gerard Manley Hopkins: a closer look at the 'terrible sonnets'. *M.A., Columbia University*, 1963.

J224 *Pike, Francis George, *Jr*. The influence of John Ruskin upon the aesthetic theory and practice of Gerard Manley Hopkins. *Ph.D., Stanford University*, 1963.
Abstracted in *Dissertation Abstracts*, vol. 25, Aug. 1964, p. 1208.

J225   *Gappa, Richard John. A critical evaluation of 'The Windhover, to Christ Our Lord', and its criticism. *M.A., University of Colorado*, 1963.

J226   *Hamilton, Seymour Charles. The unified world-vision of Gerard Manley Hopkins. *M.A., University of Toronto*, 1963.

J227   *Hill, Francis Anthony. An explication of 'Harry Ploughman' by Gerard Manley Hopkins as an inscape of cosmological motion and the unmoved mover. *M.A., Tulane University*, 1963.

J228   *Lukanitsch, Ruth Marion. The relationship of the figures of sound to the rhythm in certain poems of Gerard Manley Hopkins. *Ph.D., Northwestern University*, 1963.
    Abstracted in *Dissertation Abstracts*, vol. 25, no. 1, July 1964, p. 696.

J229   *Malloy, Margaret Gladys. Desolation and delight: a study of recurring themes in the poetry of Gerard Manley Hopkins. *M.A., University of Manitoba*, 1963.

J230   *Ochshorn, Myron Gustav. Hopkins the critic: the literary judgement and taste of Gerard Manley Hopkins; with an appendix on his verse theory. *Ph.D., University of New Mexico*, 1963.
    Abstracted in *Dissertation Abstracts*, vol. 25, no. 6, Dec. 1964, pp. 3579–80.

J231   *Olney, James Leslie. George Herbert and Gerard Manley Hopkins: a comparative study in two religious poets. *Ph.D., Columbia University*, 1963.
    Abstracted in *Dissertation Abstracts*, vol. 25, no. 3, Sept. 1964, pp. 1895–6.

J232   *Pouncey, Lorene. Gerard Manley Hopkins' sextet of 'terrible' sonnets: an analytical study. *M.A., University of Houston*, 1963.

J233   *Riley, Sister Maria Amabilis. A comparative study showing the influence of John Keats on Gerard Manley Hopkins. *M.A., Florida State University*, 1963.

J234 *Stenten, Cathryn Davis. A study of the poetic theories of Coventry Patmore, Robert Bridges and Gerard Hopkins as the basis for a system of modern prosody. *M.A., University of Nebraska,* 1963.

J235 *Townsend, Gerard James. A comparative study of 'The Wreck of the Deutschland' by Gerard Manley Hopkins and 'The Dark Night of the Soul' by St. John of the Cross. *M.A., Tulane University,* 1963.

J236 *Wills, Mary Suzanne. An analysis of the influence of the Spiritual Exercises of St. Ignatius on the poetry of Gerard Manley Hopkins. *M.A., Indiana State College,* 1963.

1964

J237 *Agnew, Francis Henry. The prosodic theory of Gerard Manley Hopkins and the philosophy of Duns Scotus. *M.A., De Paul University,* 1964.

J238 *August, Eugene R. Word inscapes: a study of the poetic vocabulary of Gerard Manley Hopkins. *Ph.D., University of Pittsburgh,* 1964.
    Abstracted in *Dissertation Abstracts,* vol. 26, no. 6, Dec. 1965, pp. 3294–5.

J239 *Augusta, Sister Paul. A commentary on the 'terrible sonnets' of Gerard Manley Hopkins. *M.A., University of New Mexico,* 1964.

J240 *Brown, Marie Patricia. The sensuous concept of nature in G. M. Hopkins' poetic images. *M.A., Georgetown University,* 1964.

J241 *Colson, Ted Donald. An analysis of selected poems of Gerard Manley Hopkins for oral interpretation and a study of his poetic theories. *Ph.D., University of Oklahoma,* 1964.
    Abstracted in *Dissertation Abstracts,* vol. 24, no. 12, June 1964, p. 5604.

J242 *Dilligan, Robert. The influence of John Keats on Gerard Manley Hopkins. *M.A., Columbia University,* 1964.

J243   *Haas, Charles Eugene. A structural analysis of selected sonnets of
       Gerard Manley Hopkins. *Ph.D., University of Denver*, 1964.
          Abstracted in *Dissertation Abstracts*, vol. 25, no. 9, Mar. 1965,
          p. 5443.

J244   *Herring, Mary Lynn. Gerard Manley Hopkins as a critic of
       poetry. *M.A., University of Tennessee*, 1964.

J245   *Marx, Carola Maxine. Gerard Manley Hopkins' 'Spring and
       Fall: to a Young Child': a study of poetic compression. *M.A., Cornell
       University*, 1964.

J246   *Murray, Neil A. The prosodic theory and practice of Hopkins,
       Patmore and Bridges. *M.A., Memorial University of Newfoundland*,
       1964.

J247   *Nielson, Sister Ancilla of the Immaculate. The Scotist element in
       Hopkins. *M.A., St. John's University*, 1964.

J248   *Orr, Paul Anthony. The artistic principles of Gerard Manley
       Hopkins. *Ph.D., University of Notre Dame*, 1964.
          Abstracted in *Dissertation Abstracts*, vol. 25, no. 5, Nov. 1964, pp.
          2965–6.

J249   *Rader, Louis. Major problems in Hopkins criticism. *Ph.D.,
       Cornell University*, 1964.

J250   *Trudeau, Sister Paul Augusta. A commentary on the 'terrible
       sonnets' of Gerard Manley Hopkins. *M.A., University of New Mexico*,
       1964.

                                  1965

J251   *Abbott, William Henry. The image of time in the poetry of
       Gerard Manley Hopkins. *M.A., Louisiana State University*, 1965.

J252   *Camp, Burr A. Gerard Manley Hopkins' sonnets of desolation:
       an analysis of the qualitative sound structure. *Thesis, Barry College*,
       1965.

J253 *Cooper, Benjamin Evans. Vertical movement in the poetry of Gerard Manley Hopkins: an insight to the poet's thought. *M.A., University of Virginia*, 1965.

J254 *Delahunty, Kenneth R. Guilt and the grail: Hopkins, poet in the active voice; Wakefield, Mon Frere. *M.A., Pennsylvania State University*, 1965.

J255 *Hart, Lucia Caroline Romberg. The poetry of Gerard Manley Hopkins. *M.A., University of Texas*, 1965.

J256 *Johnson, Ronald W. Gerard Manley Hopkins: his approach to literary criticism. *M.A., Colorado State University*, 1965.

J257 *Lovas, John Charles. The poet and his God: a study of the religious verse of Gerard Manley Hopkins. *M.A., University of Utah*, 1965.

J258 *McGowan, Madelon. The concept of nature in the poetry of Gerard Manley Hopkins. *M.A., University of Southern California*, 1965.

J259 *O'Connor, Sister M. Elizabeth Therese. Gerard Manley Hopkins' 'The Wreck of the Deutschland': a plea for structural analysis. *M.A., University of Scranton*, 1965.

J260 *Tripp, Kathryn Stewart. Gerard Manley Hopkins and the self. *M.A., Columbia University*, 1965.

J261 *Yetzer, Bernard Edward. The Victorianism of Gerard Manley Hopkins. *M.A., University of Oklahoma*, 1965.

1966

J262 *Chamberlain, Charles Martin, III. Hopkins' rejection of estheticism. *Ph.D., University of Colorado*, 1966.
     Abstracted in *Dissertation Abstracts*, vol. 28, no. 2, Aug. 1967, pp. 620–621A.

J263　*Concilio, Peter F. Gerard Manley Hopkins' 'The Wreck of the Deutschland' and the sonata-allegro: a comparative study. *M.A., Niagara University*, 1966.

J264　*De Graaff, Robert Mark. Scotism in the poetry of Gerard Manley Hopkins: a study in analogical relationships. *M.A., Miami University*, 1966.

J265　*Dumbleton, William Albert. The literary relationship of Robert Bridges to Gerard Manley Hopkins, 1889–1930. *Ph.D., University of Pennsylvania*, 1966.
　　Abstracted in *Dissertation Abstracts*, vol. 28, no. 1, July 1967, p. 227A.

J266　*Durrwachter, Carol J. John Donne and Gerard Manley Hopkins: a comparison. *M.A., Pennsylvania State University*, 1966.

J267　*Franz, Louis Joseph. The concept of the 'Mystical Body of Christ' in selected poems by Gerard Manley Hopkins. *Ph.D., University of Southern California*, 1966.
　　Abstracted in *Dissertation Abstracts*, vol. 27, no. 9, Mar. 1967, p. 3045A.

J268　*Kenneally, John Daniel. The personal and literary relationship of Gerard Manley Hopkins and Richard Watson Dixon. *Ph.D., Fordham University*, 1966.
　　Abstracted in *Dissertation Abstracts*, vol. 27, no. 2, Aug. 1966, p. 458.

J269　*Klotz, Rose Mosen. Verbal counterpoint in the poetry of Gerard Manley Hopkins. *Ph.D., University of Wisconsin*, 1966.
　　Abstracted in *Dissertation Abstracts*, vol. 27, no. 4, Oct. 1966, pp. 1058–9.

J270　*McCrossan, Sister Virginia Elizabeth. A study of two poets of faith of the nineteenth century: Christina Rossetti—Gerard M. Hopkins. *M.A., University of Hawaii*, 1966.

J271　*Moakler, Kenneth. The dark night of the self: the unifying vision in Gerard Manley Hopkins. *M.A., Western Illinois University*, 1966.

J272   *Savant, John L. The rhetorical effect of sentence patterns in Gerard Manley Hopkins' poem 'The Blessed Virgin Compared to the Air We Breathe'. *M.A., Dominican College of San Rafael,* 1966.

J273   *Snavely, Robert Carl. Gerard Manley Hopkins: mystic or metaphysical. *M.A., University of Omaha,* 1966.

J274   *Stein, Karen F. Hopkins' 'The Wreck of the Deutschland': an aesthetic analysis. *M.A., Pennsylvania State University,* 1966.

J275   *Storm, Melvin G. Gerard Manley Hopkins: the poet as critic. *M.A., University of Wyoming,* 1966.

J276   *Tamplin, John C. The forsaken forged feature: a study of Gerard Manley Hopkins' sonnet 'Henry Purcell'. *M.A., Kent State University,* 1966.

J277   *Walker, Alan. The influence of Welsh poetry on that of Gerard Manley Hopkins and Dylan Thomas. *M.A., University of Toronto,* 1966.

1967

J278   *Backscheider, Paula. The revelation of God to Gerard Manley Hopkins as expressed in his mature, complete poems. *M.A., Southern Connecticut State College,* 1967.

J279   *Bedrian, George L. Spelt from Sibyl's Leaves: a study in dichotomies. *M.A., University of Massachusetts,* 1967.

J280   *Blythe, Harold Russell. Hopkins' 'The Wreck of the Deutschland': a critical study. *M.A., University of Florida,* 1967.

J281   *Burr, Carol. Compound epithets in the poetry of Gerard Manley Hopkins. *M.A., Columbia University,* 1967.

J282   *Cohen, Edward H. A bibliography including the published works of Gerard Manley Hopkins and criticism of the works of Gerard Manley Hopkins. *Ph.D., University of New Mexico,* 1967.

This thesis was the basis of Professor Cohen's published bibliography: see F 14.

J 283   *Derrick, Mildred E. 'To what serves mortal beauty?' Hopkins' conception of nature and man in relation to God. *M.A., Vanderbilt University*, 1967.

J 284   *Elkins, Bill James. Hopkins' terrible sonnets: a study of poetic progression. *Ph.D., Ohio University*, 1967.
Abstracted in *Dissertation Abstracts*, vol. 27, no. 12, June 1967, p. 4219A.

J 285   *Hughes, Nathalie L. Gerard Manley Hopkins: toward a synthesis. *M.A., University of Miami*, 1967.

J 286   *Kaminsky, Marc. The Victorian Hopkins. *M.A., Columbia University*, 1967.

J 287   *McLaughlin, John. The pulpit rhetoric of Gerard Manley Hopkins. *Ph.D., Columbia University*, 1967.
Abstracted in *Dissertation Abstracts*, vol. 28, no. 2, Aug. 1967, p. 770A.

J 288   *Pendergrass, Paula Belcher. The dark sonnets of Gerard Manley Hopkins: a critical study. *M.A., University of Florida*, 1967.

J 289   *Smullen, George J. The sonnet forms of Gerard Manley Hopkins and Robert Bridges. *M.A., Kent State University*, 1967.

J 290   Thomas, Alfred. Hopkins the Jesuit; the years of training. *Ph.D., University of London*, 1967.
This thesis formed the basis of Father Thomas's published biography of G M H: see G 101.

1968

J 291   *Brinlee, Robert Washington. Hopkins' reconciliation of religion and poetry: its critical history and its implications for the Christian imagination. *Ph.D., University of Missouri, Columbia*, 1968.
Abstracted in *Dissertation Abstracts*, vol. 29, 1969, pp. 4479–4479A.

J292　*Mariani, Paul Louis. Artistic and spiritual development in the sonnets of Gerard Manley Hopkins, 1865–1889. *Ph.D., City University of New York,* 1968.

Abstracted in *Dissertation Abstracts,* vol. 28, no. 11, May 1968, pp. 4639A–4640A.

J293　*Riddle, Florence Kerr. Love and fear of mortal beauty: a tension in Gerard Manley Hopkins' poetry. *Ph.D., University of Washington,* 1968.

Abstracted in *Dissertation Abstracts,* vol. 29, no. 7, Jan. 1969, pp. 2276–2276A.

J294　White, Norman Everett. G. M. Hopkins: an edition of the last poems (1884–1889), with an introduction and notes. *M.Phil., University of London,* 1968.

Based on a thorough study of the MSS., this edition seeks to establish an accurate text for G M H's last poems, and includes paraphrases and commentaries.

SECTION K

CRITICISM OF INDIVIDUAL POEMS

ENTRIES in this section are arranged alphabetically by title or first line of poem, and then chronologically for each poem. The numbers in parentheses after the titles or first lines are the identification-numbers allocated to the poems in P4. It should be noted that this section overlaps with others: the entries here usually relate to one poem only, and articles on groups of poems are placed in Section I. Furthermore, certain entries elsewhere in the bibliography have a connection with one particular poem, but have not been placed in this section because their main importance lies in some other direction. There are also a few studies of individual poems in foreign languages: these have been placed in Section M. Users of this section are therefore recommended to consult the list of poems in the index, which brings all the various references to each poem together.

AD MARIAM (26)

K1 Williams, Charles. Gerard Manley Hopkins. *Times Literary Supplement*, 1 Jan. 1931, p. 12.
A letter, justifying the inclusion of 'Ad Mariam' in P2.

AS KINGFISHERS CATCH FIRE (57)

K2 Cohen, Selma Jeanne. Hopkins' 'As Kingfishers Catch Fire'. *Modern Language Quarterly*, vol. 11, no. 2, June 1950, pp. 197–204. This poem deals with 'the concept of individuality viewed first as that possessed by "each mortal thing", and then as it appears in "the just man".'

AT THE WEDDING MARCH (86) *see* G2

THE BLESSED VIRGIN COMPARED TO THE AIR WE BREATHE (60)

K 3   *Casalandra, Sister Estelle. The Blessed Virgin Compared to the Air We Breathe. *Rosary*, vol. 94, no. 10, Nov. 1943, pp. 16, 30.

K 4   *Delaney, Joan. 'The Blessed Virgin Compared to the Air We Breathe': an interpretation. *Clarke College Labarum* (Dubuque, Iowa), vol. 41, no. 3, Summer 1949, pp. 201–14.

K 5   *Klapp, F. A closer look at this masterful work: 'The Blessed Virgin Compared to the Air we Breathe'. *Marianist*, vol. 53, Jan. 1962, pp. 22–5.

BY MRS. HOPLEY (97)

K 6   Duncan-Jones, E. E. Hopkins and Mrs. Hopley. *Times Literary Supplement*, 10 Oct. 1968, p. 1159.
       Suggests a historical background for the poem.

THE CAGED SKYLARK (39)

K 7   *Friar, Kimon, *and* Brinnin, John Malcolm. Modern poetry, American and British. New York, Appleton-Century-Crofts, 1951.
       See pp. 503–4. General explication of the poem.

K 8   Giovannini, Margaret. Hopkins' 'The Caged Skylark'. *Explicator*, vol. 14, no. 6, Mar. 1956, item 35.
       The key to the poem's meaning rests in the final phrase 'bones risen'.

K 9   *Houle, Sister Mary John Bosco. Readings of two Victorian poems. *Iowa English Yearbook*, no. 10, Fall 1965, pp. 50–2.
       Meredith's 'The Lark Ascending' and GMH's 'The Caged Skylark'.

THE CANDLE INDOORS (46)

K 10   Gavin, Sister Rosemarie Julie. Hopkins' 'The Candle Indoors'. *Explicator*, vol. 20, no. 6, Feb. 1962, item 50.
       The fourth line of the octet is central to the poem's meaning.

(CARRION COMFORT) (64)

K11   Elvin, Lionel. Introduction to the study of literature; vol. 1,
Poetry. London, Sylvan Press, 1949. 224 pp.
See pp. 206–11. General explication of the poem.

K12   *Joselyn, Sister M. Herbert and Hopkins: two lyrics. *Renascence*,
vol. 10, no. 4, Summer 1958, pp. 192–5.
The poems are 'Affliction (1)' and 'Carrion Comfort'.

K13   Assad, Thomas J. A closer look at Hopkins' '(Carrion Comfort)'.
Tulane Studies in English, vol. 9, 1959, pp. 91–102.
An explication of the logical and integral meaning of the poem.

COCKLE'S ANTIBILIOUS PILLS

K14   Thomas, A[lfred]. G. M. Hopkins: an unpublished triolet.
Modern Language Review, vol. 61, no. 2, Apr. 1966, pp. 183–7.
'Even the doodles of genius are revealing': G M H found inspiration
for this triolet in a newspaper. Examines motives and methods.

K15   White, Norman E. G. M. Hopkins's triolet 'Cockle's Antibilious
Pills'. *Notes and Queries*, vol. 15 (n.s.), no. 5, May 1968, pp. 183–4.
Supplements Thomas (K14) by showing that Cockles pills were
well-known and well-mocked as far back as 1846.

EPITHALAMION (159)

K16   S, H. The poet, the Hodder and the river-bathe. *Stonyhurst
Magazine*, vol. 33, no. 415, Oct. 1960, pp. 503–4.
The poem describes the river Hodder near Stonyhurst.

FELIX RANDAL (86)

K17   Orwell, George. The meaning of a poem. *Listener*, vol. 25, no.
648, 12 June 1941, p. 841.
'The best touch . . . in this poem is due to a verbal coincidence. For
the word that pins the whole poem together . . . is that final word
"sandal", which no doubt only came into Hopkins' mind because it
happened to rhyme with Randal.'

K18 Adams, Hazard. The contexts of poetry. London, Methuen, 1965. xii, 200 pp.

See pp. 70–1. Comments on the poem.

K19 Mariani, Paul L. Hopkins' 'Felix Randal' as Sacramental vision. *Renascence*, vol. 19, no. 4, Summer 1967, pp. 217–20.

GOD'S GRANDEUR (31). *See also* M188, M217

K20 Maritain, Jacques. Poetic experience. *Review of Politics*, vol. 6, no. 4, Oct. 1944, pp. 387–402.

An essay on 'the nature of poetic knowledge', concluding thus: 'If I looked for a poem . . . manifesting in the finest way poetic experience as I have tried to describe it, I would suggest . . . 'God's Grandeur'. Comments on the poem follow.

K21 Wright, Brooks. Hopkins' 'God's Grandeur'. *Explicator*, vol. 10, no. 1, Oct. 1951, item 5.

In terms of dramatic structure the image of the dove ties together the various threads of the poem.

K22 Reeves, James. The critical sense . . . London, William Heinemann Ltd., 1956. viii, 159 pp.

See pp. 102–4. General explication of the poem.

K23 Nist, John. Sound and sense: some structures of poetry. *College English*, vol. 23, no. 4, Jan. 1962, pp. 291–5.

See particularly p. 294. Brief note on what happens in the poem when GMH shifts the consonant *d* from final position to one of alliteration.

K24 Bender, Todd K. Hopkins' 'God's Grandeur'. *Explicator*, vol. 21, no. 7, Mar. 1963, item 55.

The meaning of the first four lines, especially the phrase 'oil/crushed'.

K25 Chamberlain, Robert L. George Macdonald's 'A Manchester Poem' and Hopkin's [*sic*] 'God's Grandeur'. *Personalist*, vol. 44, no. 4, Autumn 1963, pp. 518–27.

Comparison of GMH and Macdonald.

K 26   Montag, George E. Hopkins' 'God's Grandeur' and 'the ooze of oil crushed'. *Victorian Poetry*, vol. 1, no. 4, Nov. 1963, pp. 302–3.
The meaning of the phrase and its importance in the poem.

K 27   Watson, Thomas L. Hopkins' 'God's Grandeur'. *Explicator*, vol. 22, no. 6, Feb. 1964, item 47.
The meaning of the poem as a whole.

K 28   Noel, Sister Mary. Gathering to a greatness: a study of 'God's Grandeur'. *English Journal*, vol. 53, no. 4, Apr. 1964, pp. 285–7.
A general explication, with bias towards the viewpoint and needs of the teacher of English.

K 29   Pendexter, Hugh. Hopkins' 'God's Grandeur', 1–2. *Explicator*, vol. 23, no. 1, Sept. 1964, item 2.
Explanation of the word 'foil' in l. 2.

K 30   *Ancona, Gaspar. An analysis of the sonnet 'God's Grandeur'. *Lit*, no. 5, 1964, pp. 1–5.

K 31   Giovannini, Margaret. Hopkins' 'God's Grandeur'. *Explicator*, vol. 24, no. 4, Dec. 1965, item 36.
In French, *grandeur* is also a scientific term for extension in space; thus 'grandeur of God' can refer to those aspects of God concretely demonstrated in the physical world.

K 32   Reiman, Donald H. Hopkins' 'Ooze of oil' rises again. *Victorian Poetry*, vol. 4, no. 1, Winter 1966, pp. 39–42.
The meaning of the phrase and its importance in the poem.

K 33   White, Gertrude M. Hopkins' 'God's Grandeur': a poetic statement of Christian doctrine. *Victorian Poetry*, vol. 4, no. 4, Autumn 1966, pp. 284–7.
The poem is primarily an affirmation of the doctrines of G M H's faith, and only secondarily a condemnation of nineteenth-century industrialism; *doctrine* is all.

K 34   Rosenthal, M. L. *and* Smith, A. J. M. Exploring poetry. New York, The Macmillan Company, 1966. xli, 758 pp.
See pp. 94–7, 599–600. Explication of the poem, comparing it with Shakespeare's 'Sonnet LXXIII'.

K 35 Taylor, Michael. Hopkins' 'God's Grandeur', 3–4. *Explicator*, vol. 25, no. 8, Apr. 1967, item 68.

Another explanation of the 'ooze of oil' image.

K 36 Slakey, Roger L. The grandeur in Hopkins' 'God's Grandeur'. *Victorian Poetry*, vol. 7, no. 2, Summer 1969, pp. 159–63.

A general explication of the poem's meaning.

THE HABIT OF PERFECTION (22)

K 37 Litzinger, Boyd. Hopkins' 'The Habit of Perfection'. *Explicator*, vol. 16, no. 1, Oct. 1957, item 1.

The key to the poem is an understanding of its allusions to Holy Scripture, the priestly life, and religious vows. See next entry, K 38.

K 38 Greinier, Francis J. Hopkins' 'The Habit of Perfection'. *Explicator*, vol. 21, no. 3, Nov. 1962, item 19.

Questions Litzinger's interpretation, K 37.

HARRY PLOUGHMAN (71)

K 39 Lewis, Cecil Day. The poetic image. London, Jonathan Cape, 1947. 157 pp.

See pp. 125–7. Discussion of the poem's imagery.

K 40 Mariani, Paul L. Hopkins' 'Harry Ploughman' and Frederick Walker's 'The Plough'. *Month*, vol. 40 (n.s.), nos. 1–2, July–Aug. 1968, pp. 37–44.

Examines the technique of the poem in detail, and suggests that it was inspired by Walker's painting 'The Plough'.

HEAVEN-HAVEN (9)

K 41 Howarth, R. G. Hopkins and Sir Thomas More. *Notes and Queries*, vol. 192, no. 18, 6 Sept. 1947, p. 389.

A suggested source for the poem in Psalm 107: 28–30; and in some lines by More. See also I440.

K 42   Kissane, James. Classical echoes in Hopkins' 'Heaven-Haven'. *Modern Language Notes*, vol. 73, no. 7, Nov. 1958, pp. 491–2.
G M H was influenced by Homer's description of the Elysian plain in Bk. 4 of 'The Odyssey'.

K 43   Litzinger, Boyd. The genesis of Hopkins' 'Heaven-Haven.' *Victorian Newsletter*, no. 17, Spring 1960, pp. 31–3.
G M H's craftsmanship in constructing the poem revealed by examination of his various revisions of it.

HURRAHING IN HARVEST (38)

K 44   Thomas, Roy. Hurrahing in Harvest. *in his* How to read a poem. London, University of London Press, 1961. pp. 113–16.
A paraphrase and explication, with emphasis on correct reading and scansion.

I WAKE AND FEEL THE FELL OF DARK, NOT DAY (67)

K 45   Pepper, Stephen C. The basis of criticism in the arts. Cambridge, Mass.; Harvard University Press, 1945. viii, 177 pp.
See pp. 114–41. Isolates four types of critical criteria—mechanistic, contextualistic, organistic, and formistic—and applies them to Shakespeare's 'When to the sessions of sweet silent thought . . .' and to this poem. The resulting judgements are then compared. This is very worth-while criticism, despite the jargon which disfigures it.

K 46   Allison, Alexander W. Hopkins' 'I wake and feel the fell of dark'. *Explicator*, vol. 17, no. 8, May 1959, item 54.
The poem is not a simple *cri de cœur*, but a careful description of a cultivated penitential state.

IN THE VALLEY OF THE ELWY (34) *see* 1646.

THE LEADEN ECHO AND THE GOLDEN ECHO (59). *See also* M 161, M 164, M 165, M 184, M 199.

K 47   Moore, T. Sturge. Style or beauty in literature. *Criterion*, vol. 9, no. 37, July 1930, pp. 591–603.

A condensation and adaptation of the poem; pruning its 547 words to 204 to illustrate the virtues of economy in style! The insensibility of this effort is only equalled by its complacency.

K48 Sternfeld, Frederick W. Poetry and music—Joyce's Ulysses. *in* Frye, Northrop, *editor*. Sound and poetry: English Institute Essays, 1956. New York, Columbia University Press, 1957. pp. 16–54.
See particularly pp. 38–9. A brief note on an important aspect of G M H's technique—his stressing of musical syllables and 'onrush' over unmusical ones—as illustrated in this poem.

THE LOSS OF THE EURYDICE (41). *See also* M 187

K49 Meyerstein, E. H. W. Note on 'The Loss of the Eurydice'. *Times Literary Supplement*, 11 Nov. 1949, p. 733.
Suggests a source for line 35.

K50 O'Dea, Richard J. 'Loss of the Eurydice': a possible key to the reading of Hopkins. *Victorian Poetry*, vol. 4, no. 4, Autumn 1966, pp. 291–3.
Examines the poem as an introduction to G M H's poetic procedure through its metaphorical pattern.

(MARGARET CLITHEROE) (145)

K51 Schoeck, R. J. Peine forte et dure and Hopkins' 'Margaret Clitheroe'. *Modern Language Notes*, vol. 74, no. 3, Mar. 1959, pp. 220–4.
A detailed examination of the meaning and technique of the poem.

THE MAY MAGNIFICAT (42)

K52 Ratliff, John D. Hopkins' 'The May Magnificat', 19–22. *Explicator*, vol. 16, no. 3, Dec. 1957, item 17.
The meaning of the phrase 'bugle blue'. A 'bugle' is 'a low European annual with spikes of blue flowers': G M H was trying to capture the exact colour of the eggs to which he is referring.

MOONRISE (137)

K 53 *Whitehall, Harold. Pararhyme in three poems. *West African Journal of Education* (Nigeria), vol. 11, June 1967, pp. 90–3.
'Moonrise' is one of the poems dealt with.

MY OWN HEART LET ME MORE HAVE PITY ON (69)

K 54 Riding, Laura, *and* Graves, Robert. A survey of modernist poetry. London, William Heinemann, 1927. 295 pp.
See pp. 90–4. Analysis of the sestet of the poem.

K 55 Schneider, Elisabeth. Hopkins' 'My own heart let me more have pity on'. *Explicator*, vol. 5, no. 7, May 1947, item 51.
The syntax of the sestet considered.

K 56 Schneider, Elisabeth. Hopkins' 'My own heart let me more have pity on'. *Explicator*, vol. 7, no. 7, May 1949, item 49.
Explication of the first four lines, with special reference to W. H. Gardner's views on them.

NO WORST, THERE IS NONE (65). *See also* M 179

K 57 Durr, Robert A. Hopkins' 'No worst, there is none'. *Explicator*, vol. 11, no. 2, Nov. 1952, item 11.
The metaphors in the poem progress in *qualitative* order.

K 58 Humiliata, Sister Mary. Hopkins and the Prometheus Myth. *P.M.L.A.*, vol. 70, no. 1, Mar. 1955, pp. 58–68.
The Prometheus Myth is a source for the poem's imagery.

K 59 Holloway, Sister Marcella M. Hopkins' 'No worst, there is none'. *Explicator*, vol. 14, May 1956, item 51.
This explication concentrates on the meaning of the opening and closing lines of the octave.

K 60 Mayhead, Robin. Understanding literature. Cambridge, Cambridge University Press, 1965. 189 pp.
See pp. 178–82. A general explication of the poem.

K 61   Pouncey, Lorene. An analysis of Hopkins' 'terrible' sonnet no. 65:
'No worst'. *Critical Survey*, vol. 2, no. 4, Summer 1966, pp. 242–5.
A detailed and systematic analysis of meaning and method.

(ON A PIECE OF MUSIC) (148)

K 62   Bliss, Geoffrey. In a poet's workshop: an unfinished poem by
G. M. Hopkins. *Month*, vol. 167, no. 860, Feb. 1936, pp. 160–7.
Suggestions about the poem's arrangement.

PIED BEAUTY (37)

K 63   Britton, John. 'Pied Beauty' and the glory of God. *Renascence*,
vol. 11, no. 2, Winter 1959, pp. 72–5.
A religiously motivated interpretation.

K 64   Litzinger, Boyd A. Hopkins' 'Pied Beauty' once more. *Renascence*,
vol. 13, no. 3, Spring 1961, pp. 136–8.
A general explication of the poem, written from a Catholic viewpoint.

K 65   Bernad, Miguel A. Hopkins' Pied Beauty: a note on its Ignatian
inspiration. *Essays in Criticism*, vol. 12, no. 2, Apr. 1962. pp. 217–20.

RIBBLESDALE (58)

K 66   Goodin, George. Man and nature in Hopkins's 'Ribblesdale'.
Notes and Queries, vol. 6 (n.s.), no. 11, Dec. 1959, pp. 453–4.
Notes on the poem's meaning.

ST. ALPHONSUS RODRIGUEZ (73). *See also* K 149.

K 67   Thwaites, Michael. The devoted doorkeeper . . . *Melbourne Age*
(Melbourne), 19 Jan. 1952.
This is not a detailed explication, but the central idea of the poem is
discussed in relation to the way in which it is expressed.

ST. THECLA (136)

K 68   Sharples, Sister Marian. Conjecturing a date for Hopkins' 'St. Thecla'. *Victorian Poetry*, vol. 4, no. 3, Summer 1966, pp. 204–9.

'THE SHEPHERD'S BROW . . .' (75)

K 69   Campbell, Sister M. Mary Hugh. The silent sonnet: Hopkins' 'Shepherd's Brow'. *Renascence*, vol. 15, no. 3, Spring 1963, pp. 133–42.
A critical and interpretative essay.

K 70   Clark, Robert Boykin. Hopkins' 'The Shepherd's brow'. *Victorian Newsletter*, no. 28, Fall 1965, pp. 16–18.
Another general interpretation.

K 71   Mariani, Paul L. The artistic and tonal integrity of Hopkins' 'The Shepherd's brow'. *Victorian Poetry*, vol. 6, no. 1, Spring 1968, pp. 63–8.
The poem is 'a deeply meditated vision of Man Jack's pretense to greatness seen in the unflattering light of his essential smallness'.

(THE SOLDIER) (63)

K 72   Dobrée, Bonamy. The broken cistern. London, Cohen & West Ltd., 1954. ix, 158 pp.
See pp. 109–10. A brief explication of the first few lines of the poem.

SPELT FROM SIBYL'S LEAVES (61). *See also* M 191

K 73   *Schoder, Raymond V. Spelt from Sibyl's Leaves. *Thought*, voi. 19, no. 75, Dec. 1944, pp. 633–48.

K 74   Ward, Dennis. Gerard Manley Hopkins's 'Spelt from Sibyl's Leaves'. *Month*, vol. 8 (n.s.), no. 1, July 1952, pp. 40–51.
The imagery and meaning of the poem.

K 75   Rooney, William Joseph. 'Spelt from Sibyl's Leaves': a study in contrasting methods of evaluation. *Journal of Aesthetics and Art Criticism*, vol. 13, no. 4, June 1955, pp. 507–19.

Condemns the poem for lack of 'structural integrity'; and evaluates other critical assessments of it.

K 76 Sherwood, H. C. Hopkins' 'Spelt from Sibyl's Leaves'. *Explicator*, vol. 15, Oct. 1956, item 5.

The reading of 'hornlight' in line 3 as suggesting the setting moon is an error in interpretation. Alternative reading suggested.

K 77 Thérèse, Sister. Hopkins' 'Spelt from Sibyl's Leaves'. *Explicator*, vol. 17, no. 7, Apr. 1959, item 45.

A detailed general analysis of meaning and imagery.

K 78 Gomme, Andor. A note on two Hopkins sonnets. *Essays in Criticism*, vol. 14, no. 3, July 1964, pp. 372–31.

Comments on the meaning of this poem and 'Thou art indeed just . . .' (74). See next entry, K 79.

K 79 Doherty, Francis. A note on 'Spelt from Sibyl's Leaves'. *Essays in Criticism*, vol. 14, no. 4, Oct. 1964, pp. 428–32.

Further comments, following Gomme, K 78.

K 80 White, Norman E. 'Hearse' in Hopkins' 'Spelt from Sibyl's leaves.' *English Studies* (Amsterdam), vol. 49, no. 6, Dec. 1968, pp. 546–7.

In line 2, G M H used 'hearse' firstly because of its sound, since it maintains the 'vowelling off' in the line; and secondly because of its association with the Roman Catholic office of *Tenebrae*.

K 81 White, Norman. Hopkins' 'Spelt from Sibyl's Leaves'. *Victorian Newsletter*, no. 36, Fall 1969, pp. 27–8.

SPRING (33). *See also* I 646, K 87

K 82 Phelps, Gilbert. Question and response. Cambridge, Cambridge University Press, 1969. xxii, 170 pp.

See pp. 100–4. Commentary, with questions and exercises for students, suggesting some thoughtful ways of looking at the poem.

SPRING AND FALL (55). *See also* H26.

K83 Fitzgerald, Robert. Generations of leaves: the poet in the classical tradition. *Perspectives* (New York), no. 8, summer 1954, pp. 68–85.
An essay on the classical tradition in poetry, placing GMH in that tradition with evidence adduced from this poem.

K84 *Myers, John A., *Jr*. Intimations of mortality: an analysis of Hopkins' 'Spring and Fall'. *English Journal*, vol. 51, no. 8, Nov. 1962, pp. 585–7.

K85 Louise, Sister Robert. Hopkins' 'Spring and Fall: to a Young Child'. *Explicator*, vol. 21, no. 8, Apr. 1963, item 65.
The meaning of the poem in general.

K86 Smith, Grover. A source for Hopkins' 'Spring and Fall' in *The Mill on the Floss*? *English Language Notes*, vol. 1, no. 1, Sept. 1963, pp. 43–6.
Suggests the hair-cropping episode in Maggie Tulliver's childhood ('The Mill on the Floss', Bk. 1, Chapter 7) as a possible source of the poem.

K87 Driscoll, John P. Hopkins' 'Spring', line 2; and 'Spring and Fall: to a young child', line 2. *Explicator*, vol. 24, no. 3, Nov. 1965, item 26.
Explication of the phrases 'weeds, in wheels', and 'Goldengrove'.

K88 Doherty, Paul C. Hopkins' 'Spring and Fall': to a Young Child'. *Victorian Poetry*, vol. 5, no. 2, Summer 1967, pp. 140–3.
A general explication of the poem.

K89 Calderwood, James L., *and* Toliver, Harold E., *editors*. Forms of poetry. Englewood Cliffs, N.J.; Prentice-Hall, Inc., 1968. x, 598 pp.
See pp. 591–2. The verbal structure of the poem is impressive, but the 'dramatic context in which, as a verbal action, the poem occurs' is more important to our understanding of it.

K90 Smith, Julian. Hopkins' 'Spring and Fall: to a Young Child'. *Explicator*, vol. 27, no. 5, Jan. 1969, item 36.
Take away the ninth line, and the poem becomes a sonnet.

THE STARLIGHT NIGHT (32)

K91 Scott, A. F. The poet's craft: a course in the critical appreciation of poetry. Cambridge, Cambridge University Press, 1957. xi, 219 pp.
See particularly pp. 40–1. A photograph of GMH's MS. of the poem, with facing transcription showing its revision and development.

K92 Hewett, R. P. Reading and response. London, George G. Harrap & Co., Ltd., 1960. 254 pp.
See pp. 93–6. A general explication and commentary.

THAT NATURE IS A HERACLITEAN FIRE AND OF THE COMFORT OF THE RESURRECTION (72)

K93 Holbrook, David. Llareggub revisited: Dylan Thomas and the state of modern poetry. London, Bowes and Bowes, 1962. 255 pp.
See particularly pp. 91–4. An explication of this poem is the most important of several references to GMH in the book.

K94 Grennen, Joseph E. Grammar as thaumaturgy: Hopkins' 'Heraclitean Fire'. *Renascence*, vol. 15, no. 4, Summer 1963, pp. 208–11.
The poem's meaning brought out through examination of its grammar.

K95 Stevens, Sister Mary Dominic. Hopkins' 'That Nature is a Heraclitean Fire'. *Explicator*, vol. 22, no. 3, Nov. 1963, item 18.
Suggests a philosophic basis for the poem, and considers GMH's use of the antithetical elements of fire and water as they occur in Heraclitean philosophy.

K96 *Stiles, G. W. Nature's bonfire: a brief examination of the imagery in Hopkins' 'That Nature is a Heraclitean Fire'. *Unisa English Studies*, vol. 2, 1967, pp. 49–56.

'THOU ART INDEED JUST, LORD . . .' (74) *see* K78, M206

TO R.B. (76). *See also* M 206.

K 97   Gibson, William M. Hopkins' 'To R.B.'. *Explicator*, vol. 6, Nov. 1947, item 12.

'The passionate conception of a child and the patient sure course of its gestation, representing poetic inspiration and the laborious development of an inspiration into a finished poem' constitutes the basic metaphor in the poem.

K 98   *Vogelsgang, John. Hopkins' sonnet to R[obert] B[ridges]. *Philippine Studies* (Manila), vol. 6, no. 3, Aug. 1958, pp. 315–24.

K 99   Bremer, Rudy. Hopkins' use of the word 'combs' in 'To R.B.'. *English Studies* (Amsterdam), vol. 51, no. 2, Apr. 1970, pp. 1–5.

Sets out to establish why Hopkins used the word 'combs' here, by a thorough and highly intelligent examination of his use of it in different contexts elsewhere in his poetry and prose. Explanations of the word by other critics are evaluated.

TOM'S GARLAND (70)

K 100   Silverstein, Henry. On 'Tom's Garland'. *Accent*, vol. 7, no. 2, Winter 1947, pp. 67–81.

A very detailed (if occasionally over-ingenious) explication of the meaning and underlying attitudes in the poem.

K 101   Bowra, C. M. Poetry and politics, 1900–60. Cambridge, Cambridge University Press, 1966. vii, 156 pp.

See particularly pp. 7–9. A brief but illuminating analysis of the poem.

'WHAT BEING IN RANK-OLD NATURE . . .' (141)

K 102   White, Norman. A date for G. M. Hopkins's 'What being in rank-old nature . . .' *Review of English Studies*, vol. 20 (n.s.), no. 79, Aug. 1969, pp. 319–20.

The poem was drafted on a sheet of paper containing pencil jottings about the Royal Academy's Exhibition of 1878. The poem can therefore be dated not earlier than June or July 1878.

THE WINDHOVER (36). *See also* H27, H137, H169, H179, H215, I370, M36, M95, M161, M167, M174, M183, M189, M208–9, M210, M229

K103   Downey, Harris. A poem not understood. *Virginia Quarterly Review*, vol. 11, no. 4, Oct. 1935, pp. 506–17.
One of the earliest interpretations, forming the centre-piece of this critical essay.

K104   *Grady, Thomas J. Windhover's meaning. *America*, vol. 70, no. 17, 29 Jan. 1944, pp. 465–6.
See next entry, K105.

K105   *'Cappellanus', *pseud*. Windhover. *America*, vol. 70, no. 19, 12 Feb. 1944, p. 531.
Reply to Grady, K104.

K106   *Van de Water, Charlotte. Poems to remember: Windhover. *Scholastic*, vol. 44, no. 6, 13 Mar. 1944, p. 20.

K107   Fussell, Paul, *Jr*. A note on 'The Windhover'. *Modern Language Notes*, vol. 64, no. 4, Apr. 1949, p. 271.
Correction of error in S. C. Chew's comments on GMH in H146.

K108   Nicol, B. de Bear. A Hopkins phrase. *Times Literary Supplement*, 13 May 1949, p. 313.
An interpretation of the last line.

K109   *Boyle, Robert R. A footnote on 'The Windhover'. *America*, vol. 82, no. 5, 5 Nov. 1949, pp. 129–30.

K110   Robson, W. W. Hopkins and Congreve. *Times Literary Supplement*, 24 Feb. 1950, p. 121.
A letter pointing out a possible parallel between this poem and Congreve's 'Way of the World', v.i.

K111   Lees, F. N. The Windhover. *Scrutiny*, vol. 17, no. 1, Spring 1950, pp. 32–7.
An outstandingly perceptive and closely argued interpretation. Strongly recommended as an aid to any special study of this poem.

K112   *Woodring, Carl R. Once more 'The Windhover'. *Western Review*, vol. 15, Autumn 1950, pp. 61–4.

K113   Gwynn, Frederick L. Hopkins' 'The Windhover': a new simplification. *Modern Language Notes*, vol. 66, June 1951, pp. 366–70.
    Emphasizes the *dive* of the bird to bring out the meaning of the poem.

K114   Mercer, W.C. G.M. Hopkins and Richard Jefferies. *Notes and Queries*, vol. 197, no. 10, 10 May 1952, p. 217.
    Suggests a possible source for the poem in Jefferies's *Wild life in a southern county* (1879).

K115   Wiggin, Maurice. A buyer's market. *Sunday Times*, 16 August 1953, p. 4.
    A radio review, containing only one brief remark on G MH, but one worth recording: 'It was good to hear Mr. Geoffrey Grigson, in his talk about Hopkins, puncturing those library-critics who try to discuss . . . "The Windhover" without knowing what a windhover *looks* like.'

K116   Lees, F. N. Hopkinsiana. *Times Literary Supplement*, 3 Sept. 1954, p. 557.
    A letter, concerned mainly with the meaning of 'buckle' in this poem. A long correspondence followed: see K117–26.

K117   Couldrey, Oswald. Hopkinsiana. *Times Literary Supplement*, 24 Sept. 1954, p. 609.
    A letter following Lees (K116) again mainly concerned with the meaning of 'buckle'.

K118   Empson, William. Hopkinsiana. *Times Literary Supplement*, 1 Oct. 1954, p. 625.
    A reply to Lees (K116), again about 'buckle'.

K119   Lees, F. N. Hopkinsiana. *Times Literary Supplement*, 22 Oct. 1954, p. 673.
    A further letter about the poem, following Couldrey (K117) and Empson (K118).

K 120   Empson, William. Hopkinsiana. *Times Literary Supplement*, 29 Oct. 954, p. 689.

K 121   Peters, W. A. M. Hopkinsiana. *Times Literary Supplement*, 29 Oct. 1954, p. 689.
A letter concerned mainly with the dedication of the poem to Christ.

K 122   Ritz, Jean-Georges. The Windhover. *Times Literary Supplement*, 6 May 1955, p. 237.
A letter which re-opened the debate on the poem after a lapse of several months. The poem should be read on three different levels: 1, The Bird; 2. Christ; 3. Christ's Imitator. These three levels were linked in G M H's mind, and should be linked in the reader's.

K 123   Empson, William. The Windhover. *Times Literary Supplement*, 20 May 1955, p. 269.
A letter refuting Ritz (K 122).

K 124   Gardner, W. H. The Windhover. *Times Literary Supplement*, 24 June 1955, p. 349.
A further comment following Ritz (K 122) and Empson (K 123).

K 125   Nolan, Gerard L. The Windhover. *Times Literary Supplement*, 24 June 1955, p. 349.
A further comment following Ritz (K 122) and Empson (K 123). See also next entry.

K 126   Nolan, Gerald L. The Windhover. *Times Literary Supplement*, 5 Aug. 1955, p. 445.
A letter rectifying a mistake in K 125.

K 127   Donoghue, Denis. The bird as symbol: Hopkins's Windhover. *Studies* (Dublin), vol. 44, Autumn 1955, pp. 291–9.
Suggests that 'The Windhover' in particular (and G M H's poetry in general) has been overrated by modern critics. See reply by F. G. Doyle (K 130).

K 128   Hill, Archibald A. An analysis of 'The Windhover': an experiment in structural method. *P.M.L.A.*, vol. 70, no. 5, Dec. 1955, pp. 968–78.

Examines the structure of the poem, and attempts to elucidate it by presenting it as a unified and logical whole. See also K136, K165.

K129   Ward, Dennis. G. M. Hopkins: The Windhover. *in* Wain, John, *editor*. Interpretations. London, Routledge & Kegan Paul, 1955. pp. 138–52.
'This essay is an attempt to probe the question: What did *The Windhover* mean to Hopkins?'

K130   Doyle, Francis G. A note on Hopkins's Windhover. *Studies* (Dublin), vol. 45, Spring 1956, pp. 88–91.
A refutation of Denis Donoghue's article (K127).

K131   Whitlock, Baird W. Gerard Hopkins' 'Windhover'. *Notes and Queries*, vol. 3 (n.s.), no. 4, Apr. 1956, pp. 169–71.
An interpretation and commentary.

K132   Kelly, Hugh. 'The Windhover'—and Christ. *Studies* (Dublin), vol. 45, Summer 1956, pp. 188–93.
'To exclude Christ is to throw away the key to the meaning of the poem . . .'

K133   Weatherhead, A. Kingsley. G. M. Hopkins: the Windhover. *Notes and Queries*, vol. 3 (n.s.), no. 8, Aug. 1956, p. 354.
Another general interpretation.

K134   Ayers, Robert W. Hopkins' 'The Windhover': a further simplification. *Modern Language Notes*, vol. 71, no. 8, Dec. 1956, pp. 577–84.
Explores both the meaning and the structure of the poem.

K135   King, Anne R. Hopkins' 'Windhover' and Blake. *English Studies* (Amsterdam), vol. 37, no. 6, 1956, pp. 245–52.
A source for the poem in a painting by Blake.

K136   Matchett, William H. An analysis of 'The Windhover'. *P.M.L.A.*, vol. 72, no. 1, Mar. 1957, pp. 310–11.
Comment on the article by Hill (K128).

K137   Lisca, Peter. Return of 'The Windhover'. *College English*, vol. 19, no. 3, Dec. 1957, pp. 124–6.
Another interpretation: see reply by J. D. Howard (K139).

K 138   Langbaum, Robert. The poetry of experience. London, Chatto & Windus, 1957. 246 pp.

> *See particularly* pp. 66–8. An explication of this poem underlining 'the contrast . . . between the poet's participation in the bird's aggressive life and his awareness of his own passivity or withdrawal'.

K 139   Howard, John D. Letter to the editor. *College English*, vol. 19, no. 7, Apr. 1958, p. 312.

> Comment on Lisca's interpretation (K 137), questioning Lisca's reading of G M H's words *thee, chevalier, dear*, and *here* as referring to the poet's heart.

K 140   Stillinger, Jack. Hopkins' 'skate's heel' in 'The Windhover'. *Notes and Queries*, vol. 6 (n.s.), no. 6, June 1959, pp. 215–16.

> Notes on the meaning of the phrase.

K 141   Schneider, Elisabeth. Hopkins' 'The Windhover'. *Explicator*, vol. 18, no. 4, Jan. 1960, item 22.

> Another reading of the poem's meaning, stressing the word 'buckle' as central to the whole movement of the poem. See also next entry.

K 142   Thomas, J. D. Hopkins' 'The Windhover'. *Explicator*, vol. 20, no. 4, Dec. 1961, item 31.

> Following Schneider (K 141) this interpretation stresses 'dangerous' as another key-word in the poem.

K 143   Brophy, James. The noble brute: medieval nuance in 'The Windhover'. *Modern Language Notes*, vol. 76, no. 8, Dec. 1961, pp. 673–4.

> 'Brute' in Middle English refers to a knight or a hero. Did G M H intend this meaning?

K 144   Assad, Thomas J. Hopkins' 'The Windhover'. *Tulane Studies in English*, vol. 11, 1961, pp. 87–95.

> This interpretation suggests that the poem is best approached through its literal meaning: its metaphors have a logical foundation.

K 145   Stempel, Daniel. A reading of 'The Windhover'. *College English*, vol. 23, no. 4, Jan. 1962, pp. 305–7.

> Stresses that a proper understanding of the appearance of a kestrel in flight is essential before the poem can be understood.

K 146   Eleanor, Mother Mary. Hopkins' 'Windhover' and Southwell's hawk. *Renascence*, vol. 15, no. 1, Fall 1962, pp. 21–2, 27.
Suggests a parallel (and possible source) for the poem in Robert Southwell's *A hundred meditations on the love of God*.

K 147   Templeman, William D. Ruskin's ploughshare and Hopkins' 'The Windhover'. *English Studies* (Amsterdam), vol. 43, 1962, pp. 103–6.
In writing this poem, G M H may have been inspired to use the plough as an image by a passage from Ruskin's *Ad valorem*.

K 148   August, Eugene R. Hopkins' dangerous fire. *Victorian Poetry*, vol. 1, no. 1, Jan. 1963, pp. 72–4.
The meaning of the word 'dangerous'.

K 149   McQueen, William A. 'The Windhover' and 'St. Alphonsus Rodriguez'. *Victorian Newsletter*, no. 23, Spring 1963, pp. 25–6.
A comparison of the poems which suggests that each elucidates the other.

K 150   Greiner, Francis. Hopkins' 'The Windhover' viewed as a nature poem. *Renascence*, vol. 15, no. 2, Winter 1963, pp. 68–75, 95.

K 151   Smith, L. E. W. The Windhover. *in his* Twelve poems considered. London, Methuen, 1963. pp. 119–29.
A paraphrase and explication.

K 152   Bates, Ronald. The Windhover. *Victorian Poetry*, vol. 2, no. 1, Winter 1964, pp. 63–4.
A note on the falconry image in the poem.

K 153   Huntley, John F. Hopkins 'The Windhover' as a prayer of request. *Renascence*, vol. 16, no. 3, Spring 1964, pp. 154–62.
A strongly religious interpretation.

K 154   Miller, Bruce E. On 'The Windhover'. *Victorian Poetry*, vol. 2, no. 2, Spring 1964, pp. 115–19.
Another interpretation.

K 155   Kopper, Edward A. Hopkins' 'The Windhover'. *Explicator*, vol. 22, no. 7, Mar. 1964, item 54.
　　　The last line of the poem suggests the Passion of Christ.

K 156   Bates, Ronald. Hopkins' embers poems: a liturgical source. *Renascence*, vol. 17, no. 1, Fall 1964, pp. 32–7.
　　　Finds sources for G M H's imagery in the Catholic Liturgy. The emphasis is on this poem.

K 157   Shea, F. X. Another look at 'The Windhover'. *Victorian Poetry*, vol. 2, no. 4, Autumn 1964, pp. 219–39.
　　　See answer by D. A. Downes (K 162).

K 158   *Giovannini, G. A literal gloss of Hopkins' 'The Windhover'. *in* Crisafulli, A. S., *editor*. Linguistic and literary studies in honor of Helmut A. Hatzfeld. Washington, Catholic University of America Press, 1964. pp. 203–12.

K 159   Montag, George E. 'The Windhover': crucifixion and redemption. *Victorian Poetry*, vol. 3, no. 2, Spring 1965, pp. 109–18.
　　　The poem 'depicts the specific event of the crucifixion, explicitly portrays the death of Christ, and then expounds the effect of this act [on] the redemption of man'.

K 160   Chard, Leslie F. Once more into 'The Windhover'. *English Language Notes*, vol. 2, no. 4, June 1965, pp. 282–5.
　　　Contends that line 9 is 'a concise summation of the conflict Hopkins describes in the octave of the sonnet'.

K 161   Pace, George B. On the octave rhymes of 'The Windhover'. *English Language Notes*, vol. 2, no. 4, June 1965, pp. 285–6.
　　　The stresses on the terminal syllables in the octave mirror the *a b b a*, *a b b a* of the Petrarchan rhymes, thus providing a second rhyme scheme.

K 162   Downes, David A. Hopkins and Thomism. *Victorian Poetry*, vol. 3, no. 4, Autumn 1965, pp. 270–2.
　　　Reply to Shea (K 157).

K163   Winter, J. L. Notes on 'The Windhover'. *Victorian Poetry*, vol. 4, no. 3, Summer 1966, pp. 212–13.

An interpretation of some ambiguous phrases.

K164   Driskell, Leon V. Progressive structure of 'The Windhover'. *Renascence*, vol. 19, no. 1, Fall 1966, pp. 30–6.

K165   Hill, Archibald A. 'The Windhover' revisited: linguistic analysis of poetry reassessed. *Texas Studies in Literature and Language*, vol. 7, no. 4, Winter 1966, pp. 349–59.

A detailed explication following and adapting the author's earlier article (K128).

K166   Rees, R. J. An introduction to English literature. London, Macmillan, 1966. viii, 275 pp.

See pp. 112–15. Explication of 'The Windhover'.

K167   Zillman, Lawrence John. Hopkins' *The Windhover*. in his *The art and craft of poetry*. New York, Macmillan, 1966, pp. 214–33.

An explication with special emphasis on technique.

K168   Fraser, Ronald. The Windhover again. *Downside Review*, vol. 85, no. 278, Jan. 1967, pp. 71–3.

The poem is based on the meditation on the Kingdom of Christ in the Spiritual Exercises of St. Ignatius. The text of this meditation is here set out, without commentary, alongside the text of the poem.

K169   Bates, Ronald. Downdolphinry. *University of Toronto Quarterly*, vol. 36, no. 3, Apr. 1967, pp. 229–36.

An examination of the poem's imagery.

K170   Litzinger, Boyd. Once more, 'The Windhover'. *Victorian Poetry*, vol. 5, no. 3, Autumn 1967, pp. 228–30.

Seeks to establish the literal meaning of the poem's imagery. Concludes that the poem '. . . is not about Christ, but is an act of submission of a Christlike man'.

K171   August, Eugene R. The growth of 'The Windhover'. *P.M.L.A.*, vol. 82, no. 5, Oct. 1967, pp. 465–8.

Working from the MS., the author shows how GMH revised and shaped the poem over the years, and also conjectures a precise date for it.

K172   Payne, Michael. Syntactical analysis and 'The Windhover'. *Renascence*, vol. 19, no. 2, Winter 1967, pp. 88–92.
An attempt to analyse and elucidate the poem through its grammar.

K173   Morton, William C. The harmony of verse. Toronto, University of Toronto Press, 1967. ix, 235 pp.
See particularly pp. 171–3. An explication of the poem.

K174   Haskell, Ann Sullivan. An image of 'The Windhover'. *Victorian Poetry*, vol. 6, no. 1, Spring 1968, p. 75.
Explanation of the phrase 'rung upon the reign'.

K175   Frost, David L. 'The Windhover': a commentary. *Theology*, vol. 72, no. 583, Jan. 1969, pp. 10–13.
An explication relating the falcon to Christ: in both, the 'moment of apparent collapse [is] the moment of beauty and triumph'.

K176   Baxter, Ralph C. Shakespeare's Dauphin and Hopkins' Windhover. *Victorian Poetry*, vol. 7, no. 1, Spring 1969, pp. 71–5.
Shakespeare's *Henry V* provides a source for the imagery of the poem.

K177   Pick, John, *editor*. Gerard Manley Hopkins: The Windhover. Columbus, Ohio; Charles E. Merrill Publishing Company, 1969. xiv, 146 pp. (The Merrill Literary Casebook Series.)
A collection of twenty-four critical articles on the poem (including several chapters or sections taken from full-length studies of GMH's work) all previously published.

K178   Bremer, Rudy. A new interpretation of Hopkins' 'The Windhover'. *Tijdschrift voor Levende Talen*, Mar. 1970, pp. 216–26.
A very close analysis of the poem, and examination of popular interpretations of it, help to establish the convincing and original reading offered here, the falcon standing for Loyola.

THE WOODLARK (138)

K179   Bliss, Geoffrey. In a poet's workshop: II—'The Woodlark' by G. M. Hopkins. *Month*, vol. 167, no. 864, June 1936, pp. 528–35.
A reconstruction and rearrangement of GMH's fragmentary poem. Father Bliss supplies lines of his own for the missing ones, with a surprising degree of success.

THE WRECK OF THE DEUTSCHLAND (28). *See also* M 192,
M 195, M 216, M 224–5, M 233

K 180   Gardner, W. H. 'The Wreck of the Deutschland'. *Essays and
Studies*, vol. 21, 1935 (published 1936), pp. 124–52.
The technique and meaning of the poem.

K 181   *Rose, Leslie. Plumage of far wonder. *Sentinel of the Blessed
Sacrament*, vol. 46, no. 2, Feb. 1943, pp. 65–7.

K 182   *Thornton, Francis Beauchesne. Essay on 'The Wreck of the
Deutschland.' *Catholic World*, vol. 160, no. 955, Oct. 1944, pp. 41–6.

K 183   Ryan, Francis. The Wreck of the Deutschland; an introduction
and a paraphrase. *Dublin Review*, vol. 221, no. 443, 2nd Quarter 1948,
pp. 124–41.
Includes a detailed stanza-by-stanza paraphrase.

K 184   Anon. 'Wreck of the Deutschland': Bath doctor on famous
poem. *Bath and Wilts Chronicle and Herald*, 22 Jan. 1949, p. 2.
Report of a lecture on the poem by Dr. Ray Edridge. Of interest
mainly for this remarkable comment: 'This [Dr. Edridge's] exposition
suggested an affinity with the kindred inspiration of Swinburne and
Francis Thompson.'

K 185   Schneider, Elisabeth. Two metaphysical images in Hopkins's
'The Wreck of the Deutschland'. *Modern Language Notes*, vol. 65, no. 5,
May 1950, pp. 306–11.
The meaning of the imagery in stanza 4.

K 186   D'Arcy, M. C. A note on Gerard Hopkins. *Month*, vol. 11 (n.s.),
no. 2, Feb. 1954, pp. 113–15.
Suggests a possible connection between images in this poem and in the
'dark sonnets' of G M H's last years.

K 187   [Hart], Sister Mary Adorita. Hopkins's 'Wings that spell' in 'The
Wreck of the Deutschland'. *Modern Language Notes*, vol. 70, no. 5,
May 1955, pp. 345–7.
The meaning of 'spell'; stanza 3, line 4.

K188 Martin, Philip M. Mastery and Mercy; a study of two religious poems: *The Wreck of the Deutschland* by G. M. Hopkins and *Ash Wednesday* by T. S. Eliot. London, Oxford University Press, 1957. xi, 149 pp.

See pp. 3–72. Biographical and critical essay, followed by a detailed paraphrase and commentary on the poem.

Reviews:

K189 Anon. in *Times Literary Supplement,* 28 June 1957, p. 398.

K190 Kelly, Hugh. in *Studies* (Dublin), vol. 46, Winter 1957, pp. 491–2.

For other reviews, see B204, M258.

K191 *Sullivan, Barbara. An Easter poem. *Lit,* no. 2, 1958, pp. 38–43. This article includes critical comment on the poem.

K192 Schneider, Elisabeth. Hopkins' 'The Wreck of the Deutschland', stanza 33. *Explicator,* vol. 16, no. 8, May 1958, item 46. An explanation of the last three lines of stanza 33. See also K194, K195.

K193 Brooke-Rose, Christine. A grammar of metaphor. London, Secker & Warburg, 1958. xi, 343 pp.

See particularly pp. 313–15. A grammatical survey of metaphor in poetic diction, with numerous references to this poem, and a summary of GMH's general use of metaphor.

K194 Scheve, Adelbert. Hopkins' 'Wreck of the Deutschland', stanza 33. *Explicator,* vol. 17, no. 9, June 1959, item 60. Another interpretation: see also K192, K195.

K195 Litzinger, Boyd. Hopkins' 'Wreck of the Deutschland', stanza 33. *Explicator,* vol. 18, no. 3, Dec. 1959, item 19. A further interpretation, following Schneider (K192) and Scheve (K194).

K196 Miller, J. Hillis. 'Orion' in 'The Wreck of the Deutschland'. *Modern Language Notes,* vol. 76, no. 6, June 1961, pp. 509–14. Notes on the meaning and symbolism of the phrase 'Orion of light' in stanza 21.

K 197   Litzinger, Boyd. Hopkins' 'The Wreck of the Deutschland',
stanza 19. *Explicator*, vol. 20, no. 1, Sept. 1961, item 7.
    An interpretation of 'fetch' in line 6.

K 198   McNamee, M. B. Mastery and mercy in 'The Wreck of the
Deutschland'. *College English*, vol. 23, no. 4, Jan. 1962, pp. 267–76.
    This exposition finds a basis for the poem in the Spiritual Exercises
    of St. Ignatius.

K 199   Masson, David I. Sound and sense in a line of poetry. *British
Journal of Aesthetics*, vol. 3, 1963, pp. 70–2.
    An analysis of the fifth line of stanza 15: 'And frightful a nightfall
    folded rueful a day'; seeking to show how 'the authority and power of
    a line of poetry may be precisely and closely linked to its sound-
    patterning, fine as well as gross.'

K 200   Keating, John E. The Wreck of the Deutschland: an essay and
commentary. *Kent State University Bulletin*, vol. 51, no. 1, Jan. 1963,
vii, 110 pp. (Research Series, 6.)
    This issue of the monthly bulletin is a continuation of a series of
    research projects sponsored by the University. It is a two-part study
    of the poem, consisting of an introductory essay (covering its origins,
    reception and content) followed by a detailed stanza-by-stanza
    commentary. Probably the most useful study of the poem yet pub-
    lished; but see also K 218.
For reviews, see 1628, 1639.

K 201   McLoughlin, Justin. Stratford—and a famous poem. *Franciscan*,
vol. 68, no. 2, Feb. 1963, pp. 10–11.
    A brief but useful summary of the historical background to the poem:
    four of the 'Deutschland' nuns were buried from St. Francis's
    Church, Stratford, London, and this article fills in some details.

K 202   Prosen, Anthony J. Suffering in Aeschylus and Hopkins. *Classical
Bulletin*, vol. 41, no. 1, Nov. 1964, pp. 11–13.
    A discussion of 'the basic reason for suffering in Aeschylus' *Pro-
    metheus Vinctus* and Hopkins' *The Wreck of the Deutschland* . . .'

K 203   Fiore, Amadeus. Hopkins' relation to the 'Deutschland' nuns.
Renascence, vol. 18, no. 1, Autumn 1965, pp. 45–8.
    Another account of the historical background to the poem.

K 204   Pitts, Arthur W., *Jr.* Hopkins' 'The Wreck of the Deutschland', stanza 29. *Explicator*, vol. 24, no. 1, Sept. 1965, item 7.

 The phrase 'Tarpeian-fast' may be derived from Milton ('Paradise Regained', iv.44–50).

K 205   Brett, R. L. An introduction to English studies. London, Edward Arnold Ltd., 1965. ix, 83 pp.

 A concise introduction to English studies in general, with many references throughout to this poem, which is used as an illustrative example.

K 206   Nowottny, Winifred. The common privileges of poetry. *Proceedings of the British Academy*, vol. 52, 1966, pp. 61–86.

 See particularly pp. 76–85. Detailed criticism of this poem. There are other references to G M H, *passim*.

K 207   Ong, Walter J. Evolution, myth, and poetic vision. *Comparative Literature Studies*, vol. 3, no. 1, 1966, pp. 1–20.

 A discussion of this poem with particular reference to Darwin and evolution. Reprinted in the author's book *'In the human grain', New York, Macmillan, 1967, pp. 99–126.

K 208   Schneider, Elisabeth W. 'The Wreck of the Deutschland': a new reading. *P.M.L.A.*, vol. 81, no. 1, Mar. 1966, pp. 110–22.

 The poem is here considered as an ode on conversion to the Roman Catholic Church.

K 209   Anon. Friars recall a poet. *Stratford Express* (Stratford, London), 11 Mar. 1966, p. 7.

 A brief report of the Commemoration of this poem by the Franciscan Fathers at St. Francis's Hall, Stratford, on 30 Apr. 1966. See next entry.

K 210   St. Francis Hall, Grove Crescent Road, Stratford, E.15. Festival of a Stratford poem: 'The Wreck of the Deutschland' by Gerard Manley Hopkins, S.J. (born at 87 The Grove, Stratford, 28th July, 1844). In four sessions; Saturday, 30th April 1966, 2–45 pm.

 A four-page leaflet (unpaginated) setting out the programme of the Commemoration.

K211   Barton, John M. T. Odd priest out. *Times Literary Supplement*, 20 Oct. 1966, p. 959.

This poem was rejected for publication in 'The Month' on the advice of Father Sydney Fenn Smith, S.J.—on purely literary grounds. There was no rejection of its theology. See further comment by Thomas (K212).

K212   Thomas, Alfred. Odd priest out. *Times Literary Supplement*, 27 Oct. 1966, p. 981.

Amplifies the information in Monsignor Barton's letter (K211). Father Sydney Fenn Smith once confessed himself unable to appreciate poetry. See also K216.

K213   Jayantha, R. A. A note on some aspects of The Wreck of the Deutschland. *Literary Criterion* (Mysore), vol. 8, no. 2, Summer 1968, pp. 27–34.

'The poem . . . can be regarded as the result of a compelling creative need felt by the poet to explore and express in words his inextricable involvement in the immanent and transcendent God'.

K214   Boyd, John D. Hopkins' blessed understanding: a source for a line in 'The Wreck of the Deutschland'. *English Language Notes*, vol. 5, no. 4, June 1968, pp. 293–7.

The last line of stanza 5 is a partial translation of the first two verses of Psalm 100 in the Vulgate Version of the Bible.

K215   Kelly, Hugh. 'The Wreck of the Deutschland': its spiritual thought. *Studies* (Dublin), vol. 57, Winter 1968, pp. 421–7.

A thorough examination of the spiritual thought in the poem, concluding thus: 'An analysis of the thought of "The Wreck" could not claim to reveal its greatness as poetry; but such an analysis is necessary if the poetic greatness is to be duly appreciated.'

K216   Thomas, Alfred. Hopkins and the rejection of 'The Wreck of the Deutschland'. *English Studies* (Amsterdam), vol. 49, no. 6, Dec. 1968, pp. 542–6.

The background, in detail, to the rejection of the poem by 'The Month', emphasizing the parts played by Father H. J. Coleridge, S.J., and Father Sydney Fenn Smith, S.J. See also K211, K212.

K217 Dickey, James. Gerard Manley Hopkins: The Wreck of the Deutschland. *in his* Babel to Byzantium: poets and poetry now. New York, Farrar Straus and Giroux, 1968. pp. 238–41.

An introduction to the poem, short but full of insights. 'The sea itself . . . is the most powerfully real and *active* sea in English litera- ture . . . Hopkins was able to catch the rhythms and terrors of the sea at its most murderous, as it surrounds the human spirit at its most hopeless.'

K218 Milward, Peter. A commentary on G. M. Hopkins' *The Wreck of the Deutschland*. Tokyo, The Hokuseido Press, 1968. 160 pp.

Virtually a word-by-word commentary: the author has '. . . not shrunk from considering the smallest details of vocabulary and syntax, imagery and phraseology, sound and rhythm . . .' This study invites comparison with Keating's study (K200). For scholarly purposes Keating has probably more to offer, as this study occasionally becomes bogged down in minutiae. But for 'beginners' in particular this is excellent.

For reviews, see I694, I715.

K219 Cotter, James Finn. Inscaping 'The Wreck of the Deutschland'. *Renascence*, vol. 21, no. 3, Spring 1969, pp. 124–33, 166.

An explication and commentary designed to reveal the 'inscape' of the poem so that the reader may be able to experience the impact of the *whole* poem, as with the shorter poems.

K220 Cohen, Edward H. The 'pitched' sailor and his example: a key to Hopkins' 'The Wreck of the Deutschland'. *Downside Review*, vol. 87, no. 287, Apr. 1969, pp. 172–82.

Stanza 16 'represents—as metaphor—the central theme which under- lies "The Wreck of the Deutschland" and several others of Hopkins' poems, the concept of Christ's own sacrifice as marked in all degrees and experiences of worldly existence'.

K221 Holloway, Sister Marcella. The nun's cry in 'The Wreck of the Deutschland'. *Downside Review*, vol. 88, no. 292, July 1970, pp. 288– 94.

The cry of the nun in stanza 24 'carries the burden of the ode and gives insight into the meaning of suffering as identification with Christ through love . . .'

SECTION L

MISCELLANEOUS

THIS section is a chronological list of material which does not fit into any of the categories covered by the other sections of the bibliography. It includes poems written in G M H's honour and musical settings of his works.

1874

L1 Symonds, John Addington. The blank verse of Milton. *Fortnightly Review*, vol. 16 (n.s.), no. 96, Dec. 1874, pp. 767–81.

Professor N. H. MacKenzie suggests that G M H's theory of sprung rhythm owes a debt to this remarkable essay. See H 296, pp. 106–7.

1877

L2 *Hopkins, Gifted, *pseud?* The humorous works of the late Gifted Hopkins; from manuscripts found in his desk after his decease, with eight page illustrations by Phiz. London, Jas. Blackwood & Co., 1877. vii, 268 pp.

See also L 3, L 4.

1882

L3 Lang, Andrew. The sorrows of Prince Bismarck. *Saturday Review*, vol. 54, no. 1407, 14 Oct. 1882, pp. 497–8.

See also L 2, L 4.

1888

L4 Anon. The American poet. *Saturday Review*, vol. 66, no. 1720, 13 Oct. 1888, p. 421.

See also L 2, L 3. These three entries are closely related. G M H suspected that L 3 was an attack on him by Lang, which Lang denied. Lang's remarks may have been aimed at L2. This article (L4) makes another oblique reference to 'Gifted Hopkins'. For GMH's rather hyper-sensitive comments, see LL1, pp. 153, 223–4, 294–5. The whole complex question has been ably if inconclusively investigated by W. H. Pearson in I552.

1916

L5   Kilmer, Joyce. Father Gerard Hopkins, S.J. *Studies* (Dublin), vol. 5, no. 17, Mar. 1916, p. 106.
   A poem in GMH's honour. Reprinted in *Joyce Kilmer, Vol. 1, memoir and poems,* by Robert Cortes Holliday. London, Hodder, 1917. p. 138.

1920

L6   Henson, Herbert Hensley, *editor.* A memoir of the Right Honourable Sir William Anson ... Oxford, Clarendon Press, 1920. 242 pp.
   See p. 200. 'Of a serious-minded rather hyper-sensitive man who became a Jesuit he observed, "H. has become a Jesuit and is going as a governess in a Protestant family".' This *may* refer to GMH: see JP, pp. 300–1.

1936

L7   *Millspaugh, C. A. To Gerard Hopkins. *Commonweal,* vol. 26, 13 Nov. 1936, p. 68.
   A poem in GMH's honour.

1937

L8   *Roseliep, Raymond. Two poems for Gerard Hopkins. *Catholic World,* vol. 145, Apr. 1937, p. 33.

1938

L9   *Meyer, Gerard Previn. For Gerard Manley Hopkins, S.J. *Commonweal,* vol. 27, 14 Jan. 1938, p. 318.
   A poem in GMH's honour.

1939

L10   Gordon, David. Ex voto G M H. *Tablet*, vol. 173, no. 5149, 14 Jan. 1939, p. 54.
A poem in G M H's honour.

L11   Meyerstein, E. H. W. To Gerard Manley Hopkins. *Poetry Review*, vol. 30, no. 5, May 1939, p. 184.
A poem in G M H's honour.

1940

L12   *Chavez, Fray Angelico. To Gerard Manley Hopkins (accused of exaggerated Marianism). *Spirit*, vol. 7, July 1940, p. 74.
A poem in G M H's honour.

L13   *Weiss, Theodore. On seeing a portrait of Gerard Manley Hopkins. *Columbia University Quarterly*, vol. 32, Dec. 1940, p. 332.
A poem in G M H's honour.

1941

L14   *Barber, Samuel. A nun takes the veil: Heaven-Haven. Op. 13, No. 1, four songs for voice and piano. New York, G. Schirmer, Inc., 1941.
A musical setting of G M H's work.

1944

L15   Jeremy, Sister Mary. Gerard Manley Hopkins 1844–1944. *Poetry*, vol. 64, no. 1, Apr. 1944, p. 11.
A sonnet in G M H's honour.

L16   Benét, William Rose. Centenary. *Saturday Review of Literature*, vol. 27, no. 36, 2 Sept. 1944, p. 28.
A sonnet in G M H's honour.

L17   *Quirk, Charles J. Gerard Manley Hopkins (1844–1944). *Catholic World*, vol. 160, Dec. 1944, p. 240.
A poem in G M H's honour.

1945

L18   L., H. P. C. To G. M. H., S.J. *Month*, vol. 181, no. 943, Jan.–
Feb. 1945, p. 65.
   A poem in G M H's honour.

L19   Mace, D. F. Gerard Manley Hopkins. *Poetry Review*, vol. 36,
no. 2, 1945, p. 83.
   A poem in G M H's honour.

1947

L20   Wellesz, Egon. The leaden echo and the golden echo: cantata for
high voice, violin, clarinet, violoncello and piano. Words by G. M.
Hopkins. London, Schott & Co., Ltd., 1947, 19 pp.
   A musical setting of G M H's work.

1948

L21   Hopkinson, Stephan. The pilgrimage to Holywell. *Picture Post*,
vol. 40, no. 4, 24 July 1948, pp. 25–7.
   An illustrated account of the history of St. Winifred's Well. G M H
   is not mentioned, but the background information given is interesting.

L22   *Shaw, Martin. God's Grandeur: for mixed voices and organ.
London, Oxford University Press, 1948.
   A musical setting of G M H's work.

1949

L23   Brinkley, Maxine. He gave you song (on reading Gerard Manley
Hopkins). *College English*, vol. 11, no. 3, Dec. 1949, p. 156.
   A poem in G M H's honour.

1955

L24   *Davies, Laurence H. The Bethlehem star (carol introit-unison)
words by Gerard Manley Hopkins. *in* University carol book, book 12:
Christmas. Brighton, E. H. Freeman Ltd., 1955. pp. 6–7.
   A musical setting of G M H's work.

1957

L25 Barker, George. To Father Gerard Manley Hopkins, S.J. *in his* Collected poems, 1930–55. London, Faber & Faber, 1957. pp. 174–5.
A poem in G M H's honour.

L26 *Morgan, Diane. Margaret (for high voice and piano) words by Gerard Manley Hopkins. Toronto, B.M.I. Canada Limited; New York, Associated Music Publishers, Inc., 1957.
A musical setting of G M H's work.

1958

L27 *Reizenstein, Franz. Genesis (oratorio for soprano and baritone soli, chorus and orchestra) text arranged by Christopher Hassall. London, Alfred Lengnick and Co., Ltd., 1958.
A musical setting of lines from 'The Starlight Night', pp. 15–19.

1960

L28 Gunter, G. O. To G. M. Hopkins. *College English*, vol. 22, no. 3, Dec. 1960, p. 189.
A poem in G M H's honour.

1961

L29 Brode, Anthony. Breakfast with Gerard Manley Hopkins. *in* Macdonald, Dwight, *editor*. Parodies: an anthology from Chaucer to Beerbohm—and after. London, Faber & Faber, 1961. pp. 150–1.
A very clever and amusing parody.

1962

L30 Roseliep, Raymond. With a book of verse beneath the bough. *Tablet*, vol. 216, no. 6375, 28 July 1962, p. 716.
A poem in which G M H is mentioned, and in which his influence is clearly apparent.

1963

L31 *Berkeley, Lennox. Autumn's legacy. Op. 58 for high voice and pianoforte. Part 5: 'Hurrahing in Harvest' by Gerard Manley Hopkins. London, J. & W. Chester, Ltd., 1963.
A musical setting of G M H's work.

1964

L32 *Fussl, Karl Heinz. Concerto rapsodico: words by Gerard Manley Hopkins. Wien, Universal Editions, 1964.
A musical setting of G M H's work.

L33 Warner, Oliver. English literature: a portrait gallery. London, Chatto & Windus, 1964. xvii, 205 pp.
See portrait of G M H facing p. 170. Painted by his aunt, Anne Eleanor Hopkins, this portrait is apparently little-known. See also 1618.

1965

L34 *Rubbra, Edmund. Inscape (suite for mixed voices, strings and harp, Op. 122), words by Gerard Manley Hopkins. South Croydon, Alfred Lengnick & Co., Ltd., 1965.
Musical settings of 'Pied Beauty', 'The Lantern Out of Doors', 'Spring', 'God's Grandeur', 'Summa'.

1968

L35 Jennings, Elizabeth. For Hopkins. *Month*, vol. 40 (n.s.), nos. 1–2 July–Aug. 1968, p. 49.
A poem in G M H's honour.

L36 L'Heureux, John. Some logic for my brother, G. M. H. *Month*, vol. 40 (n.s.), nos. 1–2, July–Aug. 1968, p. 65.
A poem in G M H's honour.

L37 Singleton, Frank. Stooks: a serious case of Hopkinsitis. *in his* As chimney-sweepers. Bolton, Moor Platt Press, 1968. p. 56.
A brief but brilliant parody.

PART THREE

WRITINGS ABOUT HOPKINS IN LANGUAGES OTHER THAN ENGLISH

SECTION M

FOREIGN BOOKS AND PERIODICAL ARTICLES

This section is selective, not comprehensive. The entries are grouped alphabetically by language and arranged chronologically within each language group.

DUTCH AND FLEMISH

Note: Dutch entries. The inconsistencies in spelling which will be observed in the following entries are not errors in transcription. Dutch has known five more or less drastic spelling reforms in the first half of the present century, and in one of these reforms it was ruled that '—sch' should be spelled '—s'; except after '—i', and in place-names and proper names. Thus 'Engelsche' in M 3 becomes 'Engelse' in M 6, but *Dietsche Warande* should *not* be spelt *Dietse Warande*, as it is in some bibliographies. For this explanation the compiler is indebted to Mr. Rudy Bremer of the Department of English, University of Groningen.

M 1 *Pompen, Aurelius. Gerard Manley Hopkins, S.J. *Onze Taaltuin* (Rotterdam), vol. 6, no. 1, May 1937, pp. 95–102.

M 2 *Panhuysen, Jos. De poezie van Gerard Manley Hopkins. *Boeken-schouw* (Amsterdam), vol. 32, no. 7, 15 Nov. 1938, pp. 313–18.

M 3 *Peters, W. A. M. De Engelsche dichter Gerard Manley Hopkins, S.J.; de controverse rond zijn persoon. *Studien: Katholiek Cultureel Tijdschrift* (Gravenhage), vol. 71, Nov. 1939, pp. 448–59.

M 4 *Brauns, M. De dichter Gerard Manley Hopkins, S.J. *Streven* (Brussels), vol. 12, no. 4, Aug. 1945, pp. 239–47.

M 5 *Peters, W. A. M. Gerard Manley Hopkins. *Streven* (Brussels), no. 2, Nov. 1949, pp. 200–1.

M6 *Rottiers, A. K. Engelse letteren: de kunst der dichters. *Band Kalina*, no. 4, 1950, pp. 156–8.
Review of H116 and H128.

M7 *Westerlinck, Albert. Een Onsterfelijke diamant: G. M. Hopkins. *Dietsche Warande en Belfort* (Amsterdam), no. 7, Aug.–Sept. 1950, pp. 421–6.

M8 *de Jong, Arnold. Gerard Manley Hopkins, 19de—eeuws experimenteel dichter. *Groene Amsterdammer*, 18 Sept. 1954, p.

M9 *Peters, W. A. M. 25 jaren Hopkins-critiek. *Streven* (Brussels), no. 9, 1955, pp. 208–16.

M10 *Bolsius, E. Gerard Manley Hopkins: de dichter en de religieus. *Streven* (Amsterdam), vol. 13 (n.s.), Oct. 1959, pp. 49–54.
Review of JP and SD.

M11 *Keunen, Jozef. Guido Gezelle en G. M. Hopkins. *Dietsche Warande en Belfort* (Amsterdam), vol. 9, no. 112, 1967, pp. 702–11.

M12 *Keunen, Jozef. Barbaarse bevalligheid. Een benadering van de persoon en het werk van G. M. Hopkins. Hasselt, Heideland, 1967. 192 pp.

M13 Boenders, Frans. Waarom werd Engelse jezuïet een groot dichter? Raadsel—Hopkins blijft. *Standaard der Letteren*, 26 Dec. 1969, p.
Review of B258.

FRENCH

M14 Delattre, Floris. Un poète catholique: Francis Thompson. *in his* De Byron à Francis Thompson. Paris, Librairie Payot, 1913. pp. 147–98.
    See p. 189. 'C'est cette même intensité de vie religieuse, ce même souci mistique, cette même hantise du divin que l'on retrouve dans l'œuvre poétique d'Aubrey de Vere et de Gerard Hopkins . . .' This is the earliest reference to Hopkins in a language other than English discovered by the compiler.

M15 Delattre, Floris. [Review of H9] *Revue Germanique* (Lille), vol. 10, no. 1, Jan.–Feb. 1914, pp. 92–3.

'Miss Brégy met nettement en vue la grave austérité et la dignité un peu froide d'Aubrey de Vere, et, tout à côté, l'ardeur, le pathétique poignant de Gerard Hopkins, l'ami de Newman.'

M16 Koszul, A. [Review of A72] *Revue Anglo-Américaine*, vol. 9, June 1932, pp. 451–2.

'C'est ici, l'un des plus extraordinaires trésors poétiques qui aient jamais été découverts après un long enfouissement . . .'

M17 La Gorce, Agnès de. Francis Thompson et les poètes catholiques d'Angleterre. Paris, Librairie Plon, 1932. 259 pp.

See particularly p. 216. Comment on GMH's part in Patmore's burning of *Sponsa Dei*. This book was translated into English in 1933 by H. F. Kynaston-Snell.

M18 Wolff, Lucien. [Review of H36] *Revue Anglo-Américaine*, vol. 11, no. 6, Aug. 1934, pp. 546–7.

M19 Brémond, André. La poésie naïve et savante de Gérard Hopkins. *Études* (Paris), vol. 221, no. 1, 5 Oct. 1934, pp. 23–49.

The first substantial critical essay on GMH in French, and a very perceptive one. See also I95.

M20 Cazamian, Louis. [Review of B32 and B33] *Revue Anglo-Américaine*, vol. 13, no. 4, Apr. 1936, pp. 349–50.

M21 *Cattaui, Georges. Notes sur Gerard Manley Hopkins. *Yggdrasill* (Paris), vol. 1, 25 Mar. 1937, pp. 15–16.

M22 *Brémond, André. Quelques réflexions sur la poésie et les styles poétiques. A propos d'une correspondence. *Études* (Paris), vol. 242, no. 3, 5 Feb. 1940, pp. 310–17.

Review of B113.

M23 Roditi, Edouard. Gérard Manley Hopkins. *Cahiers du Sud* (Marseilles), vol. 19, no. 223, Apr. 1940, pp. 229–35.

A critical essay in French, with a French prose translation of ten stanzas of 'The Wreck of the Deutschland'.

M 24   *Cattaui, Georges. Gerard Manley Hopkins. *Schweizer Rundschau* (Einsiedeln), vol. 44, no. 6, Sept. 1944, pp. 370–6.

M 25   *Gerard, Albert. Duns Scot et G. M. Hopkins. *Revue des Langues Vivantes*, vol. 12, 1946, pp. 35–8.

M 26   Brooke-Rose, Christine. La syntaxe et le symbolisme dans la poésie de Hopkins. *Europe* (Paris), vol. 25, no. 19, July 1947, pp. 30–9.

M 27   Cattaui, Georges. Gerard Manley Hopkins, ou un nouveau lyrisme baroque. *in his* Trois poètes: Hopkins, Yeats, Eliot. Paris, Egloff, 1947. 168 pp.
See pp. 11–44.

M 28   *Ritz, Jean-Georges. La Vierge Marie comparée à l'air que nous respirons. *Vin Nouveau* (Lyon), 3rd series, no. 13, 1949, pp. 13–16.

M 29   Valette, Jacques. Gerard Manley Hopkins. *Mercure de France*, vol. 307, no. 1035, 1 Nov. 1949, pp. 529–32.
Biographical and critical essay. 'L'effet total, qui submerge l'agacement de détail compréhensible au premier contact, est celui d'un volume compact, d'une saveur violente, d'un ébrouement de géant.'

M 30   Green, Julien. Journal, 1943–1945. Paris, Librairie Plon, 1949. 285 pp.
See particularly pp. 175–9. Thoughts on G M H interspersed with other entries in the journal.

M 31   Ellrodt, R. Grandeur et misère de Gérard Manley Hopkins. *Cahiers du Sud* (Marseilles), vol. 33, no. 306, 1951, pp. 272–89.
General critical essay, with translation of several poems into French.

M 32   Grunne, Dominique de. Technique du poète: Gerard Manley Hopkins. *Critique*, vol. 9, no. 74, July 1953, pp. 579–600.
Biographical and critical essay. '. . . l'œuvre de Hopkins a exercé une influence majeure sur la poétique anglo-saxonne depuis 1918, et bien qu'il soit encore discuté, il est reconnu avec raison comme un des grands poètes de son pays et de son époque.'

M 33   Ritz, Jean-Georges. [Review of A129, A137, B150] *Études Anglaises*, vol. 7, no. 3, July 1954, pp. 342–3.

M 34   B., L. [Review of H 179] *Vie Spirituelle*, vol. 93, no. 410, Oct. 1955, pp. 332–3.

M 35   Ritz, J.-G. [Review of H 179] *Les Langues Modernes*, vol. 49, no. 5, Oct.–Nov. 1955, pp. 465–6.
N.B. This periodical has both continuous pagination for the volume and separate pagination for each issue. The continuous pagination is quoted.

M 36   Ritz, Jean-Georges. 'The Windhover' de G. M. Hopkins. *Études Anglaises*, vol. 9, no. 1, Jan.–Mar. 1956, pp. 14–22.
An essay on the poem's meaning, with a list of critical studies, 1926–55.

M 37   Valette, Jacques. [Review of D 8] *Mercure de France*, vol. 331, no. 1132, Dec. 1957, p. 696.

M 38   *Piatier, Jacqueline. Les douloureux itinéraires du Père Gérard Hopkins. *Jésuites de l'Assistance de France*, 1958, pp. 31–3.

M 39   Thomas, Henri. Gerard Manley Hopkins. *Nouvelle Nouvelle Revue Française*, vol. 6, no. 61, Jan. 1958, pp. 122–5.
Review of D 8, with some critical comment on G M H's poetry.

M 40   Magny, Olivier de. Gérard Manley Hopkins et le cœur des choses. *Les Lettres Nouvelles*, no. 57, Feb. 1958, pp. 248–56.

M 41   *Brion, Marcel. [Review of D 8] *Le Monde*, 19 Feb. 1958, p.

M 42   Mambrino, Jean. [Review of D 8] *Études*, vol. 297, April 1958, pp. 136–7.

M 43   Chrestien, Michel. Le plus illustre des poètes méconnus de l'Angle-terre: Gerard Manley Hopkins . . . *Carrefour* (Paris), 2 Apr. 1958, p.
Review-article inspired by D 8. G M H is '. . . une sorte de Rimbaud-Mallarmé brittanique, maître d'un tel sortilège qu'il suffit de lire dix vers de lui pour que les mots anglais n'aient plus jamais le même sens . . .'

M44 Piatier, Jacqueline. Une thèse de Sorbonne sur le poète anglais:
Gerard Manley Hopkins. *Le Monde*, 14 May 1958, p.
Review of M51, in its original thesis form. Substantial critical
comment on GMH.

M45 *Ritz, Jean-Georges. Un poète anglais: le R. P. Gérard Manley
Hopkins S.J. *Bulletin des Lettres* (Lyons), vol. 20, 15 May 1958,
pp. 189–96.

M46 Ritz, Jean-Georges. [Review of H169] *Études Anglaises*, vol. 12,
no. 1, Jan.–Mar. 1959, p. 69.

M47 Vallette, Jacques. [Review of B207] *Mercure de France*, vol. 336,
no. 1150, June 1959, p. 337.

M48 Jannoud, Claude. 'Reliquiae', de Gérard Manley Hopkins, un
très grand poète anglais. *Vigie Marocaine* (Casablanca), 20 July 1958,
p.
Review of D8. Biographical and critical comment including a brief
but interesting comparison of GMH with Holderlin. 'Mais les
deux artistes ont un point commun capital: ce sont des poètes de la
globalité ... l'un et l'autre veulent exprimer le total, qu'ils considèrent
la poésie comme moyen de révélation. Ils sont, en bref, aux antipodes
de l'art impressionniste.'

M49 Danchin, Pierre. Francis Thompson: la vie et l'œuvre d'un poète.
Paris, A.-G. Nizet, 1959. 554 pp.
See particularly pp. 508–14. Some brief comparison of GMH with
Thompson.

M50 Léaud, F. [Review of H193] *Les Langues Modernes*, vol. 54, no. 4,
July–Aug. 1960, p. 321.

M51 Ritz, Jean-Georges. Le poète Gérard Manley Hopkins, S.J.,
1844–1889.: l'homme et l'œuvre. Paris, Didier, 1963. 726 pp. (Études
Anglaises, 16.)
An impressively thorough and scholarly study of every aspect of
GMH's work. There are frequent minor errors and inaccuracies,
especially in the bibliography at the end of the book, but as a whole
Professor Ritz's standards of criticism are among the highest ever

applied to G M H's work. It is regrettable that no English translation is available.

M 52   Ritz, Jean-Georges. La glorification de Dieu dans les poèmes de G. M. Hopkins. *Travaux et Jours* (Beyrouth), nos. 14–15, 1964, pp. 3–23.

M 53   Mauriac, Claude. Pierre Leyris traduit Hopkins. *Figaro* (Paris), 4 Mar. 1964, p.
Review of D 9. Brief critical comment on G M H.

M 54   Cabau, Jacques. Ce masochisme qu'on appelle la grâce. *l'Express* (Paris), 26 Mar. 1964, p.
Review of D 9, with substantial critical comment on G M H. 'L'écriture de Hopkins est la langue poétique par excellence, qui donne à voir en haussant le langage ordinaire au niveau de la vision.'

M 55   Cattaui, Georges. Gérard Manley Hopkins et 'l'inspect' des choses. *Critique*, vol. 21, no. 222, Nov. 1965, pp. 935–49.

M 56   Plomteux, R. Une nouvelle étude sur Gérard Manley Hopkins. *Revue des Langues Vivantes*, vol. 32, no. 4, 1966, pp. 434–6.
Review of M 51.

M 57   *Épiney-Burgard, Georgette. G. M. Hopkins ou le poète crucifé. *Choisir* (Geneva), vol. 7, Apr. 1966, pp. 22–4.

M 58   Thomas, Alfred. Hopkins. *in* Dictionnaire de spiritualité, vol. 7, fasc. 46; Paris, Beauchesne, 1969. pp. 744–5.
A concise biographical and critical summary, with a useful short bibliography.

GERMAN

M 59   Behn, Irene. Gerard Manley Hopkins und Seine Dichtung. *Hochland* (Munich), vol. 32, no. 8, May 1935, pp. 148–69.
Critical and biographical essay, with some translation of G M H's poems into German.

M60   Wild, Friedrich. [Review of B32 and B33] *Anglia Beiblatt*, vol. 49, no. 3, Mar. 1938, pp. 78–82.
The title of this volume is *Beiblatt zur Anglia*, but the periodical is more widely known as *Anglia Beiblatt*.

M61   Arns, Karl. [Review of *Germanisches Formgefuhl* . . . by Georg Karp.] *Anglia Beiblatt*, vol. 52, nos. 7/8, July–Aug. 1941, pp. 167–9

M62   *Clemen, Wolfgang. Die Tagebücher des G. M. Hopkins. *Merkur* (Stuttgart), vol. 3, no. 6, Jan. 1949, pp. 571–84.

M63   *Kahler, Erich. Gerard Manley Hopkins: Gedichte. *Merkur* (Stuttgart), vol. 3, no. 6, Jan. 1949, pp. 565–70.

M64   Kemp, Friedhelm. Gerard Manley Hopkins. *Hochland* (Munich), vol. 41, no. 4, Apr. 1949, pp. 385–9.
Critical essay.

M65   *Hass, Hans-Egon. Gerard Manley Hopkins. *Begegnung* (Cologne), vol. 4, no. 7, July 1949, pp. 209–12.

M66   Mühlberger, Josef. Der Englische Lyriker Hopkins. *Berliner Anzeigenblatt*, 18 Aug. 1949, p.
Short general essay.

M67   *Behn, Irene. Gerard Manley Hopkins. *Stimmen der Zeit* (Fribourg), vol. 145, no. 3, Dec. 1949, pp. 172–8.

M68   *Hansen-Löve, Friedrich. Der Dichter de Schöpfung: Ein Hinweis auf Gerard Manley Hopkins. *Wort und Wahrheit* (Vienna), vol. 7, no. 6, June 1952, pp. 457–60.

M69   *Sehrt, Ernst Th. Gerard Manley Hopkins: Eine deutsche Ausgabe. *Die Sammlung* (Göttingen), vol. 10, no. 4, Apr. 1953, pp. 215–19.

M70   *Gerlach, Erika. Zum 65. Todestag Gerard Manley Hopkins. *Welt-Stimmen* (Stuttgart), vol. 23, no. 6, June 1954, pp. 271–6.

M71 *Hässler, C. Gerard Manley Hopkins. *Die christliche Frau*, vol. 44, 1955, pp. 42–5.

M72 *Theunissen, Gert H. Schöpfergrund des Schönen. Der Dichter Gerard Manley Hopkins. *Rheinischer Merkur*, vol. 10, 1955, p. 7.

M73 *Zoller, Joseph Ottmar. Die Spuren der Schöpfung. Über Gerard Manley Hopkins. *Rheinischer Merkur*, vol. 10, 1955, p. 7.

M74 Schöffler, Heinz. Hinautgerissen in den Bannkreis der Schöpfung: Ein Unbekannter Englischer Lyriker: Gerard Manley Hopkins. *Rheinpfalz* (Ludwigshafen), 24 Feb. 1955, p.
Brief biographical and critical essay.

M75 *Gerlach, Erika. Gerard Manley Hopkins: Zur deutschen Auswahl aus Seinem Gesamtwerk. *Welt-Stimmen* (Stuttgart), vol. 24, no. 6, June 1955, pp. 260–2.

M76 *Hohoff, Curt. Hopkins, ein Dichter der Schöpfung. *Hochland* (Munich), vol. 47, no. 5, June 1955, pp. 424–31.

M77 Haas, Willy. Sprachschöpfer, Philosoph, Priester: Das Gesamtwerk Gerard Manley Hopkins' in deutscher Auswahl. *Englische Rundschau* (Cologne), vol. 5, no. 23, 10 June 1955, pp. 306–7.
Review-article dealing with D11.

M78 Hausermann, H. W. Drei Generationen über Hopkins. *Neue Zürcher Zeitung* (Zurich), 14 Aug. 1955, p.
Biographical and critical essay tracing the growth of GMH's reputation.

M79 *Horst, Karl August. Zuzang zu Hopkins. *Wort und Wahrheit* (Vienna), vol. 10, no. 9, Sept. 1955, pp. 716–19.

M80 Haas, Willy. Pater, Dichter, Philosoph. *Die Welt* (Hamburg), 24 Sept. 1955, p.
Review of D11.

M81 Wasmuth, Ewald. G. M. Hopkins' ästhetik. *Die Neue Rundschau* (Berlin), vol. 66, Winter 1955, pp. 590–604.

M82 Stenzel, H. [Review of D11] *Stimmen der Zeit* (Fribourg), vol. 157, no. 3, Dec. 1955, p. 233.

M83 Schulze, F. W. [Review of H179] *Zeitschrift für Anglistik und Amerikanistik*, vol. 4, no. 3, 1956, pp. 363–5.

M84 Spira, Theodor. Gerard Manley Hopkins: Zu einer deutschen Neuerscheinung. *Anglia* (Tübingen), vol. 74, no. 3, 1956, pp. 333–44. An essay on the problems of rendering G M H in German.

M85 Hennecke, Hans. Ritter der Unendlichkeit und Unbedingtheit: Gerard Manley Hopkins. *in his* Kritik: Gesammelte Essays zur Modernen literatur. Gütersloh, C. Bertelsmann, 1958. pp. 109–15.

M86 Stanzel, Franz. G. M. Hopkins, W. B. Yeats, D. H. Lawrence und die Spontaneität der Dichtung. *in* Brunner, Karl, *and others*, *editors*. Anglistische Studien. Festschrift zum. 70. Geburtstag von Professor Friedrich Wild. Wein, Wilhelm Braumüller, 1958. pp. 179–93. (Wiener Beiträge zur Englischen Philologie, 66.)

M87 Blume, Bernhard. Sein und Scheitern: zur Geschichte einer Metapher. *Germanisch–Romanische Monatsschrift*, (Heidelberg), vol. 9 (n.s.), no. 3, July 1959, pp. 277–87.

M88 *Kammermeir, Willibald. Des Hornisten Erstkommunion. Gedanken zu einem Gedicht von Gerard Manley Hopkins. *Seele: Monatsschrift im Dienste christlicher Lebensgestaltung* (Regensburg), vol. 36, 1960, pp. 81–5.

M89 Anon. Aus dem konzertsaal: Kammermusik. *Musica*, vol. 14, no. 12, Dec. 1960, p. 827.
A brief reference: 'Ernst Kreneks vier Lieder nach Texten von Gerard Manley wurden [*sic*] in Munster im Studio fur Neue Musik uraufgeführt.'

M90 Kock, E. Hopkins. *in* Buchberger, Michael. Lexikon für theologie und Kirche, volume 5. Fribourg, Verlag Herder, 1960. col. 481.
Compressed general account with brief bibliography.

M91 Kranz, Gisbert. Hopkins. *in his* Europas christliche Literatur, 1500–1960. Aschaffenburg, Pattloch, 1961. pp. 304–12.

M 92   Muller-Schwefe, Gerhard. G. M. Hopkins—der Victorianer. *in* Viebrock, Helmut, *and* Erzgräber, Willi, *editors*. Festschrift zum 75. Geburtstag von Theodor Spira. Heidelberg, Carl Winter, 1961. pp. 233–9.

M 93   Clemen, Ursula. Neue Ausgaben der Werke von G. M. Hopkins. *Anglia*, vol. 80, 1962, pp. 220–3.

M 94   *Balthasar, Hans Urs Von. Hopkins. *in his* Herrlichkeit: Eine Theologische Ästhetik, volume 2. Einsiedeln, Johannes Verlag, 1962. pp. 717–66.

M 95   Guardini, Romano. Ästhetisch-theologische Gedanken zu G. M. Hopkins' Sonett 'Der Turmfalke'. *in his* Sprache—Dichtung—Deutung. Würzburg, Werkbund-Verlag, 1962. pp. 84–90.

M 96   Haas, Rudolf. Gerard Manley Hopkins: Zwei Gedichte. *in his* Wege zur Englischen Lyrik in Wissenschaft und Unterricht: Interpretationen. Heidelberg, Quelle & Meyer, 1962. pp. 130–43.

M 97   Astel, Arnfrid. Ingestalt und Inkraft bei Gerard Manley Hopkins. *Neue Deutsche Heft*, vol. 93, May–June 1963, pp. 48–66.

M 98   Ludwig, Hans-Werner. Die self-Komposita bei Thomas Carlyle, Matthew Arnold und Gerard Manley Hopkins . . . Tübingen, Max Niemeyer, 1963. xvi, 243 pp.

M 99   *Zinnhobler, Rudolf. Die Aufnahme des dichterischen Werkes von G. M. Hopkins im deutschen Sprachraum. *Sonderdruk aus dem Jahresbericht des Collegiums Petrinum*, 1963/64, pp. 1–32.

M 100   Bungert, Hans. [Review of B 207] *Archiv. für das Studium der Neueren Sprachen*, vol. 201, 1964–5, pp. 221–2.

M 101   Combecher, Hans. Drei victorianische Gedichte. *Die Neueren Sprachen*, vol. 13 (n.s.), 1964, pp. 257–67.
'God's Grandeur' explicated in German.

M 102   *Piontek, Heinz. Dienst als Dank. Gerard Manley Hopkins in Neuen Übertragungen. *Zeitwende* (Hamburg), vol. 35, 1964, pp. 317–26.

M103   Liljegren, Sten Bodvar. Anglistik. *Deutsche Literaturzeitung,*
vol. 85, nos. 11/12, Nov./Dec. 1964, pp. 1030–4.
Review of M98.

M104   Fischer, Maria. Die religiöse Dichtung J. H. Newmans, G. M.
Hopkins', C. Patmores und F. Thompsons Ein Vergleich ... Tübingen,
Präzis, 1964. 200 pp.
See particularly pp. 49–76.

M105   Clemen, Ursula. [Review of G86, G91] *Anglia,* vol. 83, 1965,
pp. 114–18.

M106   *Rang, Bernhard. Gerard Manley Hopkins: Ein christlicher
Dichter. *Quatember,* vol. 30, 1965/66, pp. 24–8.

M107   Füger, Von Wilhelm. Gerard Manley Hopkins am Werk:
Zum Entstehungsprozess von 'The Starlight Night'. *Die Neueren
Sprachen,* vol. 16 (n.s.), 1967, pp. 428–39.
A detailed commentary on the poem.

M108   Jankowsky, Kurt R. Die Versauffassung bei Gerard Manley
Hopkins, den Imagisten und T. S. Eliot: Renaissance altgermanischen
Formgestaltens in der Dichtung des 20. Jahrhunderts. München,
Max Hueber Verlag, 1967. 338 pp.

M109   *Müller-Schwefe, Gerhard. Gerard Manley Hopkins: 'Spelt
from Sibyl's Leaves'. *in* Oppel, Horst, *editor.* Die moderne englische
Lyrik: Interpretationen. Berlin, E. Schmidt Verlag, 1967. pp. 39–48.

M110   *Klöhn, Gottfried. Die nominalen Wortverbindungen in der
Dichtung von Gerard Manley Hopkins. Mainz, 1968. viii, 204 pp.
Published in paperback reduced typescript.

ITALIAN

M111   Olivero, Frederico. Gerard Hopkins. *in his* Correnti mistiche
nella letteratura inglese moderna. Turin, Fratelli Bocca, 1932. pp. 73–
100.
See also M112–14.

M112   *Speranza, Ireneo. [Review of M111] *Frontespizio*, vol. 7, no. 7, July 1932, p. 6.

M113   *Gualtieri, F. M. [Review of M111] *L'Italia Letteraria* (Rome), vol. 10, no. 12, 25 Mar. 1934, p. 7.

M114   De Luca, Guiseppe. Letteratura religiosa. *Nuova Antologia*, vol. 12 (7th series), 16 Apr. 1934, pp. 633–8.
See pp. 635–8. Review of P2 and M111, with detailed biographical and critical comment, and a translation of 'Heaven-Haven' into Italian.

M115   Olivero, Frederico. Francis Thompson. Brescia, Morcelliana, 1935. 281 pp.
GMH *passim. See particularly* p. 259. 'In ginocchio dinanzi al Martirio ed alla Gloria della Croce, la sofferenza non è per il Thompson, per il Patmore e il Hopkins un tormento disperato e superbo . . .'

M116   *Baldi, Sergio. Cattolicesimo e poesia nel 'Naufrage del Deutschland'. *Frontespizio*, vol. 11, no. 3, Mar. 1936, pp. 154–64.

M117   Croce, Benedetto. Un gesuita inglese poeta: Gerard Manley Hopkins. *Critica*, vol. 35, no. 2, 20 Mar. 1937, pp. 81–100.
A critical essay containing Italian prose translations of some of GMH's poems. See also M123.

M118   *Castelli, Alberto. Il Naufragio del Deutschland. *in his* Scrittori inglesi contemporanei. Messina, Casa Editrice Giuseppe Principato, 1939. pp. 7–29.

M119   *Baldi, Sergio. Nota su una traduzione da Hopkins. *Letteratura: Rivista Trimestrale di Letteratura Contemporanea* (Florence), vol. 4, no. 2, Apr.–June 1940, pp. 111–17.

M120   *Baldi, Sergio. Gerard Manley Hopkins. Brescia, Morcelliana, 1941, 263 pp. See also M122.

M121   Olivero, Frederico. Lirica religiosa inglese; vol. 3, periodo romantico e contemporaneo, *2nd edition*. Turin, Società Editrice Internazionale, 1942.

G M H *passim. See particularly* p. 12. 'Nell' inspirazione di Gerard Hopkins fitte le stille di pioggia del ricco pensiero, del sentimento, si precipitano, battano sullo scudo bronzeo della parola e risuonano in frasi ed immagini affolate, tumultuouse.'

M 122   Castellani, G. [Review of M 120] *Archivum Historicum Societatis Iesu,* vol. 12, 1943, pp. 178–81.

M 123   Croce, Benedetto. Un gesuita inglese poeta: Gerard Manley Hopkins. *in his* Poesia antica e moderna: interpretazioni. *2nd edition.* Bari, Gius. Laterza & Figli, 1943. pp. 421–46.
A reprint of M 117.

M 124   *Alatri, Corrado da. Nel primo centenario della nascita di G. M. Hopkins, poeta gesuita cantore di Duns Scoto. *L'Italia Francescana* (Rome), vol. 19, 1944, pp. 132–48.

M 125   Croce, Benedetto. Giansenisti e gesuiti: pagine di Restif de la Bretonne e di G. M. Hopkins. *Critica,* vol. 42, no. 1–2, 20 Mar. 1944, pp. 95–8.

M 126   *Guidi, Augusto. Lettura di G. M. Hopkins. *Poesia* (Rome), vol. 1, Jan. 1945, pp. 158–60.

M 127   *Guidi, Augusto. Introduzione alla poetica di G. M. Hopkins. *Letteratura* (Florence), vol. 8, May–June 1946, pp. 93–102.

M 128   Guidi, Augusto *and* Baldi, Sergio. Problemi di interpretazione in G. M. Hopkins. *Anglica: Revista di Studi Inglesi e Americani* (Florence), vol. 1, no. 5, Oct. 1946, pp. 208–11.
Notes on translating 'The Wreck of the Deutschland' into Italian.

M 129   *Guidi, Augusto. Persone e cose nella poesia di G. M. Hopkins. *Humanitas,* vol. 1, Sept. 1946, pp. 934–8.

M 130   *Guidi, Augusto. Poeti cattolici dell'inghilterra moderna. Rome, La Spiga, 1947. pp. 70–5.

M 131   *Melchiori, Giorgio. Poeti cattolici in inghilterra. *Fiera Letteraria* (Milan), vol. 3, no. 12, 28 Mar. 1948, p. 4.

M 132   *Anon. [Review of D 15] *La Civiltà Cattolica*, vol. 99, 4 Sept. 1948, pp. 529–30.

M 133   Forté, Felix. Omaggio a Hopkins. *l'Avvenire d'Italia* (Bologna), 20 Nov. 1949, p.
A tribute for the sixtieth anniversary of G M H's death, with biographical and critical comment.

M 134   Guidi, Augusto. [Review of G 64] *Rivista di Letteratura Moderne*, vol. 1 (n.s.), 1950, p. 71.

M 135   Guidi, Augusto. Undici gesuiti attorno a Hopkins. *Fiera Letteraria* (Rome), 26 Mar. 1950, p.
Review of H 137, with some critical comment on G M H.

M 136   Baldi, Sergio. Hopkins. *in* Enciclopedia cattolica, vol. 6. Vatican City, Ente per il Libro Cattolico, 1951. cols. 1479–81.
A compressed general article, with short bibliography.

M 137   *Melchiori, Giorgio. Due manieristi: Henry James e G. M. Hopkins. *Lo Spettatore Italiano* (Rome), vol. 6, Jan. 1953, pp. 20–7.

M 138   Lombardo, Agostino. La letteratura inglese nella critica di Croce. *Rivista di Letteratura Moderne*, vol. 4, no. 2, Apr.–June 1953, pp. 128–44.
See pp. 134–5. A note on Benedetto Croce's criticism and appreciation of G M H.

M 139   *Guidi, Augusto. Luci e riflessi nel linguaggio di G. M. Hopkins. *Dialoghia* (Rome), Dec. 1953, pp. 51–7.

M 140   Guidi, Augusto. [Review of A 137] *Idea* (Rome), 28 Feb. 1954, p.
This review includes a substantial amount of critical comment on G M H.

M 141   *Bertolucci, Attilio. La poesia inglese contemporanea da Gerard M. Hopkins a Dylan Thomas. *Radiocorriere* (Rome), 1 May 1954, p.

M142   D'Agostino, Nemi. Due formazioni: Hopkins e Joyce. *Fiera Letteraria* (Rome), 28 Nov. 1954, p.
Review of *Tra letture e lezioni di lingua inglese* and *Il primo Joyce* by Augusto Guidi, with detailed comparisons of G M H and Joyce, and critical comment on both writers.

M143   Guidi, Augusto. Milton e Hopkins. *English Miscellany* (Rome), vol. 6, 1955, pp. 31–43.

M144   Guidi, Augusto. Due schede Anglosassoni: la poesia di Hopkins; il pensiero di Coleridge. *Fiera Letteraria* (Rome), 15 May 1955, p.
Review of H 179, with some detailed critical comment, and of a book on Coleridge. The books are dealt with separately; no comparison of G M H and Coleridge is attempted.

M145   *Spellanzon, Giannina. Gerard Manley Hopkins. *l'Indice d'Oro* (Rome), Oct. 1958, pp. 369–70.

M146   Spellanzon, Giannina. Il dramma di Hopkins: la vita estranea. *l'Avvenire d'Italia* (Bologna), 27 Nov. 1958, p.
Biographical and critical essay in Italian; brief, but interesting through its use of quotations from G M H in *French* translation—'per facilitarne la comprensione . . .'

M147   Novelli, Gino. Discorso su Hopkins. *Giornale di Sicilia* (Palermo), 10 Dec. 1958, p.
Biographical note, with only a little critical comment.

M148   Zamboni, Armando. Un grande poeta inglese: Gerard Hopkins. *Realta Politica* (Rome), 5 Dec. 1959, p.
Brief biographical and critical essay.

M149   Guidi, Augusto. Fortuna e attualità di un poeta gesuita inglese: una portentosa ricchezza di immagini nel linguaggio 'difficile' di Hopkins. *Giornale d'Italia* (Rome), 6 Dec. 1959, p.
A review-article inspired by recent Hopkins scholarship and translation, with detailed and comparative critical comment.

M150   *Morati, Luciano. Spiritualità e inspirazione nella poesia di Gerard Manley Hopkins. *Letture* (Milan), vol. 15, no. 8–9, Aug.–Sept. 1960, pp. 563–70.

M 151   Scudder, Giuliana. R. Bridges e G. M. Hopkins: storia di un' amicizia. *Humanitas* (Brescia), vol. 15, no. 12, Dec. 1960, pp. 929–32. Review of G 86.

M 152   Cambon, Glauco. Concettismo esistenziale di Rebora. *Paragone: Letteratura*, vol. 12, no. 138, June 1961, pp. 43–51. G M H *passim*. Brief comparison with Clemente Rebora.

M 153   Zellochi, Rosanna. La 'barbarica bellezza' di Gerard Manley Hopkins. *Convivium*, vol. 29 (n.s.), July–Aug. 1961, pp. 461–71. A detailed critical essay.

M 154   Anderson, Robin. Gerardo Manley Hopkins. *L'Osservatore Romano*, 24 June 1964, p. 3. Critical essay in Italian.

M 155   *Badin, Donatella A. L'epistolario di Gerard Manley Hopkins. *in* Lombardo, Agostino, *editor*. Studi e ricerche di letteratura inglese e americana. Vol. 1. Milan, Ist. Editoriale Cisalpino, 1967. pp. 221–72.

M 156   *Anon. Gerard Manley Hopkins, S.J. (1844–89): centenario della sua entrata nella Compagnia di Gesu. *Societas* (Naples), vol. 20, 1968, pp. 107–10.

JAPANESE

Note: Virtually all the Japanese entries listed here are taken directly from Mr. Kazuyoshi Enozawa's invaluable bibliography. For full details of this bibliography see F 16a.

M 157   *Kitamura, Tsuneo. Namari-iro no Kodama: Kin-iro no Kodama; Gerard Manley Hopkins ni tsuite. *Shi to Shiron*, no. 13, 1931, pp. 119–21, 161.

M 158   *Kitamura, Tsuneo. Gerard Manley Hopkins: Gendaishi Kansho no Test toshite. *Eigo Kenkyu*, vol. 26, no. 8, 1933, pp. 126–31.

M 159   *Fukunaga, Kazutoshi. Hopkins no Shi. *in Eigo-Eibungaku Koza*. Tokyo, Eigo-Eibungaku Kanko-kai, 1934. pp. 3–39.

M160 *Kit *pseud.?* G. M. Hopkins no Shi. *Eibungaku Kenkyu*, vol. 14, no. 3, 1934, pp. 435–7.

M161 *Murase, Shunsuke. Hopkins no Shi Ni-hen: 'The Leaden Echo'; 'The Windhover'. *Oberon*, no. 10, June 1935, pp. 37–40.

M162 *Mori, Toru. C. Day Lewis: Hopkins no Tegami. *Oberon*, no. 11, Sept. 1935, pp. 30–3.
A translation of B56.

M163 *Murase, Shunsuke. Herbert Read: Hopkins no Shi. *Oberon*, no. 13, 1936, pp. 23–9.
A translation of H43.

M164 *Teranishi, Takeo. The Leaden Echo. *Eigo Seinen*, vol. 78, no. 5, 1937, p. 137.
Japanese translation with notes.

M165 *Teranishi, Takeo. The Golden Echo. *Eigo Seinen*, vol. 78, no. 6, 1937, p. 169.
Japanese translation with notes.

M166 *Noguchi, Keisuke. Seinen Hopkins. *Shinryodo*, vol. 4, no. 20, 1938, pp. 104–9.
Translation of B80.

M167 *Teranishi, Takeo. The Windhover. *Eigo Seinen*, vol. 79, no. 10, 1938, p. 304.
Japanese translation with notes.

M168 *Nagiri, Tetsuo. C. Day Lewis no Hopkins Ron. *Shinryodo*, vol. 6, no. 31, 1939, pp. 51–60.

M169 *Shiga, Masaru. Bungaku to Shinnen. Tokyo, Risosha, 1940, pp. 159–289.
Several chapters devoted to Hopkins.

M170 *Ogawa, Jiro. Gerard Manley Hopkins. *Eigo Kyoiku*, (Hiroshima), vol. 4, no. 4, 1940, pp. 63–8.

M171   *Karita, Motoshi. Hopkins Dansho. *Catholic Kenkyu*, vol. 21, no. 1, Feb. 1941, pp. 56–60.

M172   *Okumura, Mifune. Hopkins to Gengo. *in* Ritsumeikan Daigaku Hobun-gakubu Bungaku-ka Sosetsu Kinen Rombun-shu. Kyoto, Ritsumeikan Daigaku Shuppan-bu, 1941. pp. 227–43.

M173   *Campbell, Roy. Eikoku no Shinkan. *Eibungaku Kenkyu*, vol. 26, no. 1, 1949, pp. 108–11.
Review of H120.

M174   *Yagi, Tsuyoshi. The Windhover. *Eigo Kenkyu*, vol. 40, no. 3, Mar. 1951, pp. 12–13.
Japanese translation with notes.

M175   *Maekawa, Shun'ichi. Letter to the 'Salon Eiken' column. *Eigo Kenkyu*, vol. 40, no. 5, May 1951, p. 77.

M176   *Habara, Yukio. Gerard Manley Hopkins. *Eigo-Eibungaku Kenkyu*, vol. 2, no. 2, 1955, pp. 166–76.

M177   *Milward, Peter. Gendaishijin toshite no Hopkins no Keisei. *Sophia*, vol. 4, no. 3, Mar. 1955, pp. 35–54.

M178   *Yamamura, Takeo. Hopkins to Bridges. *Eibungaku Hyoron*, no. 2, Mar. 1955, pp. 88–106.

M179   *Fukase, Motohiro. Kanashimi no Kiwami. *in* Gendai Sekai Shi Sen. Tokyo, Mikashobo, 1955. p. 153.
On 'No worst, there is none'.

M180   *Osawa, Minoru. Maguso Daka; Madara no Bi; Shu yo, Ware wa Aragaedo; Haru. *in* Gendai Sekai Shi Sen. Tokyo, Mikasa-shobo, 1955, pp. 154–6.
Translations of 'The Windhover', 'Pied Beauty', 'Thou art indeed just, Lord . . .', 'Spring'.

M181   *Yamamura, Takeo. Hopkins ni okeru Kansei no Mondai. *Jimbun*, no. 2, Mar. 1956, pp. 73–95.

M182 *Yamamura, Takeo. Dolben no Shi o megutte no Kosatsu. *Eibungaku Hyoron*, no. 3, Mar. 1956, pp. 34–51.
On the poetry of D. M. Dolben: GMH is discussed.

M183 *Saito, Takeshi. Hopkins: The Windhover. *Eigo Seinen*, vol. 102, no. 5, May 1956, pp. 10–12.
A critical essay.

M184 *Tatsuma, Minoru. 'Namari no Kodama' to 'Ogon no Kodama' Kenkyu. *Niigata Daigaku Kyoiku-kagaku*, vol. 6, no. 1, Oct. 1956, pp. 9–16.
Notes on 'The Leaden Echo and the Golden Echo.'

M185 *Tatsuma, Minoru. Eishi ni okeru Sprung Rhythm—Sono Seishitsu to Hattatsu (I). *Niigata Daigaku Jimbun-kagaku Kenkyu*, no. 10, 1956, pp. 25–52.
An essay on sprung rhythm in English poetry. GMH is discussed. Continued in M186.

M186 *Tatsuma, Minoru. Eishi ni okeru Sprung Rhythm—Sono Seishitsu to Hattatsu (II). *Niigata Daigaku Jimbun-kagaku Kenkyu*, no. 13, 1957, pp. 1–26.
Continuation of M185. See also M198.

M187 *Tatsuma, Minoru. 'The Loss of the Eurydice' Kenkyu. *Niigata Daigaku Kyoiku-kagaku*, vol. 7, no. 1, 1957, pp. 1–9.
Notes on the poem.

M188 *Kato, Masao. G. M. Hopkins no sonnet 'God's Grandeur' Oboegaki. *Eibungaku Shicho*, vol. 29, no. 1, Jan. 1957, pp. 182–93.
Notes on the poem.

M189 *Tatsuma, Minoru. 'The Windhover' Kenkyu—G. M. Hopkins no Sonnet-kan. *Niigata Daigaku Jimbun-kagaku Kenkyu*, no. 12, Mar. 1957, pp. 1–21.
Comments on GMH's idea of the sonnet.

M190 *Okumura, Mifune. Mokichi, Rilke, Hopkins. *Potonamu*, vol. 34, no. 8, Aug. 1957, pp. 8–11.

M 191 *Tatsuma, Minoru. 'Spelt from Sibyl's Leaves' Kenkyu. *Niigata Daigaku Kyoiku-kagaku*, vol. 8, no. 1, 1958, pp. 1–9.
Notes on the poem.

M 192 *Yamamura, Takeo. 'Deutschland-go no Nampa' o Toshite Mita Hopkins no Shiteki Honshitsu. *Eibungaku Hyoron*, no. 5, Mar. 1958, pp. 96–118.
An essay on the qualities of G M H's poetry as found in this poem on the 'Deutschland'.

M 193 *Soda, Minoru. G. M. Hopkins no Kachi. *Eigo Seinen*, vol. 104, no. 5, May 1958, pp. 32–4.

M 194 *Egawa, Toru. G. M. Hopkins Sobyo—Sono Kenkyo-sei to Mikkyo-sei tono Kankei. *Metropolitan*, no. 2, 1958, pp. 27–42.
The relation between the exoteric and the esoteric tendencies in G M H.

M 195 *Tatsuma, Minoru. 'The Wreck of the Deutschland' Kenkyu. *Niigata Daigaku Nagaoka Bunko Kenkyu Kiyo*, no. 3, Dec. 1958, pp. 60–74.

M 196 *Hayashi, Shigeko. Gerard Manley Hopkins ni okeru Self to Bi to Kincho. *Ei-Bei Bungaku Hyoron*, vol. 6, no. 2, 1959, pp. 93–127.

M 197 *Tatsuma, Minoru. Heraclitus no Hi. *Niigata Daigaku Jimbun-kagaku Kenkyu*, no. 16, 1959. pp. 1–14.

M 198 *Tatsuma, Minoru. Eishi ni okeru Sprung Rhythm—Sono Seishitsu to Hattatsu (III). *Niigata Daigaku Jimbun-kagaku Kenkyu*, no. 17, 1959, pp. 1–31.
Continuation and conclusion of M 185 and M 186.

M 199 *Osawa, Minoru. Namari no Kodama; Kin no Kodama. *Metaphysic Shi*, nos. 3–4, June 1959, pp. 1–3.
On 'The Leaden Echo and the Golden Echo'.

M 200 *Kano, Hideo. Suki Kirai to Bungaku-teki Kachi—Hopkins to Cowper. *Eibumpo Kenkyu*, vol. 3, no. 8, Nov. 1959, pp. 81–2.

M 201 *Hayashi, Shigeko. Hopkins no 'Terrible Sonnets' ni tsuite. *Ei-Bei Bungaku Hyoron*, vol. 8, no. 1, 1960, pp. 83–101.

M 202 *Masutani, Sotoyoshi. G. M. Hopkins Byosha. *Hitotsubashi Daigaku Kenkyu Nempo*, no. 2, 1960, pp. 35–62.

M 203 *Egawa, Toru. G. M. Hopkins Ron. *Ei-Bei Bungaku*, no. 21, Mar. 1960, pp. 1–36.

M 204 *Shima, Yoshio. Kami, Jiko, Chowa—Hopkins no Shizen-shi ni tsuite. *Hobun Ronso* (Bunka-hen), no. 12, June 1960, pp. 16–38.

M 205 *Shima, Yoshio. 'Fumetsu no Diamond' e no Michi—Hopkins Shiron. *Kumamoto Daigaku Eigo-Eibungaku*, no. 4, Dec. 1960, pp. 69–92.

M 206 *Tatsuma, Minoru. 'Thou art indeed just, Lord' oyobi 'To R. B.' Kenkyu. *Niigata Daigaku Jimbunkagaku Kenkyu*, no. 20, 1961, pp. 13–29.

M 207 *Yamamura, Takeo. Hopkins Junrei. *Eibungaku Hyoron*, no. 9, Mar. 1961, pp. 153–9.

M 208 *Egawa, Toru. 'Maguso Daka' ni okeru Shukyo Keiken. *Oberon*, vol. 5 (n.s.), no. 3, Oct. 1961, pp. 81–7.
Religious experience in 'The Windhover'.

M 209 *Masutani, Sotoyoshi. 'The Windhover' no Kaishaku o megutte. *Oberon*, vol. 5 (n.s.), no. 3, Oct. 1961, pp. 70–5.
On interpretations of the poem.

M 210 *Iwasaki, Soji. G. M. Hopkins: The Windhover—Hitotsu-no Kaishaku. *Kiyo* (Aichi Kenritsu Womens' College), no. 12, Dec. 1961, pp. 37–55.
An interpretation of the poem.

M 211 *Nakamura, Toru. G. M. Hopkins Bannen no Sonnets ni tsuite. *Kaijo Hoan Daigaku Kenkyu Hokoku*, Mar. 1962, pp. 265–91.

M 212 *Tatsuma, Minoru. Gerard Manley Hopkins Kenkyu. *Niigata Daigaku Kyoiku-gakubu Kiyo*, vol. 3, no. 1, Mar. 1962, pp. 70–80.

M 213   *Omichi, Suekichi. Hopkins no Shukyo Shiso no Ichi Dammen. *Hakusan Eibungaku*, no. 8, Apr. 1962, pp. 15–33.
On G M H's religious thought.

M 214   *Haya, Ken'ichi. Hopkins no 'Romanticism'. *Oberon*, vol. 7 (n.s.), no. 2, 1963, pp. 71–9.

M 215   *Sawasaki, Junnosuke. G. M. Hopkins Ron—Shuji no Imi. *Jimbun Gakuho*, no. 34, Mar. 1963, pp. 95–126.
The meaning of rhetoric in G M H.

M 216   *Milward, Peter. Deutschland-go no Nampa. *Seiki*, no. 158, July 1963, pp. 65–72.

M 217   *Kawanishi, Susumu. Kami no Sogon. *Tokyo Dokuritsu Shimbun*, no. 48, 1964, p. 4.
On 'God's Grandeur'.

M 218   *Yasuda, Shoichiro. Hopkins Kenkyu to Eliot. *Nagoya Daigaku Bungakubu Kenkyu Ronshu*, vol. 34, Mar. 1964, pp. 93–114.
On Hopkins and T. S. Eliot.

M 219   *Omichi, Suekichi. Hopkins to Shizen Byosha. *Hakusan Eibungaku*, no. 10, Apr. 1965, pp. 17–38.
G M H and his depictions of nature.

M 220   *Shima, Yoshio. G. M. Hopkins—Bi no Shito toshite no. *Essays*, no. 20, June 1966, pp. 57–65.

M 221   *Omichi, Suekichi. Hopkins, no Shi ni okeru Cho-shizen-kan ni tsuite. *Hakusan Eibungaku*, no. 11, Oct. 1966, pp. 1–19.
Aspects of the supernatural in G M H's poetry.

M 222   *Milward, Peter. Hopkins to T. S. Eliot—Gendai ni okeru Futari no Christ-kyo Shijin. *Oberon*, vol. 10 (n.s.), no. 2, 1967, pp. 10–21.
G M H and Eliot as two modern Christian poets.

M 223   *Yasuda, Shoichiro. 'Victorian Hopkins' Saiko—Hitotsu no

'Inscape' Ron. *Nagoya Daigaku Bungakubu Kenkyu Ronshu*, vol. 43, Mar. 1967, pp. 75–87.
G M H as Victorian reconsidered: an essay on inscape.

M 224   *Furukawa, Takao. 'Deutschland-go no Nampa' ni okeru Shudai to Shijin no Shiten tono Kankei ni tsuite. *Phoenix*, no. 6, June 1967, pp. 38–50.

M 225   *Furukawa, Takao. 'Deutschland-go no Nampa' ni okeru Image Toitsu to Kimpaku-kan ni tsuite. *Lumina*, no. 11, Feb. 1968, pp. 20–9.

M 226   *Ogata, Toma. Gerard Manley Hopkins ni okeru Dichotomy no Imi. *Kansai Gaikokugo Daigaku Kenkyu Ronshu*, no. 13, Apr. 1968, pp. 55–74.

M 227   *Yasuda, Shoichiro. G. M. Hopkins Kenkyu. Tokyo, Shimizukobundo, 1968.
This book contains Japanese translations of all the major poems, with essays on the nature of G M H's poetry and its background.

M 228   *Yasuda, Shoichiro. Hopkins Kenkyu Bessatsu—Yakushi no Chukai. Tokyo, Shimizukobundo, 1968.
A variorum-type commentary on G M H's major poems.

M 229   *Enozawa, Kazuyoshi. Hopkins no Shi 'Taka'. *Eigo Kyoiku*, vol. 17, no. 10, Jan. 1969, p. 38.
On 'The Windhover'.

M 230   Yasuda, Shoichiro. Eigo. *Rising Generation* (Tokyo), vol. 115, no. 7, 1 July 1969, pp. 434–5.
Review of H 293.

M 231   *Ogata, Toma. Muishiki-teki Kakumei Shijin toshite no G. M. Hopkins no Ichi-men—Sono Jesus-kai tono Kanren ni oite. *Albion*, no. 16, 1970, pp. 35–66.

M 232   *Omichi, Suekichi. Hopkins no Shi 'Kansei no Shukan' hoka Ni-hen. *Takachiho Ronso 1969*, 1970, pp. 1–20.

M 233　*Shimane, Kunio. Deutschland-go no Nampa. *Soundings*, no. 2, Nov. 1970, pp. 86–100.
On 'The Wreck of the Deutschland'.

PORTUGUESE

M 234　*Durão, Paulo. A poesia de G. M. Hopkins. *Brotéria* (Lisbon), vol. 58, Mar. 1954, pp. 294–309.

M 235　Grilo, J. Monteiro. O Rev. Gerard Manley Hopkins S.J., precursor do modernismo poetico ingles. *Diario de Noticias* (Lisbon), 25 Oct. 1955, p. 7.
Critical essay and biographical comment.

M 236　Durão, Paulo. Os exercícios Espirituais no poesia de G. M. Hopkins. *Brotéria* (Lisbon), vol. 61, no. 6, Dec. 1955, pp. 520–31.
A discussion of the Ignatian exercises and their influence on G M H.

M 237　Sena, Jorge de. 'O poeta é um fingidor' . . . Lisbon, Ediciões Atica, [1961]. 153 pp.
G M H *passim*.

SPANISH

M 238　*Muñoz Rojas, José Antonio. Gerard Manley Hopkins. *Cruz y Raya* (Madrid), no. 34, Jan. 1936, pp. 107–18.

M 239　*Lind, L. Roberto. Gerard Manley Hopkins: poeta menor de la Edad Mediavictoriana. *Universidad de la Habana Publicacion Bimestral*, vols. 36–7, May-Aug. 1941, pp. 48–55.

M 240　*Muñoz Rojas, José Antonio. En al centenario de Gerard Manley Hopkins, S.J. *Rázon y Fe* (Madrid), vol. 132, no. 7, Nov. 1945, pp. 569–74.

M 241　Alonso, Dámaso. Seis poemas de Hopkins. *Trivium* (Monterey, Mexico), vol. 1, no. 3, Jan. 1949, pp. 10–17.
Critical commentary followed by translations of six poems into Spanish. See also M 250.

M 242   *Revol, Enrique Louis. La poesia de Gerard Manley Hopkins. *in his* Al pie de las letras: pequenos ensayos literarios. Buenos Aires, Reunion, 1949. pp. 55–71.

M 243   *Baron, Ronald. Traduciendo a Hopkins. *Criterio* (Buenos Aires), vol. 23, 21 Dec. 1950, pp. 1005–10.

M 244   *Gutierrez Mora, José Manuel. Dos poetas ingleses: Alfred, Lord Tennyson, 1809–92; Gerard Manley Hopkins 1844–89. *Et Caetera* (Guadalajara), vol. 1, no. 2, Apr.–June 1950, pp. 1–15 (supplement).

M 245   Aldama, Ant. M. de [Review of G 64 and M 27] *Archivum Historicum Societatis Iesu*, vol. 20, no. 40, July–Dec. 1951, pp. 346–9.

M 246   *Navarro Sánchez, Adalberto. Poemas de Gerard Manley Hopkins. *El Occidental*, 26 Aug. 1951, pp. 7, 15.

M 247   Aldama, Ant. M. de [Review of A 110, H 91, H 120] *Archivum Historicum Societatis Iesu*, vol. 21, no. 41, Jan.–June 1952, pp. 212–17.

M 248   Aldama, Ant. M. de [Review of H 128]. *Archivum Historicum Societatis Iesu*, vol. 21, no. 41, Jan.–June 1952, pp. 217–21.

M 249   *Gutiérrez Mora, José Manuel. Diez sonetos de Hopkins. *Ábside* (Mexico City), vol. 16, no. 3, July–Sept. 1952, pp. 305–20.

M 250   Alonso, Dámaso. Seis poemas de Hopkins *in his* Poetas españoles contemporáneos. Madrid, Editorial Gredos, 1952. pp. 403–22. (Biblioteca Románica Hispánica, II. Estudios y ensayos, 6.)
Reprint of M 241.

M 251   Gutiérrez Mora, José Manuel. Hopkinsiana: la vida, la obra y la supervivencia de Gerard Manley Hopkins. Mexico City, Aldina, 1952. 239 pp.
The most substantial critical work on G M H in Spanish, but very difficult to obtain. Includes some translations of G M H's poems. See I 470, M 252.

M 252   *Pujals, E. [Review of M 251] *Arbor* (Madrid), vol. 25, 1953, pp. 136–8.

M253 Castellani, Leonardo. Gerardo Manley Hopkins (1844–1889). *Revista de la Universidad de Buenos Aires*, vol. 7 (cuarta época), no. 28, Oct.–Dec. 1953, pp. 559–68.
General essay.

M254 *Roig, José Antonio, *and* Bonet, José Vicente. Dos poemas marianos de Hopkins. *Razón y Fe* (Madrid), vol. 150, 1954, pp. 110–16.

M255 Aldama, Ant. M. de [Review of A129, A137, B150] *Archivum Historicum Societatis Iesu*, vol. 23, no. 45, Jan.–June 1954, pp. 186–9.

M256 Aldama, Ant. M. de [Review of B179] *Archivum Historicum Societatis Iesu*, vol. 27, Jan.–June 1958, pp. 178–9.

M257 Aldama, Ant. M. de [Review of D8] *Archivum Historicum Societatis Iesu*, vol. 27, July–Dec. 1958, pp. 408–10.

M258 Aldama, Ant. M. de [Review of K188 *and* H206] *Archivum Historicum Societatis Iesu*, vol. 28, Jan.–June 1959, pp. 259–60.

M259 Aldama, Ant. M. de [Review of B207 *and* B208] *Archivum Historicum Societatis Iesu*, vol. 28, July–Dec. 1959, pp. 395–7.

M260 *Traversi, Derek. La poesia di Gerard Manley Hopkins. *Nuestro Tiempo* (Madrid), vol. 15, 1961, pp. 1330–47.

M261 Aldama, Ant. M. de [Review of G86] *Archivum Historicum Societatis Iesu*, vol. 30, 1961, pp. 305–6.

M262 *Pol, Osvaldo. Hopkins: una extrana experiencia. *Estudios* (Buenos Aires), Jan.–Feb. 1964, pp. 52–60.

M263 Aldama, Ant. M. de [Review of M51] *Archivum Historicum Societatis Iesu*, vol. 35, Jan.–June 1966, pp. 265–6.

M264 *Gutiérrez Vega, Zenaida. La obra poética de Hopkins a través de algunos poemas. *Cuadernos Hispanoamericanos* (Madrid), vol. 75, 1968, pp. 691–9.

SWEDISH

M265   Gyllenbåga, Nils. Jesuiten contra diktaren. *Expressen* (Stockholm), 5 Apr. 1950, p. 4.
Review of H116 and H128, with substantial critical comment.

M266   Fleisher, Frederic. Gerald [*sic*] Manley Hopkins. *Sydsvenska Dagbladet* (Malmo), 23 Dec. 1953, p.
Review of A137, B150.

M267   Soderberg, Lasse. Prast och poet: G. M. Hopkins. *Arbetaren* (Stockholm), 16 Jan. 1954, p.
Brief critical essay.

M268   Melin, Lars. Gerard Manley Hopkins. *Credo* (Uppsala), vol. 48, no. 4, 1967, pp. 174–8.
Biographical and critical essay.

PART FOUR

NOTES ON LOCATIONS OF SOURCE MATERIALS

SECTION N

COLLECTIONS OF SOURCE MATERIALS IN LIBRARIES AND IN PRIVATE HANDS

N1   THE BODLEIAN LIBRARY, OXFORD

An extensive and important collection of MSS., consisting of:

MS. Eng. poet. d. 149. MS. book B—for details, see P4, pp. 232–3.

MS. Eng. poet. d. 150. MS. book H—for details, see P4, p. 233.

MS. Eng. poet. c. 48. A collection of papers containing drafts and copies of poems in Latin, Welsh, and English.

MS. Eng. lett. e. 40.; MS. Eng. lett. e. 41. Letters from G M H to his family.

MS. Eng. lett. d. 143. Letters from Bridges to G M H's mother, mainly about G M H's poems and the preparation and publication of P1.

MS. Mus. c. 97. For details, see JP, pp. 463–5.

MS. Eng. poet. e. 91. Poems by R. W. Dixon copied by G M H. See LL2, pp. 171–2.

MS. Eng. poet. e. 90. G M H's 'Commonplace Book'.

MS. Eng. misc. a. 8. Miscellaneous papers, including the only extant letter from Bridges to G M H.

N2   CAMPION HALL, OXFORD

An extensive and important collection of MSS.; including G M H's early diaries, his journals, sketch-book and sermon-book, his school note-books, Oxford essays, and miscellaneous papers. This collection has been catalogued in detail by Humphry House: see JP, pp. 529–35.

N3   *MANUSCRIPTS IN THE KEEPING OF LORD BRIDGES

Robert Bridges's own collection of MSS. is now in the keeping of Lord Bridges, and consists of:

MS. book A—for details, see P4, p. 232.
G M H's letters to Robert Bridges.
G M H's letters to R. W. Dixon.

N4   STONYHURST COLLEGE, Nr. BLACKBURN, LANCASHIRE

The College library possesses a copy of P1, with two autograph poems inserted. An annotated transcript of one of these poems ('The Kind Betrothal', a version of 'The Habit of Perfection') is included in A100. The other poem is a version of 'Lines for a Picture of St. Dorothea'. There are no other Hopkins MSS. at the College, but the library is rich in Catholic and Jesuit periodicals and other material of value to the student of G M H.

N5   *THE ORATORY, BIRMINGHAM

The Oratory holds some letters from G M H to Cardinal Newman, and one from G M H to Father Ignatius Ryder.

N6   BALLIOL COLLEGE, OXFORD

The College library holds a letter from G M H to Francis de Paravicini. See FL2, pp. 61–3.

N7   THE LANCASHIRE RECORD OFFICE, BOW LANE, PRESTON, LANCASHIRE

One letter from G M H to the Archbishop of Liverpool is held here. See *Guide to the Lancashire Record Office* by R. Sharpe France; Preston, Lancashire County Council, 1962, p. 241. For an edited transcript of this letter, with commentary, see B268.

N8 *35 LOWER LEESON STREET, DUBLIN

The Jesuits of the Irish Province keep a small but important collection of MSS., including the MS. of 'St. Thecla' (see P4, p. 309), and several books containing marginal annotations by G M H.

N9 *UNIVERSITY LIBRARY, UNIVERSITY OF TEXAS, AUSTIN, TEXAS 78712

The most important part of this growing collection of MSS. is a group of four letters from G M H to Katharine Tynan, which form G M H's side of the letters from her in FL2. These letters are currently being edited by Professor D. J. DeLaura. For transcriptions of these letters, with commentary, see B 206.

N10 *PARISH RECORD BOOKS

G M H's autograph entries exist in the parish records of ST. ALOYSIUS' CHURCH, OXFORD and ST. FRANCIS XAVIER'S CHURCH, LIVERPOOL. These entries are merely records of baptisms, marriages, visits to the sick, and other church business.

N11 114 MOUNT STREET, LONDON W1Y 6AH

The library at the headquarters of the English Province of the Society of Jesus holds no Hopkins MSS., but it includes a number of books, offprints, and reference works of value to students of G M H, some of them very rare.

N12 *FOURIER LIBRARY, COLLEGE OF NOTRE DAME OF MARYLAND, 4701 NORTH CHARLES STREET, BALTIMORE, MARYLAND 21210

The library includes a special Hopkins collection. Its MSS. are listed in *National Union Catalogue of Manuscript Collections* (Library of Congress, 1966), and the bound volumes are covered by a short-title list available from the librarian. The collection also contains numerous unbound periodicals, photographs and photocopies of which there is as yet no official catalogue.

N13 *CROSBY LIBRARY, GONZAGA UNIVERSITY, EAST 502 BOONE AVENUE, SPOKANE, WASHINGTON 99202

The library includes a special Hopkins collection, which has been catalogued by Ruth Seelhammer. This catalogue (F16) covers the very extensive collection of published materials, but does not cover MSS.— the following extract from Mrs. Seelhammer's *Preface* explains the scope of her work:

One limiting element has been that it is published works, principally, which are included here although theses and dissertations have not been excluded. There are of course manuscript materials and original documents in the collection and others belonging to it which are not available at this time since they have not yet been deposited in the collection itself. In their entirety these are of such scope as to make them, when they do become available, the source of great value in a different way.

INDEX

This index includes all AUTHORS of books and periodical articles, all TITLES of periodicals, TITLES of selected primary works, and NAMES of persons connected with GMH or whose work has been discussed in relation to his.

Poems and prose by GMH, and subjects relating to him and to his work are grouped together under his name in the following subdivisions:

HOPKINS, GERARD MANLEY
1. BIOGRAPHICAL
2. PERSONAL AND SPIRITUAL
3. AS A POET
4. AS A WRITER OF PROSE
5. AS A CRITIC
6. AS A MUSICIAN
7. AS AN ARTIST